James, Brother of Jesus, and the Jerusalem Church

To John + Diane

Good friends

and fellow pilgrims on the Way.

Best wishes

John.

James, Brother of Jesus, and the Jerusalem Church

A Radical Exploration of Christian Origins

Alan Saxby

FOREWORD BY
James Crossley

WIPF & STOCK · Eugene, Oregon

JAMES, BROTHER OF JESUS, AND THE JERUSALEM CHURCH
A Radical Exploration of Christian Origins

Wipf and Stock
An Imprint of Wipf and Stock Publishers
199 W. 8th Ave., Suite 3
Eugene, OR 97401

www.wipfandstock.com

ISBN 13: 978-1-4982-0390-6

Manufactured in the U.S.A.   04/07/2015

In Memoriam

Fay
1937–2003
Wife, Mother, and Grandmother

Contents

Foreword

ALAN SAXBY HAS WRITTEN a social history of the early Christian movement associated (or not) with James, brother of Jesus, and with a particular emphasis on historical *change* from below and how people can get omitted from history. Such combinations are still somewhat unusual in New Testament studies, let alone studies associated with James. Histories of Christian origins are still largely static in that they are typically descriptions of how things and theology "really were." Even social-scientific criticism does what its title implies: provide exegetical illumination. There are numerous reasons for this but one is quite simple: it remains highly unusual, certainly in the UK, for people with strong connections to working class communities to have a significant present in New Testament studies.

Having known Alan for several years and seen his ideas develop, it is notable that his historical thinking was always grounded in social events and social change. This is not to say, of course, that Alan was not interested in theological issues (Bultmann still remains a favorite of his). Indeed, he stands close to a once strong English radical tradition where the combination of reading texts such as the Bible in the light of labor history is second nature. This sort of tradition has a strong history in his native Yorkshire where Alan has received memories of, and witnessed first-hand, some of the most prominent events and changes in English social and labor history. For instance, Alan's hometown of Barnsley was one of the nerve centers for Arthur Scargill, another local, who was leader of the National Union of Mineworkers during the devastating Miners' Strike of 1984–85, the effects of which are felt across the north of England to this day. During that bitter twelve-month struggle, Alan could look across the road from his place of work to the Miners' Union Headquarters—"Camelot," as the locals christened it (King Arthur's Castle). For someone like Alan, how could history and historical change *not* be about the realities of everyday life and how could they not have a deep impact on people who ordinarily do not have a voice?[1]

This is not to say that we reduce Alan's research into Christian origins to some kind of mirror image of twentieth-century social history or the like. Manifestly, it is not. But Alan's background has clearly contributed to his sensitivity towards lost voices, as well as the ways in which human beings understand and interpret their environment in less than luxurious circumstances. Alan told me that, on completion of his PhD, his childhood sweetheart sent him a note with "Rev Dr—not bad for a lad from Linburn Road." It certainly isn't! But, as is implicit in her words, we should also see the publication of Alan's work as a bittersweet moment. What it shows, in part, is that more and more people with perspectives and backgrounds such as Alan's would add so much more to academic life. As an analogy we only need to look at the impact feminist studies have had in the field. But the worry in the UK is that, with the increasing neoliberalism and privatization in higher education, more people with such close connections to working class communities will be even less likely to be involved pursuing such intellectual activities (statistics concerning social mobility more broadly over the past thirty years support this). We might casually suggest that this must be resisted as much as possible, as well as finding new ways to increase working class educational engagement after the decline of the organized labor movement. Indeed we should; and it is the success of someone like Alan that reminds us why.

James Crossley

University of Sheffield

---

1. We might also note that the radical British New Testament scholar, Chris Rowland, is from just down the road in Doncaster.

Preface

The Birth of a Thesis

IT BEGAN IN A period of tedium and boredom. I was an examiner for GCSE Religious Studies marking scripts on *The Life and Teaching of Jesus,* which included questions focused on the story of the Rich Young Ruler. For one mark, candidates were asked to name a modern day person who was a good example of Christian living.

Aside from one candidate who said, "my grandmother is a good example," my frustrations mounted as four hundred to five hundred scripts repeatedly informed me that "Mother Teresa is a good example of Christian living." Much as I admire Mother Teresa, didn't they know anyone else?

It was in this state of acute mental torpor and lassitude that I found myself hearing the injunction of Jesus to "Go, sell, and give to the poor" in a completely fresh way—was Jesus in fact telling the young man to give his wealth to "the poor"—the group in Jerusalem we meet later as led by his brother James? Was James already leader of a group in Jerusalem?

Imagery from the Prodigal Son parable poured in—the Elder Brother was a "dead ringer" for James—who then was the Younger Son? Was Jesus saying, "No use giving me the money—you know my record with that—better give it to my brother James, he'll be much safer with it." Other images and fragments of texts crowded in and within twenty minutes or so I had the outline for a novel on a piece of scrap paper.

It was fantasy. I knew it, but I was hooked onto James. Long hours caring for my wife through chronic illness gave me space to return, after many years, to serious and extensive reading in NT scholarship, and I found myself particularly alert to what was being said about James, the Lord's brother. The more I read, the more the notion of James being leader of a movement in Jerusalem contemporary with that of Jesus in Galilee began to make sense, even more sense than what most books I read offered me. And equally frustrating was that no scholar seemed to be addressing my question.

My fantasy had generated a hypothesis, which was maturing into a credible thesis—and with the time becoming available, I was ready to engage as a partner in the conversation.

Acknowledgments

I COUNT MYSELF FORTUNATE in living within traveling distance of Sheffield University, which, at the time, was the only secular university in the UK to support a department solely devoted to Biblical Studies—a department held in high esteem by practitioners in the field throughout the world. Having a personal lifetime faith-commitment, I wanted the academic rigor and intellectual challenge of such an environment, and have not been disappointed.

I wish to express warm appreciation to my supervisors for their support and guidance during the past years of study and exploration:

- to Rev. Canon Professor Loveday Alexander for putting on the necessary pressure to trigger my brain into stepping up a gear for the task I had set my hand to; for her guidance in connecting me into the contemporary world of New Testament scholarship; and, prior to her retirement, recommending me . . .

- . . . to Dr. (now Professor) James Crossley who took on the role, journeying with me on a voyage of exploration and discovery—challenging, suggesting, warning, guiding, listening, and sharing insights.

If Professor Alexander was my "Peter"—providing the foundational "rock" for my study, then Professor Crossley has been my "Paul," encouraging me to journey out into fresh territory. They have facilitated and helped to energize my search but, as one of the canonical *dramatis personae* fatefully said, "What I have written, *I* have written".

As one who commenced his education in a world before the Biro, and was pensioned off from work before the advent of email, I wish to express my appreciation to Matthew Wimer and his colleagues at Wipf and Stock for their support and patient guidance through this, my first venture into the mysteries and intricacies of book publishing.

I also thank my family—both young and those of more mature years—
for their love, support, and understanding; Janet, the "companion of my
autumnal years," for her encouragement and recognition that she shares me
with a rather shadowy figure from the distant past; my son-in-law Martin,
for bringing me into the modern electronic age along with his never-failing
help across cyber-space in all things IT ("every family needs a Martin");
Monica, for proofreading the text; Linda, for keeping my domestic space
habitable; Gill and Jan, for their supportive friendship over many years, and
my many friends at church for their continuing love and interest.

Abbreviations

All abbreviations in the text conform to the standard set by the Society of Biblical Literature:

> Patrick H. Alexander, John F. Kutsko, James D. Ernest, Shirley A. Decker-Lucke and David L. Petersen, eds. *The SBL Handbook of Style: For Ancient Near Eastern, Biblical, and Early Christian Studies*. Peabody, MA: Hendrickson, 2006.

Except where indicated, all transcripts of the biblical text are from the NRSV.

References/excerpts from the writings of Josephus:

> *Josephus*. Translated by H. St. J. Thackeray, *et al.* 10 vols. Loeb Classical Library, Cambridge, MA: Harvard University Press, 1926–1965.

References/excerpts from the writings of Eusebius:

> *The Ecclesiastical History 1: Books I—IV.* Translated by Kirsopp Lake. Loeb Classical Library, Cambridge, MA: Harvard University Press, 1926.

Note on Cross-References

Cross-references are placed within the text and direct the attention of the reader to a relevant Chapter and Section.

They are recorded in the following format:

§ 1. 2.3

The initial number refers to the Chapter, followed (as appropriate) by a section/subsection reference. Multiple references are indicated by the following symbol: §§

Introduction

JAMES, THE BROTHER OF Jesus, is a marginalized character in the pages of the New Testament (NT), and yet during the first thirty years or so of the nascent Christian movement he, not Peter and Paul, was its most dominant personality. Few books and articles are written about him, which is unsurprising given the fragments of hard information we possess, and even when the spotlight of NT scholarship brings James into view it is usually as part of a broader project which is as little interested in James *per se* as are the NT documents themselves. The interest in him is mainly as the *brother* of Jesus, and of *his* relationship to Jesus—never the other way round. We contextualize James within the context of the Lucan narrative flow in Acts, which again is understandable as it is the only attempt to write a history of this new movement we have from that early period, but it is a document where the absence of James is more noteworthy than his presence, and reflects the concerns of a generation long after James's death and far removed from Jerusalem—the scene of James's presence.

This contrasts markedly from the rich vein of stories and tradition about James in circulation during the second to fourth centuries. Despite the difficulties, this giant of a Christian leader from the earliest days deserves to be studied in his own right and in his own context. Fortunately, the limited evidence we have for James, especially that in Paul's Galatian letter, is of the finest kind—incidental primary historical evidence—better than anything we have for Jesus, remembrance of whom is wholly received through the distorting lens of cultic veneration. In addition there are a small number of early traditions involving James embedded in the Gospels, Epistles, and Acts that are of value because the interest of the writer is focused elsewhere—for example, on Paul.

We need to listen to that evidence through the distortions of the context in which we receive it, through the mists of Paul's anxieties about his

churches, free of the structuring of the history in Acts, and free—a tall order—of our normal dominant interest in Paul, Peter, or the Gentile mission;
and persistently ask of these mainly incidental references what they tell us
about James and the movement in Jerusalem that was gathered around him.

Drawing on my experience in counseling, I call this "focused listening"—listening to the words, their expression, the moods, the spaces between the words, and entering with imagination into the world of the other,
without injecting my own (or other's) premature pre-suppositions, interpretations, and rationalizations.

This study of James has the occasional flavor of the popular detective novel in which the evidence is presented in such a way that the total
scenario seems fairly clear (in a similar way to how the Lucan history in
Acts frames our gaze). There are a few inconsistencies that are generally not
noticed or easily glossed over—it is the master detective (male or female)
who not only notices them, but makes them the key around which she or he
restructures the evidence and, in the final act—*voila!*—the truth is revealed.
Sherlock Holmes, of course, always has the distinct advantage of possessing
all the relevant evidence; the student of James only has a fraction of what
she or he needs and cannot produce the same certainty of outcome (and
no "*voila!*" moment), but the process is very similar—to press very limited
material for evidence and on this foundation seek to construct a framework,
contextualizing James and his people within *their* world, rather than trying
to fit sometimes dissonant material into a superimposed framework. In this
study, the person and history of James and the Jerusalem church do begin
to emerge, albeit, in Paul's imagery, "seen through a glass darkly." We find
a group in Jerusalem, gathered around James and his brothers a few years
before the fateful visit of Jesus to the city. Fired by the preaching of John the
Baptist, they experienced the events surrounding the execution of this other
brother of James as fulfilling the message of John and consequently they
became the kernel of that vigorous early Christian movement in Jerusalem
referred to by Paul and by traditions and remembrances embedded within
Luke's later history in Acts.

As the prologue to Mark's gospel intimates—we need to think of two
locations for the "beginning of the gospel": Jerusalem and Galilee.

Our focus is Jerusalem—and James.

Notes on Some Terms Used

1. Relating to the World of the Incipient Christian Church

Two millennia of (mainly) European usage has bestowed a heavy legacy of meanings and associations on the word "Church." Except where the context of use is clear, I seek to restrict terms such as "church" and "Christian" to usage in the closing years of the first century CE and later, when the movement associated with Jesus Christ shows signs of a growing self-awareness in distinction from the Judaism in which it was birthed. "Christianity" is even less usable within this period.

Although the words "Christian" (Acts 11:26) and "church" were in use from the middle years of the century we need to take great care in how we use them. Terminology such as "early Christianity," "primitive church," "church of Jerusalem," all embed assumptions about Christian origins within their very language. Although absolute consistency is difficult, to reduce this risk and to aid clarification I use the following terms:

Proto-Christian

Particularly in the early years following the life/death/rising of Jesus, before any significant ingress of Gentiles to their movement—the period which is the focus of this study—it is highly likely that "Christian" groups continued to think of themselves as fully "Jewish" and part of the broader movement for the restoration of Israel that was vigorously looked for by many sons of Israel during this period. For them the events surrounding and flowing from Jesus marked a significant fulfillment within Judaism. I introduce the term "proto-Christian" therefore to refer to those movements of restoration and reform within Second Temple Judaism, principally pre-70 CE in Palestine (or spreading from there), that flowed and linked together eventually into that movement which increasingly identified itself, and was identified by others, as "Christian" over against the formative Judaism that was developing in the same post-70 CE period. Although the term is clearly teleologically driven, it seeks to avoid an anachronistic use of "Christian" within pre-70 CE Judaism before any "parting of the ways".

Church / ἐκκλησία

"Church" carries a heavy load of two millennia of usage. It carries connotations of institution and organization, building and "gathered congregation." Paul, in his opening epistolary salutations, often describes the coming together of those who respond to his message as "the church," a term he also applies to the comparable groupings in Jerusalem. It is also the word used in Revelation. Needing distance between NT usage and our contemporary imagery of "church," in most instances I retain the word in its Greek format of ἐκκλησία.

Jakobusgemeinde

The description of the community in Jerusalem that we encounter in the NT and later Christian tradition as being led for many years by James as the "Church of Jerusalem" is anachronistic and pre-judges questions about its historical origination and self-identity. I introduce a German term *Jakobusgemeinde* ("The Community of James") for this critical group as being both historically accurate and theologically neutral.

"Jesus Movement"

A number of NT scholars use the phrase "Jesus-Movement" to meet the need I address in using the term "proto-Christian" as a descriptor of those very earliest "Christian" groupings. But, as in the case of descriptions such as "Primitive Christianity," this also embeds assumptions about Christian origins that need to be challenged. I restrict "Jesus Movement" specifically to the movement in Galilee that can be ascribed to the leadership and initiation of Jesus of Nazareth, continuing there beyond his death/rising. The epithet "Galilean" can usefully be added to it.

The Council / Conference of Jerusalem (Acts 15)

I use the word "Conference" rather than the traditional "Council of Jerusalem" to describe the meeting in Acts 15. "Conference" is the better contemporary word for the meeting which Luke describes, and also avoids confusion with the "council of the *Jakobusgemeinde*" ("apostles and elders") that I suggest as part of the latter's structure (§ 5. 9.2). The description of the Acts 15 meeting as a "Council" is retrojected from later ecclesiastical practice (and suspect of ecclesiastical interest). Luke provides no such descriptor (πλῆθος in Acts 15:12 is the only candidate).

James, The Epistle of James, and EpJas

In some scholastic writing, the epithet "James" sometimes has an ambiguous referent—either to the historical personage of James or to the epistle ascribed to him. Here, "James," without qualification, refers to the historical brother of Jesus, distinguishing him from "James bar Zebedee" (of the Galilean Twelve) and several others briefly mentioned in the NT who bore the same common Judaic name. I use the abbreviation *EpJas* when referring either to the Epistle of James, or its eponymous author (without prejudice to the question of the letter's authorship).

2. Relating to the World of Second Temple Judaism

As with the Christian vocabulary and its history of use, which both enriches and bedevils it, so language associated with Judaism has its own distinctive "baggage" of use and abuse, added to which is the twentieth century experience of the Holocaust. Problems of language usage are important.

Jew, Jewish, Judaism

I have sought to restrict usage of terms such as "Jew," "Jewish" to a minimum because of their frequent anti-semitic associations; and I have taken care to limit my use of the term "Judaism" because our NT period precedes the development of the more familiar rabbinic Judaism, which is in part defined in contradistinction to Christianity.[1] Although it seems that whilst the preferred self-description of a first century Jew was "Israelite," the epithet

---

1. Jackson-McCabe, *Jewish Christianity Reconsidered*; Gregory, "Hindrance or Help," 389–90.

"Jew" was more likely to be used by Gentiles. Unfortunately the reality on the ground was more complex.[2] Whilst reflecting this range of use where it feels appropriate, I have tried to use the term *"Israelite(s)"* (or a cognate) in preference to "Jew"; and to use the descriptor *"Judaic"* in preference to "Jewish," or the more locational "Judean".

Circumcision / περιτομή

The word "circumcision" can refer to the rite or practice of circumcision; or be used as an ethnic or group label; or to indicate a particular ideological position and/or those who hold to it. The context usually clarifies the usage. I retain the Greek form of περιτομή to try to reflect its ethos and use.

The End Time / ἔσχατον

There was a widespread belief in late Second Temple Judaism that they were living in the final days before a final decisive divine intervention in the affairs of humanity, but, as Martin Goodman observed: "There is no evidence of an agreed coherent eschatology within any ancient Jewish group. It is, however, striking that expectation of some dramatic change in the world was so widespread."[3] I therefore retain the Greek format of ἔσχατον for this generalized expectation of the imminence of the "last days," without prejudice to any associated eschatology.

Synagogue / συναγωγή

"Synagogue" (in a similar way to "church") easily evokes an image of a building as a meeting place for religious purposes. Archaeological evidence for synagogue buildings in Palestine pre-70 CE is absolutely minimal: the "Theodotus" inscription discovered in Jerusalem is firm evidence of one such building in that city,[4] whilst the evidence from Galilee is also fragmentary.[5]

2. Elliott, "Jesus the Israelite," 119–54.

3. Goodman, *Rome and Jerusalem*, 199; Cooper, "Adaptive Eschatological Inference," 62–63, offers a useful summary of the range of understanding of the ἔσχατον in Second Temple Judaic literature.

4. Charlesworth, "Jesus Research and Archaeology," 50–51; Kloppenborg, "Theodotus Synagogue Inscription," 223–82; Hengel, *Pre-Christian Paul*, 56.

5. Dunn, "Did Jesus Attend the Synagogue?" 217; Charlesworth, Review of *Settlement and History*, 283. Zangenberg, "Archaeological News," 471–84; Freyne, "Jesus of Galilee," 400.

The village synagogue was the name of the village meeting concerned with the whole range of community issues, including Torah reading and instruction[6]—to retain that primary focus I retain the Greek συναγωγή to cover Judaic gatherings for community purposes, debate, decisions, justice, teaching, prayer.

The Zealots / "zealots"

The *Zealots* is a term ascribed by Josephus to a specific group of resistance fighters in the War of 66–73 CE, and that *is* its primary connotation. During the last century, there was a misleading (though understandable) practice by many NT scholars in extending the term to cover all the various warlords and resistance groups that Josephus had labeled as "fourth philosophy."[7] This was, however, quite a useful shorthand practice, which I retain by the use of inverted commas and the small-case opening letter—"zealots"—when invoking that more generalized reference.

---

6. Horsley, *Archaeology, History and Society*, 131–53; Moxnes, *Putting Jesus in His Place*, 152–53; Dunn, "Did Jesus Attend the Synagogue?" 218–21.

7. E.g., Wainwright, *Guide to the New Testament*, 14–15. "The rebels were usually members of a nationalist group called Zealots."

Foundations

1

The Lost Brother

1. The Forgotten Brother

"I NEVER KNEW THAT Jesus had a brother," said Dave, my barber. He is not alone—James, the "Lord's brother" (Gal 1:19) is a largely forgotten character in the early Christian story despite traces of him having occupied a leading role in that unfolding drama.

1.1 Jacobean[1] Anomalies

In the canonical story, James mainly occupies the shadows on the edge of the stage,[2] only moving center-stage once—for the Conference of Jerusalem—yet his appearances betray a discordant picture. In the Gospel of Mark he appears as being at least unsympathetic to Jesus and is compared unfavorably (along with Jesus' family) to the family of Jesus' disciples (Mark 3:31–35; 6:3–4) and the fourth Gospel specifically states that "not even his brothers believed in him" (John 7:5), yet the earliest tradition (1 Cor 15:7) records an individual resurrection appearance to James and he seems to be referred to as an "apostle" (Gal 1:19). In Acts he emerges into the story (Acts 12:17) as a key person without explanation, a position that is soon clarified as being the presiding figure of the "Mother Church" of Jerusalem (Acts 15:13–21; 21:18), confirming much earlier evidence where James is

1. "Jacob" is the original Jewish form of the name: "James" is the familiar English version.

2. Hengel, *Saint Peter,* 10–11, computes eleven references to James' name in the NT compared with 177 occurrences of Paul's name and 181 of Peter's.

named first amongst the Jerusalem "Pillars" (Gal 2:9). A "general epistle" was ascribed to him, albeit after considerable hesitation in a later period.

Beyond the New Testament canon, the execution of James in 62 CE is reported by Josephus.[3] Otherwise, the person of James is overshadowed in the developing "orthodox" traditions of nascent Christianity who saw Christ's authority as being transmitted to later generations through the "chief apostle" Peter, whilst memories of James were revered mainly amongst inheritors of what we now often term as "Jewish Christianity," such as the traditions of Hegesippus reported by Eusebius and the Pseudo-Clementine literature, as well as by sects such as the Ebionites.

This anomalous presentation of James is found within the overall presentation of the origins of the Christian movement in the New Testament. Its grand design, sacralized through scripture, begins with the event of Jesus' life, death, and resurrection from whence the saving word is taken throughout the known world by a very focused primitive church. As in so many grand schemes however, historically, the devil is in the detail of an evidently more complex situation. John the Baptist and Jesus, Galilee and Jerusalem, Jewish and Gentile Christians, Paul and James present a cluster of dualities which disturb and sometimes disrupt the smooth surface narrative of the text and are indicative of tensions and stresses experienced within the movement.

1.2 Corporate Amnesia

Aside from those movements in the early Christian centuries that valued Jacobean traditions, a pattern of corporate amnesia (perhaps encouraged by the authorization vested in the canonization of the Lucan *Acts of the Apostles*) settled around the person of James, including the world of biblical scholarship, until very recently. In a bibliography of nearly two hundred authors in his comprehensive study of James,[4] John Painter lists only one book in English (by a journalist) devoted exclusively to James in the twentieth century prior to 1980: a slender volume (115 x A5 pages in a font-12 script)—Guy Schofield, *In the Year Sixty Two*.[5] From the same period there are just two volumes in German with a similar focus: the first by J. Blinzler (1967),[6] followed by L. Oberlinner (1975),[7] though the more significant

---

3. *Ant.* 20.200.

4. Painter, *Just James,* 292–302.

5. Schofield, *In the Year Sixty-Two.*

6. Blinzler, *Die Brüder und Schwester Jesu.*

7. Oberlinner, *Historische Überlieferungen.*

work from the mid-twentieth century is arguably Ethelbert Stauffer's paper exploring a Jacobean Caliphate[8] which Matti Myllykoski, in his extensive survey of Jacobean scholarship, described as "the only more or less programmatic article that sought to revalue the role of James in the history of early Christianity."[9] Prior to the 1980s, we have to go back as far as 1906 for an extensive study of James in English—W. Patrick, *James the Lord's Brother*.[10]

1.3 The Excluded Brother

The past thirty years have witnessed a remarkable surge of interest in the person of James and the movement that gathered around him. However, old habits still seem to die hard: around the turn of the century a major symposium—the Christian Origins Project—offered a new take on Christian beginnings, mainly drawing on the work of prominent North American scholars of the caliber of Burton Mack,[11] John Kloppenborg,[12] James Robinson and Helmut Koester,[13] Ron Cameron and Merrill Miller,[14] Elizabeth Castelli and Hal Taussig.[15] They question whether the diversity evident in the early Christian movement can originate from one point of singularity—the "Lucan paradigm"—and that question is valid and relevant to our quest.

In an impressive critique of the position of contemporary scholars of Christian origins such as E. P. Sanders, Dominic Crossan, and Richard Horsley, Miller argues that all attempts to found the origin of the Christian movement in Jerusalem founder on such incompatibilities as that between the political execution of Jesus and the description of a continuing vigorous messianic movement led by his close followers in that same city of Jerusalem.[16] Miller argues that the primacy of the Jerusalem church in our canonical records is rather a product of "the internal disputes and competing claims for legitimation of individuals and communities engaged in a

8. Stauffer, "Zum Kalifat des Jacobus."

9. Myllykoski, "James the Just in History and Tradition."

10. Patrick, *James the Lord's Brother*.

11. Mack, *Myth of Innocence*; Mack, *Lost Gospel*; Mack, *Christian Myth*.

12. Kloppenborg, *Formation of Q*; critiqued by James Dunn in his presidential address to the *Studiorum Novi Testamenti Societas* at Durham University (2002). Dunn, "Altering the Default Setting," 139–75.

13. Robinson and Koester, *Trajectories through Early Christianity*.

14. Cameron and Miller, *Redescribing Christian Origins*.

15. Castelli and Taussig, *Reimagining Christian Origins*.

16. Miller, "Beginning from Jerusalem," 3–30; Miller, "Antioch, Paul, and Jerusalem," 177–236.

mission to the Gentiles beginning in the late forties and the decade of the fifties."[17] James is not forgotten, he is excluded from the story.

Miller's focus on the unlikelihood of the followers of Jesus being able to operate openly in Jerusalem after the execution of their leader on a charge of treason does not consider a simpler alternative scenario: that James and the *Jakobusgemeinde* may have been an established and accepted grouping/ movement in the city, known to present no threat.

In the same time period as the Project, and responding to a similar sense of unease to the Lucan account of Christian beginnings in Acts, D. E. Smith diminishes the existence and role of a Jerusalem church in Christian origins, even suggesting that there were no Christophanies in Jerusalem, and so no original congregations in Jerusalem and no mission that spread out from there. The Pillars were not local, but missionary leaders whom Paul met on festival visits.[18]

But those who would exclude James and the *Jakobusgemeinde* from the story of Christian origins have to account for the passion, anxieties, and commitment Paul exhibited in carrying through his collection project for "the poor in Jerusalem," known to us in his contemporary, spontaneous memos embedded in his letters.

2. The Rediscovered Brother

That this absence of James is exclusion rather than amnesia has to be the diagnosis for these scholars were writing at the end of two decades that had seen an unparalleled resurgence of interest in James of Jerusalem, with a renewed emphasis that the origin(s) of Christianity must be situated in the world of Second Temple Judaism in the years leading up to 70 CE.

This reflects the seismic shift in biblical studies in the post-holocaust world from our previous Liberal-Protestant Establishment to a fertile collaboration of Gentile and Jewish scholars. With the seminal work of scholars such as E. P. Sanders[19] and Jacob Neusner,[20] as well as the window into the period furnished by the material now available from the Dead Sea Scrolls, it is recognized that the "orthodoxy" of Rabbinic Judaism cannot be projected back into that earlier period. Indeed, prior to 70 CE there were a number of

---

17. Miller, "Beginning from Jerusalem," 15.

18. Smith, "Was there a Jerusalem Church?" 57–74.

19. See Sanders, *Jesus and Judaism.*

20. See Neusner, *Rabbinic Traditions*; see "Neusner, Jacob" in Collins and Harlow, *Dictionary of Early Judaism,* 995–96 for an overview and appreciation.

differing persuasions about the implications of belonging to the Covenant People, hence the occasional use of the plural *Judaisms*.

Yet, in the same period, there has been a significant focus on a Hellenistic model for interpreting Jesus seen generally in the work of the Jesus Seminar[21] but more specifically in the "Cynic Jesus" proposals of Burton Mack,[22] qualified by John Dominic Crossan,[23] leading into the Christian Origins Project. In classical Hegelian mode[24] these developments helped stimulate the establishment of a comparable consultation on James under the guidance of Bruce Chilton, Craig Evans, and Jacob Neusner (§ 1. 2.3).[25]

This interest in James nourishes two concerns—first, to explore in this broader context his significance and contribution to the origin and development of early Christianity; and secondly, to assess the contribution a study of James can make to our understanding of Second Temple Judaism, of which the movement associated with his name was a part.

At the more populist level the adventitious discovery of the "James Ossuary"[26] certainly gave the Just One his fifteen minutes of fame—actually, slightly longer.[27]

2.1 The Challenge

The specific impetus to this renewed interest in James must be credited to the controversial publications on the Dead Sea Scrolls and Christian origins in the 1980s by Robert Eisenman.[28] He argues that the Qumran sectarian

21. Funk, et al., *Five Gospels*.

22. Mack, *Myth of Innocence*; Mack, *Christian Myth*.

23. Crossan, *Historical Jesus*, 421–22.

24. Chilton, in Preface to Chilton, Evans, Neusner *The Missing Jesus* vii.

25. Chilton and Evans, *James the Just*; Chilton and Evans, *Missions of James, Peter, and Paul*.

26. Shanks and Witherington III, *Brother of Jesus*; Silberman and Goren, "Faking Biblical History"; Tabor, *Jesus Dynasty* 15–23.

27. Oded Golan, an Israeli antiques collector, was charged with forty-four counts of forgery in 2004 (including that he faked the Ossuary inscription). Court proceedings concluded in October 2010, but it was not until March 2012 that the verdict was given with Golan being acquitted. The Judge ruled that the Prosecution had "failed to prove any of the serious charges" against him; however, adding that this verdict does not prove the authenticity of the inscription, and he anticipated that it will continue to be subject to further research (*Independent*, 15.03.12).

28. Eisenman, *Maccabees, Zadokites*; Eisenman, *James the Just*. These texts were combined in an expanded volume—Eisenman, *Dead Sea Scrolls and the First Christians*. His final most fully detailed presentation of his thesis (1073 pages, including

literature contains material from the *Jakobusgemeinde* (my descriptor) and implies[29] that the Qumranic Teacher of Righteousness may be James—a thesis of enormous import were it to be established.[30]

As Burton Mack and the Christian Origins Project had done, Eisenman totally dispenses with the dominant Lucan paradigm of Christian Origins which he argues is the creation of the Pauline/Gentile Christian movement, a betrayal of the strongly nationalistic "Torah-zealous" movement he finds associated with James.

Although his thesis is not completely dependent on his interpretations of the *Habbakuk Pesher* in the Dead Sea Scrolls,[31] it has been seriously undermined by radio-carbon dating of this and other key scrolls to a date in the first century BCE.[32] Additionally, the main thrust of his argument has received little support from other Scrolls' scholars.[33]

---

fifty-two pages of endnotes) is *James the Brother of Jesus*.

29. In his final book of the series on James, he displays significantly more caution—"Whether James is to be identified with the Righteous Teacher at Qumran or simply a parallel successor is not the point—the Scrolls allow us to approach the Messianic Community of James with about as much precision as we are likely to have from any other source." (Eisenman, *James the Brother of Jesus*, 963).

30. The presentation of his thesis is not helped by his marked dependency on Michael Baigent for whom he accords fulsome praise—"a bastion of support for me over many years" (Eisenman, *James*, xv). Baigent's characteristic literary fingerprints are all over *James the Brother of Jesus*. Baigent and Richard Leigh gained (with Henry Lincoln) a degree of notoriety with their popular book *The Holy Blood and the Holy Grail*, which was the inspiration for Dan Brown's novel, *The Da Vinci Code*, and the occasion of Baigent's failed damages claim in court for plagiarism. From *Holy Blood*, Baigent and Leigh went on to write their (discredited) conspiracy-theory book, *The Dead Sea Scrolls Deception*. Undeterred, Baigent's proven penchant for the conspiracy-theory genre never seems far from the surface of Eisenman's *James*.

31. "(I)n his recent work on James, Eisenman has in fact moved the emphasis away from the Scrolls and onto classical and patristic sources, particular (sic) the Pseudo-Clementine *Recognitions*."—Davies, "James in the Qumran Scrolls," 17–32. It is significant that in the introduction to his major work—*James*—Eisenman begins his *Introduction* by confidently asserting that "In so far as the 'Righteous Teacher' in the Dead Sea Scrolls occupies a similar position (to James), the parallels between the two and the respective communities they led narrow considerably, *even to the point of convergence*" (xix) (my italics) and urges that "Readers are encouraged to make judgments for themselves and, where possible, to go to the primary sources directly and not rely on secondhand presentations" (xxxv). However, in the *Epilogue*, almost a thousand pages later—heavily informed by the Dead Sea Scrolls—he claims that "The Scrolls (are) being used peripherally for purposes of external comparison and verification only." Eisenman, *James*, 959.

32. For example, 1QpHab is dated by Accelerator Mass Spectrometry between 88–2 BCE. See Vanderkam and Flint, *The Meaning of the Dead Sea Scrolls*, 30. The validity of these results (Oxford and Zurich, 1989–91 and University of Arizona, 1994–95) has been challenged—Atwill and Braunheim, "Redating the Radiocarbon Dating in the Dead Sea Scrolls," 143–57.

33. Davies, "James in the Qumran Scrolls," 20–21.

Eisenman's writing is strongly polemical[34] but his "hermeneutic of suspicion" is hardly pursued with equal vigor across all his sources; whilst his penchant for codes,[35] "over-writing" and allusions seems to have more affinity with the world of cryptic crossword puzzles:[36]

> Once one gets the knack of it, the Eisenman method proves itself as scientific (sic!)[37] as any employed in form and redaction criticism.[38]

In a paper analyzing the *Kittim* references in the Dead Sea Scrolls, George Brooke cautions against too easy an identification of passages with contemporary events:

> ... to derive history from the use of such texts in a commentary like 1QpHab seems foolhardy. . . . We can learn little or nothing of the history of the Qumran community from these texts, and little enough about the Romans.[39]

On the positive side, Eisenman does seek to place James within the social and political dynamics of Judaic Jerusalem in the turbulent years leading up to the Jewish War of 66–74 CE:

> One of the central theses of this book will be the identification of James as the center of the "opposition alliance" in Jerusalem, involved in and precipitating the Uprising against Rome in 66–70 CE.[40]

> We have placed James at the center of sectarian and popular agitation ending up in the fall of Jerusalem and we have identified the basic issues involved in such strife.[41]

---

34. Thiede, in an endnote in his *Dead Sea Scrolls*, drawing on a "conversation in Rome, 14 December 1999" describes Eisenman as "driven by a love for what he calls 'Jamesian Christianity,' uniting Judaism, Christianity, and even Islam, against the errors of the Pauline church" (247 n.44).

35. Related to codes is his characteristic penchant for linking names with the mantra: "In our view . . ." ("Paul as Herodian," 110–22).

36. In a positive review of his thesis, Robert Price describes Eisenman as being "armed with a hermeneutic of suspicion . . . (showing) . . . us how to crack the codes of theological disinformation, to listen to the long-faded echoes . . . to view the hitherto-unseen landscape of early Christianity" (Price, "Eisenman's Gospel," 186–97).

37. Whilst form and redaction criticism may not claim to fulfill Popperian verification criteria, they do work within clearly defined principles and a system of checks and balances.

38. Price, "Eisenman's Gospel," 196.

39. Brooke, "Kittim in the Qumran Pesharim," 158–59.

40. Eisenman, *James*, xxi.

41. Ibid., 963.

He portrays James as ultra-zealous for the Torah and thereby wielding a considerable moderating influence on the situation. It was the removal of James from the Jerusalem scene as a result of his execution that expedited the final slide into revolution. Unfortunately, Eisenman does not engage with a range of modern scholarship in this area[42] (a characteristic which runs all through his writing) and opts for a simple polarity[43] of a corrupt ruling elite in cahoots with the Roman occupying power over against a populace "zealous for Torah" for whom Gentile ownership and control of their holy land was an offense that cried to heaven for rectification.

Eisenman challenges us to take seriously the thoroughly Judaic nature of the Jacobean movement:

> Eisenman does not think in terms of a distinctive, novel "Jewish Christianity"—a sectarian movement that is not yet a religion separated from other forms of Judaism—but a stage in the evolution of the (one single) messianic movement in Palestine . . . The earliest Christianity, then, is marked not by any new departure but by an ongoing affirmation of long-held and purely Jewish values.[44]

However, following his failure to recognize the variety within late Second Temple Judaism, he can only affirm the thorough Judaic character of the *Jakobusgemeinde* at the cost of rejecting Paul and the Gentile mission as being irredeemably compromised with the pagan world and the Roman Imperium. Eisenman identifies Paul with the person of the Liar (or "spouter of lies,"[45] in his preferred translation) of the *Habakkuk Pesher*, linking this with a later Jewish-Christian labeling of him as the "enemy." Unfortunately, although some associated with James could well have used the invective[46] of the *Habakkuk Pesher*, the primary evidence of the authentic Pauline letters, which do indeed reveal real tensions between Paul and both James and Cephas, clearly demonstrates those tensions as being within a mutually owned relationship.

One final critique of Eisenman is that by bringing James out of the shadows so that he completely fills the stage, it is difficult to see how his

42. For example, Horsley, *Jesus and the Spiral of Violence*; Goodman, *Ruling Class of Judaea*; Hengel, *Zealots*.

43. Davies, "James in the Qumran Scrolls," 21.

44. Ibid., 25.

45. Eisenman, *James*, xxxiv.

46. Cf. Albert Baumgarten: " . . . the pool of terms used by groups of that era to describe themselves was quite small and . . . there was a significant overlap between the terms used by different groups. It seems as if there was a competition between groups which had the right to appropriate these favorable terms for itself" (Baumgarten, *Flourishing of Jewish Sects,* 34). Presumably the same applies to the slanderous terms they used of each other.

thesis can account for the "Jesus phenomenon"—that in the post-70 CE world both Judaic Christians (including Ebionites) and Gentile Christians centered their faith in Jesus. He completes his massive book with the enigmatic, but empty, phrase: "Whatever James was, so was Jesus."[47]

Equally enigmatic and tantalizing is his promise of a second volume that, in 1997, "has already been prepared." It is yet to appear. As early as 2004, Patrick Hartin produced *James of Jerusalem*[48] in which Eisenman is simply ignored.

However, scholarship owes a debt to Eisenman for his singular focus on James himself and the exploration of him within a thoroughgoing Judaic context, albeit too narrowly defined.

2.2 The Response

That James, the brother of the Lord, was now on the agenda of biblical scholarship is evidenced by Martin Hengel's provocatively titled paper "Jakobus der Herrenbruder—der erste Papst?"[49] as early as 1985—whereas Eisenman located James within the world of late Second Temple Judaism, Hengel stressed his place as a central and primal figure within the earliest years of the Christian movement.

Following Hengel and before Eisenman's definitive *James the Brother of Jesus* saw the light of day in 1997, other approaches to the *Jakobusbild* were entering the field:

First, Wilhelm Pratscher's *Der Herrenbruder Jakobus und die Jakobustradition* (1987)[50] carried out a wide and thorough survey, at considerable depth, of what can be known of James from contemporary and near-contemporary writings, through to the developing traditions centering around him, particularly in the Gnostic and Judaic-Christian writings. Evidence in the gospels (both Synoptic and Johannine) is strongly colored by the Evangelists' redactional presentation but does carry indications of a certain distancing between Jesus and his family, which was to change. James became a disciple following Jesus' resurrection appearance to him, only to become leader of the Jerusalem community after Peter moved away.

The best historical information is in Acts and Paul's letters, especially Galatians. Pratscher, following a suggestion initially made by Adolf Harnack,[51] sees the Cephas/James parallelism of 1 Cor 15:7 arising out of a conflict for

47. Eisenman, *James,* 963.

48. Hartin, *James of Jerusalem.*

49. Hengel, "Jakobus der Herrenbruder," 71–104.

50. Pratscher, *Der Herrenbruder Jakobus.*

51. Harnack, "Die Verklarungsgeschichte Jesu," 62–80

the leadership of the Jerusalem church between a "Peter group" and a "James group." His leadership of the Jerusalem church was a gradual process through the exercise of an administrative, rather than missionary, role.

Although their relationship was not close, Pratscher detects no antipathy between Paul and James and discounts the notion that James was behind the opposition that Paul faced in Galatia, Corinth, and Philippi.[52]

In Britain, Richard Bauckham was independently very active in Jacobean research. In *Jude and the Relatives of Jesus* (1990)[53] he brings together wide-ranging evidence from both Christian and rabbinic literature with Palestinian archeology to provide fresh insight into the role of the Dominical family in the early church within which James must find his place.

He followed this in 1995 with a major article on "James and the Jerusalem Church."[54] Anchoring himself firmly in a critical evaluation of the text of Acts he describes the initial leadership of the Jerusalem church being provided by the Twelve who are replaced by the Elders (who first appear in Acts 11:30) as the originating Apostles progressively disappear from the Jerusalem scene through a mixture of missioning, persecution, martyrdom and natural mortality. It is only after the attack on their leadership by Agrippa I, leading to the execution of James (Zebedee) and the imprisonment of Peter, that James (the brother of Jesus) emerges as the undisputed leader of the Jerusalem church, along with a council of twelve Elders. Bauckham contends that James' immunity from Agrippa's persecution was not because of his strict Torah-observance (a feature that was also true of Peter and the other James) but "simply that the Twelve were recognized as the leaders of the Christian community (whereas) James was not yet sufficiently prominent to attract such attention, but became prominent precisely during, and in the aftermath, of the persecution."[55]

The mid-nineties of the last century saw the almost contemporaneous publication of two major works, from France and Australia, centering on James—*Jacques, Frère de Jésus* by Pierre-Antoine Bernheim (1996),[56] and *Just James* from John Painter (1997).[57] Although Chilton describes them as responding "directly and indirectly to the controversial thesis of Robert H.

---

52. Best, Review of *Der Herrenbruder*, 377–82; Barrett, Review of *Der Herrenbruder*, 122–23; Myllykoski, "James the Just in History," 77–78.

53. Bauckham, *Jude and the Relatives of Jesus*.

54. Bauckham, "James and the Jerusalem Church," 415–80.

55. Ibid., 441.

56. Bernheim, *Jacques, Frère de Jésus*.

57. Painter, *Just James*.

Eisenman"[58] there is no overt evidence of this, other than an appendix in Painter's book.[59] Both seek to draw a historical portrait of James, founded on good critical scholarship.

Bernheim is interesting as he is not a member of the academy but a "writer and publisher" who nonetheless combines a high level of professional skill as a communicator with a wide grasp of contemporary scholarship in both French and English on James and Christian origins, demonstrating finely balanced judgments on the issues raised.

Unlike Eisenman, his focus is largely on the canonical material—after an initial excursion into the problematical sibling status of James in the first Christian centuries during which commitment to Mary's "perpetual virginity" strengthened. In good biographical style he attempts to piece together the setting of James' childhood in a pious, relatively comfortable and Torah-observant family of craftsmen living within the culture of first-century Palestinian Judaism, before treating James' (and the family's) relationship with Jesus. He notes that the resurrection appearance to him in 1 Cor 15:7 is not portrayed as a "conversion."

He travels familiar territory in dealing with the Antioch incident, arguing that Paul's Judaizing opponents in Galatia were probably organized from Jerusalem and therefore with some support from James. Amidst ongoing tension and alienation, he further argues, Paul had to go to Jerusalem on that final visit to seek an accommodation with James if he were to have any hope of continuing his distinctive mission program. Luke's silence about the collection suggests it was not accepted.

John Painter presents a balanced and comprehensive review of what can be known of James in his 1997 book, *Just James*. He goes beyond Bernheim in dealing extensively with the early church traditions about James through to the time of Jerome, as well as with the canonical material.

He distances himself from the widely accepted assumption that James changed from unbelief during the time of his brothers' ministry through an appearance of the risen Jesus, only rising to leadership in the movement after Peter's enforced flight from Jerusalem (Acts 12:17).[60]

Recognizing that the references to James in the New Testament are few and (with the qualified exception of his eponymous epistle) not written from his position, he proceeds to a detailed exegesis of the relevant material in the four Gospels, Acts, and Paul's letters. He argues that "the evidence

58. Chilton and Evans, *James the Just,* 3.

59. Painter, *Just James,* 277–88.

60. Painter, *Just James,* 13. Also, Painter, "James and Peter," 143–210. "The early emergence of James as the leader of the Jerusalem church is inexplicable if James and the brothers were unbelievers during Jesus' ministry" (146).

used to document the unbelief of the family, the brothers in particular, will not bear the weight of the case that has been built on it."[61]

Turning to Acts:

> James is portrayed as the leader of the Jerusalem church (and) there is nothing to suggest that this view represents a radical change within the Jesus movement. There is no evidence of a "conversion" of James from unbeliever to follower, nor is it clear that Peter was the first leader of the Jerusalem church, giving way to James only after a decade or so of leadership.[62]

Painter recognizes evidence of a leadership struggle between Peter and James, despite their close association in the circumcision mission. Looking back to Canon Streeter's classic work,[63] he accepts that Streeter's 'M' material represents traditions brought to Antioch by refugees from Jerusalem after 70 CE[64] where they have been assimilated into the Antiochene Petrine tradition, and the leadership of Peter is asserted against the ongoing influence of James and the Family.[65] Material, which originally expressed the position of James *vis-à-vis* Paul (e.g., Matt 5:17–20), is taken up into the Petrine position of intensification of the Law over against the emerging formative Judaism.

The middle section of *Just James* continues with an equally detailed and judicious exegesis of the largely later traditions of the church preserved in the writings of Eusebius[66], and the Nag Hammadi Library[67], along with apocryphal writings such as the gospels of *Thomas* and *to the Hebrews,* with a variety of later Christian evidence including *The Pseudo-Clementines,* Origen, and Jerome.[68] He draws out how James is gradually domesticated and placed within the orthodoxy of the developing Great Church, in contradistinction to his supreme position in Gnostic-Christian writings and in the Judaic-Christian tradition. He completes his work with a section on the Epistle of James and Jewish Christianity (with a critique of Eisenman[69]).

---

61. Painter, *Just James,* 41.

62. Ibid., 42.

63. Streeter, *Four Gospels.*

64. Also Meier, in Brown and Meier, *Antioch and Rome* 15–27, 45–72 (cf. Gerd Lüdemann, *Primitive Christianity,* 116).

65. Painter, *Just James,* 86–88.

66. Ibid., 105–223.

67. Ibid., 159–81.

68. Ibid., 182–223.

69. Ibid., 230–34, 277–88.

The strength of Painter's work lies in its comprehensive and detailed examination of all the early textual references to James—an invaluable resource—but therein inevitably lies its limitation: in the main, James is contextualized ecclesiastically. Painter is to be congratulated on seeking to situate James within the spectrum of pre–70 CE proto-Christian movements: it is equally (if not more) important to try to place him within the spectra of Judaic movements and practice in the Jerusalem of late Second Temple Judaism.

The social and economic dimension of this had been succinctly and suggestively explored by Ralph Martin (1988) within the very thorough introduction to his commentary on the Epistle of James.[70] He argues for a two-layered development of the Epistle, with original testamentary material from James being "edited and adapted to meet the pastoral needs" of an Antiochene community.[71] This original social context is viewed as being within the socio/economic situation of Palestine-Syria in the mid-sixties where James, "a Jewish Christian pietist and leader,"[72] is caught between his support for the oppressed poor (both people and priests) and opposition to the revolutionary manifesto of the "zealots."

Also coinciding with the appearance of Eisenman's final *magnum opus* came the release, significantly, of an English translation of Stauffer's 1952 paper: "The Caliphate of James."[73] From the evidence in Eusebius[74] that, following the death of James, the *Jakobusgemeinde* prioritized the election of a further member of the dominical family—Simeon—as the successor to James, Stauffer argued for the existence of a family dynasty (a "Caliphate") within the Jerusalem movement: Jesus is succeeded by James, with Simeon as next in line.

Similarly, James Tabor in 2006 builds on Stauffer's thesis of the standing and supreme authority of James and the dominical family within the *Jakobusgemeinde*, and from Jerusalem over the movement spreading from there. He asserts that, far from being distant from their ultimately more famous sibling, James and his brothers were disciples of Jesus during his ministry and claims that their names can be discerned near the end of the traditional listing of the Galilean "Twelve." James is also the "beloved disciple" of the fourth Gospel into whose care Jesus gave his mother from the cross.[75]

70. Martin, *James*.

71. Ibid., lxxvi–lxxvii.

72. Martin, *James,* lxviii.

73. Stauffer, "Caliphate of James," 120–43.

74. *Hist. eccl.* 11.1.

75. Tabor, *Jesus Dynasty*.

Recognition of the strength and significance of this primitive dynastic tradition tends to cut across the older scholastic tradition that viewed James as a later (post-resurrection) convert to his brother's movement, a position clearly reflected (with more sobriety than Tabor) in the title of Patrick Hartin's work of 2004—*James of Jerusalem: Heir to Jesus of Nazareth*: "In fact, James is the true heir to the message and way of life of Jesus. On him the mantle of Jesus truly rests."[76]

2.3 The Consultation

It was the religious and cultural dimension that became the focus for a significant series of consultations sponsored by the Institute for Advanced Theology at Bard College between 1997 and 2001, centering on the person of James, under the chairmanship of Bruce Chilton.[77] It is mainly a response, not to Eisenman, but to the writings of Mack and Crossan and the work of the Jesus Seminar,[78] particularly the hellenizing "Cynic thesis," to which Craig Evans gives a strong riposte.[79]

The literary outcome is a wide-ranging series of papers under the editorship of Chilton and Evans exploring (in the first volume) James within the context of pre-70 CE Judaism,[80] and then (in the succeeding volume) within the context of the early Christian movements.[81]

In his introduction to the first volume, *James the Just and Christian Origins,* Chilton outlines the necessary inter-relationship between the two focal issues of whether "Christianity (was) in fact *as well as in its self-awareness, a species of Judaism,*" following which "the question of James' standing in Jesus' movement obviously becomes crucial"[82] (italics original).

But "a merely historical approach offers no prospect of success," and even "the issue of (social) context is at least as problematic as the evidence concerning the particular person involved." The literary evidence is

76. Hartin, *James of Jerusalem,* xvii.

77. Chilton and Evans, *James the Just*; Chilton and Evans, *Missions of James, Peter, and Paul.*

78. Chilton, et al., *Missing Jesus,* vii.

79. Evans, "Misplaced Jesus," 14–27; Evans, "Assessing Progress," 35–54; cf. Hanson and Oakman, *Palestine in the Time of Jesus,* 125; Bernheim, *James,* 118–19; Pearson, "A Q Community in Galilee?" 476–94; Horsley, *Sociology and the Jesus Movement,* 116–19.

80. Chilton and Evans, *James the Just.*

81. Chilton and Evans, *Missions of James, Peter, and Paul.*

82. Chilton and Evans, *James the Just,* 4. Chilton appears to be using the descriptor "Jesus movement" in a wider sense than is adopted in this book (See "Notes on Some Terms Used").

fragmentary and "even were they to be taken at face value, (they) do not provide a coherent . . . account of Jesus' brother."[83] Rather, "they all make James into an image which comports with their own programs."[84]

Chilton urges that for James:

> (The) generative question . . . involves specifying the practices and beliefs which attach to James within the sources, and seeking to understand his place within them. Not every practice, not every belief may be assumed to be correctly attributed to James, but the various streams of tradition the documents represent do come together in what may be called nodes, to constitute stable associations of practices and beliefs with James. The nodal issues of practices and beliefs, not "facts," represent our point of departure. Just those nodal issues are addressed in our papers . . .[85]

The first set of seminar papers is therefore focused on the primary issue of seeking to situate James within Palestinian Judaism prior to the destruction of the Temple, first through "Issues of Background and Context" as epitomized by Neusner's paper on the Nazirite vow[86], followed by papers grouped under the heading of "James and Jewish Christianity" including an analysis by Markus Bockmuehl on "Antioch and James the Just" and an investigation by Richard Bauckham on the indictment that led to James's execution.[87]

The result is a stimulating broadening of awareness of the Judaic context of James, with no precipitous rush to conclusions. However, the socio-political context of pre–70 CE Jerusalem remains untouched (even by Bauckham's paper) and this has to be part of the James context—after all he was significant enough on the broader Jerusalem stage for the Judaic leadership to want to be rid of him.

The consultation produced two interim sets of "less technical"[88] papers in 2000—*The Brother of Jesus*[89] and *The Missing Jesus*[90] before the publication

---

83. Ibid., 5.

84. Ibid., 9.

85. Chilton and Evans, *James the Just,* 10–11.

86. Neusner, "Vow-Taking," 59–82.

87. Bockmuehl, "Antioch and James the Just," 155–98; Bauckham, "For What Offence," 199–232.

88. Chilton and Evans, *Missions of James, Peter, and Paul.*

89. Chilton and Evans, *Brother of Jesus.*

90. Chilton, et al., *Missing Jesus.*

in 2005 of their second major volume—*The Missions of James, Peter, and Paul*—which is nearly double the length of the first volume.

In *The Missions,* the focus of attention moves from viewing James within the context of Second Temple Judaism to his placing within the incipient, developing and expanding "movement which came to be called Christianity in its various cultural settings."[91]

With more data available, though still very limited, than for their first stage of enquiry—and none (except possibly his eponymous epistle) written from a Jacobean standpoint—the consultation chose an approach that I would describe as "triangulation" (a model from cartography). Through an exploration of his relationships with the other two major players in the story—Peter and Paul—we can look for a more balanced description of James specifically in those areas where their "lines of vision" intersect:

> Given James's own eminence, those relationships must have been hallmarks of his own stance and status, and they open the prospect that we might delineate James's theological perspective more precisely than otherwise possible by means of this contrast with Peter and Paul.[92]

Such an approach involves a more careful and nuanced approach to the positions of Peter and Paul on the major points of tension, particularly those surrounding the Gentile question, and only then might we begin to perceive the dim outline of James. This approach is epitomized by the papers of Bauckham,[93] Painter,[94] and Neusner.[95]

The Bard Institute's interest in James has continued into the establishment of the *Center for the Study of James the Brother* in 2007 "to address a critical period in the study of both Judaism and Christianity: the thirty years between 32 CE and 62 CE, when the Jesus movement was directed from the Temple in Jerusalem by James, the brother of Jesus."[96]

It is with the Consultations' papers on Paul and James[97] that we encounter a problem that is endemic to all study of James—the need to care-

---

91. Chilton and Evans, *Missions of James, Peter, and Paul,* vii.

92. Ibid.

93. Bauckham in Chilton and Evans, *Missions of James, Peter, and Paul,* 91–142.

94. Painter, "James and Peter," 143–210; Painter, "Power of Words," 235–75.

95. Neusner, "Israel's Gentile Problem," 275–306.

96. Bard College Press Release. October 11, 2007. The inaugural lecture was delivered by Sean Freyne, *Retrieving James/Jakov.*

97. Cf, Painter, "Power of Words," 235–74; Chilton, "Wisdom and Grace," 307–22; Davids, "Test of Wealth," 355–84; and "Why Do We Suffer?" 435–66; Davids, "James and Peter," 29–52.

fully clarify how the Epistle of James (EpJas) is perceived as relating to the historical person of James, the brother of Jesus. This is not done by any contributor, nor by Chilton in his introductory preface to this second volume. The only possible reference occurs in the introduction to the earlier volume where it could be included in his concept of "nodal issues" in "the various streams of tradition the documents represent."[98]

2.4 The Epistle

Yet, during this last quarter of a century, there has been a marked re-evaluation of the Epistle of James, shadowing the renewed interest in James of Jerusalem. With the benefit of hindsight, the publication in 1976 of the English translation of Martin Dibelius's magisterial commentary[99] on James was the finale to a long period of majority scholarly opinion[100] asserting the pseudonymity of the Epistle, from a date in the latter years of the first century well on into the second century. Pheme Perkins (1995)[101] and Sophie Laws (1980),[102] who argues for a second century setting in Rome, continue this earlier trend: otherwise there has been a strong resurgence of affirmation of the authenticity of the Epistle as deriving from James, and therefore to be dated before 62 CE in Palestine as seen in the commentaries of James Adamson (1976),[103] Luke Timothy Johnson (1995),[104] Richard Bauckham (1999),[105] Douglas Moo (2000),[106] Patrick Hartin (2003),[107] William Brosend (2004),[108] Ben Witherington III (2007),[109] Craig Blomberg/Mariam Kamell

98. Chilton and Evans, *James the Just*, 10–11.

99. Dibelius, *James*.

100. Davids, *Epistle of James*, 2–5. "The views expressed in fifty-five works since the end of the last (i.e., nineteenth) century: seven authors think that it is a lightly Christianized Jewish text; twenty-three in effect attribute it to James; for the twenty-five others, the letter will have been written after the death of James; however, seven of these consider that the anonymous author will have composed the letter on the basis of authentic writings of James" (Bernheim, *James, Brother of Jesus*, 309 n.3).

101. Perkins, *First and Second Peter, James, and Jude*.

102. Laws, *Epistle of James*.

103. Adamson, *Epistle of James*.

104. Johnson, *Letter of James*.

105. Bauckham, *James*; Bauckham, *Jude*, 133 n.233.

106. Moo, *Letter of James*.

107. Hartin, *James*.

108. Brosend II, *James and Jude*, 6.

109. Bird, Review of *Letters and Homilies*, 115.

(2008)[110] and Dan McCartney (2009);[111] whilst Peter Davids (1982),[112] Ralph Martin (1988),[113] Robert Wall (1997),[114] Freeman Sleeper (1998),[115] and Dale Allison[116] adopt variations of what could be termed a redactionist approach—memories and traditions originating from James/Jerusalem being shaped up to meet the needs of diasporan post–70 CE situations.

In a similar manner, Painter sees the Epistle as being the product of a Greek-speaking diasporan Jew intent on communicating the tradition of James from Jerusalem to the diaspora[117] and "in agreement with R. P. Martin it is argued that the tradition in EpJas is best understood against the background of the issue of poverty within the Jerusalem church before 66 CE."[118] Bernheim regards the Epistle as written by a Hellenized Jewish Christian, 60–70 CE, in touch with the traditions associated with James and the Jerusalem church.[119]

What is common to all these contemporary scholars, as well as to the James Consultation, is the belief/recognition that the Epistle of James preserves early Judaic/Christian tradition that can be treated as characteristic of traditions embedded in the *Jakobusgemeinde* and shared by the Lord's brother.

Strongly confronting this convergence is the argument of David Nienhuis (2007)[120] that we need to move away from the literary-historical paradigm that undergirds all these approaches. Emphasizing that there is no clear external evidence for the Epistle before Origen he presents a strong argument for contextualizing EpJas within the formation of the canon, heading a collection of letters linked with the names of the three Pillars (James, Peter, and John) to counterbalance those associated with the name of Paul, as the church responded in the mid-second century to the challenge presented by Marcion.

The lack of consensus on the provenance and dating of the Epistle advises caution in its use for a historical study of James.

---

110. Blomberg and Kamell, *James*, 35.

111. Lalleman, Review of *James*, 117.

112. Davids, *James*, 7–22.

113. Martin, *James*, lxxvi–lxxvii.

114. Wall, *Community of the Wise*.

115. Sleeper, *James*, 39–41.

116. Allison, *James*, 29.

117. Painter, *Just James*, 245–48; Painter and deSilva, *James and Jude*.

118. Painter, *Just James*, 247.

119. Bernheim, *James, Brother of Jesus*, 244.

120. Nienhuis, *Not By Paul Alone*.

2.5 A Dying Ember

Christopher Rowland's overview of *Christian Origins*[121] in 2002 could only find two paragraphs for James. This emphasizes that the explosion of interest in James initiated by Eisenman in the 1980s seems to have peaked at the turn of the century with the Bard Consultation and is now dying away with an occasional flare from the embers—Jeffrey Butz published his *The Brother of Jesus*[122] (2005) which is largely a more readable presentation of Eisenman's position but with a clearer polemical objective that the rediscovery of James and his tradition of teaching may form a bridge between Judaism, Islam and Christianity, healing the wounds of the centuries.[123]

3. Evaluation

In summary, an older scholarship on James tended to structure its reading of James around three key foci preserved in the NT:

- the alienation of James and his family from Jesus (expressed particularly clearly in Mark 3:19–35; 6:1–6);

- the appearance of the risen Jesus to James (1 Cor 15:7);

- the later emergence of James in Acts as the recognized leader of the Jerusalem church, co-incident with Peter's departure from Jerusalem (Acts 12:12–17).

Radically simplifying, the older consensus read this sequentially as describing a transformation of James from unbelief during the lifetime of his brother to faith in him following his encounter with the risen Jesus, and his gradual rise to leadership of the Jerusalem community in the succeeding years (especially as "the Lord's brother"), taking control of the movement there, after Peter fled from Jerusalem. Vestigial remains of this older consensus are still common. It is an approach strongly conditioned by the Lucan history of Christian beginnings in Acts.

The explosion of interest in James that marked the closing years of the twentieth century, whilst not delivering "assured results," has nonetheless witnessed movement away from this earlier framework and seems to be reaching towards new consensual positions on a number of issues:

121. Rowland, *Christian Origins,* 264–65.

122. Butz, *Brother of Jesus.*

123. This does appear to reflect a specific concern of Eisenman, though coming from a different direction to Butz. See n.34 above.

- the locus and identification of James to be found within the world of late Second Temple Judaism (e.g., Eisenman, Chilton, Evans, Neusner, and the Bard Consulation and Institute);

- the foundational importance of James for the Christian movement in Jerusalem and his continuing importance for later "non-orthodox" Christian traditions (e.g., Pratscher, Painter);

- a re-evaluation of the relationship between Jesus and his family during the time of his ministry with a greater openness to his brothers being, to some degree, followers of Jesus during that time (e.g., Painter, Bernheim, Hartin, Bauckham, Eisenman, Tabor);

- the appearance of the risen Jesus to James (1 Cor 15:7) is not viewed as a "conversion experience" (e.g., Painter, Bernheim, Hartin);

- James is the leader of the Jerusalem congregation: Peter's role is seen more as leader of the church's mission (e.g., Painter, Hartin).

3.1 The Omission

Gaps inevitably remain. Two significant ones are:

- With the exception of Eisenman, all this latter group who are working towards a new understanding of James continue to largely set their work within the much later historical framework provided by Luke in the *Acts of the Apostles*. This particularly affects discussion of how James came to leadership of the *Jakobusgemeinde*, which is a central concern of this book.

- Missing from all this historical interest in James is any interest in the question I became captivated by (see *Preface*)—did James have a life before Jesus, and what might its implication be for our understanding of the origins of the "mother church" of Jerusalem?

4. The Quest

4.1 Problem and Proposal: A Tale of Two Brothers

The New Testament bears clear evidence of diversity within an idealized unity. The traditional (canonical) model is that the Christian movement flows from what cosmologists would describe as a "singularity"—Jesus of Nazareth whose life and work was mainly in Galilee, but who was killed in

Jerusalem. Within this narrative James is presented as unbelieving during the lifetime of Jesus and then emerges as the natural and undisputed leader of the Christian movement from Jerusalem. Galilee disappears totally from the story and is replaced by a vigorous assertive community of followers (led by Jesus' own brother, of all people) in the very city where their leader had been executed for alleged treason only a short time before. This is widely recognized as dissonant.

4.1.1 An Eighteenth-Century Analogy

The Evangelical Awakening of the eighteenth century in England provides an interesting analogy, for today John Wesley is routinely referred to as the founder of the Methodist Church, and the latter community annually celebrate a distinct experience and even a precise point in time as its originating moment. It is also a story of two brothers. But the reality was more complex:

- A time of social and economic change and stress saw the emergence of a number of renewal groups within and on the fringes of the church, of which the movement linked with the Wesley brothers simply proved the most durable.[124]

- There were a number of other significant leaders from within this groundswell of renewal (both within and outside Wesley's "connexion"), whose names are now only recognized by the historically interested.[125] Some nurtured their own movements, whilst others continued to minister within the Established Church.

Wesley's movement emerged as a church out of all this creativity. Some of the other renewal groups merged in with the Wesleyan movement, whilst

---

124. For example, the Moravians were a major influence on Wesley. The "Evangelical Awakening" of the eighteenth century preceded Wesley's experience of 1738—a spontaneous revival movement had begun three years earlier in 1735 in a Welsh village following the conversion of Howell Harris, who both initiated "field-preaching" and gathered his converts into "Societies," practices that were later adopted by Wesley. Independently, a movement of revival occurred in England in the same year of 1735 under the preaching of George Whitefield following his own conversion. It was only in 1739 that Wesley came at the request of Whitefield to support him in work amongst the Kingswood miners of Bristol whose "awakening" was occurring through Whitefield's preaching.

125. In addition to Harris, Whitefield, and John's brother Charles there is the Countess of Huntingdon, William Grimshaw of Haworth, Vincent Perronet, John Fletcher of Madeley, and John Berridge (center of the "Everton revival" of 1756–59)—all Anglican parish priests—Thomas Maxfield, Captain Foy, John Nelson, John Haime, Thomas Olivers, Mary Bosanquet, et al. (Davies, *Methodism,* 78–83).

others maintained a separate existence with varying degrees of success. But all that historical complexity is now truncated into the logo: "John Wesley is the Founder of Methodism."[126] Traditions in their usage become streamlined, augmented and focused[127]—a gestalt effect whereby as the spotlight falls on the central action it fills the arena of our awareness and other actors blur into the background. Accordingly, words, actions and initiatives of other actors tend to accrue to the name and credit of the central figure (§§ 3. 5.2; 7. 7.2).[128]

4.2 A Fresh Perspective

This eighteenth-century analogy is suggestive of a differing way of looking at Christian origins:

4.2.1 Overview

We must locate Christian origins firmly within the social situation of first-century Palestinian Judaism, also a time of economic and social stress. The challenge of Hellenistic culture and the issues raised by the reality of Roman

126. Dunn, *Beginning from Jerusalem*, 133–35. Dunn notes the Methodist analogy (with others), and that Luke's "presentation of a single day and place of origin for the whole of what was to follow" may result from "giving exclusive attention to what was a much messier and more fragmented beginning." He briefly notes such "Hints within the New Testament" (135–37) but pursues it no further.

127. Even in our literary age it is a process which continues: in a book devoted to the sayings of Winston Churchill, Richard Langworth devotes a final chapter to *Red Herrings*—sayings and aphorisms originating elsewhere which have become attached to the great man through popular usage (Langworth, *Churchill's Wit*, 201–06). In a very different context, Jim Perrin, in his recent biography of the iconic British climber, Don Whillans, offers a detailed analysis of one of the many legends that grew around him within the climbing community, laying bare the original event. He details how characters and names from other stories blend with imagery from *Dandy/Beano* strip-cartoons and the psychological need of the storytelling community in a time of social change for a "working class hero" to produce the final story (in this case, Whillans prowess at brawling as a diminutive fifteen year old). He stresses that legends such as this developed within the very small community of climbers in the 1950s when (without a linked media industry) information exchange depended largely on oral transmission. Perrin observed: "The oral tradition, when recounting human performance, has never valued the accurate above the imaginative in its reportage. And so myths grow, *reflecting as they do something of their community's essential yearnings*" (my italics). Perrin, *Villain*, 84–89.

128. This focusing on to a central figure is even extended into hymnody—"Hark, the Herald Angels Sing," is a redaction by George Whitefield and Martin Madan of a Charles Wesley original, but is solely ascribed to Charles Wesley in the authorized Methodist hymn-books. *The Methodist Hymn Book* (1932), *Hymns and Psalms* (1983), and *Singing the Faith* (2011)—a practice not followed by other denominations.

Imperialism produced a range of responses. One significant reaction was a renewed affirmation of the fundamentals of Judaic faith and traditions. This developed into a groundswell of renewal that manifested itself over time in a variety of groupings with differing levels of permanence and identity. The figure of John the Baptist has particular significance. It is within this context that the movement associated with Jesus of Nazareth must be located, along with other proto-Christian movements, which eventually coalesced into the movement(s) that would later be identified as "Christian."[129] Such was the eventual strength of the Jesus-tradition that it absorbed these parallel traditions into itself leaving only shadows of their original provenance.

James and Jerusalem represent one such proto-Christian stream. It is proposed that James was already leader (even founder) of a Torah-observant renewal movement in Jerusalem, strongly affected by the Baptist's message, and contemporary with (even prior to) the activity of his brother in Galilee. This would, alongside location in Jerusalem and his sibling relationship to Jesus, both account for the strength of the *Jakobusgemeinde* with its particular ethos, and the unquestioned eminence of James in Jerusalem and within the developing Christian movement.

In pre–70 CE Palestine it is anachronistic to use the descriptor "Christian" with its connotation of self-identity and distinctiveness. The primary assumption must be that these proto-Christian groupings saw themselves, and were treated as such by their contemporaries, as being within the broad stream(s) of late Second Temple Judaism, albeit with varied tolerance-levels.

4.2.2 Outline of Process

- **Ground Survey**

  We begin by mapping out the world of James to guide and alert us in our search (§§ 2.–3.):

  – it is the world of late Second Temple Israel experiencing the impact on its fabric and traditions from the incursion of Hellenistic culture and the imposition of Roman Imperial rule (§ 2. 1–5).

  – Into this picture is drawn an analysis of a range of responses developed within Israel as it sought to hold the conflict between its strong sense of national/tribal identity and the *realpolitik* of

---

129. "(A) growing conviction amongst students of Christian origins that earliest Christianity was diverse." Paget, "Marcion and the Resurrection," 74–102.

its situation, with a particular focus on the sectarian response (§ 2. 6).

- The "Ground Survey" is completed by a closer consideration of two significant movements of Judaic reform that are contemporaneous with both James and Jesus—the Essenes and John the Baptist (§ 3.).

- **Locating James (§§ 4.–7.)**

We view:

  - The primary contemporary evidence of Paul (§ 4.);

  - The limited narrative-tradition involving James in *Acts;* joined with the Lucan portrayal of the *Jakobusgemeinde* (§ 5.);

  - The fragmentary evidence relating to James and his family (§ 6.);

  - The significance of the lack of interest in the Galilean Jesus that is present in all the tradition trajectories originating from Jerusalem (§ 7.).

- **Evaluation (§§ 8.–9.)**

  - A review and summary of the main evidence concerning James and the *Jakobusgemeinde.* (§ 8.);

  - A re-valuation of Luke's foundation myth of the church. (§ 9.)

2

The World of James

THE TASK OF DISCOVERING James of Jerusalem is similar to that of an archeologist investigating a site that has been subject long ago to a massive upheaval. On the ground occasional fragments are found that don't belong in their present setting and point to a different origination. In first century Palestine, that upheaval is the Jewish War of 66–73 CE.

Our archeologist's first task is a ground survey, scanning the morphology of the site with mental antennae attuned by training and experience of comparable excavations for any site indicators and surface markers that might repay careful excavation and investigation. That is our initial task as well—to map out the world of James of Jerusalem, identifying those surface markers that are promising for more detailed investigation and for clarifying the questions (our scholastic "tool") we need to bring to bear on the material.

1. A Problem of Historiography

In approaching a study of James we immediately confront a problem: a distinct lack of data—a few fragmentary pieces of information and allusions caught up and dragged along like flotsam into a diverging and strengthening stream of tradition. Their evaluation is determined within that current, rather than from the source which gave them original significance. Even a modern biography, drawing on an abundance of data, can only operate meaningfully through exploration of the person-in-context. With James the data is so sparse that biographical writing as commonly understood is a non-starter, even if it were good or relevant historical methodology.

1.1 Site Morphology

Our approach to James therefore is to explore his world of first-century Palestine as prelude to an attempt to contextualize his relationship to it and his place within it. This will involve an exploration of the socio-economic-political realities of that far-off world[1] and the perceptions, particularly within the Judaic culture,[2] of those whose life experiences were circumscribed by the Roman Imperium.

We need to place the proto-Christian movement(s) in that world with special attention to a locus in Jerusalem, apart from which no understanding of James is possible (§§ 2.–3.). Only then can we turn our attention to James himself (§§ 4.–7.).

1.2 Contextualization—A Quantum Leap

Contextualization is important, it highlights the significance and relevance of available data, it enables a possible placing of fragmentary information, and it is a recognition that people are, at both micro- and macro-level, a product of their social context and of the social forces operating around and through them.[3]

Amongst the immediate problems this raises is the level of technology available in the first century CE, which did not support an "information society." Information that might be available for later generations was sparsely recorded in the first place, and material evidence through archeology is inevitably partial, subject to the favors of Lady Luck, and very expensive (pro rata). Further, the social sciences did not exist as a discipline, so the information we have, literary and epigraphic, was addressed to other concerns

---

1. Cf., Crossan, *Historical Jesus*; Horsley, *Jesus and the Spiral of Violence*; Horsley, *Archeology, History and Society*; Stegemann and Stegemann, *The Jesus Movement*; Theissen, *Gospels in Context*; Mack, *Christian Myth*; Bauckham, *Book of Acts*; Crossley, *Why Christianity Happened*; Goodman, *Rome and Jerusalem*.

2. Cf., Freyne, *Jesus, a Jewish Galilean*; Nickelsburg, *Ancient Judaism and Christian Origins*; Thiede, *Dead Sea Scrolls*; Vanderkam and Flint, *Meaning of the Dead Sea Scrolls*; Moxnes, *Putting Jesus in His Place*.

3. In connection with historical Jesus scholarship James Crossley has argued that the traditional focus on the person of Jesus overlooks "the questions of why the Jesus movement emerged when and where it did and whether the individual historical figure of Jesus had any causal importance in the emergence of what was to become Christianity." (Original paper presented at the 25th Annual Conference of the British New Testament Society in Sheffield, 2006. Published in amended form—Crossley, "Writing about the Historical Jesus," 63–90.

and (especially the literary component) is the product of upper elite controlling groups, embodying their perceptions of social reality.

There is a great gulf (not simply two millennia) between the world of first-century CE Palestine within the Roman Empire and the twenty-first century CE world of Western liberal democracy and global capitalism—a quantum leap.

2. Community and Association

2.1 *Gemeinschaft* and *Gesellschaft*

In approaching that far-off world of James we must recognize that one fundamental difference between all ancient societies and our contemporary Western society and culture lies in the relationship between an individual and their community—a distinction focused for us by Ferdinand Tönnies[4] in the late nineteenth century in the concepts of *Gemeinschaft* (community) and *Gesellschaft* (association[5]).

Gemeinschaft describes a conception of social organization and being in which the group, tribe, nation is the basic unit and the individual understands his or her existence only as a member of the group. An extreme expression of this in the last century was the Japanese *kamikaze*. *Gemeinschaft* is described by Raymond Plant as:

> based on kinship, shared habitat and a set of common attitudes, experiences, feelings and dispositions. Once a member, he can never leave it, unless physically, but remains tied.[6]

By contrast, *Gesellschaft* highlights the primacy of the individual whose social life is experienced through a rainbow assortment of groups and associations to which s/he belongs through some degree of choice for the instrumental purpose of achieving individual goals. A *Gesellschaft* society derives its energy and direction through the competitive/co-operative interplay of such groupings. An extreme form of *Gesellschaft* was in Margaret Thatcher's dictum that "there is no such thing as society. There are individual men and women, and there are families,"[7] whilst a more sober statement is enshrined in the United Nations' Charter of Human Rights.[8]

---

4. Tönnies, *Gemeinschaft und Gesellschaft*, 223–31.
5. Sometimes translated as "Society."
6. Plant, "Community," 88–90.
7. The Lady had clearly never experienced football terraces on a Saturday afternoon.
8. "Everyone has the right to freedom of thought, conscience and religion; this right

Tönnies recognized that *Gemeinschaft* and *Gesellschaft* were conceptual tools and although in the real world there is always a degree of mix,[9] they do nonetheless highlight essential features of how communities and cultures—and individuals within them—function and understand themselves and others:

> Both village and town retain many characteristics of the family; the village retains more, the town less. Only when the town develops into the city are these characteristics almost entirely lost. . . . But as the town lives on within the city, elements of the *Gemeinschaft*, as the only real form of life, persist within the *Gesellschaft*, although lingering and decaying.[10]

First-century CE Palestine clearly embodies one self-understanding and twenty-first century Western culture, its clearest expression in North America, the other—a great gulf. Bruce Malina, writing from the perspective of the cultural anthropology of first century Mediterranean society similarly draws a contrast between modern Western concepts of personal individuality and a concept of the individual embedded in the group.[11]

These twin concepts of *Gemeinschaft* and *Gesellschaft* are crucial to any understanding of the relationship between religion and the society in which it is embodied. With *Gemeinschaft*, religion is an integral and necessary component of the tribal/national mythology through which the self-identity and self-understanding of its members are understood, expressed and reinforced. For a person to choose another religious system is to reject (and be rejected by) the very community that has nurtured them. In societies where *Gesellschaft* dominates, religious belief and practice is a matter of personal (even private) choice and its social expression involves joining an *association* which (any theology notwithstanding) is a voluntary group defining itself over against other *associations* and its overall society. To change religion does not involve rejection of, or incur rejection by, the broader community (other than some possible disapprobation by members of the previous face-to-face grouping).

---

includes freedom to change his (*sic*) religion or belief, and freedom, either alone or in community with others and in public or private, to manifest his religion or belief in teaching, practice, worship and observance." (The Universal Declaration of Human Rights: Article 18.)

9. Crook, "Structure versus Agency," 251–75; Lawrence, "Structure, Agency *and* Ideology," 277–86.

10. Tönnies, *Community and Society,* 223–31.

11. Malina, *New Testament World,* 54–55.

2.2 From *Gemeinschaft* to *Gesellschaft*:
A Historical Illustration

Within European history the displacement of a predominantly *Gemeinschaft* orientation by the first stirrings of a *Gesellschaft* understanding flowed from the social and intellectual upheaval of the Renaissance, and the English Reformation can be described as the story of a period during which the dominant orientation within society began to move from *Gemeinschaft* to *Gesellschaft*. Yet deep tension between the two perceptions was experienced at both individual and communal levels, so ingrained in the human psyche was the older understanding, even though the days described by Bede[12] when the conversion of a king was naturally followed by the baptisms of his people were long gone.

The anomalous position within a liberal democracy of the Church of England as the National Church inter-meshed with the traditional power structures, voicing the prayers of the nation on occasions such as Remembrance Day, "established by Law" and therefore subject to Parliament, is a vestigial remnant of this earlier *Gemeinschaft* society. The same traditional understanding underlies the practice of parish priests who vicariously offer the life and prayers of their parish to God in their daily observance of the Divine Office.

A key dimension of the religious struggles of the English Reformation (from an Anglican perspective) can be seen as the attempt to retain the Church of England as just that—the *Church* of *England*, with the soul of the Church as well as political power at issue in the Civil War. First, Presbyterianism[13] and then, in the days of the Commonwealth, Puritanism sought to see their tenets and concerns embedded in and expressed through the national Church.[14] Thus, common to all was still the understanding that the Church was integral to any expression of the community's being.

Common to all, that is, except the dissenting congregations amongst whom we can see the emergence of a *Gesellschaft* concept of society. Yet the strength of the *Gemeinschaft* sentiment can be demonstrated both in the way the dissenters were seen as threatening the stability of the traditional social order[15] whilst defining themselves largely within the crucial parameters of Trinitarian Christianity,[16] which was still being viewed as

12. Bede, *History of the English Church*, 123–26.

13. Leading to Milton's famous dictum: "New Presbyter is Old Priest writ large."

14. Oliver Cromwell never belonged to a dissenting congregation.

15. Roman Catholics were a special case, whose rejection of the legitimacy of Anne Boleyn's offspring was *de jure* treason.

16. Unitarians and Quakers were significant exceptions.

an essential component of the community's Christian self-understanding and expression.

The Society of Friends ("Quakers") present an interesting case. Authority was not vested in scripture, dogma or church hierarchy but in the "inner light" (understood as the light of Christ within). Although historically rooted in Christianity and still seeing themselves within that tradition,[17] theirs was essentially an affirmation of the autonomy of the individual over against external authorities (bishops were very concerned at its spread[18]— they were right!), but it was an affirmation that could still at that time only be made within the framework of a Christian Faith understood as a crucial expression of English self identity.[19]

2.3 *Gemeinschaft* and the World of James

This way of interpreting the progress of the English Reformation highlights features that are germane to our understanding of the world of James. It demonstrates the power of *Gemeinschaft* in defining perceptions of social reality with the associated communal and personal conceptions of self-identity and strong internalization of those perceptions, seen in its continuing power long after its social and economic rationale has begun to move in the direction of *Gesellschaft*.

Religion is seen as integral to the community's self-understanding and corporate expression with dissent experienced and viewed as a threat to the social structure. Therefore any new movements in religion are likely to be seen (i.e., to see themselves, and probably be seen by others) as movements of reform within the normative pattern of religious expression of that culture, drawing upon that culture's shared traditions for its inspiration, strength and direction and, initially at least (if at all), will organize itself within the community's recognized structures, rather than over against them.

Therefore in trying to get a grip on the proto-Christian community in Jerusalem we should not use the word "church" nor think the concept "church" (especially with images of congregations)—that inevitably

17. It can be argued that they are not specifically or essentially Christian—there is no necessity for scripture or prayers to Christ "as to a god" (with apologies to Pliny) in their meetings.

18. During the 1980s I chanced upon an exhibition at Hope Parish Church (Derbyshire) which included copies of the Incumbent's response to a Diocesan inquiry by his Bishop (seventeenth–eighteenth century) concerning the state of his parish, prominent in which were questions about the number of Quakers known to be in the parish.

19. It took another 150 years before Charles Bradlaugh and Annie Besant could publicly affirm an atheist position.

transposes material from a later (not necessarily much later) period into a world where they do not belong. Similarly, we must not transfer images from the contemporaneous communities in the urban diaspora, addressed by Paul in his letters. We need to think in terms of currents and movements within Judaic society, whilst recognizing that development (possibly rapid) might mature into something more recognizable as a "sect" prior to 70 CE.[20]

Thus, movements triggered by the complex of events surrounding John the Baptist and Jesus could not have developed within Israelite society other than by seeing themselves and being accepted by others as within the Abrahamic/Mosaic traditions and Torah-informed practices of their society, particularly within the Temple-city of Jerusalem. It is not that anything else would have resulted in a rejection and excommunication, which would have snuffed out the tremulous beginnings of a new movement, but it was simply unthinkable.[21]

It was only later with the Pauline mission, coming to its climax in his visit to Jerusalem and its Holy Places with the offering from (of?) his dominantly Gentile communities, that this development of what is becoming an identifiable Christian movement goes "a bridge too far" with its challenge to two of the central concerns of Judaic religion and society—ethnicity (with its related rite of circumcision) and Torah.

Although some elements of the Christian movement almost certainly experienced increasing tension with other expressions of Judaic belief and practice (cf., the hostility between the movement and those represented by the Pharisees reflected in the Gospels) it was still intra-Judaic conflict (a sign of vigor and commitment on all sides) and within the binding ties symbolized by *Gemeinschaft*.

The proto-Christian movements (even that of Paul's Gentile mission) must be seen as movements within this Judaic/Israelite self-understanding, extending beyond the Josephian canon of Sadducees, Pharisees, Essenes and "Fourth Philosophy"[22] to include those who valued and preserved

20. A "sect" has a heightened sense of self/group identity over against the wider community from which its membership is drawn, with significant "boundary markers" identifying who is "in" and who is "out." Before the end of the first century Luke describes the Christian movement associated with the Pauline Gentile mission as a "sect" (Acts 28:22).

21. When such excommunication from the synagogue did eventually occur later in the century, a maturing sense of separate identity was developing within the Christian movement, giving both psychological and social protection, although writings such as the Epistle to the Hebrews bear witness to the deep anxieties, so typical of a *Gemeinschaft* orientation, this "parting of the ways" did incur for many.

22. See "Notes on Some Terms Used": *Zealots*.

the Enochian literature[23] and the sign-prophet/messianic movements (§ 2. 6.2.3) that Josephus so disliked but could not ignore. The varied proto-Christian movements need factoring in; otherwise, we are perpetuating the paradigm that views Christianity as a self-conscious new religious movement from the outset. There is a need to understand and locate proto-Christian movements both within and contributing to the spectrum of movements and ideas within late Second Temple Judaism—and to locate them as Judaic movements, expressive of a Judaic *Gemeinschaft*.[24]

We note too that observers (contemporary and modern) label all these movements for us and this can mask a reality of greater boundary-porosity. For example, the *Jakobusgemeinde* seems to be largely at home within Pharisaic streams of dialogue and to have been the proto-Christian movement most "at ease in Zion"—theologically and geographically (§ 5. 9.1).[25]

2.4 Group Identity within *Gemeinschaft*

As Tönnies had recognized, *Gemeinschaft* should not be taken to imply an undifferentiated sameness throughout society: rather it provides the overarching frame of reference within which individuals, kinship networks,

23. Nickelsburg, *Ancient Judaism and Christian Origins,* 179–81.

24. These Judaic streams were not necessarily exclusive. For example, at the time of the Jewish War we encounter John the Essene as a "zealot" leader (*J.W.* 2.567) (Marcus, "*Birkat Ha-Minim* Revisited," 543) and there is explicit evidence in Acts (Acts 15:5) and inferential evidence in Galatians (Gal 2:4) of Pharisees belonging to the Christian movement. Priests could be associated with any stream of Judaism, including the *Jakobusgemeinde* (Acts 6:7). There are also allusions indicating "zealots" amongst the Jesus people:

- "Simon the Zealot" is listed amongst the Twelve (Luke 6:15). However, this may be an anachronism on Luke's part, or a nickname enshrining his enthusiasm, or a reference to his "zeal for the Law" in the way that Paul describes an earlier phase of his Judaic commitment (Phil 3.6).

- More intriguing is the call to "take up their cross" (Mark 8:34, et al.) which is surely more credible as a call to resistance on the lips of such a one as John of Gischala. (cf. S.G.F. Brandon, *Trial of Jesus of Nazareth,* 147). That it has entered into Christian tradition is probable testimony to the porosity of boundaries between resistance and kindred groups in the Israelite society of this period.

- Castigation of the rich in Jas 5:1–6 may betray the trace of a "zealot" presence in the *Jakobusgemeinde*

25. This is perhaps the reality behind a story Hegessipus relates that can be too easily dismissed (*Hist. eccl.* 2.23.1–18)—the occasion when James (of all people) is asked by the Temple authorities to caution the Passover crowds about their over-enthusiastic attachment to Jesus as the Christ. This may preserve a historical reality that the Judaic authorities saw James as "Us" rather than "Them"—perhaps a "safe pair of hands."

villages, tribes, regions, nation, and scattered ethnic groups have a shared sense of belonging together. "In-group" over against "out-group" factors are essentially involved at all levels of human community awareness: "Galileans" were definitely not "Judeans" but nonetheless shared a common identity as Israelites over against "the Gentiles." And Nazareth certainly had its own identity—"can anything good come out of Nazareth?" (John 1:45).

This "in-group"/"out-group" factor positively exults in the practice of labeling, which frequently originates with the out-group, even though the in-group may take it and own it (as, for example, the label "Christian," Acts 11:26). Within a small village community such as Nazareth primary group face-to-face relationships would be almost coterminous with the population of the whole village. The label "Nazarene" is more likely to have been used of the inhabitants of Nazareth by "outsider" Galileans, rather than initially by themselves, although they might readily adopt and own the term in interaction with other Galileans. It would then, for instance, be available as a ready badge of identity for any grouping of migrant workers from the Nazareth region living in Jerusalem.

It is within urban areas[26] that new associations, perhaps initially rooted in kinship/geographic or occupational identities, but spreading beyond that, begin to develop:

> The emergence of a diversity of groups in Jewish society fits the pattern of agrarian empires when they become large and complex. Society became differentiated and stratified and that led to the development of social groups in addition to basic kinship and political groups.[27]

But that differentiation remains within the broader *Gemeinschaft* complex.

3. The Socio-Economic World of Late Second Temple Judaism

3.1 An Advanced Agrarian Society

The economy of first-century Palestine, common to the ancient Mediterranean region, is an *Advanced Agrarian Society*.[28] This is beyond a basic

---

26. Stark, *Rise of Christianity,* notes that a deviant sub-culture develops more easily in a large urban area where it is easier to achieve a critical mass (134).

27. Saldarini, *Pharisees Scribes and Sadducees,* 60.

28. Stegemann, *Jesus Movement,* 7–14; Horsley, *Sociology and the Jesus Movement,* 68–80.

subsistence level—the technology and social organization allow for a very modest surplus giving possibilities of small amounts of local trade (and taxation) and hence the need for a social structure and a control of these fairly elementary manifestations of economic activity which were provided through the urban centers.

Thus agrarian societies, where rural societies were the vast majority, were involved in agriculture and its related activities, but living in a symbiotic relationship with their neighboring cities that were a market for their produce:

> Socially and politically . . . cities also shaped the character of Mediterranean agrarian societies, since in them lived the elite, who as owners of property and wealth, and as possessors of social control, ruled both country and city. This detailed definition of the agrarian type of society can call attention to the fact that agricultural production—and not it alone—was subject to a political and social governance system that through *redistribution* concentrated the wealth of society in the hands of a small number of the elite.[29] (italics original)

A need for social structure and its control was thus an opportunity, readily grasped, so that the essential "symbiotic relationship" was easily experienced by the rural population as more akin to a parasitic one.

3.1.1 Social Structure

An agrarian society is basically divided into two groups with virtually zero social mobility between them[30]—the very small, very rich, very powerful elite in the cities (3 percent of the total[31]), who use that position and power to exploit the peasant agrarian economy of the surrounding region for their own benefit and in so doing consolidate their power even more.

Analysis of status discrimination within this tiny elite grouping has been comparatively straightforward—they have left their literary footprint on the records. The footprints of the less literate majority are much harder to discern. Steven Friesen has proposed in relation to the Roman Empire a more detailed "Poverty Scale" (PS),[32] which, despite its limitation, does

---

29. Stegemann, *Jesus Movement*, 7.

30. Ibid., 67.

31. Friesen, "Poverty in Pauline Studies," 323–61.

32. Ibid.

open up the possibility of a more nuanced discussion of social distinctions amongst the non-elite majority.[33]

This has facilitated the identification of two groups (PS 4&5)[34] in the middle of the scale who are generally, or even comfortably, above a minimum subsistence level. Friesen tentatively estimates that these constitute about 29 percent of the population.[35] Bruce Longenecker, whilst accepting the Scale as a working tool, has presented evidence that these "middling groups" were a significantly higher proportion of the population, suggesting a figure of about 42 percent.[36]

3.1.2 Social Mobility

This figure of 42 percent is what we might expect in view of the impact of urbanization on employment opportunities and structure. The growth of the cities, whether Jerusalem or Sepphoris, with their associated needs of social organization and control; economic, financial and commercial life; legal expertise and enforcement; plus the cultural and entertainment desires of powerful, affluent and often competing cliques of the elite created an expanding employment market, especially in the "retainer" and associated sector. This expansion could not be serviced from among the existent ranks of retainers etc. and therefore provided one of the few possibilities of upward social mobility, as part of their recruitment has to be from other non-elite sectors (§§ 2. 5.2.5+n.100; 2. 6.2.4).

3.1.3 Social Dislocation

But social mobility is evident in other directions. The vast majority of society is the rural peasantry who lived in poverty or, at best, on or near its margins. Even those who still tilled their traditional family fields were never more secure than their most recent harvest. One bad summer (or a tax levy

33. We must caution that his "PS" scale, confined to economic criteria, is an imposition on the evidence by modern scholars and so will not necessarily reflect actual status discriminations recognized at the time amongst the mass of the population which can be very complex (cf. Oakes, "Constructing Poverty Scales for Graeco-Roman Society," 367–71) and have a significance not immediately apparent to the casual observer; e.g., see the description of status ascriptions amongst face workers in a coal mine and their projection into the community in Andy Caves' description of his underground mining apprenticeship just prior to the 1984 strike—Cave, *Learning to Breathe*.

34. Not to be confused with our socio-economic class concepts.

35. Friesen, "Poverty in Pauline Studies," 347.

36. Longenecker, "Exposing the Economic Middle," 264.

that could not be met) and loans had to be sought, which was the beginning of the slippery slope into becoming a tenant-farmer, and then a day-wage laborer with its seasonality and associated periods of unemployment, even permanent unemployment and the thought of opting-out and joining one of the bandit groups based in the nearby hills (§ 2. 6.2.2.). Alternatively, there was the possibility of leaving the home village and migrating to the diaspora (like the Prodigal Son) (§ 6. 1.2), or joining one of the labor gangs in one of the major construction works sponsored by the Herods. (§ 2. 4.).[37] Jesus' comment on those leaving home and family (Mark 10:29–30) may reflect this familiar social scene of a son leaving home. The developments at Sepphoris would surely have attracted labor from the nearby villages, such as Nazareth, but the overwhelming magnet was the Temple Project in Jerusalem that could conceivably account for some of Jesus' brothers being no longer resident in Nazareth (§ 6. 2.2).[38] Compounding this situation was the fact that the providers of loans had to come from the already rich and powerful elite, thus consolidating their wealth and power as they took possession of land from defaulting peasants, entrenching even further divisions in society.

The gospel parables are full of pictures reflecting this world, from those using illustrations taken from farming practice and experience to tales of absentee and/or harsh landlords; debt and day laborers waiting in the market place for the offer of work; retainers (dressed "in a little brief authority") abusing tenants, or using their position to protect themselves; or a tenant farmer trying to re-purchase his land when he "hits gold."[39] Building work is familiar as are the perils, problems and opportunities of some entrepreneurial activity.

3.2 A Province of Empire

3.2.1 Roman Occupation

Superimposed upon the existent structure was the Roman presence. On the one hand the *Pax Romana* did enable a development of trade, though

37. Moxnes, *Putting Jesus in His Place*, 43: "This was a situation that weakened the authority of the male head of the household, and that increased the opportunities and choices for younger males." (§ 6. 1.2).

38. Implied by Mark 6:3 ". . . and are not *his sisters here* with us."

39. Evidence from archeology questions the existence of large estates in Lower Galilee contra the implications (e.g., loss of land) often derived from Jesus' parables, but the valley north of Nazareth does reveal the presence of medium sized estates, probably owned by the urban elite of Sepphoris—Fiensy, "Did Large Estates Exist," 133–53.

this was mainly of value to the minority elite with a particular distortion towards the fleshpots of Rome itself. On the other hand, Rome looked to its occupied territories, in good colonial style, as a resource to be exploited for its own needs which introduced an extra tax burden on the peasantry who were additionally expected to pay for the "protection" of the Roman army. In this, the experience of Judea, Samaria, and Galilee was the same as the rest of the Roman Empire—Rome's wealth was at the impoverishment of her colonies.

One particularly hard nut to swallow by the descendants of Abraham was the physical presence of Gentile (Roman) troops in the sacred land of promise given by Yahweh. Ownership of the land was asserted through an assumption of the right to taxation, consequent upon the imposition of direct rule following the incompetencies of Archelaus. This was a festering sore fueling the various occurrences of protest and resistance throughout this period.

3.2.2 Taxation and Tribute

The native inhabitants of Nazareth around the year 30 CE would have identified with Samuel Johnson's wry observation on the "two unavoidable things" in life, the other being death. As in most custom and excise systems, taxation in first century Palestine was characteristically complex and multi-layered with the tax-creators and principal beneficiaries hardly missing an opportunity.[40]

In brief there were three principal layers of taxation: there were the traditional tithes and levies (Neh 10:35–39) for the support of the priests and Levites and the half-shekel temple tax for the support of the temple and its cultus (Exod 30:13; Matt 17:24). Added to this were the dues extracted from their own secular, indigenous rulers to entrench their own power and prestige, exampled particularly by Herod the Great with his grandiose building projects like Caesarea Maritima at home, and gifts to other rulers with whom he needed to curry favor. Above all, however, was his project of re-building the Jerusalem Temple with the larger project of his Jerusalem Palace. The tax-burden experienced can be measured by the unrest and demands for relief made following the death of Herod in 4 BCE, yet the Temple Project (with its exactions) rumbled on for a further seventy years, being completed just in time for its destruction in the Great Rebellion—rather like

---

40. Jeremias, *Jerusalem in the Time of Jesus,* 124–26; Stegemann, *Jesus Movement,* 114–23; Dunn, *Jesus Remembered,* 310–11; Horsley, *Galilee: History, Politics, People,* 139–44, 177–78, 217–19; Sanders, *Judaism,* 146–69.

a sand-castle before the oncoming tide. Similarly in Galilee Herod Antipas, following his father's example, pursued his own building projects—especially at Sepphoris and Tiberias—though, as Morten Jenson has argued, on a more modest scale than the on-going work in Judea, facilitating a more stable period of government,[41] and probably contributing to a lower level of revolutionary activity in Galilee compared to Judea:

> All the various sign and prophetic movements mentioned by Josephus, as well as the circles that provided the scriptural warrant for the rejection of foreign rule, were either from Judea or were active there. What of Galilee? With the exception of the disturbances that occurred on the death of Herod the Great, the Jesus movement is the only other native Galilean one that could plausibly be seen as a direct protest against Herodian rule.[42]

Onto this burden of taxation was imposed the third layer of taxation—the levy to Caesar for the maintenance of the army and the glorification of Rome. After all, the point of having an Empire was as a rich resource to meet their perceived needs—"Rome lives well at her subjects' expense."[43] It was precisely this levy by an occupying imperial power that fueled underlying resentment as it reinforced the reality of their subjugation and was seen as an offense against Yahweh, the true owner of the land. Often associated with Fourth Philosophy ideology it could be used as a debating point by a much wider fraternity as a test-case of one's Judaic identity and commitment (Mark 12:14–17//Matt 22:15–22//Luke 20:20–26).

At such levels of taxation, subsistence farmers were always in danger of running into debt; smallholders would often have to sell out and become tenant farmers and day laborers, or worse.[44]

Thus, one of the first acts of the revolutionaries in taking control of the Temple in 66 CE was to burn the records of debt.[45]

4. Cities and Construction Projects

In addition to their impact on tribute and taxation already noted, the ambitious building projects and urban developments of the Herodian dynasty had consequences in the politico-socio-economic and cultural sphere. His

41. Jensen, "Herod Antipas in Galilee," 7–32.

42. Freyne, "Galilee as Laboratory," 157.

43. Bauckham "Economic Critique of Rome," 78.

44. Dunn, *Jesus Remembered*, 311.

45. *J.W.* 2.427.

building projects were an expression of his allegiance to Rome, but they distorted the local economy, introduced new layers of retainers (e.g., the Herodians), and increased the burden of taxation, thus undermining the perilous economic balance of the peasant landholder, pushing him into the cycle of debt, tenancy, day laboring, and even begging or social banditry.[46] The injection of capital involved in the actual construction process and the pursuant ingress of a new urban elite was a further destabilizing factor within the fragile rural economy of both Galilee and Judea.

4.1 Galilee

Horsley argues from numismatic and pottery evidence that the traditional economy of Galilee was that of a peasant subsistence economy where trades were part of the local village economy and trading being direct from producer to consumer.[47] Freyne describes the rural economy of Nazareth as intensive, small-scale farming by peasant landowners.[48] The urban *nouveau riche* had the resources to stimulate a certain amount of new trade and employment into the dominantly subsistence economy, a process that would favor the larger estates over against the traditional small-holding peasant family, further exacerbating the latter's perilous economic insecurity:

> The values of a market economy with all the attendant signs of exploitation of the weak and ostentatious living of the wealthy are easily documented; specialization in terms of more intensive harvesting of produce both from the land and lake, as well as production of goods for inter-regional trade . . . clear signs of the extension of monetization as a means of exchange . . . It seems possible to link these developments with Antipas' foundations of Sepphoris and Tiberias, as symptomatic of the more complex changes occurring within the whole region.[49]

Four miles from Sepphoris, the tiny village of Nazareth, the home of James, must have felt the reverberations.

Sepphoris, clearly visible from James' back door, materially and symbolically was the ever-present daily reminder of the reality of Antipas' rule as client-king of the Roman Imperium. It was a constant reinforcement of

46. Freyne, *Jesus, a Jewish Galilean*, 134.

47. Horsley, *Archeology, History and Society*, 66–76. Further, Chancey, *Myth of a Gentile Galilee* draws on extensive archeological evidence to demonstrate a dominant Jewish population and associated Jewish milieu in Galilee.

48. Freyne, *Jesus, a Jewish Galilean*, 44–45; Freyne, "Jesus of Galilee" 388–89.

49. Freyne, "Herodian Economics."

the Israelite position as a subjugated people. It was the political, administrative, military and (increasingly) economic center of the region. Compulsory acquisition of peasant land must have been involved in its foundation (a problem Antipas partially avoided in his Tiberias project by the even more noxious policy of building over a burial ground). As resources flowed from the rural peasantry to the urban elite:

> . . . there would have been a visible gap between the wealth of
> the urban centers and the countryside at the expense of the rural
> peasantry, coupled with an even greater economic burden. The
> very building of Sepphoris and Tiberias meant this asymmetri-
> cal relationship was at times literally cast in stone.[50]

Finally, both the construction process as well as the very presence of the new urban centers created a continuing demand for labor, possibly better paid but certainly more stable than the seasonal and often marginal existence in the fields. The building programs may have attracted some young men,[51] anxious to break out from the increasingly dismal prospects offered in the rural peasant economy but they would certainly have drawn off many of the permanently and perhaps also the seasonally unemployed with the additional benefit, from the rulers' point of view, of limiting the degree of social unrest. It may not be coincidental that the Great Revolution broke out during the decade that saw the completion of the Temple project with the laying-off of a large number of workers not all of whom would be soaked up by hastily organized short-term job-creation schemes.[52]

However, we must note Mark Chancey's caution against over-dogmatic evaluations of the economic relationships and outcomes in the Galilee of Antipas. He asserts that the situation is more complex than our interpretive models allow and hard data is too sparse for a univocal assessment, reflected in differing contemporary scholastic judgments of the evidence.[53]

Were James and his brothers caught up in this labor-mobility, perhaps having lost their family land-holding (the parables of Jesus display a close knowledge and empathy with the life of peasant farmers) (§§ 2. 3.1.3; 6. 1.2, 2.2)? Jesus is described as a τέκτων—traditionally translated as "carpenter," but in fact having a broader reference to skills associated with the building trade.[54] Was Jesus for a period attracted/impelled into build-

---

50. Crossley, *Why Christianity Happened*, 45.

51. Stegemann, *Jesus Movement*, 85–86; Zangenberg, "Archeological News," 474–75.

52. *Ant.* 20.219–222.

53. Chancey, "Disputed Issues," 53–67.

54. "The most common meanings of τέκτων are mason, carpenter, woodworker." Davies and Allison, *Saint Matthew*, 2:456. We owe "carpenter" to the early English

ing work in nearby Sepphoris (his parables also show acquaintance with building—houses built on rock and sand—Matt 7:24–27//Luke 6:47–49)? And James? And the other brothers?

4.2 Judea and Jerusalem

Rural Judea shared much of the same economic and social problems as rural Galilee, but with the superimposed consumer demands of proximity to the city.

What was distinctive in Judea was its domination by Jerusalem—unlike Sepphoris, the foundations of Jerusalem are lost in the mists of myth and legend, but from the time of David and particularly following the post-exilic establishment of a Temple-based theocracy by Ezra, Jerusalem, centered on the Temple, was the dominating economic factor for the whole Judean hinterland.[55] Support for the Temple personnel, building maintenance, provision of animals for sacrifice, hospitality services for large numbers of pilgrims, especially at festival times, as well as the presence of a much wider range of associated trades and crafts all contributed to this economic dominance which was serviced by the extensive capital in the Temple Treasury built on the regular tithes and tributes from both Palestinian and diasporan Israelites.

Jerusalem was thus very different in age, in focus, and in its relationship to the Imperial power from Sepphoris, Tiberias, Caesarea Maritima, and Caesarea Philippi; but the experience of economic alienation and subjugation was much the same—with the important distinction that the affluent elite were their own indigenous rulers, the chief priests. Thus the ambivalent position of the Sadducean High Priesthood in being both the political appointees of a foreign power as well as "God's Chosen" was matched by an ambivalent attitude from the rural peasantry who experienced them as the guardians of Zion and as their exploiters.

Hellenistic influences filtered into Jerusalem rather than being structured into its plan and design. As elsewhere the breach was initially through its affluent elite[56]—in Jerusalem, the priesthood. But Herod, always sensitive to his dubiously Jewish Idumean ancestry and perhaps learning from the

---

translation of Miles Coverdale. Joinery is part of the skills of a τέκτων. Bernheim (*James*, 41) notes that Justin Martyr (*Dialogue with Trypho*, 88) says that Jesus made yokes and ploughs. Casey (*Jesus of Nazareth*, 152) considers, "both Joseph and Jesus may have worked as builders and stonemasons as well." See also Taylor, *Mark*, 300; Bernheim, *James*, 42; Tabor, *Jesus Dynasty*, 89–90; Jeremias, *Jerusalem in the Time of Jesus*, 14–22.

55. Cf., Jeremias, *Jerusalem in the Time of Jesus*.

56. Baumgarten, *Flourishing of Jewish Sects*, 87–89.

folly of Antiochus IV, in addition to the pagan Caesarea Maritima, made the other major building project of his rule the re-building of the Temple on Mount Zion. This, while embodying the central sacred spaces of the Temple, integrated Hellenistic architectural features such as the colonnade of Solomon's Portico into its design. Commencing in 20 or 19 BCE and not completed until 62–64 CE it was a major construction project employing initially 10,000 men plus 1,000 priests, rising eventually to a total of 18,000 before completion.[57] It has not passed notice that the associated building of Herod's Palace was on an even grander scale—and presumably it did not pass notice at the time either.

We have already noted the problems that were created for the city authorities by the laying-off of these building workers consequent on the completion of the Project in 62–64 CE, which underlines its previous economic importance for Jerusalem.

We have little evidence on how the Jerusalem populace viewed Herod's project. The Galilean disciples of Jesus are portrayed as marveling at the great buildings: with greater perception Jesus was less impressed (Mark 13:1–2). In the War of 66–73 CE the Sanctuary itself was fanatically defended to the end,[58] but some of its associated buildings (the high priest's house and the palaces of Agrippa and Bernice) had been the first to be torched by the insurgents at the start of the uprising, even before the archives repository was burned down.[59] This suggests a very strong commitment to the *place* of Zion with its buildings (whatever their provenance), which was not extended to associated structures symbolizing their *ancien régime*.

We should also note the belief that in the ἔσχατον a new magnificent Temple would be built to replace the somewhat modest building put up on the return from Exile.[60] Was this new structure seen, perhaps by the Sadducees, as a fulfillment of prophecies, heralding in the New Age? It would certainly have been an impressive piece of "spin" for Herod.

We can only speculate about the psychological impact upon the men themselves who had spent perhaps the greatest part of their adult life on the creation of this magnificent edifice. Tradition closely associates James with the Temple[61]—could it be that James initially came to Jerusalem for work in the Temple project and that this left an indelible impression on his psyche?

57. *Ant.* 20.219–22; Jeremias, *Jerusalem in the Time of Jesus*, 22.

58. *J.W.* 6.244–53.

59. *J.W.* 2.426–27.

60. *1 En.* 90.28–29; Hag 2.9; Tob 14.5.

61. *Hist. eccl.* 2.23.5–6.

There is one fragile piece of evidence to support this suggestion—Hegessipus is reported by Eusebius describing how James "used to enter alone into the temple and be found kneeling and praying for forgiveness for the people, so that *his knees grew hard like a camel's* because of his constant worship of God, kneeling and asking forgiveness for the people."[62] Without detracting from his piety, may not his condition have its origin in years as a τέκτων on the Temple building project—a case of "builder's knee"?[63]

5. Insight from Islam

Having surveyed the world of James our next stage in contextualization is to bring in a comparative social model, both to check preliminary observations and to focus on further significant features—two cameras give depth of vision.

Study of ancient societies has to use comparative models (that may only match some of the significant data), which must then be checked against, supplemented and filled out by contemporary information (literary, epigraphical, archeological) that was not produced for sociological purposes.

> In the social sciences there are two broad types of comparison between two phenomena. The first, the so-called "close comparison" of phenomena existing together in time and place, is generally aimed at bringing out differences between them and not similarities, given that their cultural contiguity already make some likeness inevitable. The second, the so-called "distant comparison," is conducted between phenomena that are remote in time or place or both. Here the interest lies in similarities, since differences are only to be expected. The phenomena to be compared include any cultural data susceptible of social analysis.[64]

This latter approach has to be our dominant one.

---

62. *Hist. eccl.* 2.23.6. As Hartin, *James of Jerusalem*, 123, commented: "The idea of 'camel's knees' resulting from long periods of kneeling does not reflect a Jewish form of piety."

63. A Google search produced nearly 400,000 entries for "builders knee pads."

64. Esler, "Socio-Redaction Criticism of Luke-Acts," 135; Esler, "Paul and Stoicism," 108; See also Duverger, *Introduction to the Social Sciences*, 261–67.

5.1 Through an Islamic Lens

Although very distant from first-century Palestine in time, albeit very close geographically, and certainly much closer culturally than our contemporary Western world, Islamic society in its oriental heartlands offers a lens through which we might bring into clearer focus the world of late Second Temple Judaism.

This closer cultural proximity is partly a product of the lengthy life and dominance of the Ottoman Empire and partly a result of the post-Crusades schism of European Christendom from a Muslim Orient which has retained roots in an older culture from a time and region much closer to first-century Palestine than ours, sustaining a greater degree of affinity.

5.1.1 Islam and Gemeinschaft

At the primary level of personal and community self-identity both first century Judaic society and contemporary Islamic society display a fairly distinct orientation to *Gemeinschaft*.

For Islam, the health and well-being of the group has primacy over that of the individual, indeed it is through the group that the individual finds his identity and his sense of well-being. Islam is the whole within which the individual finds his place.[65] It is a universal brotherhood that can only be fully practiced within a society structured by Islamic law and precept:

> . . . Islam emphasizes the group and community. Three of the five injunctions of Islam—prayers, fasting and *haj*—are directly related to group activity and participation. . . . It is the relationship between individualism and equality which differentiates the Muslim and Western, especially American, systems. . . . Islam presents an interesting if somewhat contradictory picture: although there is minimum premium to the individual the highest value is placed on equality. The individual is clearly subordinate to the *ummah* (brotherhood). God is the focus, the pivot, of creation and everything else takes its cue from this reality. But before God human beings are equal. The egalitarianism in Islam is genuine and pronounced. The daily prayers, and the very formation in which they are said, confirm this.[66]

---

65. In discussing Islam I am consciously gender-specific. Indeed Islamic paternalism strongly mirrors the all-pervasive paternalism of first century CE Judaic society.

66. Ahmed, *Discovering Islam,* 220–21.

This is an expression of a *Gemeinschaft* perception of society where religion forms part of the warp and woof of its existence, an essential part of the community's self-definition with the individual finding his place and meaning within that bonding. In the main the individual does not choose his religion, he is born into it and grows with it.[67] Individuals will vary in their degree of personal enthusiasm and commitment[68] but to choose another religion, or to deny Islam is perceived as traitorous. Shortly after the *fatwa* against Salman Rushdie was issued during the 1980s for his book *Satanic Verses*, I was in conversation with an Islamic friend who was very active in inter-faith relationships. He explained that the insult felt by Muslims was because Rushdie was himself a Muslim (i.e., he was brought up and reared in a Muslim society). "Would that offense have been felt if I, a Christian, had written it?" — "No."[69]

With changed referents, this could be a description of first century Judaic society where not just "zealots" but peasants from the field preferred death with their families to any dishonoring of Torah or Temple.[70] Similarly, the anger, which irrupted against Paul on his final visit to Jerusalem, was triggered by the conviction that he had reneged on his Judaic inheritance by preaching against Torah and circumcision, and by defiling the sanctity of the Temple (Acts 21:27–36).

5.1.2 Situational Affinities

This underlying *Gemeinschaft* affinity is further reinforced by a significant number of congruent experiences.

Both societies have experienced radical economic change and integration into a "global"[71] economy. In Judea/Galilee we have charted the breakdown of a traditional subsistence economy with land being seen

67. Something of the same relationship persists in parts of Ireland. In the mid-1990s I was marking GCSE Religious Studies papers from a school that clearly belonged to the Catholic/Nationalist community in Northern Ireland. In a question about the sacraments of baptism and communion I found myself transported into what, for me, was an alien world where growing up in the Church and in the community were one, and the progressive sacraments of the Catholic Church marked the *rites de passage* through childhood into adulthood.

68. Being a suicide-bomber is fortunately not a very popular calling, although it does accrue honor within some sectors of the tradition.

69. This response would appear to need modification in the light of more recent experience.

70. *J.W.* 2.192–98.

71. In the case of first-century Palestine the word "global" has an obviously more restricted reference.

as a commodity to be exploited whereas the Islamic heartland has been impacted by oil and everything that has flowed from that—and oil is a commodity eminently suited for exploitation by the most powerful. This exploitation of oil has produced a plutocracy with economic polarization even more pronounced than that of Judea/Galilee and has been associated with a similar process of urbanization involving a marked movement from the countryside into the cities.

Both societies are in a world dominated by a global super-power which uses its economic and military power to impose its will and exploits the human and material resources of its empire for its own benefit and ends, covered by a moral veneer of bestowing the benefits of peace and civilization. Imperial rule in both cases is normally exercised through indigenous client-rulers with a supporting military presence where necessary to remind both ruled and client-rulers where power really resides. Direct (military) rule can be imposed when the core interests of the Empire are seen to be at risk and these concerns have led to the presence of alien occupying forces on land held to be "holy."[72]

Overarching the more direct economic/political/military imposition, both societies are faced with the attractions and challenge of a culture whose values are perceived by many as undermining their own traditional foundations, a culture of more successful economic systems whose ingress predates direct super-power imposition. In the case of Galilee/Judea it is Hellenism: with Islamic society it is "Western Values," narrowing down to the "American Way of Life." This invasion of a powerful alien culture is culturally disruptive and leads to a loss of identity.[73]

In both cases reactions to the invading culture vary, but insofar as they are seen to threaten the well-being or even very existence of their society, resistance principally occurs through a re-emphasis on their traditions expressed via various "boundary-markers" and "purity" rules; with resort to violence where no other agency seems possible. Modern militant Islam can be traced back to Sayyid Qutb,[74] with a call to:

> (W)ithdraw from mainstream *jahili*[75] society and create a dedicated vanguard . . . an enclave of pure faith, where they could prepare for the coming struggle . . . (eventually) Muslims would

---

72. The removal of American troops from the land of Saudi Arabia is a core issue for Al Qaeda.

73. Armstrong, *Muhammad*, 42–43.

74. An Egyptian intellectual who was executed in 1966.

75. *jahiliyya*—"the term used by Muslims to describe the corrupt barbarism of pre-Islamic Arabia" (Armstrong).

be forced to fight a *jihad*, a holy war, confident of their eventual success—just as Muhammad was when he conquered Mecca in 630.[76]

Finally, in both cases the ways and desires of the more powerful culture are being imposed on a traditional society with ancient traditions that define their identity and are embodied in their sacred writings: and both traditions and scriptures contain a built-in critique of injustice, and of those whose power permits or enables it.

We are now in a position to explore elements of the Islamic experience that will aid the identification of critical features in the world of James.

5.2 The Islamic Focus

> It is possible to disagree about the extent, homogeneity or irreversibility of this trend (secularization) . . . but, by and large, it would seem reasonable to say that it is real. But there is one very real, dramatic and conspicuous exception to all this: Islam.[77]

With these words Ernest Gellner in *Postmodernism, Reason and Religion* seeks for explanation of why Islam is the only major world religion to "buck the trend" of declining religious conviction and practice.

He sets current movements of revitalization of Islam within the context of Western global economic and political dominance:

> The urge to reform, ever present in Islam, acquired a new vigor and intensity. No doubt it also acquired some new themes and additional motivation: why has the West overtaken us, why is it such a menace to us? . . . But the dominant and persuasive answer . . . commended a *return* to, or a more rigorous observance of *High* Islam.[78]

During both the colonial and post-colonial period,

> Reformed Islam has played a role very similar to that played by nationalism elsewhere . . . (it) confers a genuine shared

---

76. Armstrong, *Muhammad*, 13–14. There is a distinct echo from both the Maccabean uprising and the War Scroll from Qumran (Flusser, *Judaism of the Second Temple Period*, 140–58).

77. Gellner, *Postmodernism*, 5.

78. See § 2. 5.2.3.

identity on what would otherwise be a mere summation of the under-privileged.[79]

But under-developed countries, particularly under Western hegemony, face a dilemma:

> . . . should we wish to equal in power (thereby spurning our own tradition), or should we, on the contrary, affirm the values of our own tradition, even at the price of material weakness?[80]

The Islamic response has been:

> . . . a return to, or a more rigorous observance of High Islam . . . self-correction did not need to go outside the society . . . it could find it in its own perfectly genuine and real Higher Culture, which had indeed only been practiced by a minority in the past, but which had been recognized (though not implemented) as a valid norm by the rest of society. Now, seemingly under the impact of a moral impulse and in response to preaching, but in fact as a result of profound and pervasive changes in social organization, it could at last be practiced by all. Self-reform in the light of modern requirements could be presented as a return to the genuinely local ideal, a moral home-coming, rather than a self-repudiation. . . . this vision . . . has a number of very considerable and striking advantages. *It does not appeal to an alien model; it appeals to a model which has unquestionable, deep, genuine local roots.* (my italics).[81]

The humiliation of Islamic defeat by Israel in the "six days war" of 1967 has been seen as a major stimulant to current Islamic vigor, defeat being attributed to lax Islamic practice. Likewise, two millennia earlier many in Israel found the explanation of their humiliation under Roman occupation within their traditions—e.g., a Deuteronomic reading of history, a critique of the impurity of the Temple and its Priesthood, and a failure in Torah observance.

5.2.1 "It's the Economy, Stupid" (President Clinton)

Just as the world of James was experiencing significant economic change and social disruption through its incorporation into the global economy of its

---

79. Gellner, *Postmodernism*, 15.

80. Ibid., 18–19.

81. Ibid., 19–20.

day with wealth and power centering in the cities, so the oil-fueled economies of the Islamic heartland have led to an accompanying growth of cities
and their increased specialization at the expense of the traditional tribal/
rural areas. Implicit in this is a high degree of labor mobility as people move
from the struggling rural economies towards the attractions of the growing
urban areas—a mobility which extends to an Islamic "diaspora," facilitated
by improved communications and ease of movement under *Pax Americana*.

With little imagination one can see very similar factors operative within first-century Palestine—part of the (imposed) Roman Empire whose *pax
Romana* provided unprecedented means of communication (evidenced, for
example, by the Jewish diaspora and the rapid spread and inter-connections
of the early Christian movements). At the same time the exploitation of
the land, traditionally viewed as sacred, led to alienation as peasants were
forced through taxation and debt to yield their inheritance.[82] Meanwhile
the continuing penetration into all parts of society by Hellenistic culture
intruded an awareness of broader horizons whilst the establishment of new
urban centers encouraged the movement into them of dispossessed peasants from the countryside, particularly to the historic Temple-city of Jerusalem with its major Herodian building project. This brings us to the critical
issue of urbanization.

5.2.2 Urbanization

Urbanization was a global phenomenon in the twentieth century. Most of
the Islamic world was affected—and in ways that are suggestive for our understanding of social processes within first-century Palestine, especially the
Judaic world of Jerusalem and James:

> . . . cities throughout history have been seats of Christian, Jew-
> ish and Islamic piety. Furthermore, there is evidence from the
> recent past and the contemporary period that social disloca-
> tion—migration from villages to towns—is accompanied by
> increased religious practice which could, under favorable con-
> ditions, sustain movements of religious revival. The Method-
> ist revival spread hand in hand with the growth of industrial
> cities in England.[83]

82. Freyne, *Jesus, a Jewish Galilean,* 46.

83. Arjomand, "Social change," 93, noting in support, Hobsbawm, *Primitive Rebels,*
and Thompson, *The Making of the English Working Class.* However, Thompson's was
a nuanced approach relating episodes of religious revival to the frustration of movements for social reform/revolution. See also the study by Ted Wickham of religious life
in the growth and industrialization of Sheffield (Wickham, *Church and People in an*

New religious movements provide a community structure in urban areas where family and close friends are lacking.[84] This is a pattern that has been observed in West Africa during the twentieth century where migrants into the growing industrial urban areas, with their associated anomie, found within the vitality of Pentecostal churches that warmth and closeness of human relationships previously experienced in the rural communities from which they had come.

What is of particular interest is that in the Islamic heartlands the response to such experiences as new technology, urbanization, education, centralization and exposure to modern communications has not been a growth in secularism but a return to their traditions and a reaffirmation of Islam, which mirrors very clearly first century Judaic abhorrence and opposition to the process of Hellenization through a stress on their very living traditions, centered in the Torah—"a model which has unquestionable, deep, genuine local roots" (§ 2. 5.2).

5.2.3 "High Islam" and "Low Islam"

A critical aspect of the Islamic urbanization experience which uncannily resonates with Israel in the first century is a distinction of religious styles, reflecting urban/rural patterns, between:

> . . . a High Islam of the Scholars and the Low Islam of the people. The boundary between the two was not sharp, but was often

---

Industrial City). Wickham demonstrated that the bulk of the working-class remained "unchurched." The early Methodist movements appealed to the more socially mobile groups (what one might call "aspirant artisans") whilst the "great congregations" of late-Victorian nonconformity were dominantly made up of skilled workers and the newly developing lower middle class, who may have found in a time of rapid social change that the nonconformist emphasis upon individual salvation and responsibility provided divine sanction for their newly embraced lifestyle of economic individualism. (How else could the Eucharistic Chalice be replaced by tiny individual communion glasses?) It needs also to be remembered that the era of the "great congregations" (post-1851 census) actually recorded a continuous decrease in the proportion of church attendance due to the demographic distortions of the period. Likewise, the Methodist movement which engaged the working classes most intensively—the Primitive Methodists—providing leadership, language and organizational models for nascent Trade Unionism—made little headway in the large industrial cities. Their strength was in the mining, manufacturing and mill towns and villages in regions such as the Potteries and Lancashire. (Wearmouth, *Some Working-Class Movements*; *Methodism and the Struggle of the Working Classes*; *Methodism and the Trade Unions*). All this should caution us that history "in the buff" is inevitably complex and should alert us to the presence of similar complexity in the Jerusalem of 30–70 CE.

84. Clarke, "Japanese New Religious Movements," 201.

very gradual and ambiguous, resembling in this respect the related but not identical line of demarcation between territories
governed effectively from the political centre and territory governed by local tribes and their leaders.[85]

> High Islam is carried by urban scholars, recruited largely from
> the trading bourgeoisie . . . and reflects the natural tastes and
> values of urban middle classes . . . Those values include order,
> rule-observance, sobriety, learning . . . an aversion to hysteria
> and emotional excess . . . stresses the severely monotheistic and
> nomocratic nature of Islam . . . and is generally orientated to-
> wards puritanism and scripturalism.[86]

Conversely, Low Islam (or Folk Islam) is non-literate and stresses
magic more than learning, ecstasy more than rule-observance:[87]

> There has been an enormous shift in the balance *from* Folk Islam
> *to* High Islam. The social bases of Folk Islam have been in large
> part eroded, whilst those of High Islam were greatly strength-
> ened. Urbanization, political centralization, incorporation in a
> wider market, labor migration, have all impelled populations
> in the direction of the formally (theologically) more 'correct'
> Islam.[88] (italics original)

This is strongly scripturalist and puritan.[89]

5.2.4 Torah and Urban Literacy

Similar to the emergence of "High Islam," the Ezraic legacy in Israel was a
"re-formation" centered on the Torah, the *book* of the *Law*. But, writings
demand literacy. Cities, with their greater wealth and concomitant leisure,
have always been attractive to scholars, and in the more complex urban context literacy is at a higher premium than in the peasant subsistence economy
of the rural villages. Literacy in post-Ezra Judea was restricted to the priests

---

85. Gellner, *Postmodernism*, 9.

86. Ibid., 11.

87. Ibid.

88. Ibid., 15.

89. Similarly, Arjomand notes that as cities have always been the centers of Islamic
orthodoxy, movements out of rural areas become associated with adherence to more
rigorous forms of Islam: "The decline of this peripheral variant (Sufism) of Islam has
gone hand in hand with the growth in the urban centers of what Geertz (Geertz, *Islam
Observed*) has termed 'scripturalism'" (Arjomand, "Social Change," 93–94).

but following the success of the Maccabean revolution with its war cry of "zeal for the Law," literacy and the literate acquired a new status—and a baseline for critique of the established order. Of particular relevance, highlighted for us by the seminal work on orality and literacy by Walter Ong, is the perceptual shift that occurs with accession to literacy:

> A sound dominated verbal economy is consonant with aggregative (harmonizing) tendencies rather than with analytic, dissecting tendencies (which would come with the inscribed, visualized word).[90]

Albert Baumgarten draws out the significance of this insight for the late Second Temple period:

> A feel for precision and for analytic exactitude is created and interiorized . . . If more widespread literacy in the ancient Jewish case produces results similar to those studied by anthropologists in other cultures, and yields a passion for precision, that desire for exactness among ancient Jews should find its expression in a commitment to studying the law, interpreting its provisions, and living by those interpretations as accurately as possible.[91]

Although the Ezraic foundations of post-exilic Judaism had placed the authority for interpretation of the Torah as well as the performance of the cultus on the high priests, the concomitant codification of Torah and gathering together and creating of their written traditions encouraged a further growth of scribes and a literate retainer class. Although a small proportion of the total population, they nonetheless included many of what we would term the "movers and shakers in society."[92] Consequently, when the Hasmonean High Priesthood was felt to have moved from the pristine purity of Judaic society Mattathias and his sons were believed to have striven for, there developed a critique based on Torah and its interpretation amongst the literate retainer classes, a critique that was to feed into a more violent conclusion under direct Roman rule.

With the Torah being in the hands (symbolically, if not always literally) of a wider section of the community, there comes a fundamental shift of power—from being the authorized interpreters of Torah, the priestly rulers are now also subject to its judgments in the hands of at least the literate groupings of their society (and there are many levels of literacy to be

---

90. Ong, *Orality and Literacy,* 73–74.

91. Baumgarten, *Jewish Sects,* 123–24.

92. Ibid., 47–48.

found).[93] It is a process of democratization and the empowerment, initially, of the non-elite retainer class.

Central to this critique was the delineation of what it meant to be a true "son of Abraham" in the face of the ingress of Hellenism and, secondly, the legitimacy of the priesthood and the performance of the cultus. All this was centered in Jerusalem,[94] with its Temple, and was expressed through patient and detailed interpretation of their scriptures, as the Dead Sea Scrolls so patently demonstrate.

Just as the "High Islam" of the *Qur'an* emerges as the normative expression of Islamic society undergoing the experience of urbanization, so the scribal *Torah* was guide for the first-century Israelite. And in both cases adherence to the central tenets and symbols of their faith enabled them to affirm their self-identity and resist the challenge of an economically more powerful alien culture—"a model which has unquestionable, deep, genuine local roots."

Jerusalem—"City of our God" and center of the cosmos—defined by and offering the Torah in a world where new forces had been unleashed—was the environment in which James and the *Jakobusgemeinde* were nourished and, for a time, flourished.

5.2.5 Urban Associations

A further element in the contemporary Islamic experience of urbanization with significance for our mapping-out of the world of James lies in the remarkable growth of religious organizations within its expanding cities.

In the post-war period, with its expanding oil-fueled economy, Iran has shared in the phenomenon of urban growth, which has been associated with a growth of orthodox Islam.[95] Interestingly, there has also been a marked increase in the number of religious associations, many with titles indicating membership of "two quite possibly overlapping social groups: lower-middle-class guilds and professions associated with the bazaar economy, and recent migrants from the provinces."[96]

93. Keith, *Jesus' Literacy*, 71–123.

94. Even the Qumran community in the desert defined itself *vis-à-vis* Jerusalem and its Temple.

95. Arjomand, "Social Change," 95, based on data produced in his "Social Movements."

96. Ibid., 96. Arjomand invites comparison with Methodist experience in nineteenth century England (n.83 above).

A similar pattern is affirmed in First century Jerusalem[97]—Luke refers to "members of the synagogue called the Synagogue of Freedmen, comprising Cyrenians and Alexandrians and people from Cilicia and Asia" (Acts 6:9). And it was a pattern repeated in cities across the Diaspora (as it is in British "ex-Pat" enclaves around the world today).

The move from a rural to an urban environment is always unsettling. Left behind are those primary face-to-face group relationships that were an expression of the community structure of the rural village, supplying identity and giving both support and significance to its individual inhabitants. To its incomers a city can be experienced as impersonal, overwhelming, and marked by a sense of anomie. Those primary face-to-face group relationships that formed their rural village communities are much less characteristic of the larger urban complex: rather, *they have to be sought, or created*.

In his analysis of the origin and development of Jewish sects in the Hasmonean period (§ 2. 6.1) Baumgarten identifies this as a key process:

> While migration from small to very large places of life strips some people of traditional beliefs, it causes others to redouble their devotion to tradition, especially to more extreme versions or interpretations of their faith. . . . the disrupted and uprooted new urban population seek a master who can guide them in their new and confusing circumstances . . . these new urbanites are especially prone to join sects, which provide them with the master they seek.[98]

He also links this process with the factor of greater levels of literacy in the urban context:

> Literacy often goes hand in hand with urbanization: perhaps those who learn how to read are not satisfied with a life of subsistence agriculture and therefore move to the city, perhaps the dynamic is in the other direction—those who move to the city for any number of reasons need to be able to read to survive there, hence acquire the skill. . . . That pool of newly literate people, experiencing the effects of literacy . . . are also the newly urban and thus subject to the changes engendered by their move to the city.[99]

---

97. Riesner, "Synagogues in Jerusalem," 179–211. First-century synagogues in both Rome and Jerusalem were associations marked by a common identity or language, or with a common theology and interpretation of Torah (e.g., Essenes). Goodman, *Rome and Jerusalem*, 238–39.

98. Baumgarten, *Jewish Sects*, 138.

99. Ibid., 137.

These processes are not unique to the world of late Second Temple Judaism.

What was the effect of the urban experience on those migrant workers employed on the Temple project? What was the effect of their daily involvement in building the Temple and spending their working hours within the Temple environment? What did they do during the regular Sabbath rest? Would the boys from a Torah-observant family in Nazareth have taken the educational opportunities offered by the range of activities centered on the Temple (e.g., teaching/preaching within the Temple precincts seems to have been an accepted activity—Mark 14:49; Acts 3:11—4:42)? Could such migrants become recognized (among their peers at least) as interpreters of Torah, proficient in Hebrew/Aramaic (even Greek?), and thereby move into the retainer class (§§ 2. 5.2.4; 2. 6.2.4)?[100] Could James . . .?

Further, was it this urban Jerusalem[101] environment, spawning a range of associations amongst its teeming migrant workers (some identified by occupation/craft, others by place of origin), that brought into being an association of workers from Nazareth and its environs who replicated the gatherings of their village community?[102] Might something like this—"the συναγωγή[103] of the Nazarenes"[104]—be the core community of that which finally emerges onto the pages of history as the community led by James, the *Jakobusgemeinde* (§§ 6. 2.2; 8. 2.1.5)? Indeed, could Christianity as a dis-

---

100. Although social mobility in agrarian societies was very restricted, during a time of urban expansion the retainer class could not maintain itself solely by recruitment from within its own ranks. A limited level of recruitment of the more capable from the lower strata would be inevitable.

101. Not simply Jerusalem, but it was throughout the diaspora that Jewish people maintained their sense of identity and belonging through the developments of their synagogues in the urban centers of the Empire. Also, it was as an urban movement spreading from the urban setting of the Nazarene *Jakobusgemeinde* (despite the centering of the Jesus-movement itself in rural Galilee) that early Christianity spread through the Roman Empire (Meeks, *First Urban Christians*).

102. In his study of 1920s Chicago (Allsop, *Bootleggers*, 352–53) Kenneth Allsop describes how migrant workers from the rural setting of Sicily brought the social structure of their home villages into the alien urban setting of Chicago, providing them with meaning, identity and a communal support mechanism. See § 2. 6.2.2 n.157.

103. See "Notes on Some Terms Used": *Synagogue*.

104. "Nazarene" is held by many scholars to have probably been the earliest name attached to the Christian movement. It is there that the difficulty begins as there are problems in accounting for its form as originating in either Nazareth or Nazirite. May it not simply be, in origin, the slang term used by others of such an association of migrant workers from the Nazareth area: the ambivalence in our received tradition about its spelling being a product of its origination and continued usage in an oral culture outside of literary convention? (§ 6. n.44).

tinct movement, with the potential for organizational expression and identity, have developed in anything other than such an urban environment?

These are hypothetical questions, but they may alert us to the possible presence of indicators in the James' story that we might otherwise miss.

There is one further element in the contemporary Islamic urbanization experience that is pregnant with possibility for illuminating some of the tragedy of first-century Jerusalem: in Iran during the days of the Shah the religious associations in Tehran "were harnessed to support Khomeini's movement for the establishment of Islamic theocracy."[105] Were some of the groups of the newly urbanized Jerusalem residents similarly radicalized by exposure to 'Fourth Philosophy' ideology to provide additional backbone to the Revolution? This raises questions about the role of the *Jakobusgemeinde* in pre-revolutionary Jerusalem. For example, was it a major focus of passive resistance to the pro-Roman Hellenization policies/practices of the Priestly aristocracy—hence the motivation for James' execution,[106] his remembrance as the "Oblias" of Jerusalem[107] and the (disputed) tradition[108] that his death opened the door for the extremist militant leadership of popular disaffection, accelerating the inexorable decline into war?[109] Or, did the *Jakobusgemeinde* identify with "Fourth Philosophy" thinking and become tragically involved in the nemesis of 70 CE?

6. The Judaic Response

A marked feature of the later period of Second Temple Judaism was its sectarian development in reaction to the hegemony of Greco-Roman culture and influence. Noted by both Josephus and Philo, and out of phase with both antecedent and subsequent Judaic history, a number of movements/sects developed and achieved significant position and influence within Israel and its leadership.[110]

---

105. Arjomand, "Social Change," 97.

106. Ananus may have expected the support of Albinus for his illegal execution of James?

107. *Eccl. hist.* 2.23.7.

108. *Eccl. hist.* 2.23.18–20; Origen, *Contra Celsus*, 1.47, 2.13; 2.17; Eisenman, *James*, 395–99.

109. *Eccl. hist.* 3.7.8–9.

110. Baumgarten, *Jewish Sects,* 1–4.

6.1. Hasmonean Sectarianism

Noting that "the exegetical situation and social circumstances (are) mirror images of each other,"[111] Baumgarten recognizes that the sects enumerated by Josephus[112] and Philo (Sadducees, Pharisees and Essenes) all emerged into what he terms their maturity in the mid-second century BCE Hasmonean period, and can be understood in reference to the situations of that era whereas the assortment of groups (including "Fourth Philosophy," related protest groups and proto-Christian movements) arising during the first century CE are all conditioned by an Imperial Roman context.[113]

Baumgarten demonstrates that the older movements were always a minority of the population—but a significant minority as their membership

> . . . were men[114] likelier to come from the economic, social and educational elite . . . who could afford the "luxury" of indulgence in affairs of the spirit, and who had sufficient background to become sensitive to and interested in issues of a certain character, appropriate to their status. These were people well integrated into the social structure, among its natural leaders, while also open to the possibility of criticizing it, and thus harboring a potential for disobedience . . . either working to change the culture from a position of advantage, and sometimes even succeeding in achieving dominance, or being the most obstinate opponents of the establishment.[115]

In line with this, Baumgarten describes Sadducees, Pharisees and Essenes originating as urban movements in Jerusalem, as indicated by their variant foci on the Temple, although eventually, in the Roman period, there was some migration to other urban centers.[116]

Baumgarten discerns this flourishing of Jewish sects in the dissonance experienced between the high hopes for the restoration of Israel, which fired

---

111. Ibid., 126.

112. Evidence from the Dead Sea Scrolls supports Josephus in recognizing three principal sects in Second Temple Judaism–Flusser, *Judaism of the Second Temple Period*, 214–57.

113. Baumgarten, *Jewish Sects*, 9.

114. Baumgarten remarks that the early Christian movements seem to be the only instance of female inclusion (Baumgarten, *Jewish Sects*, 45 n.19). Josephus does record that Simon bar Giora, a rebel war-lord in the Uprising came to Masada with "his following of women" (*J.W.* 4.503–508), but they seem to be more in the tradition of "camp-followers."

115. Baumgarten, *Jewish Sects*, 47–48.

116. Ibid., 46.

the Maccabean revolution, and the betrayal (in their eyes) of those hopes by the succeeding Hasmonean dynasty as they embraced much of the Hellenism their martyrs had died to resist.[117]

6.1.1 A Question of Identity

The assault of Antiochus IV on the religious center of their national life that precipitated the uprising of the Maccabees brought to a head the increasing challenge posed by Hellenism to the traditional Judaic way of life and self-understanding as Yahweh's elect people. Ever since the Babylonian exiles had returned to Jerusalem they had found it necessary to protect their way of life by drawing boundaries of purity around themselves, initially at the time of Nehemiah to keep separate from both the Samaritans and the residents of Jerusalem whose families had not been deported in 586 BCE. With the establishment of the Temple-state of Judea under Persian hegemony Jewish identity was simply a combination of residence and ethnicity. Despite the gradual encroachments of Hellenism, this traditional understanding continued until the crisis of 168 BCE when the Maccabean reaction led to a strong reaffirmation of traditional boundary-markers such as circumcision and Sabbath, with a renewed emphasis on the Torah as the control over the whole Judaic community. But military victory did not alter the fact that Hellenism was "in the air" of the times, so with the Maccabees and movements such as the Hasidim there occurred the beginning of the need to define what it meant to be a true Israelite—ethnicity and (with a growing diaspora) residence were no longer sufficient.

Loyalty to Torah and obedience to Torah, as expressed through such critical markers as circumcision, marriage, Sabbath, food and hospitality customs became the criterion by which the "true Israelite" was identified. Study of the Torah and its tenets was at the heart of this endeavor, encouraging the growth of the scribal and literate class we have noted (§ 2. 5.2.4) —initially, and always dominantly, an urban, nay, Jerusalem phenomenon. Casuistry is endemic to this process: the stronger the drive for holiness, the tighter the boundaries groups draw around themselves. The greater the demands of Torah are felt, the greater the number of ethnic Jews are denied (by the sectarians) the status of "true Israelite." Qumran is one end game of this process.

An inevitable byproduct of this is that the greatest animosity is always felt towards the kindred sects that are seen as betraying/compromising the

---

117. Ibid., 81–91.

truth[118]—for example, for Qumran: "the Lying Preacher,"[119] "the Liar,"[120] "Spouter of Lies,"[121] "scoffer,"[122] "traitors."[123]

6.1.2 Sadducees, Pharisees, and Essenes

Our information about Sadducees is so sketchy that little can be safely said, other than noting their membership of the ruling class and close association with the high priests, but both the Pharisees and the (probably) Essene community at Qumran display concerns relating to purity and the Temple.[124] On the one hand, the Qumran community with a priestly/Zadokite leadership has withdrawn from the Jerusalem cultus as protest against both the legitimacy of the Hasmonean priesthood and the legality of its cultic performance whilst the Pharisees, a lay movement, sought to renew the purity of Judaic life through extending into secular living purity practices intended for priests in the performance of their cultic duties.[125] Qumran saw themselves as preserving "in the wilderness" a true, living Temple with a legitimate Zadokite priesthood, a correct calendar for Festival celebrations and right ritual in preparation for "The Day" when God would enable them to return and perform their priestly office in the actual Temple on Mount Zion. On the other hand, the Pharisees lived within the secular world and sought the reformation of Jewish society through example, teaching and persuasion. In contemporary sociological terms they are prototypical examples of the "reformist sect," who seek to work within society to change it, contrasting with the "introversionist sect" that gives up on the world and turns in on itself.[126]

Both were critical of the current state of affairs, both believed in its renewal to a pristine purity with a responsibility towards its achievement—and

118. Vermes, *Complete Dead Sea Scrolls in English*, 54–57; Knibb, *Qumran Community*, 16–25. It is also a feature seen in the fissiparous nature of many fundamentalist sects, both religious and political—gloriously parodied in the scene on the Coliseum terraces in the Monty Python film "Life of Brian."

119. CD VIII, 13; 1QpHab X, 9.

120. CD XX, 15; 1QpHab II, 1–2; VI, 11–12.

121. 1QpHab X, 9.

122. CD I,14; BII, 11–12.

123. CD V, 11.

124. For the origins of Sadducees, Pharisees and Essenes, see Rofe, "The Onset of Sects," 39–49.

125. Grabbe, *Jewish Religion and History*, 44.

126. Wilson, *Religious Sects*, 21–47.

both were keenly committed to the Torah, the scriptures and its interpretation, and in good sectarian fashion Qumran dismissively referred to the Pharisees as "seekers after smooth things"[127]—i.e., not faithful interpreters of Torah. Pharisaic comments on Qumran are still buried in the sand somewhere![128]

But the Josephian triad of Sadducees/Pharisees/Essenes (which he carefully distances from the "Fourth Philosophy"[129]) is demonstrably too simplistic. Not only has the Dead Sea Scrolls library alerted us to the range and variability of ideas preserved by one small highly-disciplined religious community along with the implications for our understanding of the Essenes, but also they "provide our best data for imagining some of the diverse social aspects of Second Temple Judaism."[130] For example, the Enochic literature represents a developing, cumulative tradition over three centuries which:

> presupposes an ongoing context in which the traditions were transmitted. Unfortunately we know almost nothing about the specific identity, structure, and daily life of this Enochic community. . . . While, for the most part, we cannot specify names or clearly define communities, we can trace continuities in the theological and intellectual traditions that funneled into the Enochic group and out of it, and we know that the contexts that transmitted this material split in various directions.[131]

It is a picture which portrays a rich and vigorous society and discourse—but a discourse dominantly within the priestly, scribal and retainer classes in or, (in the case of Qumran) centered on Jerusalem.[132]

6.1.3 What About the Workers?

We only know of these vigorous dialogues through the literature that has come to us (by both intention and accident)—yet that was a dominantly oral society and culture. Were the artisans of Jerusalem so brain-dead through the struggle for survival that no intellectual vitality occurred, as Ben-Sira

127. CD I, 18; 4QpNah III, 7.

128. The *Birkat ha-Minim*, which was used post-Jamnia against the Christians, may have an earlier history and setting revealing the Pharisaic reaction against the Qumran sect. Flusser, *Judaism of the Second Temple Period*, 108–09. Cf. Marcus, "*Birkat Ha-Minim*," 545–48.

129. *Ant.* 1–24; *J.W.* 2.118–21; 162–66.

130. Nickelsburg, *Ancient Judaism and Christian Origins*, 179.

131. Ibid.

132. Saldarini, *Pharisees, Scribes, and Sadducees,* 46, 277–308.

suggests (Sir 38:25–33)? Surely not—manual work, particularly when rou-tinized, can leave much space for mental reflection, thought and intellectual creativity. And there was much in Jerusalem to stimulate the brain cells.

We also must note that Ben Sira's reference to working people whom he cannot envisage as being intellectually active (Sir 38:24–34) is almost exclu-sively defined by individual craftsmen (the ploughman, seal-cutter, smith, and potter)—there appears no awareness of the vigor of debate (probably in a different "language code") that can occur within manual laboring groups.

Consider the Edwardian Welsh slate miners of Llechwedd—like the Temple building workers they worked with stone: their work was danger-ous, their life-span short, long hours, little leisure, poorly paid, on the eco-nomic edge of survival in a society whose economy was skewed towards the demands of the wealthy who had little expectation of "culture" amongst those they thoughtlessly exploited. In the archives of the University College in Bangor, North Wales, there is the minute book of a quarrymen's *caban*—the small stone hut where they took their all-too-brief lunch breaks. One month (October 1902) it records:

> There's singing—either serious solos, or more playfully the mu-sical contortionism of setting the words of *O Fryniau Caersalem* to the tune of *Crug-y-bar*. There's recitation—of a poem that had been read only twice, and of an abbreviated *Dafydd Brenin Israel*. There are competitions on grammatical themes—read a passage from which all the punctuation had been removed, spell difficult words, create new ones. There are discussions—should ministers of religion have a lifetime's or a defined term's appoint-ment to office; should the measures of the 1902 Education Act as they affect Wales be opposed; is the taking of a wife a matter of choice, or a necessity? There are lectures too—"How much greater is a man than a sheep" runs the title of one; in another, Owen Morris talks about his holidays. All this took place in dank tunnels, in crude huts 600 metres up a mountain, in rain and wind, as the men slaked their thirst with bottles of cold tea and ate probably no more than dry bread. . . . Was the breadth, the awareness, the pride evinced through those activities an ex-pression of the men's proud knowledge of difference, of cultural resistance, of intrinsic superiority to the vain, philistine and greedy proprietors who allowed them so meagre a living?[133]

Mutatis mutandis, the probability must be high that in the *cabans* of Jerusalem there would be "expressions of proud difference, of cultural

133. Perrin, *Visions of Snowdonia*, 88–92.

resistance and of intrinsic superiority to the vain, philistine and greedy" aristocracy, the agents of Roman Imperial power.

The likelihood needs also to be raised that the presence of massed labor on the Temple rebuilding project may have encouraged a radicalization of the migrant temple workers,[134] with associated structures of organization, perhaps through their *cabans* or *soviets* (συναγωγαί[135]), or the Temple working teams themselves may have provided the social context for the development and articulation of resistance.[136] The sign prophets did not emerge out of a social vacuum.

The thesis of Margaret Barker is worth noting, although she is a minority voice.[137] She argues that older pre-exilic traditions were worked over in the post-exilic period by the priestly aristocracy in their interest. Reading with a "hermeneutic of suspicion," traces of these older traditions can be detected within the material and this, with other trace-evidence (as with a palimpsest), suggests the persistence at a popular level of an older tradition, centered on the Temple, over against the official cultus of the Establishment. If she is indeed overhearing (with inevitably distorted reception) some of the oral chatter of the Jerusalem "taverns" and "soviets" one cannot help but wonder about the effects on the eighteen thousand Temple builders, craftsmen and laborers—what did they think about, and talk about during their work (or on the Sabbath rest)?[138]

But the possibility/probability of deviant oral traditions and scripts does lead us into the first century CE scenario:

6.2. An Unpacific Pax?

The imposition and presence of Imperial Roman rule, as we have seen, brought a new and overtly alien actor onto the scene: it also added a fresh,

---

134. Unionization in British industry was always more easily facilitated within industries where men worked together in their thousands. Compare the difficulties faced in the early unionization of workers in the mining and knife-grinding industries where workers were typically located in isolated small groups—Machin, *Yorkshire Miners*; Cullen, *Stirrings in Sheffield on a Saturday Night*.

135. See "Notes on Some Terms Used": *Synagogue*. One is reminded of a similar usage of "chapel" in the printing industry.

136. Horsley, "Jesus and the Politics," 126–27.

137. Barker, *Older Testament*.

138. If Barker is correct, the reason for our oft-confessed lack of knowledge about the Sadducees might be because we actually have it—in the priestly post-exilic redaction of the traditions.

and ultimately fatal, ingredient to the unstable socio-economic pressure cooker that was Palestine at the turn of the centuries:

> ... there can be no doubt that Christians, the Fourth Philosophy and the Zealots were products of the first century CE ... the causes for the rise of the sects ... are fairly clear, intimately connected with the imposition of direct Roman rule ...[139]

We are greatly indebted to Josephus for our information on the panoply of sects, movements and charismatic individuals that add so much color to our view of the period, and also indebted to the clarity of his overt concern to exculpate his Judaic religion and people from any war-guilt that enables us to see through and beyond his frequent negative judgments.[140]

But it is to Eric Hobsbawm that recent scholarship is indebted for providing the key for restructuring these references through his ground-breaking study of peasant resistance;[141] and to scholars such as Richard Horsley[142] and Dominic Crossan[143] for pioneering the use of that key to open up the social realities embedded beneath the Josephian text.

> In addition to large main currents and basic movements, whose beginnings reach back into the early stages of the Jewish people's disagreements with the Hellenistic kingdoms, there were a number of religious phenomena in the Herodian-Roman period that ... are interpretable as indirect protest reactions to the socio-economic and religio-political chaos in the land of Israel. ... Unlike the main religious groups, however, they found their main supporters not in the elite but in the lower stratum and among the underprivileged.[144]

Although there are many interconnecting themes and links between these various non-elite movements, not least that none had a formal/hierarchically legitimized leadership, it will be useful to discuss them through

---

139. Baumgarten, *Jewish Sects,* 19.

140. We need to remember that for most of the peasants, for most of the time, getting on with the daily problem of survival would have been the paramount behavior—"Give us *this day* our daily bread." Ben Macintyre, in his account of a French village under German Occupation during World War I, notes the general acceptance that "accommodation rather than confrontation was the best approach" (Macintyre, *Foreign Field,* 45–46).

141. Hobsbawm, *Primitive Rebels.*

142. Horsley, *Jesus and the Spiral of Violence;* Horsley and Hanson, *Bandits, Prophets, and Messiahs;* Horsley, "Popular Prophetic Movements" 3–27.

143. Crossan, *Historical Jesus.*

144. Stegemann, *Jesus Movement,* 162.

a focus on the principal nature and social legitimization of that leadership. It is important also to keep in mind that there were interconnections and overlaps between these new first century CE movements and with those movements having longer historical roots, such as the Pharisees[145] and Enochian movements, who maintained ongoing activity and vitality. Whilst recognizing that within all classification systems imposed on human material there are degrees of overlap and general untidiness, I propose using a continuum with classification ranging from short-term "leaderless" mass movements, through those where leadership of more permanent groupings results from the group dynamics involved in their foundation and development, to movements appearing to be dominantly brought into being by the personality, charisma, or popular status of an individual, shading over into groups resourced by some degree of routinized leadership:

1. 6.2.1 Spontaneous Reactive Movements;

2. 6.2.2 Emergent Leadership—Groups "Beyond the Pale";[146]

3. 6.2.3 "Inspirational-Leader" Movements;

4. 6.2.4 "Quasi-rabbinic" Leadership.

6.2.1 Spontaneous Reactive Movements

The period experienced spasmodic occurrences of spontaneous mass demonstrations or riots mainly triggered by insensitive actions by the Roman power, or its agents—such as the destruction of a Torah scroll by a Roman soldier,[147] or a fellow squaddie exposing his nether regions in the Temple precincts.[148] More deliberately Pilate ordered his troops' imperial ensigns to be taken into Jerusalem and on another occasion robbed the Temple treasury to finance an aqueduct.[149] On the former occasion a "vast number" of Judeans (not from "rent-a-crowd") traveled all the way to Caesarea to petition for their removal which they achieved through an impressive display of passive resistance: on the latter occasion they thronged round his tribunal in Jerusalem only to be violently dispersed.

---

145. Josephus recognizes the Pharisaic/"Fourth Philosophy" nexus. *Ant.* 18.23.

146. I use this phrase in its original Irish connotation of the (large) area of Ireland that was outside the protection of the English forces operating from Dublin.

147. *J.W.* 2.228–31.

148. *Ant.* 20.105–12; *J.W.* 2.223–27.

149. *Ant.* 18.55–62; *J.W.* 2.169–77.

In both cases it was an offense against the Temple and Holy City that triggered the demonstrations which give every impression of being a spontaneous response of the populace, producing its own temporary (un-named—probably retainer) leadership. Feelings centered on the Temple ran deep amongst ordinary Judeans who were prepared to defend its sanctity with their lives.

The strength of these feelings was most seriously tested in 40/41 CE when Caligula ordered his army to place a statue of himself in the Temple (echoes of 168 BCE).[150] His army was met by a massed demonstration from all levels of Judaic society, such that the fields were abandoned and the harvest in danger of being left to rot. Another courageous display of non-violent resistance created a stand-off during which time Caligula conveniently died.

As with all popular demonstrations when feelings run high, however, serious violence provoking violent counter-repression could readily occur, as happened shortly after the death of Herod.[151]

> No agitator can produce . . . unrest. Unrest may be utilized by a potential leader, but the causes of unrest lie in the frustrations which are already there.[152]

Such occasional, spontaneous movements of the populace, without pre-planned organization, were by their nature very transient but they do demonstrate the depths of feeling, in both elite and non-elite sectors of their society, surrounding their sacred symbols of community bonding. They were feelings that could be tapped by the right man, or the right organization, at the right time, which leads us to emergent leadership.

6.2.2 Emergent Leadership—Groups "Beyond the Pale"

Such spontaneous reactive movements threw up their own equally transitory leadership, which in some cases would be provided by members of the retainer class; but we now need to consider more permanent groupings, predominantly of peasants and the dispossessed (the "outlaws") for whom there was little or nothing in the way of traditional legitimization of authority and leadership and for whom leadership was achieved and accorded through the inter-personal dynamics of the group itself in its particular situation.[153] This remains true even where the leadership is accorded to one of the retainer

---

150. *Ant.* 18.261–309.

151. *J.W.* 2.4–13.

152. Brown, *Social Psychology of Industry*, 238.

153. Brown, *Social Psychology*, 275–91.

class[154]—leadership is accorded to the person who is experienced as best fitted to protect the group and help it achieve its objectives.

Banditry was endemic in Palestine during the Herodian-Roman period. We have noted (§ 2. 3.1.3) that one major effect of the economic transitions of these times was the increase in the number of landless and jobless peasants whose options (for males, at least) were principally begging, moving to the newer employment opportunities in the cities (whether the homeland or the diaspora), or joining one of the groups of desperate men operating beyond the normal reach of the legions and the law from caves in the mountains.[155] It is mostly in relation to these groups that we are indebted to Hobsbawm[156] who introduced the concept of "social bandits"—groups who operate beyond the boundaries of mainstream society and law, even though they are a product of that same controlling socio/economic/political system, abhorred by the authorities, yet remain in an ambivalent relationship of threat and protection with the communities of the non-elite.[157]

These groups emerge onto the pages of history with the suppression, by Herod on his way to power (c. 47 BCE), of Hezekiah,[158] whose "manor" (to use the jargon of the British criminal underworld) was in the northern

154. Many/most revolutionary movements are led by a disaffected member of the elite.

155. Moxnes, *Jesus in His Place*, 97.

156. Hobsbawm, *Primitive Rebels;* Hanson and Oakman, *Palestine in the Time of Jesus,* 86–88.

157. (1) There is an interesting parallel in Kenneth Allsop's description of 1920s Chicago (Allsop, *Bootleggers*). Written almost contemporaneously with Hobsbawm's thesis, and betraying no awareness of it—and twelve years before the publication of Anton Blok's study on the Sicilian Mafia (Blok, "Peasant and the Brigand," 494–503), Allsopp offers an explanation of the American public's fascination with the Mobsters in the way they *embodied core American values* of entrepreneurialism, albeit in very deviant ways (19–24); contextualizes them within the Italian-Sicilian urban immigrant communities who can turn to them as defenders of their alienated community (318–19) and providers of basic social-welfare facilities (e.g., Capone set up the first soup-kitchens and block restaurants in Depression Chicago "and you didn't have to listen to any sermons or get up and confess."—332, 384–85, 426). Allsop reports the transference of the social structure of their native Sicilian villages into the Chicago ghettos (352–53), and there are also references to characteristic styles of clothing and language such as B.D. Shaw was to identify in "The Bandit" (Giardina, *Romans,* 300–41). (2) "Robin Hood and his merry men" is the prototype of this in Anglo-Saxon mythology, but that should not blind us to the recognition of acts which by any criterion are criminal—we should not assume that all Josephus' "bandits" are "social bandits" (or that "social bandits" are consistently "social"!). Cf. Crossley, *Why Christianity Happened,* 52–53.

158. *Ant.* 14.158–60; *J.W.* 1.203–05.

borderland with Syria.[159] But in the following century they become an increasing presence on the edge of the stage with the accelerating deterioration of Judaic society after the re-imposition of direct Roman rule. When "the dogs of war" were finally loosed in 66 CE they moved inexorably center stage, now more as warlords, displacing the traditionally legitimized Jerusalem leadership of the Revolt as prelude to periods of internecine warfare before the imminent approach of Titus cautioned saner policies.[160] These bandit groups provided the backbone and the muscle of Jewish resistance to Rome. From the story of Jesus the name of Barabbas may come to mind (Mark 15:7).

This coming together with the Sacred Center of hardened fighters from the hill-country,[161] imbued with a folk-history of resistance from Maccabean days and a hatred of both Imperial power and its puppet-rulers has remarkable echoes with Islamic experience. Gellner writes that in Islamic history:

> The urban mob can riot under the leadership of a respected scholar, but this is not too grave a danger for the established authorities: the real danger for them lies in the alliance between a respected scholar and the militarily formidable peripheral tribes. Ironically, it is these tribes, whose daily practices and knowledge of religion, from the viewpoint of urban orthodoxy, leave much to be desired, who also provided the sword-arm which, from time to time, endowed that same orthodoxy with military and political clout, and made possible a great renewal. The preacher unites a group of tribes, upbraids them for their own ignorance and laxity, but at the same time urges them to support him in cleaning up the corruption in the city and its court, which incidentally means booty for *them*.[162] (italics original)

This could almost be a description of the City of Jerusalem in 66–70 CE.

The identification of the several resistance groups in Jerusalem during this time and their relationships and shifting alliances are as confusing in Josephus as they no doubt were during the siege itself. Although the rebellion originated within Jerusalem under the instigation of a section of the lower priesthood, the ruling elite proved unable to maintain control over the passions that had been unleashed so that as the City lost its social cohesion and discipline (and the legions were successfully subjugating the hinterland) the

---

159. Schurer, *History of the Jewish People*, 275–76.

160. *J.W.* 4.135–42; 5.248–57.

161. Freyne, "Bandits in Galilee," 50–68. "The combination of the Jerusalem populace and the bandits from the country is repeatedly affirmed" (63).

162. Gellner, *Postmodernism*, 12–13.

more radical groupings were drawn in, none of whom were strong enough to impose its own will, inducing ever more chaos.[163]

The resistance groups homed in on Jerusalem from the mountains and rural areas throughout Palestine—Galilee, Judea, Idumea—partly under pressure from the army of Vespasian, partly for the defense of Zion (and sometimes—the Idumeans—by invitation), and "endowed that same orthodoxy," in Gellner's words, "with military and political clout." Three of these groupings are named—the *Sicarii*,[164] the *Zealots*[165] and the *Idumeans*[166]; but most are known to us by the name of their leader, such as John of Gischala,[167] Menahem,[168] or Simon bar Giora.[169]

From whence comes their leadership? It is not *primarily* charismatic for the initial stages of their group formation, determined by their social context as outlaws seeking survival in an extreme and consistently hostile environment, inevitably preceded the development of the unquestioned leadership role we encounter in Josephus. "Leadership is specific to the particular situation."[170] Where there is no given formal or traditional structure of power, leadership is developed and accorded to "the person who furthers the interests of the group, and who comes closest to their ideals in his behavior."[171] Even where groups, such as the army, possessing a formal hierarchy, face *in extremis* situations a new leadership can emerge through the recognition of that complex of abilities inherent in some of their members which can ensure their survival and viability as a group.[172]

Leadership of such outlaw groups might well have had its genesis in the social interactions and traditional relationships occurring in the village(s) from which the original core of outlaws came, and the establishment of effective leadership would attract others to join, presumably through that

163. The practices which led to accusations of "tyranny" in Josephus probably resulted from attempts to impose the level of control necessary to successfully withstand a long siege—the Soviets imposed comparable harsh discipline on the citizens of Leningrad to enable them to withstand the three year siege of the German army, 1941–44.

164. *J.W.* 2.254–57 The *Sicarii* appear to be an urban guerilla group. ". . . (the Zealots) should not be confused with the Sicarii . . . they are kept separate by Josephus." (Grabbe, *Jewish Religion and History*, 62; also, Baumgarten, *Jewish Sects*, 19 n52).

165. *J.W.* 2.651; 4.135–61. See "Notes on Some Terms Used."

166. *J.W.* 4.224–35.

167. *Life* 189–90. *J.W.* 4.1–37; 159–207; 355–65.

168. *J.W.* 2.433–48.

169. *J.W.* 2 652–53. 4.503–44; 577–84.

170. Brown, *Social Psychology of Industry*, 220.

171. Sprott, *Human Groups*, 153.

172. Dixon, *On the Psychology of Military Incompetence*.

same network of family and village. And it is also true that success in leadership did encourage some of them to claim "anointed one's" (messiah/royal) status,[173] but their leadership was the product of the interpersonal dynamic of group formation and development.[174]

There is evidence of family connection[175] underpinning some of these outlaw groups: Menahem[176] the "son (probably grandson) of Judas the Galilean" and Eleazar ben Jair[177] of the same family, and their brothers—James and Simon[178]—all appear to be descended from their dynastic "godfather" Hezekiah[179] whom, we have seen, Herod the Great had "taken out" in c. 47 BCE.[180] It is by no means a universal feature but it does reflect the shaping influence of primary socialization with a degree of ascribed status accorded through the family connection. However the ability to provide effective leadership would still be the main criterion for recognition by men living at the "boundaries."[181]

---

173. *Ant.* 17.269–85; *J.W.* 2.55–65; 4.510; 575; 7.29–30.

174. A remarkable example of leadership coming out of the needs of the situation in recent UK history was the emergence of Arthur Scargill into the effective leadership of the National Union of Mineworkers (NUM) during the 1970s. At the beginning of the 1972 Miners' strike, officially called by the Union, Scargill was simply the Compensation Agent for the Yorkshire Area of the NUM. He quickly moved into virtually uncontested leadership of the strike whilst not holding any nationally elected office. Despairing of an official leadership that appeared to have little idea of organizing a national strike, the Union membership turned to and responded to Scargill who offered the leadership they were looking for. They accorded him the leadership as the man with *the bundle of skills, abilities and confidence that was needed* if they, as a Union, were going to succeed (or, indeed, survive) in their conflict. *He said the things they were looking to hear: he demanded the commitment and organized the actions they knew were necessary.* (It was only after the strike—1973—that he was elected as President of the Yorkshire Area, and much later—1981—to national office as NUM President). It was only in the aftermath of his "leadership by acclamation" that some of the trappings of "messianism" started to be accorded him—more than one Union branch commissioned a new banner featuring a portrait of Scargill, whilst the appearance of £10 notes in their pay-packets led miners to describe them for some time as "Scargills," whilst the local community affectionately christened the Yorkshire HQ building of the NUM in Barnsley as "Camelot—King Arthur's Castle."

175. Kennard, "Judas of Galilee and his Clan," 281–86; Grabbe, *Jewish Religion and History*, 58–60.

176. *J.W.* 2.433.

177. *J.W.* 2.447.

178. *Ant.* 20.102.

179. *J.W.* 2.56.

180. *Ant.* 14.158–60; *J.W.* 1.203–05.

181. The name of "Cromwell" was insufficient to maintain Oliver's son Richard in power.

Close kinship to Jesus was certainly germane to the recognition of James as leader of the *Jakobusgemeinde,* but may not have been either necessary or sufficient of itself to establish and, particularly, maintain him in it.[182]

6.2.3 *"Inspirational-Leader" Movements*[183]

Under the previous heading we encountered strong charismatic personalities whose leadership emerged out of their situation: we now need to recognize those individuals whose charisma, ability or claim of divine mission[184] called forth a disparate range of movements.

There were a number of leaders who initiated fairly short-lived, but sizable, movements by the power of their personality and preaching. These are the "sign prophets" who, according to Josephus, "under the pretext of divine inspiration evoked unrest and uproar and through their words instilled demonic enthusiasm in the masses. Finally, they led the people into the wilderness, where God wanted to show them signs of liberation."[185] But "no agitator can produce unrest" (§ 2. 6.2.1)—they tapped into existent depths of feeling. The activities of Theudas[186] and "the Egyptian"[187] are particularly noted by Josephus. However, whether pacific or militarist, the Roman military soon abbreviated the life of such movements, but while they lasted the authority of the leader was clearly in his claim, and its acknowledgment by the crowds, to be in the tradition and succession of the Hebrew prophets—a claim that was reinforced through their re-enactments and the locations (such as the *wilderness* motif) that were redolent of Yahwistic salvation-history. The movements surrounding John the Baptist and Jesus may not have seemed too dissimilar to a casual Gentile observer (§ 3.).

182. James maintained his leadership of the *Jakobusgemeinde* over a period of at least twenty years, probably more.

183. I am using the term "inspirational" generically in preference to "charismatic" as that latter term can enjoy specific, but regrettably varied, definitions.

184. Kee, *Christian Origins,* 54–75 describes four types of charismatic leader—ethical prophet, miracle worker, teacher/philosopher, and astrologer/diviner/prophet.

185. *Ant.* 20.167–88; *J.W.* 2.258–63.

186. *Ant.* 20.97–98.

187. *Ant.* 20.169; *J.W.* 2.261.

6.2.4 "Quasi-rabbinic" Leadership[188]

As we have moved from short-lived intensive movements responding to a particular crisis to movements exhibiting a more ongoing character, it is not surprising that we should find a more routinized[189] form of leadership developing alongside the initiating charismatic stimulus. This is seen in the expanding teaching role of the leaders and thus a corresponding convergence with patterns established in the older retainer-dominated groupings (such as the Pharisees).

One outcome of the Maccabean revolution was a new intensity surrounding Torah and its interpretation. With the increased levels of literacy associated with the experience of urbanization, this facilitated the critique and challenge to the traditional priestly custodians of the Law by the sectarian movements during the following Hasmonean period (§ 2. 5.2.4). In that context those with the ability to read, master, understand and interpret the Law and the Prophets (with associated *halakah*) inevitably rose in social status (formal and informal) and influence[190]—a role that was later to mature in the Talmudic period into that of "Rabbi." This was significantly true amongst the Pharisees who, according to Josephus, "are considered the most accurate interpreters of the laws"[191] and whom Jeremias describes as belonging to the new "ruling class of scriptural interpreters" who represented the common people over against the aristocracy.[192]

This is the interface where the retainer-class interacts with and is interpenetrated by some at least of peasant origin,[193] and within Jerusalem this would have embraced some of the displaced migrant workers such as those attracted by the Temple Building Project as they sought for new meaning and community within an alien environment.[194]

Not all leaders have charismatic personalities. Some are looked to for leadership mainly on account of their sheer competence and ability in those

188. I am using the modified descriptor of "Quasi-rabbinic" in preference to the simpler "Rabbinic" as that shares the same problems of anachronism as "Christian."

189. A reference to the latter stages of Weber's classic description of the development of movements from charismatic beginnings through to institutional expression. Osiek, *What Are They Saying*, 78.

190. Sir 38.34b—39.11; *Ant.* 20.264–65; Saldarini, *Pharisees, Scribes, and Sadducees*, 247–66.

191. *J.W.* 2.162.

192. Jeremias, *Jerusalem in the Time of Jesus*, 266.

193. "Sociologically most of them (scribes) would have been retainers, that is, *people who had left the peasantry* but did not have an independent place and power in society." (my italics) (Saldarini, *Scribes, Pharisees and Scribes*, 274).

194. Baumgarten, *Jewish Sects*, 138.

areas that are needed/valued by the group members. It is thus as "interpreters of Torah" that some other leaders can be recognized, for example, Bannus, the John-the-Baptist-like ascetic figure so tantalizingly mentioned by Josephus in his *Life*.[195] Josephus tells that he spent three years in his late teens with Bannus, learning from him. This is very suggestive of a small group of acolytes gathered around their mentor. There is no suggestion of "prophet" in the description (though Josephus would probably have been reluctant to admit it, were that the case): it was a case of learning from a man notable for his holy living—"I imitated him in those things and continued with him three years." There was probably a Pharisaic underpinning to what Bannus was doing as Josephus records that on his return to Jerusalem "I . . . began to conduct myself according to the rules of the sect of the Pharisees."

That Pharisees could be in such roles of leadership and respect, with a more permanent group gathered round them, is born out by the incident of the Golden Eagle emblem over one of the Temple Gates at a time of political weakness when Herod was mortally ill:

> There were in the capital two doctors with a reputation as profound experts in the laws of their country,[196] who consequently enjoyed the highest esteem of the whole nation; their names were Judas, son of Sepphoraeus, and Matthias, son of Margalus. *Their lectures in the laws were attended by a large youthful audience*, and day after day they drew together quite an army of men in their prime.[197] (my italics)

We are given no information about the social composition of such a group. Presumably the core would be the sons of Pharisees and Scribes (including those from the Diaspora—contemporaries, say, of Saul of Tarsus), but the larger the group the greater the likelihood of it including members of the non-elite classes, including recruits from amongst the many thousands of uprooted migrant workers in the city.

A very similar (probably identical) scenario in *Antiquities* is the short-lived rebellion at the time of the 6 CE census led by Judas the Galilean with the Pharisee Saddok.[198] Josephus identifies this as the point of emergence of his "Fourth Philosophy" that was to mature into the tragic harvest of the

---

195. Josephus, *Life*, 11–12.

196. I.e., Pharisees *J.W.* 2.162.

197. *J.W.* 1.648–50.

198. Schurer, *History of the Jewish People I*, 381–82. Schurer identifies Judas (son of Sepphoris) (4 BCE) with Judas the Galilean (6 CE). Also, Kennard, "Judas of Galilee and his Clan" 281.

Great Revolt in 66 CE.[199] Given a fair degree of ideological convergence between the revolt of Judas and the issues of the Great Revolt with the troubles preceding it, nonetheless it seems that this earlier event was a discrete occurrence rather than the beginning of a movement (as Josephus seems to imply) though it did no doubt become part of the folk-memory of the period. What is important for us is to recognize that although the "P.B.I." of the revolt were undoubtedly (as ever) drawn dominantly from the displaced peasant classes, the leadership seems to be drawn from the retainer class (Saddok, a Pharisee), a perception that is reinforced by Josephus' later information that "this school agrees in all other respects with the opinions of the Pharisees."[200] This suggests that, without denying the possibility/probability of a charismatic element in someone such as Judas, the legitimation of the leadership was derived from Saddok, at least, being recognized as an expert in the interpretation of Torah.

Examples of "direct action" should not blind us to the probably more pacific norm of such "rabbi"/disciple groupings where it is expertise in Torah that is the attraction to and reward of such leadership—from the "school" of Ben Sira[201] through to Saul of Tarsus who was "brought up in (Jerusalem) at the feet of Gamaliel, (and) educated strictly according to the Law" (Acts 22:3).[202] The aforementioned Bannus is another example.

We must also take cognizance of the possibility/probability that in a city the size of Jerusalem there would be a number of such locally recognized "self-educated" people[203] who, despite Ben Sira's pessimism,[204] developed a very real expertise in Torah interpretation.[205] We have a clear record

199. *Ant.* 18.1–10; 23–25.

200. *Ant.* 18.23.

201. Sir 51.23–30.

202. Freyne, *Jewish Galilean*, 129–30, draws attention to a group (in Daniel)—"the wise ones"—which he distinguishes from the *maskilim* and sees it as a sort of analogue/prototype for understanding the Jesus-group(s).

203. The story of one working-class movement with a religious focus in nineteenth century England—the Primitive Methodists—is replete with examples of working men, especially miners or agricultural workers, who were self-educated and thereby became leading figures not only in their chapels but in their wider communities. (Wearmouth, *Methodism and the Trade Unions*, 37–68). This was an expression of a feature that was characteristic of the whole working-class movement during that period (Wearmouth, *Methodism and the Struggle*; Wearmouth, *Some Working Class Movements*). Maurice Casey argues that Jesus and his brothers were probably literate in Aramaic and Hebrew (Casey, *Jesus of Nazareth*, 158–164), contra Crossan, *Jesus*, 25. ". . . it must be presumed that Jesus also was illiterate."

204. Sir 38.24–34.

205. Keith, "Claim of John 7:15," 44–63. Keith's argument is equally applicable to James.

of this in the NT in the shape of the "Nazarene" James[206] and the community of people gathered around him in Jerusalem who looked to him for leadership (Acts 15:13–21).

There was the opportunity to listen to and engage with Torah interpreters in the Temple precincts (e.g., Mark 14:49; Luke 2:46–47; Acts 5:42), if not elsewhere, and the space afforded by the weekly Sabbath. Chris Keith, in his comprehensive study of Jesus' literacy,[207] noted the wide and complex spectrum of language and literacy skills variously held, and argues that Jesus does not exhibit "scribal literacy," but what he defined as "craftsman's literacy." He recognizes, nonetheless, that Jesus was able to effectively engage with the scribes in public in their own area of expertise such that the crowds exclaimed "what authority!"[208] *Mutatis mutandis*, what is true for Jesus must be broadly true for James, with the proviso that through living in Jerusalem he may have had more opportunity to develop a facility in scribal literacy. On the occasion of James' execution, Josephus reported on the respect in which he was held by the Pharisees,[209] which (amongst other things) may point towards him having had a level of scribal literacy on a par with their own.[210]

Bauckham has described this "son of Nazareth" as "a wisdom teacher in his own right."[211] But this leaves completely open the question of where, how, and over what period of time James acquired such expertise and recognition (§ 8. 1.2.1).

206. E.g., Kloppenborg, "Diaspora Discourse," 242–70, notes that, in a pseudonymous writing, credibility demands consonance between the fictive author and the historical person (especially a contemporary or one of recent memory). This carries a clear inference that, whether pseudonymous or authorial, EpJas testifies to James, at this later time, being recognized as an interpreter of Torah in his own right, independent of his relationship with Jesus (EpJas significantly makes no play on the sibling relationship). And if his authority is thus independent of Jesus, it is likely that it does in fact pre-date Jesus (§ 6. 3).

207. Keith, *Jesus' Literacy.*

208. Freyne, referring to DSS 4Q 416–18, affirms, "For Jesus also, wisdom and understanding (were) not the preserve of upper-class scribes. (They) can be mediated in and through the everyday circumstances of home and village life . . . (The) emphasis (is) on the gift-nature of wisdom, . . . subverting the elite notions of scribal wisdom being the preserve of those who have time for leisure." Freyne, *Jewish Galilean*, 141.

209. *Ant* 20.200–03

210. Goodacre, *Thomas and the Gospels*, 142

211. Bauckham, "James and Jesus," 117.

6.3. Summary

James is historically significant as the undisputed presiding figure of the *Jakobusgemeinde*. Having mapped out the socio-historical site of our investigation we need to highlight those surface markers that will both facilitate a more coherent framing for both James and the *Jakobusgemeinde* and guide our further examination.

6.3.1 *The Jakobusgemeinde*

We would anticipate the *Jakobusgemeinde* to exhibit in some measure the following markers:

- as part of a *Gemeinschaft*-oriented society to understand itself:
  - as an integral part of that society;
  - defining itself *vis-à-vis* that society;
  - structuring its movement in patterns derived from that society.
- within the sectarian ethos of late Second Temple Judaism:
  - to orientate itself relative to the agenda of concerns common to most of the sectarians, which principally center around the maintenance of Israelite/Judaic identity (national and individual) in face of the infiltration of Hellenistic culture and their incorporation into the Roman Empire;
  - to associate themselves with like-minded groupings, whilst opposing those they considered to be seriously deviant.
- in the Jerusalem heading towards the irruption of 66 CE:
  - to have a strong, empowering, commitment to Torah;
  - to develop its own leadership, capable of interpreting the Torah for its situation;
  - to be sensitive to the boundary markers of a "true" son of Israel such as circumcision and food purity.

6.3.2 James of Jerusalem

How did James of Nazareth become James of Jerusalem?

We have identified a number of relevant markers of processes that were endemic in first century Palestine:

- economic/social dislocation;

- debt/unemployment/migrant labor;

- Temple Rebuilding Project;

- urbanization experience, loss of familiar community, search for new meaning and community;

- "educational" opportunities—proximity of Temple, Teachers of Torah, self-education;

- συναγωγή formation, governed by craft, region of origin, facilitating empowerment of non-elite groupings;

- acquisition of informal/formal status through "Mastery of the Torah."

Historical social science, of course, is no replacement for hard data, but it can help us to develop frameworks of understanding where data is sparse, and, like "profiling" in criminology, can guide us in our search and alert us to the possible significance of otherwise unremarkable fragments of information.

These markers, with differing levels of significance, indicate the clear possibility that the son of a Torah-observant family from rural Galilee could well emerge as leader of a συναγωγή in Jerusalem, perhaps centered round a core of fellow migrants. That such a grouping emerged in Jerusalem, around the Nazarene James and his brothers, is clear from the New Testament and early Christian tradition. What is less clear from the data is how and when.

3

John the Baptist

REFORM WAS VERY MUCH in the air in Palestine in the first century CE. Before we turn our focus on to James we need to bring into the frame two contemporary movements looking for the restoration of the true Israel in the light of the imminent ἔσχατον—the Baptist, and the longer established Essenes, especially those in the towns and villages of Israel.

1. The Essenes (outside Qumran)

We have already noted the significance of the wilderness group encamped at Qumran (§ 2. 6.1.2). Since the discovery of the Dead Sea Scrolls scholars have been able to fill out the observations of contemporary writers such as Philo and Josephus with writings from a reform group within late Second Temple Judaism that is almost certainly to be identified with the previously elusive Essenes:[1] a description conferred by others but whose preferred self-designation was "Community (*yahad*) of God."[2] The fact that the bulk of this material comes from the Qumran caves inevitably carries a danger of distorting our perception of the Essene movement as a whole,[3] which both Philo and Josephus[4] report as being found through the towns and villages of

1. Rofe, "The Onset of Sects in Post-Exilic Judaism" 42–46, presents evidence discerning the roots of the later Essene movement c. 300 BCE.

2. 1QS I.12, II.22–25.

3. "The most economical solution to the various statements . . . is to say that the Qumran community (was) a small branch of the Essenes." VanderKam and Flint, *Meaning of the Dead Sea Scrolls,* 250; Hengel and Barrett, *Conflicts and Challenges,* 17.

4. *J.W.* 2.119–161; Philo, *Apologia pro Iudaeis*—in Eusebius, *Praeparatio Evangelica,*

Judea, in what John Collins has described as "multiple settlements" of which Qumran is just one.[5] The *Damascus Document* (CD), originally discovered in a Cairo Genizah and then amongst the Qumran documents, particularly offers insight into how the Essene "rule" was expressed for living within everyday Judaic society.[6]

It is remarkable that complete silence envelops the Essenes in the New Testament. This may reflect their geographical spread—being much thinner on the ground in Galilee (the principal focus of Jesus' activity in all the canonical gospels) than in Judea. Or, given that we usually encounter Pharisees, Sadducees, Scribes/Lawyers, and Herodians[7] in situations of conflict, it may be that there was either a degree of sympathy between the Essenes and the nascent Christian groupings, or, at least, a lack of competition for membership or popular appeal and influence.[8]

Justine Taylor and Etienne Nodet,[9] arguing for greater attention to be paid to rites and liturgies as conservers of traditional practice, note that the "baptism" of converts and the sacred meal with the blessing of the cup and the bread are "common to early Christianity and the Essenes (and) are to be found also in rabbinic Judaism"[10] which suggests an original setting for these practices within Second Temple Judaism. Thus, "the occurrence in rabbinic Judaism of features shared with the Essenes and the followers of Jesus, points rather to the emergence of the rabbinic tradition itself from an original environment which was close to the Essenes, and therefore to Jesus' disciples, but equally distant from official circles." Hence:

> (I)f the original environment of Christianity was close to the Essenes, then we can immediately see why they would not be

---

VIII.11.1, quoted in Knibb, *Qumran Community,* 15.

5. Collins, "Site of Qumran," 11–13. Even the "sectarian" writings among the DSS probably have a wider Essene reference than a uniquely Qumran one, for ". . . these rules were not written for the inhabitants of Qumran, since the settlement was established only around 100 BCE, but for other Essene groups" (Frey, "Essenes," 600).

6. Esler, *First Christians,* 75–78, views CD as reflecting an earlier stage in the Qumran community.

7. Otto Betz has suggested that "Herodians" may have been a derogatory term in use for the Essenes, deriving from the favor in which Herod (the Great) had held them (*Ant.* 15.373). Betz, "Jesus and the Temple Scroll," 75–103. Taylor, *Essenes, the Scrolls and the Dead Sea,* 109–30.

8. For possible links between the Essene community and the *Jakobusgemeinde,* see Capper, "The Palestinian Context," 341–50; Charlesworth, "Jesus Research," 31; Pixner, "Mount Zion, Jesus, and Archeology," 309–22; Riesner, "Jesus, the Primitive Community," 198–234; Bernheim, *James,* 209–12.

9. Taylor and Nodet, *Origins of Christianity,* 88–126.

10. Taylor, "Original Environment," 214–24.

mentioned by name in the New Testament: the "insiders" would not use the term used by others to refer to them.[11]

We noted that the community at Qumran had a passionate concern with the Temple cultus and sought its reform[12]—priesthood, rites and calendar.[13] The *Damascus Document* is suggestive of a boycott of the Temple cultus during the "age of wickedness"[14] although there is a later reference to Temple offerings,[15] and Josephus refers to their continued payment of the Temple levy.[16] The Essenes extreme critique of the contemporary Temple cultus arose specifically from their passionate commitment and belief in the Temple and its cultus as gifted by Yahweh, presently corrupted by the illegality of the Hasmonean priesthood and its practices. They had separated themselves from the Jerusalem hierarchy and establishment, and at Qumran sought to preserve and develop the true Zadokite priesthood with the authentic festival calendar in the wilderness of Judea against that "Day" when Yahweh would restore true priesthood and worship on Zion.[17] In the interim their community (the *yahad*—not just at Qumran) could itself be considered as the true Temple[18], which therefore inevitably involved great care in acceptance and training of novitiates with an ongoing discipline of community life.

The organization of the Essene "camps" within the broader community of Israel is instructive. Authority was vested in the person of the *mebaqqer* ("guardian") who will instruct, guide, care for, and discipline the members of the Community,[19] in terms that would be recognizable through the centuries as the episcopal ideal:[20]

11. Ibid., 219–21.

12. 4Q394—399.

13. Knibb, *Qumran Community,* 9.

14. *CD* 6.11–14.

15. *CD* 11.17–21. "This contradiction is perhaps to be explained by the assumption that the collection of laws reflect different stages in the evolution of the beliefs and attitudes of the movement."—Knibb, *Qumran Community,* 53.

16. *Ant.* 18.19 cf. Matt 17.24–27; 4Q159 sanctions a "one-off" payment of the Temple Tax to comply with the Law, rather than the later tradition which understands it as an annual tax, thus "withholding regular support from the Temple in Jerusalem." (Vermes, *Dead Sea Scrolls,* 529).

17. *CD* 1.4–12; 3.12—4.12; 5.20—6.11

18. *CD* 3.19; Knibb, *Qumran Community,* 33–35.

19. *CD* 13.8–14.

20. Jeremias, *Jerusalem,* 265.

> He shall love them as a father loves his children, and shall carry
> them in all their distress like a shepherd his sheep.[21]

There is also reference to a group of "twelve men and three priests" who have received two years intensive training in the Torah and the way of the *yahad*.[22] Their formation was essential for the establishment of the community as "Israel."[23] They may have been the nucleus around which a new settlement was generated[24] and thus been a normative feature of Essene "camps," not solely that at Qumran (§ 5. 9.2.4).

Essenes accepted and practiced a stern discipline based on a thoroughgoing adherence to Torah as interpreted by their leader,[25] the "Teacher of Righteousness," and embedded both in the minutiae of their "Way"[26] and their heroic efforts to establish and maintain purity in their communal life.[27] Included in this was the relinquishing of all individual goods and wealth into the common ownership of the community[28]—a practice that was also a feature of the Essene camps[29] in the wider Judaic society.[30] Thus their self-description as "the Poor"[31] may have been both a material and spiritual form of expression. It has recently been argued by Brian Capper[32] that the non-Qumranic ("secular") Essenes operated a series of "Poor Houses" just outside Jerusalem and throughout rural Judea, providing a social support facility where the kinship network was failing. The reference to the ubiquity of poverty on the occasion of Jesus being anointed (Mark 14:3–9) may have this as its context.

Not only the books of Moses but the writings of the Prophets (with their "Righteous-Teacher inspired" interpretations) are well represented

21. *CD* 13.9.

22. 1QS VIII.1–16 (4QSe); Abbreviated to "fifteen men" in one fragment of the *Damascus Document* (4Q265 fr. 7 ii,7–8).

23. 1QS VIII 5, 12.

24. Knibb, *Qumran Community*, 129; Collins, *Site of Qumran*, 13–15; 1QS VIII 14–16.

25. *CD* 4.8.

26. *CD* 1.10,13; 4Q398.14–17.

27. *CD* 6.11—8.2.

28. 1QS VI.19–20.

29. *CD* 7.6–8.

30. *J.W.* 2.122, 127; *Ant.* 18.200; Philo, *Every Good Man Is Free*—quoted in VanderKam and Flint, *Meaning of the Dead Sea Scrolls*, 246–47). Also a feature traditionally ascribed to the *Jakobusgemeinde* (Acts 2:44–45, 4:34—5.11. Capper, "Palestinian Context," 327–35).

31. *CD* 19.9.

32. Capper, "Essene Community Houses," 472–502.

in the Qumran library—indicative of the importance of sacred writ for their self-understanding. They were the "true Israel," albeit a "Righteous Remnant,"[33] living in the shadow of the ἔσχατον which gave both meaning and motive[34] for their severe discipline and commitment, understood as a preparation, and possibly facilitation, of the prophetic "Day of Yahweh."

2. The Baptizer and the Galilean

In our analysis of leadership patterns of popular movements within Second Temple Judaism we recognized that leadership could be accorded on more than one dimension.[35] This is certainly true of both John the Baptist and Jesus of Nazareth both of whom display, with different emphases, that charismatic attraction associated with being recognized as a prophet along with a more routinized quasi-rabbinic teaching role.

In company with the "sign prophets" they both utilized motifs from that same salvation-history: John centered his work in the wilderness, dressing in a form that was reminiscent of Elijah (Mark 1:4–6), whilst Jesus fed the multitude (Israel) in the wilderness (Mark 6:30–44//Matt 14:1–21// Luke 9:10–17; Mark 8:1–10//Matt 15:32–39) and, near the end, symbolically entered Jerusalem (Mark 11:1–10//Matt 21:1–9//Luke 19:28–38). Although accorded a similar legitimation as prophets by the common people, the closely related movements springing from the leadership of John the Baptist and Jesus of Nazareth went further than the sign prophets in gathering a close band of disciples, whom they taught, in addition to the mass following of the crowds, and perhaps as a consequence of this their movements demonstrated greater durability, in both cases surviving, even flourishing, after the death of their leader.

Beyond the Matthean and (particularly) the Lucan birth narratives we have little information about the early years and influences on Jesus—growing up in Nazareth, a visit to the Temple at the age of twelve (Luke 2:39–51) along with inferences deriving from two brief intrusions into the text of his family (Mark 3:20–21, 31–35; 6:1–6)—and we have nothing about John. Luke covers the years before he bursts on the scene with the essentially contentless phrase ". . . he was in the wilderness until the day he appeared publicly to Israel" (Luke 1:80).

---

33. *CD* 1.4.

34. *CD* 4.10–12.

35. The descriptor of "sign prophet" is, of course, a modern scholastic category imposed on the ancient texts.

It is unlikely that John and Jesus came from the lowest levels of society.[36] The Lucan birth narratives present a tradition that John belonged to a priestly family which might place him in the retainer class;[37] whilst Jesus' artisan[38] background as a τέκτων (Mark 6:3) [or the son of a τέκτων (Matt 13:55)] is clearly remembered. Indeed, there is a possibility that Jesus' family originally were of higher (though still non-elite) status—James McGrath, in examining the evidence for claims of Jesus' illegitimacy through an analysis of his adult social interactions argues that the shock recorded by his friendship with "sinners" implies that he had a higher status, he was not a *mamzer*.[39] Similarly, Paul Foster has argued that there are "indicators that Jesus' background did not reflect the lowest echelons of Galilean peasantry," and that "Jesus did not originate in the social class of illiterate Galilean peasantry as has been suggested by a number of recent reconstructions of the historical Jesus."[40] Maurice Casey, noting the naming pattern of the brothers (§ 6. 1.3), describes Jesus (and therefore James) as "born into an observant Jewish family"[41] and stresses the evidence for Jesus (and his brothers) being literate in both Aramaic and Hebrew.[42] In his more nuanced study of Jesus' literacy, Chris Keith concluded:

> The Markan portrayal of Jesus as a τέκτων who is outside the scribal-literate class but nevertheless occupies social positions associated with scribal literacy, and meets various receptions for doing so, most clearly reflects the actual past.[43]

Bernheim summarized:

> . . . Joseph's family was a family of craftsmen living in a degree of comfort, compared to most of the inhabitants of Nazareth, who will have been agricultural workers or farmers working a minuscule plot of land . . . (Joseph's trade) called for considerable technical knowledge. Moreover it is probable that Joseph and his sons found work at Sepphoris . . . The parables of Jesus

---

36. Contra Crossan, *Historical Jesus.*

37. Stegemann, *Jesus Movement*, 185.

38. In Sir 38.27, τέκτων is translated as "artisan" by the NRSV translators, suggesting a wider skills-base than our "carpenter"; see § 2. 4.1 n.54.

39. McKnight, "Calling Jesus *Mamzer*," 73–103; McGrath, "Was Jesus Illegitimate," 81–100.

40. Foster, "Educating Jesus," 7, 12.

41. Casey, *Jesus of Nazareth*, 143–45, 169.

42. Ibid., 158–64.

43. Keith, *Jesus' Literacy*, 188.

show us someone who was very familiar with the mechanisms of the monetary economy.[44]

We should note that what is true for Jesus must also be true for his brothers, including James. Whilst Horsley tentatively concludes:

> One might conclude that Jesus himself was a socially marginal figure insofar as his family must have lost its family inheritance at some point and had to make a living as artisans.[45]

A feature of many historical peasant protest and resistance movements is that the leadership frequently originates from higher social groupings—and the John/Jesus movement(s) may indeed be a limited example of this.

John, in classic prophetic style, "appeared in the wilderness, proclaiming . . ." (Mark 1:4). Following the discovery of the Qumran Scrolls the question of possible connections between John and the Essenes was quickly raised to fill in some of his "hidden years," even the possibility of John having belonged to the Qumran community: for example, John emerges "fully developed" in the same general wilderness area of the lower Jordan valley as Qumran, his practice of baptism recalls the ritual washings of the Qumran community with their concern for ritual purity; there is a shared ascetic life-style; and, significantly, both the Isaianic call to "prepare in the wilderness the way of Yahweh" (Isa 40:3) is specifically applied to both the *Yahad* and John (1QS VIII.15; Mark 1:3). Jean Steinmann proposed that the links and disconnections (e.g., John's baptism was a singular event) could be explained by John having been a novice at Qumran, from where he received his grounding in the scriptures, but at some point left the community.[46]

However, the features (such as the strong concern for purity), which they share, are also widely found across the spectrum of Second Temple Judaism.[47] As Joan Taylor observed in her extensive and detailed study of the Baptist:

> (W)e would have to prove not only that parallels exist between John and the Essenes, but also that these parallels are neither found in regard to other groups within Second Temple Judaism nor traceable to common source material. The parallels between

---

44. Bernheim, *James,* 43.

45. Horsley, *Hidden Transcripts,* 16.

46. Steinmann, *Saint John the Baptist,* 58–62; cf. Brownlee, "John the Baptist in the New Light," 71–90; Betz, "Was John the Baptist an Essene," 205–14.

47. Taylor, *Immerser,* 15–100.

John and the Essenes would have to be unique and explicable only in terms of direct relationship.[48]

She concluded her examination of the proposed linkage between John and Qumran:

(T)he overwhelming impression is that John should probably not be seen as having any direct relationship with the Essenes, least of all the isolated group at Qumran, whether prior to or during his own prophetic activity by the river Jordan.[49]

2.1 The Baptizer's Movement

John the Baptist made a deep impression on his contemporaries—half a century later Josephus can write of him in connection with the defeat of Antipas in war with Aretas of Nabatea with a precision not evidenced in his allusions to Jesus.[50] He describes the occasion and reason for the Baptist's execution as Herod's fear of John's hold on the general populace, recording the popular opinion that the defeat of Antipas was a divine judgment for his execution of John—strong independent witness to John's impact on his fellow Israelites, both in his lifetime and for at least a generation later. Josephus' only secure mention of Jesus is a passing reference on the occasion of the execution of James, the brother of Jesus.[51]

The Synoptic tradition, with a Hellenized resonance in Josephus, rooted both the Baptist and his message within the prophetic salvation-history of Israel, summoning the people of Israel to repent. John's message was prefaced by a profound conviction that they were living in the shadow of the impending ἔσχατον—"Even now the axe is lying at the root of the trees." (Luke 3:7–10). It was a belief that was common to many at that time, especially those within the movements for the restoration of Israel (including the hope for the ingathering of the exiled tribes[52]) within Second Temple Judaism. In that light John issued his call to renewed faithfulness to the Torah and the covenant-relationship, with a call for zekhut—"the protecting influence of

48. Ibid., 16.

49. Ibid., 15–48.

50. *Ant.* 18.116–19. As a Jerusalem resident Josephus may have been more aware of the Baptist, and the peoples' estimation of him, than he would have been of the Galilean Jesus.

51. *Ant.* 20.200. (The *Testimonium Flavianum* —*Ant.*18.63—bears clear marks of Christian redaction).

52. Ferda, "John the Baptist," 154–88.

freely chosen good conduct over and above what was required by the Law."[53] John's concern was the urgent renewal in covenant faith of the whole Judaic community in view of the imminence of the ἔσχατον, to "prepare the way of the Lord, make his paths straight" (Mark 1:3). Those baptized were to return home to live it out—"a huge web of apocalyptic expectations, a network of ticking time bombs all over the Jewish homeland"[54]—at least in Jerusalem and Judea (Mark 1:5).

Like others seeking the renewal of Israel within the land given them by Yahweh—whether Judas and Matthias (of "Golden Eagle" fame)[55] or Jesus of Nazareth—there gathered around the Baptist a nucleus of disciples whom he taught to pray (Luke 11:1) and presumably much else besides. It is likely that both Jesus and some of his later Galilean nucleus of followers were originally in the disciple group around John. There is no indication that John sought to establish a new discrete movement (any more than Jesus did during his Galilean ministry[56]): he sent penitents, *mainly from Jerusalem and Judea*, back to their sedentary occupations to express in their lives the fruits of repentance in a life of fidelity to Torah.

3. John and Jesus: The Issue of Status

"Jesus was baptized by John the Baptist" famously heads the list of E. P. Sanders' "almost indisputable facts" about the life of Jesus.[57] It was an event deeply embedded in the tradition, but one that early created unease in the developing Christian movement, clearly revealed in the Matthean addition portraying John's reluctance to baptize this particular candidate (Matt 3:15). The *Gospel of the Hebrews* similarly betrays awareness of tension in the picture of a sin-free Christ undergoing baptism "for the forgiveness of sins."[58]

53. Taylor, *Immerser*, 124. We find it reflected also in the traditions of Jacobean teaching embedded in EpJas and the Sermon on the Mount (§ 7. 7.2).

54. Crossan, *Jesus: A Revolutionary Biography*, 43–44; Twelftree, "Jesus the Baptist," 103–25.

55. *J.W.* 1.648.

56. The implication of Jesus' actions at the Last Supper are not germane here.

57. Sanders, *Jesus and Judaism*, 11.

58. *Gos. Heb.* 2.1–2. The Christian doctrine of the "sinlessness of Christ" is probably derived theologically from the interpretation of the death of Christ as the perfect sacrifice "for our sins" projected onto the tradition of Jesus. To be recognized as a "righteous one" (as Jesus was—Matt 27:19; Luke 23:47; Jas 5:6) does not equate with having never sinned—James, his brother, became known as "James the Just/Righteous" but this did not carry any notion of "sinless perfection," such as the church has imputed to Jesus.

But this unease is about more than Jesus apparently repenting of sins for, more significantly, it raises questions of primacy, status and power:

- the very act of baptism expresses a power relationship;
- it implies Jesus as already a disciple of John, receiving his teaching, and continuing as a disciple;
- John's movement precedes that of Jesus—and age conveys primacy.

Nothing can erase the impact of the visual symbolism inherent in the very act of baptism by immersion. The action eloquently expresses a power relationship between the one who performs/supervises the act of baptism and the one who is submerged.

For those baptized by John, it was neither an isolated act, nor the beginning of a turning back to Yahweh, but a significant step in that process. Notwithstanding the distinctiveness of his baptizing activity in the light of the impending ἔσχατον Taylor has demonstrated that John's immersion would be fully understood within the world of Second Temple Judaism as a cleansing of the body from physical impurity completing the process of inner cleansing acquired through repentance along with a renewal of Torah observance—"a baptism of repentance for the forgiveness of sins" (Mark 1:4).[59] Not only does this place John's actions as fully understandable within the Judaic practice of his time but also underscores that the people whom John baptized had been under the influence of his preaching and teaching prior to their immersion:

> Certainly, those who had been to John for immersion considered themselves to be his disciples. Put simply, one could be John's disciple and still not yet be immersed, but one probably would not be immersed by John without being his disciple.[60]

The unavoidable implication of this is that Jesus also was a learner, a disciple, of John for a period before his own immersion—a relationship that may have continued for a time afterwards.[61] The Fourth Gospel significantly records a period of simultaneous activity by John and Jesus (John 3:22–26,[62] 4:1–3), which is an inherently credible scenario.[63] Indeed Maurice Casey

---

59. Taylor, *Immerser*, 49–100.

60. Ibid., 106.

61. Casey, *Jesus of Nazareth*, 178–85.

62. Pryor, "John the Baptist and Jesus," 23–25.

63. Twelftree, "Jesus the Baptist," 109–12: "(I)t is probable that Mark or his tradition has suppressed the idea that Jesus had been a baptist in league with John in the wilderness."

asserts "a very strong argument of cumulative weight for supposing that the ministries of John the Baptist and Jesus overlapped, and that this is where some of Jesus' sayings belonged."[64] The Fourth Evangelist also refers to a transfer of loyalty by some from John to Jesus (John 1:35–42), which may reflect his theological agenda of exalting Jesus of Nazareth *vis-à-vis* John the Baptist, but is nonetheless also historically credible, reflecting a porosity of boundaries between reform movements in Israel.

This clearly establishes a position of seniority by John over Jesus to which the nascent Christian movement was to become very sensitive, preserving/creating sayings to counter this implication. For example, Mark 1:7 says, "The one who is more powerful than I is coming after me." Or, John 1:30 reads, "After me (John) comes a man who ranks ahead of me because he was before me."

After describing how crowds from Jerusalem and Judea flocked to hear and receive baptism from John, Mark describes how, in similar fashion, "in those days Jesus came from Nazareth of Galilee" (Mark 1:9), an experience that was to lead on to his own activity in Galilee (Mark 1:14–15). It could not be clearer—John's mission chronologically preceded that of Jesus, and in the first century Mediterranean world age and temporal precedence bestowed status.[65]

3.1 Tradition Dissonance and Development

This tension in understanding and status, inherent in the setting and symbolism of Jesus' baptism by John, is firmly embedded in the gospel tradition.

On the one hand, there are sayings where the Baptist and Jesus are spoken of "in the same breath":

- "For John came neither eating nor drinking . . . the Son of Man came eating and drinking . . ." (Matt 11:18–19//Luke 7:33–34; also—Mark 2:18//Matt 9:14//Luke 5:33; Mark 11:28–30//Matt 21:23–25//Luke 20:1–4);
- Echoes of a "John *revividus*" sentiment in both the popular and the official mind (Mark 6:14–16//Matt 14:1–2//Luke 9:7–9; Mark 8:27–28//Matt 16:13–14//Luke 9:18–19).

---

64. Casey, *Aramaic Approach to Q*, 145.
65. Barclay, "Neither Old nor Young," 225–41.

- And Jesus himself, when challenged in Jerusalem about his authority stymies his opponents with a counter-challenge focused on John (Mark 11:27–33).

At other times, contrasting with that strain that would limit John's role to that of forerunner to Jesus, John is spoken of in impressive terms of eschatological significance:

- "For all the prophets and the law prophesied until John came; and if you are willing to accept it, he is Elijah who is to come." (Matt 11:12–14; cf., Mark 9:11–13//Matt 17:10–13).

- "Among those born of women no one has arisen greater than John the Baptist; yet the least in the kingdom of heaven is greater than he."(Matt 11:11)

—and especially—

- "The law and the prophets were in effect until John came; since then the good news of the kingdom of God is proclaimed, and everyone tries to enter it by force." (Luke 16:16)

> The available sources are witnesses to their striking similarities, in their messages . . . their radical personalities, their destinies, and their reception by their contemporaries. John and Jesus can and should be understood as two apocalyptic preachers who shared a great number of characteristics, and who can and should be categorized as two examples of the same religious type in the landscape of Second Temple Judaism.[66]

Thus, as the tradition about the person of the Baptist developed there is evidence of tension experienced by the emergent Christian movement in honoring John. He is embraced within its new *Heilsgeschichte*, whilst at the same time it endeavors to restrict him within a position of clear subordination to Jesus, about whom a high Christology was developing.[67]

It should be noted that this dissonance in handling the memory of John the Baptist occurs across a broad spectrum of NT witnesses—Mark, Q, the Matthean and Lucan redactions, and the Fourth Gospel—an outstanding example of multiple attestation from sources that emanate from c. 50 CE? (Q) to c. 100 CE? (Fourth Gospel). This is strong evidence for the continuing presence and influence of a living Baptist tradition—evidence that

---

66. Bermejo-Rubio, "Why is John the Baptist Used," 195.

67. Wink, *John the Baptist*, 42–43, 105; Tuckett, *Q and the History*, 119.

is reinforced by consideration of the Lucan Nativity Narratives that, being inserted before what appears to be the original start of his gospel (Luke 3:1) possibly had a significant period of independent transmission and development within a Baptist milieu, which would include the *Jakobusgemeinde* (§ 8. 2.1.3).

3.2 The Curious Case of the Nativity Narrative

The Lucan nativity narrative contains "two exactly parallel infancy accounts, one of John and the other of Jesus."[68] The story of John can stand by itself, which suggests that the story of the conception and birth of Jesus is modeled on that of John.[69] Further, "it is clear that the story of Jesus, whatever its exact origins, has been integrated into that of John, and not *vice versa*."[70]

Walter Wink summarizes:

> Elsewhere in Luke 1 scholars have noted what Kraeling calls the absence of "the common Gospel tendency to subordinate John to Jesus and to regard him as Jesus' Forerunner."[71] John plays so exalted a role that a Baptist milieu of composition seems to be indicated. John will "turn many of the sons of Israel to the Lord their God," he will "make ready for the Lord a people prepared" (1:16f.)—for the Lord, not the messiah.[72]

H. L. MacNeill, with a passionate outpouring of adverbial fecundity, asserted that:

> . . .there is nothing whatever that is distinctively, necessarily, Christian. Everything in these two chapters, on the contrary, is definitely, positively, patriotically, and enthusiastically Jewish.[73]

The focus needs to be on the songs Luke has embedded into his narrative, particularly those familiar from Christian liturgy as the *Magnificat* and the *Benedictus*. (Luke 2:46–55, 2:68–79). Liturgy, by its very nature is conservative, and these songs, steeped in the ethos of Palestinian messianic

---

68. Scobie, *John the Baptist*, 51; Brown, *Birth of the Messiah*, 243, 250; Richards, *First Christmas*, 48; Martin, "Progymnastic Topic Lists," 39–40.

69. Bultmann, *History of the Synoptic Tradition*; Dibelius, *From Tradition to Gospel*; Creed, *St Luke*, 7; Brown, *Birth of the Messiah*, 281.

70. Scobie, *John the Baptist*, 50.

71. Kraeling, *John the Baptist*, 16.

72. Wink, *John the Baptist*, 60.

73. MacNeill, "*Sitz im Leben*," 126–27 (quoted in Scobie, *John the Baptist*, 52–53).

Judaism, preserve tradition from a time much earlier than when Luke was writing. Raymond Brown (noting the Temple/piety connection[74]) suggests that they may have their origin in the Judaic Christianity of Jerusalem—the *anawim* ("the poor")—and that the source of the traditions about John in the Lucan narrative may originate with followers of John.[75]

Charles Scobie notes anomalies within those two ancient hymns that are suggestive of a Baptist interest:[76]

- The presence of a significant textual variation (Luke 1:46) attributing the *Magnificat* to Elizabeth whilst the inter-textuality framing of the childless Hannah (1 Sam 2:1–10) is consonant with Elizabeth's condition rather than the "young virgin" Mary.

- The *Benedictus*—the hymnic celebration of the birth of his son, John, by Zechariah—contains the confusing reference to John's Davidic descent (Luke 1:69) which is inconsistent with both parents being presented as of priestly descent (Luke 1:5).

Taking this on board, the *Magnificat* and *Benedictus* become celebrations originally and uniquely of John and their content resonates with the earliest presentations we have of the public ministry of John in the Synoptic tradition. They are pregnant with anticipation and hope of the renewal of Israel in the imminent ἔσχατον for:

> He has shown strength with his arm . . .
>
> He has brought down the powerful from their thrones,
>
> and lifted up the lowly . . .
>
> He has helped his servant Israel . . .
>
> He has raised up a mighty savior for us
>
> in the house of his servant David.
>
> He . . . has remembered his holy covenant . . .
>
> to grant us, that we, being saved from the hands of our enemies,
>
> might serve him without fear, in holiness and righteousness
>
> before him all our days.
>
> (Luke 1:51–54, 68–75)

---

74. Brown, *Birth of the Messiah*, 350–63.

75. Ibid; Bovon, *Luke 1*, 28–30.

76. Scobie, *John the Baptist*, 54–55; Brown, *Birth of the Messiah*, 334–35.

Given the well-recognized tendency we noted of hymns/liturgy to be the *residuum* of older traditions we may be in touch here with an original tradition about John, which gives him the highest honors:[77]

> In Luke 1 there is a very high estimate of John. Up to a point the infancy narrative agrees with the Christian view of John as a prophet (1:76), the new Elijah (1:17), who will preach repentance (1:17, 77). But it goes further than this and further than any other part of the new Testament, for, since "the Lord" means God himself,[78] John is presented as the forerunner of God, and not the Messiah. . . . He will "be the Lord's forerunner to prepare his way" (1:76). *There is no room here for a Messiah,* indeed John himself is virtually cast in that role; his birth is due to an act of divine intervention, he is filled with the Holy Spirit from his mother's womb (1:15), and with his birth God has already 'turned to his people, saved them and set them free' and 'raised up a deliverer of victorious power' (1:68, 69), John's position in Luke 1 could hardly be more exalted.[79]

The preservation of such a memory of the Baptist within a foundational document of Christianity which otherwise downplays the significance of John in the interests of a developing Christology is persuasive testimony to a powerful set of traditions about him that could not be ignored because they were treasured by a vigorous, *distinct,* but *related* movement of Judaic reform that looked to John as their origin and exemplar (§ 8. 2.1.3).[80] Luke preserves, in somewhat dramatic form, that memory of John as "the beginning of the gospel" (Mark 1.1), to be subsumed within the greater narrative of Jesus (cf. § 3. 5).

3.3 The Prologue of John

From the latter years of the first century and later than when the Synoptic gospel tradition was beginning to circulate we get further confirmation that the memory and person of John continued to be venerated. At a time when

77. The evocation of Judaic nationalist sentiment embedded in the *Magnificat* and the *Benedictus* would have found a ready audience in the *Jakobusgemeinde* (§§ 5. 6.4; 5. 10.).

78. Scobie's reference is to Luke.1.46.

79. Scobie, *John the Baptist*, 53.

80. Wink, *John the Baptist*, 60–72 offers a detailed critique of the theory of a Baptist source behind Luke 1. Webb, *John the Baptizer*, 197, 353; Brown, *Birth of the Messiah*, 245, 273–81.

the nascent Christian movement was adjusting to the realization of its distinctive being from its Judaic parentage there were some who found such high views of John threatening.

The Fourth Gospel, in line with its high Christology, presents a more restricted view than the Synoptics of John, presenting him as a key witness to Jesus as "Messiah" and "Son of God" (cf. John 20:31) as well as the "Coming One," "Lamb of God," "King of Israel," "he about whom Moses and the prophets wrote," and "Son of Man" (John 1:26–51).

However, the preceding Prologue (John 1:1–18) interrupts its poetic flow with what can best be described as footnotes, e.g.:

> There was a man sent from God whose name was John.
>
> He came to bear witness to testify to the light,
>
> so that all might believe through him.
>
> He himself was not the light,
>
> but he came to testify to the light.
>
> The true light, which enlightens everyone,
>
> was coming into the world. (John 1:6–9, also v.15)

This underlines John's secondary relationship to Jesus, all of which only makes sense on the assumption, adopted by many commentators, that towards the end of the first century there was a virile movement within early proto-Christian communities, especially perhaps those whose core traditions emanated from the *Jakobusgemeinde* (§ 8. 2.1.3), honoring the Baptist in a way that the Evangelist considered threatening to the unique position he ascribed to Jesus "the Messiah, the Son of God" (John 20.31). After the climax to the Prologue, asserting that ". . . it is God the only Son . . . who has made (God) known" (John 1:18), the Evangelist begins his narrative with an immediate more explicit denial on the lips of the Baptist that he is neither the Messiah nor Elijah (John 1:20)—a denial that is pointless unless some were making that sort of claim for the Baptist at the time of writing many years later.[81]

4. Pre-Pauline Ephesus

Writing at a similar period to the *Gospel of John*, Luke records the presence at Ephesus, about fifteen to twenty years after John's execution and before

81. Cullman, "Significance of the Qumran Texts," 8–32.

Paul arrived, of "disciples" (including Apollos) who "knew only the baptism of John" (Acts 18:24—19:9).[82] Apollos came from Alexandria and presumably reflected the theology and practice of that proto-Christian community for "He had been instructed in the Way of the Lord . . . and taught accurately the things concerning Jesus" (18:25).

This is a long way from evidence of a Baptist sect but it does reflect a period when both the theology and practice of the proto-Christian movements enjoyed significant variation within a consciousness of being part of the same development: Alexandria differed from the Pauline Mission whilst sharing "the things concerning Jesus," whilst pre-Pauline Ephesus seems to have nurtured/allowed variant understandings of "being Israel." We are presented with a picture of a proto-Christian movement in Ephesus (and in Alexandria?) in mid-century (or Luke's experience—or historical understanding—half a century later, projected back into his narrative), which comfortably included those whose understanding and practice of "the Way" was markedly influenced and driven by traditions venerating the Baptist. Indeed, Luke's narrative in Acts 18:1–21; 18:24—19:9 clearly indicates that the proto-Christian movement in Ephesus (whether that of Apollos, Priscilla and Aquila, or the "Baptist-disciples," each representing an expression of "the Way" differentially grounded and pursued) was not only tolerant of significant variation but was also *an integral part of the Synagogue and Judaic community* within that town. Those who only know "John's baptism" are nonetheless recognized as "disciples" (19:1), whilst Apollos, Priscilla, and Aquila seem fully at ease and able to share "the Way of God" (18:26) within the community of the Judaic συναγωγή.

In fine this incident probably reveals the presence within the Ephesus synagogue of a proto-Christian grouping (under Apollos[83]) whose understanding and knowledge of "the Way" was derived from the Judaic mission (Gal 2:5–7) of the *Jakobusgemeinde* (via Alexandria?). This included the tradition and practice of "John's baptism." Indeed, some of this evidence we often consider to point to the ongoing existence of a vigorous Baptist sect may be better understood as derived from the *kerygma* and teaching of the Jerusalem *Jakobusgemeinde* (§§ 5. 10; 7.; 8. 2.1.4) But Apollos's teaching,

82. Twelftree, "Jesus the Baptist," 112. He suggests this feature as arising from a period early in Jesus' ministry when he was baptizing alongside John. Meggitt, "Madness of King Jesus," 383 n.12 speculates that a possible persecution of John's disciples "might explain the rapid emergence of a diaspora of followers of John evident in Acts of the Apostles"—Acts 18.25 (Alexandria) and 19.7 (Ephesus).

83. Gunther (*Die Fruhgeschichte*, 35–38) argues that "*before* Paul's mission (1Cor 16.9) a non-Pauline community existed in Ephesus under the leadership of Apollos"— quoted in Lüdemann, *Primitive Christianity*, 132–33.

though "accurate," was deficient—"Priscilla and Aquila . . . took him aside and explained the Way of God to him more accurately" (Acts 18:25–26). This deficiency, of course, was from the later viewpoint of Luke, whilst Paul's move away from the synagogue "taking the disciples (now 'baptized in the name of the Lord Jesus') with him" (19:9) enshrines the Lucan sub-text of placing distance between the emerging Gentile-Christian movement of the late first century from its historic roots in the *Jakobusgemeinde* (see § 9.).

5. The Beginning of the Gospel?

Wink concluded his critique of the theory of a Baptist source behind Luke 1 (§ 3. 3.2):

> There are only Baptist traditions, probably brought over to the church by former Baptists. . . . the church possessed these traditions from the very beginning by virtue of the fact that it was itself an outgrowth of the Baptist movement.[84]

This reflects a broadly representative perception of the relationship between John and Jesus as a sequential progression from John to Jesus to Church. But *this is essentially a theological sequence*: it is not necessarily a historical sequence, which requires a view of John and Jesus (and their followers) as distinct yet related parts of a wider reform and restoration movement within late Second Temple Judaism, with the added factor that many venerated both.

This view involves a shift away from focusing on how the Baptist, Paul, and the various groupings later identified as "church" relate to Jesus of Nazareth, to a focus instead on how these various persons and movements (including that of Jesus) relate with and to each other within Second Temple Judaism.

John Drury has drawn attention to the chiastic structure of the prologue to Mark's gospel (Mark 1:1–15),[85] being framed within "The begin-

---

84. Wink, *John the Baptist*, 71.

85. In 1934, R. H. Lightfoot had observed that "(T)he prologue . . . puts into the *readers'* hands at the outset the key which is designed to unlock the meaning of the contents of the book (italics original) . . . In the case of St. Mark this has been obscured for us by the arrangement of the paragraphs in Westcott and Hort's Greek Testament, which is probably the text most familiar to English students of the gospels in the original." (Lightfoot, *History and Interpretation*, 61–62) This textual imposition is continued in many modern translations through the insertion of chapter headings, with breaks after v.8 and v.13 being very common (e.g., NEB, GNB, JB, NIV—cf., NRSV which has only a line-break after v.15).

ning of the good news (v 1) . . ." and "Jesus came to Galilee, proclaiming the good news of God: 'The time is fulfilled' (vv 14–15). . ."[86]

Prologues set the scene and alert the reader to significant themes in the ensuing narrative. Markan commentaries have rightly focused on the setting of the gospel account within the *Heilsgeschichte* of Judaic tradition and on the diachronic/theological relationship between the two principle characters of John and Jesus, but few take note that *location* is also of significance[87]—this, despite the fact that the prologue climaxes with Jesus proclaiming the gospel in Galilee, forming an *inclusio* with the end of the gospel where "Jesus is going ahead of you to Galilee (where) you will see him . . ." (Mark 16:7).

From a much fuller analysis of the prologue's structure that Drury offers[88] I select the synchronic thread of "place" (*Fig 1*).

For our present purposes the potential significance of this lies in the central couplet (C/C1). Given the significance of Galilee for Mark (above), the balancing of "Judea/Jerusalem" with "Galilee" cannot be accidental—it points to *two* locations of significance for "the beginning of the gospel":

- Jerusalem, under the direct impact of John's preaching;

- Galilee, the site of Jesus' ministry;

Galilee is, of course, well documented as having both geographical and kerygmatic significance. But Jerusalem (antecedent to the crucifixion)?

We must take seriously (allowing for narrative exaggeration) as more than scene-setting Mark's description of "people from the whole Judean countryside and all the people of Jerusalem" responding to the message of the Baptist (Mark 1:5). It is the very first scene in the story he is setting out to relate and we should rightly anticipate that it is not just an incidental reference. That John's preaching made a serious impact on the streets of Jerusalem is verified by the later incident Mark recounts when Jesus, on the

86. Drury, "Mark 1.1–15: An Interpretation," 25–36.

87. The significance of *location* in Mark's prologue is overlooked by Rawlinson, *St Mark*; Taylor, *Mark*; Hunter, *Saint Mark*; Nineham, *St Mark*; Moule, *Mark, 7–14*; Cranfield, *Mark, 33–68*; Lane, *Mark, 39–66*; Hooker, *Message of Mark, 1–16, 25–26*; Hurtado, *Mark, 1–11*; Iersel, *Mark, 88–108*. Painter, *Mark's Gospel, 23–35* places the emphasis on the diachronic relationship of John the Baptist and Jesus (33). The significance of *place*, although coupling "Galilee" with "Wilderness," occurs in Marxsen, *Mark, 59–60*; and in Bryan, *Preface to Mark*, 87; whilst the comparison is between "Wilderness" and "Jerusalem" in Juel, *Mark*, 31. Guelich, *Mark*, 42, protests that "The geographical location of the outset of Jesus' ministry has its roots in the tradition of Jesus' earthly ministry rather than the redactional interests of Mark."

88. Drury, "Mark 1:1–15," 28.

day after he created mayhem in Jerusalem by his attack on the marketing activities of the Temple, returned to the Temple and was challenged about his authority for such action by the Temple authorities themselves. Jesus trumps them with a counter challenge relating to John, and "they were afraid of the crowd, for all regarded John as truly a prophet" (Mark 11:27–33).

A	Gospel: Text	v 1
B	Wilderness	vv 2–3
C	Jordan: Judea/Jerusalem	vv 4–8
C¹	Jordan: Nazareth of Galilee	vv 9–11
B¹	Wilderness	vv 12–13
A¹	Gospel: Galilee	vv 14–15

Fig.1. Mark 1.1–15

This impact of John on the common people of Israel is further attested by Josephus who writes of Herod's fear of the preaching and influence of John over the people as the occasion for him executing John; so much so, that when an army of Herod, many years later, was defeated by Aretas "some Jews thought the destruction of Herod's army came from God as a just punishment of what he did against John, called the Baptist."[89]

So, how had John's message impacted on the streets of Jerusalem? It would certainly have strengthened the movement for the renewal of Israel there, especially with its heightened sense of the impending ἔσχατον. We can surely anticipate a renewed and more demanding commitment to Torah, including a call for *zekhut*—freely chosen good conduct over and above what was required by the Law (Luke 3:8–14; § 5. 9.1). To be living in the shadow of the ἔσχατον, prepared for by a keen practice of Torah and the valuing of what was later called *zekhut* are precisely the core characteristics of those we meet in Paul's letters, EpJas (§ 7. 7.2) and the book of Acts as members of the *Jakobusgemeinde*, and there is one further linkage:

5.1 The Baptism Nexus:

Apart from the possibility of a period when John and Jesus were both baptizing in the Jordan (John 4:1–3) there is a complete and significant silence

89. *Ant.* 18.116–19.

in all the gospel traditions of any baptizing activity by Jesus, or his disciples, during his ministry in Galilee.[90] It is therefore remarkable that baptism was to be the almost universal and unquestioned practice of the nascent Christian movements from the very beginning, *contra* this evident non-practice of Jesus.[91]

It is likely that John's baptisms were normally of groups/crowds of people and therefore that the physical act of baptizing involved assistance from his closer disciples, such as Jesus appears to have been. That the "baptism of John" continued to be performed after John's execution is both inherently probable and is borne out by the later incident at Ephesus centering on Apollos and the "disciples who only knew the baptism of John" (Acts 18:24—19:7).

A vigorous, continuing movement in Jerusalem, initiated through John's mission and continuing his practice of "a baptism of repentance for the forgiveness of sins" provides the necessary connecting link bridging the hiatus between the practice of baptism by the nascent Christian movement despite its non-observance by Jesus in Galilee.

Taking the hint from the Markan prologue—did an embryonic *Jakobusgemeinde* have its origin in the stimulus and excitement of those times? Or, if it was already an identifiable group in Jerusalem, did their experience by the Jordan provide them with a renewed sense of identity and purpose? May not the possible existence of a grouping such as the *Jakobusgemeinde* (whom we are to meet in the pages of the New Testament), strongly influenced by (and maybe emulating) the preaching and practice of John the Baptist,[92] provide the historical link between the baptismal practice of John and that of the early Christian movements?[93]

---

90. Twelftree, "Jesus the Baptist," 118–22, links cessation of the practice of baptism by Jesus in Galilee to a development in his message from one (like John) of preparation—signified through baptism—for the coming End, to a proclamation that the End was already inbreaking, as evidenced by his exorcisms etc. "Conducting baptism—a sign of preparedness for the ἔσχατον—was no longer relevant." (125). Taylor and Adinolfi, "John the Baptist," 247–84—arguing that "narrative patterns can be indicative of history masked by overt rhetoric" note that "Mark includes the persistent presence of water, often in combination with wilderness places and crowds. . . . replicates the same features associated with John the Baptist, creating a narrative template for Jesus continuing John's baptism . . . yet explicit mention of Jesus' baptizing is avoided." Cf., France, "Jesus the Baptist," 94–111.

91. Tuckett, *Q and the History of Early Christianity*, 124.

92. There was no shortage of *miqva'ot* facilities for ritual cleansing in the Jerusalem area.

93. Mark saw the "beginning of the gospel" in the ministry of the Baptist (Mark 1:1–6)—defensible as both a theologically valid and historically accurate statement.

5.2 A Gestalt Postscript

Joan Taylor raises the possibility that some of the Baptist's teaching may have become embedded within the traditions attributed to Jesus.[94] On the one hand the fact that Jesus had initially been a disciple of John and presumably taken on board some/much of his teaching plus the way they both inhabited a similar theological milieu (despite their contrasting lifestyles) would have made discrimination between their logia difficult within early oral tradition. On the other hand she also notes a number of echoes within the gospels (e.g., Matt 3:10//Luke 3:9 with Matt 7:19, 15:13; Matt 3:7//Luke 3:7 with Matt 12:34, 23:33), especially within the Matthean tradition:

> The Gospel writers do not seem to have felt any concern about similarities between Jesus' and John's teaching, but they ensured that John's teaching was completely eclipsed by Jesus' and incorporated into the *kerygma* of the early Church.[95]

Similarly, Dale Allison has argued for a greater degree of continuity between John and Jesus than is normally recognized. He particularly draws attention to the occurrence of parallels that have no echo in other Judaic writings—for example, the linking imagery of baptism and fire (Luke 3:16; 12:49–50).[96]

> . . . Only the most cynical view would assert that, despite chronology and the attested dependence of Jesus and his earliest disciples on John's work, his teaching and prophecy were recast from scratch along Christian lines, so that nothing of John's real message remains for us to distinguish, except perhaps something entirely doom-laden and severe. It seems likely that much more of John's message has remained than has hitherto been recognized and that it is embedded in the heart of the Christian ethos.[97]

This would certainly be the case if many/most of the *Jakobusgemeinde* had their faith and practice initially grounded in the strong Baptist traditions circulating in Jerusalem. Whilst allowing for Taylor's suggestion that "there may have been a policy of assigning doubtful traditions to Jesus rather than to John, just to be on the safe side"[98] I suggest that it is more likely to be an

---

94. Taylor, *Immerser*, 149–54. See also, Rothschild, *Baptist Traditions in Q*, which is severely critiqued by Downing, 35–36.

95. Taylor, *Immerser*, 151.

96. Allison, "Continuity between John and Jesus," 6–27.

97. Taylor, *Immerser*, 151.

98. Ibid., 150.

example of the simplifying gestalt effect in remembering history (§ 1. 4.1.1) where traditions (original to what were to become secondary characters) become clustered around the principal figure.[99]

6. The Baptizer - Summary, Inferences and Questions

- The movement associated with John the Baptist finds its setting within the culture of a late Second Temple Judaism seeking the renewal and restoration of Israel.

- His message is of the imminence of the ἔσχατον, preparation for which calls for repentance, marked by the cleansing of immersion, and a return to observance of the Torah interpreted in a spirit that goes beyond minimal adherence. We encounter these same concerns and emphases amongst the *Jakobusgemeinde* whom we meet in the NT.

- The influence of John's mission was particularly strong and continuing in Jerusalem and Judea, and may be the soil in which the nascent Christian movement embedded itself in that location.

- Some of his followers came to place supreme significance on the person of John, affirming virtual messianic status to him.

- The Jesus Movement emerged out of that of the Baptist, becoming autonomous and distinct after Jesus returned to Galilee following the arrest and execution of John.

- The movements surrounding John and Jesus were conscious of a close relationship within the broader renewal movement in Israel, as is evident in the "boundary porosity"[100] permitting the movement of disciples from the one to the other, as well as the frequent linkage of their names in the mind of friend and foe alike. This closeness seems to have

99. This raises the question of whether something similar has occurred between James and Jesus for there are strong echoes between teaching in EpJas and Q—see § 7.7.

100. This element of boundary porosity continues as a significant feature between Judaic groups (including proto-Christian groups) into the apostolic and post-apostolic period. It is implicit in Paul's angst with the Galatian community and a little later (post–70 CE) in the situation confronting the author of Hebrews. The warnings against "heresy" that start surfacing in the later NT letters and some of the criticisms in the seven letters in Revelation also reflect boundary ambiguity and movement between various long-forgotten proto-Christian movements. Boundary ambiguity and porosity is also apparent in the movements between ἐκκλησία and συναγωγή which continued into the second century and later (Wilson, *Related Strangers*, 166–168; Skarsaune, "History of Jewish Believers," 747–49).

continued well after the deaths of both leaders (the Ephesus scenario), only taking on more adversarial tones later in the first century.

- This close association between John and Jesus may have facilitated the transference of logia from John to the ultimately dominant figure of Jesus.

- Receiving baptism from John carried the clear implication in the world of late Second Temple Judaism that Jesus was secondary to John, reinforced by his status as a disciple of John (and possibly being one of his lieutenants after his baptism).

- The presence of a movement in Jerusalem originating in John's mission (in whatever form it expressed itself) earlier than that of Jesus in Galilee may, in like manner, have fed into the sense of the *Jakobusgemeinde*'s primacy as we later encounter it in the writings of Paul and Luke.

- The interrelatedness of the John and Jesus movements combined with their contrasting focus in Galilee and Jerusalem is projected by Mark in his prologue to identify them as twin loci for the "beginning of the gospel."

- The likely continuance of John's baptism amongst those seeking to live out his teaching within Jerusalem is sufficient to account for its apparently ready adoption within the emergent proto-Christian movements developing from Jerusalem.

- The movement initiated by the Baptist is a clear example of a proto-Christian movement that is chronologically earlier to, independent of, and prior to that of Jesus. And if we can recognize it in John, may we not also find it in the person of James, the brother of Jesus, and the group in Jerusalem that is associated with his name, albeit seeing itself as part of that broader movement stemming from John?

Locating James

4

The Primary Evidence: Paul

1. Selection of Sites

1.1 Site Indicators

WE HAVE SURVEYED THE world of first century Palestine inhabited by James, and it has provided us with a frame within which to locate James and the *Jakobusgemeinde*. It suggests the probability that we shall find the place for James within the movements dedicated to the renewal and restoration of Israel that spawned within the late Second Temple period, including movements associated with Jesus of Nazareth.

However, we must be open to the possibility that the origin of the *Jakobusgemeinde* was distinct from the movement stimulated by Jesus within that culture of renewal and restoration, with James as a key person around whom its first nucleus gathered.

1.2 The Boundary

As with any archeological excavation, consideration of available time and space imposes limits on the area for investigation, so in our search for James and his position in that complex of events out of which Christianity was born, I am proposing to *focus* on evidence within the New Testament canon:

- most of the information we possess about James that originates in writings within the first century or so from the death of Jesus of Nazareth is within this text;[1]

- within this text is encapsulated the central conundrum of the presence and the absence of James;

- this text became the foundational text for Christianity.

1.3 Key Textual Sites

Not only is the information we possess from the first and early second centuries about James virtually restricted to the New Testament, even there it is limited, fragmentary and of varied quality. That is our problem. Jesus and Paul, with Peter to a lesser extent, occupy the center of the stage in the New Testament. Very occasionally, James moves in—almost as an "extra."

1.3.1 Prime Sites: Paul and Acts

There are two prime textual sites:

- Paul's correspondence (especially 1 Cor 15:3–11 and Gal 1—2)—contemporary evidence of the finest kind from within the "heat of the battle";

- The *Acts of the Apostles*—written forty or more years later, it alone presents itself as a history of the early Christian movement for, *crucially*, a post-70 CE audience. Its later inclusion in the canon served to confirm its paradigmatic status in structuring our understanding of the first century Christian movement for two millennia.

---

1. One clear exception to this is the reference in Josephus to the execution of James in 62 CE (*Ant.* 20.197–203). Writings centering on the memory and honoring of James from the second to the fourth centuries are extant: *The Apocryphon of James*; *The Apocalypse of James I and II*; *The Protevangelium of James*; The Pseudo-Clementine *Homilies* and *Recognitions*. Of these only *The Apocryphon*, and *The Ascents of James* with the *Kerygmata Petrou* (both included within the later Pseudo-Celementines) may have roots overlapping with the latest NT writings. [Rappe, "Secret Book of James," 332–42; Williams, "Apocryphon of James," 29–37; Schoedel and Parrott, "(First) Apocalypse of James," 260–68; Hedrick and Parrott, " (Second) Apocalypse of James," 269–76; Sim, *Gospel of Matthew*, 183–86]. The *Gospel of Thomas* is similarly placed, although some scholars argue for a core text of first century provenance. (Koester and Lambdin, "Gospel of Thomas," 139–60; DeConick, *Original Gospel of Thomas*, 7–9; cf. Goodacre, *Thomas and the Gospels*; *JSNT* 36.3, 2014).

1.3.2 Secondary Sites: The Jacobean Epistles

In secondary position to those prime canonical sites we must include the Epistles of James (EpJas) and Jude. Although a small number of scholars defend the authorial integrity of these letters (making EpJas the earliest of our NT writings),[2] most accept them as pseudonymous (but with little consensus on dates). This is particularly frustrating in the case of EpJas, where the position can be summed up by saying that the internal evidence strongly suggests a date within a few years of James' death[3] whereas the external evidence equally strongly indicates a significantly later second century date.[4] Similar uncertainty, though less polarized, is felt about the date and provenance of the very brief letter of Jude.[5] This lack of consensus renders them unsatisfactory as prime historical witnesses on a comparable level with Paul and Acts. Nonetheless, as they come at an early period from within that vigorous proto-Christian tradition who looked back to James as their father-in-God and sustained a significant level of literary output honoring his memory,[6] rather than from the ultimately normative Pauline-Lucan trajectory, their memory of James and their expression of the continuing Judaic-Christian tradition both complement and provide an invaluable check on the picture that emerges from and between the lines of the Gentile Mission writings. Also, though of less significance, is the *Epistle to the Hebrews*, which likewise stands outside the Pauline/Lucan trajectory, and its contents suggest a degree of affinity and interaction with concerns and tradition emanating from Jerusalem (e.g., the meaning and significance of the cultus).

---

2. Adamson, *James*; Johnson, *James*; Bauckham, *Wisdom of James*; Moo, *James*; Hartin, *James*; Brosend, *James and Jude*, 6.

3. Davids, *James*, 2–22; Martin, *James*, lxxvi–lxxvii; Hartin, *James and the Q Sayings*, 233–44; Wall, *Community of the Wise*; Sleeper, *James*, 39–41; Sawicki, "Person or Practice?" 387.

4. Dibelius, *James*; Perkins, *Peter, James, and Jude*, 83–85; Laws, *James*; Nienhuis, *Not by Paul Alone*.

5. Bauckham, *Jude*, 168–78; Perkins, *Peter, James and Jude*, 142–43; Green, *Jude and 2 Peter*, 1–18.

6. E.g., *Epistle of James*; *Gospel of Thomas*; *Gospel of the Hebrews*; *Gospel of the Egyptians*; *Apocryphon of James*; *First Apocalypse of James*; *Second Apocalypse of James*; *Protevangelium of James*; *Pseudo-Clementines*.

1.3.3 Secondary Sites: The Canonical Gospels

Apart from the Nativity (and possibly the Resurrection) narratives, the family of Mary in the synoptic text only surfaces briefly twice—Mark 3:19–35 (Matt 12:46–50; Luke 8:19–21) and Mark 6:1–6, which latter is the only place in the Gospels where James is acknowledged by name (cf. Matt 13:54–58; Luke 4:16–30). Because of their incidental character it is better to draw them in to enhance our understanding after we have a frame for understanding James based on our prime sites.[7]

2. Listening to our Witnesses

Paul and Luke are therefore our prime witnesses. As a counselor, I learned the importance of listening intensively to a client's story, seeking with imagination to enter into their world and see things as they see them, without a too premature intrusion of my interpretations or other relevant material. As scholars we must do no less: we need scholastic "tunnel vision." Paul and Luke are independent of each other (even if they were sometime traveling companions), and that independence, their story, must be respected—*only then can we challenge.*

Recognition of the independence of these key textual sites from each other carries with it the recognition that each is viewing James from different vantage points. Each vantage point has its own validity and our first task must be to let the "James" in each viewing point be foregrounded. In brief, Paul's writings are excellent primary evidence from a major player who had met and debated with James, and was in conflict with at least some of the *Jakobusgemeinde*, whilst Acts is positioned on a later and different tradition-trajectory—from a perspective having affinities with the Hellenist Gentile mission.[8]

A rich tradition of scholarship on these two textual sites has understandably had its principal focus on Paul and hence, quite rightly, the connection between the Lucan history and Paul's own writings has had to be explored, analyzed and evaluated to aid our understanding of Paul and his significance in the early Christian movement. Much of this scholarship has

---

7. The same is true of John's Gospel, but additionally its heavy and overt theological restructuring makes its use for historical information surrounding the lives of Jesus and James very difficult. Casey, *Jesus of Nazareth*, 511–24; Foster, "Memory, Orality, and the Fourth Gospel," 191–227. This is not to deny the possibility of some independent historical information.

8. I.e., the mission to Gentiles associated with the "Jerusalem Decree" of Acts 15 with its base possibly at Antioch.

expended itself upon the interconnections between Paul's Gentile mission, the Jerusalem Conference, the *Jakobusgemeinde* and the identification of his opponents in Galatia and Corinth.

Although we shall need to take cognizance of these scholarly reconstructions of "Paul-with-Acts" we cannot use them as primary evidence for James and the *Jakobusgemeinde*. To do so would contaminate both sources. Therefore our task is not to tackle the familiar inter-textual problems, but *to ask of each text* what is its picture of James and the *Jakobusgemeinde*.

Only after we have listened to the testimony of both these witnesses can each be challenged with the evidence of the other. *But the purpose of such challenge must be to point up the picture of James and his community.*

We can *then* bring in evidence such as that from the "Judaic-Christian" trajectory preserved in EpJas and Jude, and from the gospel narratives. Significant extra-canonical evidence can also be fed in during this process, but our focus must always return to James—and, if necessary, live with unresolved dissonance.

3. Listening to Paul

Paul's letters are clearly original.[9] We are privileged to have in the letters of Paul primary historical evidence about James of a kind that is rare in the historiography of the ancient world—the actual writing of a key participant from within the flow of events, which thereby becomes part of them. We have nothing comparable for Jesus, tradition of whom we receive through the lens of cultic veneration within an oral culture, albeit with a degree of eyewitness control.[10] Paul and James had met face to face (Gal 1:19).

The dominance of the Lucan framework for Paul's life, reinforced by generations of teaching on "Paul's missionary journeys" supplemented in many older bibles by maps (a rare visual aid), was broken by John Knox's ground breaking *Chapters in a Life of Paul* with its dictum that:

> (A) fact only suggested in the letters has a status which even the most unequivocal statement of Acts, if not otherwise supported, cannot confer.[11]

9. I follow the broad consensus, in identifying as authentic, letters from Paul to his ἐκκλησίαι in Thessalonia, Galatia, Philippi, Corinth, Rome, and the personal note to Philemon.

10. Bauckham, *Jesus and the Eyewitnesses*.

11. Knox, *Chapters in a Life of Paul*, 33.

This axiom however must be modified with the recognition that, beyond any hard information Paul might provide, his writings inevitably give us *Paul's* own perceptions of people and situations and *Paul's* own recollection of events. Atsuhiro Asano states:

> Paul's narration of historical events (in Galatians) can be regarded as a retrospective interpretation of history, shaped by the exigency in the Galatian community.[12]

Similarly, in confronting "too static a conception of Paul" and his movement, Nicholas Taylor asserts:

> Paul's self-conception as reflected in his letters, and his accounts of and allusions to events, are to be understood in the context of the specific circumstances in and to which he wrote, and not as objective historical truth.[13]

That is a timely reminder of the dynamic and developing nature of the relationships, perceptions, interpretations, memory and understandings defining an individual's *Sitz im Leben*. Paul's perception of James and the *Jakobusgemeinde* is colored by his emotion and his understanding (which may only be partial) of the situation facing himself and his communities at the time of writing. That is datum and not defect.

However, this does not preclude totally "objective historical data" (as Taylor seems to imply).[14] As is frequently pointed out, Paul had to get the details of his limited contacts with "Jerusalem" correct or his position *vis-à-vis* the conflict in the ἐκκλησία of Galatia would be in ruins: it is in his perceptions and presentation that "spin" occurs. The historiographical task is to assess the degree of "drift," as navigators in the days before satellite navigation had to allow for changing climatic factors affecting their course—and the degree of "drift" (the writer's "spin") is the product of "climate" (the current context of the writer, the issues at stake, the level of emotional commitment, with his perception and evaluation of it). But it is important to recognize that the originating events and the author's perceptions and presentations of it are both invaluable data for our task.

We also have to take on board the fact that in our interrogation of Paul's text for information about James and the *Jakobusgemeinde* we are hunting for information that is largely "off the radar" of Paul's recitation of these past events in his personal biography—we are asking questions of

12. Asano, *Community-Identity Construction in Galatians*, 115.

13. Taylor, *Paul, Antioch and Jerusalem*, 14.

14. As others have noted, there are many variant and inconsistent accounts of what occurred in a Dallas Street on 22 November 1963—but President Kennedy *was* shot.

Paul that he is not setting out to answer. Where his retelling of events in the 30s and 40s CE is critical for his position in the 50s CE we must allow for, and attempt to assess, the degree and direction of distortion occurring; but we need to note the significance of any elements (probably minor) in the narration that, although part of the scene, do not feed into the issues confronting the writer; and to sensitize ourselves to the presence of what we could almost think of as "quasi-Freudian slips."

In order to keep this study within its limits, I emphasize that it is Paul's perceptions of James and his people that interest us, not Paul himself (except insofar as Paul's life history, current situation, and self-perception color the issue). This also allows us the methodological simplification of discounting questions such as those relating to the precise historical sequencing of the authentic Pauline epistles—they were all written within a period of less than ten years (c. 48–58 CE), within about fifteen to twenty years of Paul's conversion (much less from the critical "Antioch Incident") and some fifteen to twenty-five years from the execution of Jesus—the period of Paul's epoch making activity in Asia Minor and Greece.[15] Likewise, questions concerning the relationships between Paul and Luke's accounts of the Jerusalem Conference—very important for the history of the early church—need not detain us. We need to listen to what Paul and Luke individually tell us about James, then evaluate their level of consonance.

4. The Earliest Tradition

Our very earliest introduction to James is in the oral tradition Paul recounts as having "received" and "handed on" to his Corinthian converts:[16] "He appeared to Cephas . . . then to James" (1 Cor 15:5–7). There is strong scholarly consensus that this "James" refers to "the Lord's brother."

Cephas and James are the only named persons in the list of recipients of appearances by the risen Jesus in 1 Cor 15:3–7, as they are on the occasion of Paul's first visit to Jerusalem after his conversion (Gal 1:18–24). It may indeed have been on this latter occasion that Paul "received" the

---

15. Riesner, *Paul's Early Period*; Lüdemann, *Paul Apostle to the Gentiles*, 262–63; Longenecker, *Galatians*, lxxiii; Taylor, *Paul, Jerusalem and Antioch*, 51–59.

16. Habermas, "Resurrection Research," 135–53. "The vast majority of critical scholars . . . place Paul's reception of this material in the mid-30s CE," 141–42. The terms "received" and "handed on" became established in rabbinic Judaism for describing the transmission of Torah; Byrskog, "Transmission of the Jesus Tradition," 449–50).

Jerusalem-centered tradition he recounts,[17] little more than three years after the crucifixion of Jesus, c. 33–34 CE.[18]

Following Adolf Harnack[19] there has been vigorous debate about whether the Cephas/James parallelism in these verses reflects a Peter/ James rivalry within the early Movement, with an emphasis on the similar construction of "Cephas and the twelve" and "James and the apostles."[20] It is an approach to reading history that reflects the historic influence of Hegelian dialectic that had previously spawned the Peter/Paul dichotomy of the Tübingen school. The textual tradition is secure. The suggestion is made that the tradition Paul received ended with "was raised on the third day, in accordance with the scriptures" (v. 4) and that the apostolic appearances list (vv. 5–7), with its repetitive εἶτα and ἔπειτα "suggest that each of them (v. 5 and v. 7) may represent a tradition expressing some rivalry between the supporters of Cephas and James."[21] But the distinction Paul is making here is not between Cephas and James, but between the "apostolic" appearances and his own much later one. Further, Paul's attention at this point in his letter is with a real problem in Corinth, not some hypothetical problem in Jerusalem, about which he also gives no indication in his Galatian correspondence (the only occasion in the New Testament where James and Cephas share the stage together) not many years earlier—or even in the "Antioch Incident" (Gal 2:11–14). Myllykoski, in his review of *James the Just in History and Tradition* concludes by limply referring to "these separate pieces of tradition picked up by Paul,"[22] but parallelism is a feature of oral transmission, and the exclusive occurrence of the same two named persons in both the tradition "received" with Paul's autobiographical account in Gal 1:18–19 forms a very coherent link.

What this debate has obscured is the more important fact that in Paul's recitation of the resurrection appearances of Jesus (and you cannot get much earlier than that in the history of the church!), James is on a par with Cephas[23] and there at the focal center from the very start, as he is on the

17. Robertson and Plummer, *I Corinthians*, 335–36.

18. Riesner, *Paul's Early Period*, 322. I am using the chronology proposed by Riesner as a basic framework for Paul. The chronology favored by Lüdemann is broadly consistent with Reisner on the dating for Paul's early relationship with Jerusalem, our focus here—Gerd Lüdemann, "A Chronology of Paul," 289–308.

19. Harnack, "Die Verklärungsgeschichte Jesu," 62–80.

20. Myllykoski, "James the Just," 84–86; Painter, "Who Was James?" 29–31.

21. Painter, "Who was James?" 30.

22. Myllykoski, "James the Just," 112.

23. "Paul does not say that the Lord appeared *first* to Peter." Robertson and Plummer, *1 Corinthians*, 335.

occasion of Paul's first visit. The tradition carries no indication of this appearance being the occasion of a hypothesized "conversion" for James into being a follower of his brother.[24]

4.1 A Later Fragment

Although from a much later period it is relevant at this point to draw in the tradition of the appearance of the risen Christ to James found in the *Gospel of the Hebrews*, quoted by Jerome:

> The Lord, after he had given the linen cloth to the priest's slave, went to James and appeared to him. (Now James had sworn not to eat bread from the time that he drank from the Lord's cup until he would see him raised from among those who sleep.) Shortly after this the Lord said, "Bring a table and some bread." And immediately it is added: He took the bread, blessed it, broke it, and gave it to James the Just and said to him, "My brother, eat your bread, for the Son of Adam has been raised from among those who sleep."[25]

From a tradition that clearly venerated the memory of James, this account accords to James the honor of being the very first to receive an appearance of the risen Jesus. We must suspect hagiographical interest, but it does preserve a tradition of James' involvement with the movement that was to become Christianity from the very outset. References to the Last Supper in this tantalizing fragment may resonate from the Synoptic text[26]—but their implication that James was present at that Meal may not be dismissed so easily (§ 6. 2.2).[27]

5. Paul's First Visit to Jerusalem:

The principal textual site for Paul's witness is the letter to the Galatians:

---

24. Bruce, *Paul and Jesus*, 48; Rowland, *Christian Origins*, 265; Painter, "James and Peter," 155; Bernheim, *James*, 97–100; Bauckham, *Jude*, 56–57.

25. *Gos Heb* 9.1–4. Miller, *The Complete Gospels*, 434.

26. *Gos Heb* 9.1–4. Miller, *The Complete Gospels*, 434.

27. Painter, *Just James*, 185–186.

5.1 Cephas and James

The ἐκκλησίαι in Galatia were founded by Paul (Gal 1:6; 4:13–14). He is writing to them some time later (c. 48–56 CE[28]—the precise dating is not relevant for our purpose) to counter the influence of some whom he sees as undermining his gospel: "I am astonished that you are so quickly deserting the one who called you in the grace of Christ and are turning to a different gospel . . . You foolish Galatians! Who has bewitched you?" (1:6; 3:1).

In the opening passages of the letter he anecdotally prepares his argument by a priceless piece of autobiography from the days when he "was violently persecuting τὴν ἐκκλησίαν τοῦ Θεοῦ and was trying to destroy it" (1.13), to a recital of an incident in Antioch when he confronted Cephas [a Pillar of the *Jakobusgemeinde* (2.9)] about his withdrawal from table fellowship with Gentiles (2.11–14).[29]

Underlining the authenticity of his message he emphasizes that it "is not of human origin; for I did not receive it from a human source, nor was I taught it, but I received it through a revelation of Jesus Christ" (1:11–12). It quickly becomes clear that it is specifically the human source of "Jerusalem" that is crucial: "I did not confer with any human being, nor did I go up to (ἀνῆλθον εἰς) Jerusalem to those who were already apostles before me" (1:16–17), which includes James (1:19). "Going up to Jerusalem" portrays a syntactic affinity with later Christian usage of "Rome" or "Canterbury."

There follows descriptions of two occasions when he did "go up to" (ἀνῆλθον/ἀνέβην εἰς) Jerusalem (1:18; 2:1). This language of "going up"[30] preserves at the very least the psychological eminence of the Holy City as the focal point of the Judaic faith and is also a word of pilgrimage[31], as by nations at the ἔσχατον—"Come, let us go up (ἀναβῶμεν. LXX) to the mountain of the Lord" (Micah 4:2). The two sentiments coalesce.

Added to this emotional ascendancy of Jerusalem for the Israelite, Jerusalem is also the place for "those who were already apostles before me" (1:17), specifically Cephas (1:18) and James, "the Lord's brother"(1:19). It is likely that the "apostles before me" has a much broader reference than the "Twelve" of Synoptic (especially Lucan) tradition[32] (cf., Rom 16.7;

---

28. Riesner, *Paul's Early Period,* 322; Cousar, *Galatians,* 6; Longenecker, *Galatians,* lxxiii; Betz, *Galatians,* 12; Lüdemann, *Paul Apostle to the Gentiles,* 262–63; Taylor, *Paul, Antioch and Jerusalem,* 51–59.

29. Betz, *Galatians,* 37–112.

30. Also used by Luke at Acts 11:2, 15:2 and 18:22.

31. " . . . used as a 'pilgrimage' word " Barrett, *Acts of the Apostles,* 536.

32. Lightfoot, *Galatians,* 92–101; Betz, *Galatians,* 74–75; Leuba, "Apostle," 21–23; Taylor, *Paul, Antioch and Jerusalem,* 90–94, 154–160; Asano, *Galatians* 89–90;

§ 5. 9.2.4), though they may be included within it. Thus, by the mid-30s CE, "Jerusalem" was already established within the proto-Christian Movement as a focal presence with a developing authority on account of both its central significance in the City of Zion and the presence there of the witnesses to the events surrounding the execution of Jesus and the guarantors of the tradition of his risen appearances.

The purpose of this first visit (33–34 CE[33]) was "to visit Cephas[34] and (Paul) stayed with him for fifteen days" (1:18), adding almost as an aside, "but I did not see any other apostle, except James the Lord's brother" (1:19). The assumption seems to be that Cephas is resident in Jerusalem [an inference supported by his inclusion in the Pillars triumvirate (2:9)], although fourteen or more years later (2:1) he turns up in Antioch (2:11). Later still, Paul also refers to Cephas as traveling with his wife on apostolic tours (1 Cor 9:5).

Paul's other contact on that visit, as we have seen, was with "James the Lord's brother." Paul "stayed" with Cephas: he "saw" James. For whatever reason, this suggests a more distant relationship between Paul and James than with Cephas—a relationship possibly strained by Paul's earlier hostility to the memory of James' brother. It may be that Paul was paying a courtesy visit on James as one whose position could not be ignored?[35] That Cephas is named before James is often taken to imply the precedence of Cephas over James[36] but it may equally be a matter of simple temporal sequence.

Identification as the brother of Jesus serves to distinguish James from others of the same name who were prominent in these early days.[37] That it is precisely "the brother of the *Lord*" strongly suggests also that the family relationship bestowed a degree of prestige upon James and his brothers.[38] The "brothers of the Lord" appear in 1 Cor 9:5 as an identifiable group, separate from the "other apostles . . . and Cephas," but there is a significant, though unremarked, distancing there between "the brothers" (§ 6. 3.) who

---

Witherington III, *Grace in Galatia*, 116.

33. Riesner, *Paul's Early Period*, 322.

34. The identity of Cephas with Peter has been suspect since the second century at least [Clement of Alexandria (*Hist. eccls.* 12.2)]. The methodology of *focused listening* to each witness (§ 4. 2.) requires that we use the names as in the text, despite any possible dissonance. See further §§ 4. 6.1.4; 4. *Excursus*.

35. Painter, *Just James*, 60.

36. Betz, *Galatians*, 76.

37. Eight individuals called James are referred to in the NT—though some of these instances probably refer to the same person. Painter, *Just James*, 2–3.

38. We also need to register that Jesus is already designated as "ὁ κυρίος" at this early stage.

are engaged on something akin to a mission or pastoral visitation whilst James remains firmly in Jerusalem.

In that case Paul would have had some quality time with James but the greater time was spent with Cephas. Dunn reflects a common assumption[39] that this time may have been used by Paul in gaining acquaintance with the Galilean traditions about Jesus,[40] but if he did it is not reflected in this letter (§ 7. 3.). Richard Bauckham went further in advocating that during this first visit Paul "learned such traditions from Peter by a formal process of learning,"[41]—a proposal that was summarily dismissed by Stephen Patterson:

> (W)hen we look for evidence of the Jesus tradition Paul might have actually learned from Peter—sayings of Jesus, stories about him, perhaps a parable or miracle story—Paul's letters have next to nothing . . . not compelling evidence of a formal education spent committing the words and deeds of Jesus to memory.[42]

With reference to James, Paul writes that apart from Cephas "I did not see any other apostle except (εἰ μὴ) James the Lord's brother" (1:19). Most commentators rule out any identification here between "the apostles" and "the twelve."[43] The ambiguity lies in James' apostolic status, for the preposition . . .

> . . . εἰ μὴ (can) be rendered inclusively ("apart from") or exclusively ("but"); in the first instance James would be regarded as one of the "other apostles," while in the latter case he would fall into another category.[44]

A strong argument is made for the inclusive use to be the most natural interpretation here.[45] However we must recognize that at the time Paul was writing (and all his letters generally recognized as authentic by scholars were written within the very short space of time of less than ten years) the word "apostle" was still fluid in use.[46] As this letter pre-dates the time when apostle/Apostle becomes an issue, we can allow for Paul not being totally

---

39. E.g., Robertson and Plummer, *1 Corinthians*, 336.

40. Dunn, "Relationship between Paul and Jerusalem," 465.

41. Bauckham, *Jesus and the Eyewitnesses*, 271.

42. Patterson, "Can You Trust a Gospel?" 206.

43. Betz, *Galatians*, 78; Fee, *Corinthians*, 729.

44. Betz, *Galatians*, 78.

45. Lighfoot, *Galatians*, 84–85; Longenecker, *Galatians*, 38.

46. Taylor, *Paul, Antioch and Jerusalem*, 90–91, 146–70, 227–28.

precise when his focus was on emphasizing the strict limits of his contacts with Jerusalem (1:20)[47].

5.2 The *Jakobusgemeinde* (Gal 1:6–24)

What about the *Jakobusgemeinde*? Although Paul's principal concern focuses on the strictly limited nature of his meetings with Cephas and James, he does make passing references to the proto-Christian groupings in the Jerusalem area in those years of the early 30s CE:

- 5.2.1 I was violently persecuting τὴν ἐκκλησίαν τοῦ Θεοῦ and was trying to destroy it. (Gal 1.13).

- 5.2.2 I was still unknown by sight to ταῖς ἐκκλησίαις τῆς Ἰουδαίας ταῖς ἐν Χριστῷ. (Gal 1.22)

5.2.1 τὴν ἐκκλησίαν τοῦ Θεοῦ (1.13)

Paul is referring back to the period, about twenty years previously,[48] before "God . . . was pleased to reveal his Son" to him (1:15–16) when he "was violently persecuting τὴν ἐκκλησίαν τοῦ Θεοῦ and was trying to destroy it" (1:13). Being an "ex-offender" is part of his regular c.v. as an apostle (1:23; Phil 3:6; 1 Cor 15:9). We cannot discount physical coercion on Paul's part, given the legitimation extended by the example of the "zeal of Phinehas" within the traditions of Israel, even to the taking of life when deeply held and deeply felt religious sensitivities are perceived as being flouted.[49] Nevertheless we must beware of reading into Paul's words here the more colorful descriptions of his persecuting activities placed on his lips in the Lucan account (Acts 22:4–8; 26:9–14): descriptions of persecuting activities/experiences in the remainder of this same letter (Gal 4:49; 5:11; 6:12) seem to refer more to the severe and intense social/psychological pressuring that can occur in some sects from previous companions towards those seen as apostatizing.[50] In a similar way, and for similar purposes, Paul is looking back on his past to a time when he was a definite thorn in the side and op-

---

47. Asano, *Galatians*, 90 n.37.

48. Riesner, *Paul's Early Period*, 322.

49. Kim, *Origin of Paul's Gospel*, 41–50; Legasse, "Paul's Pre-Christian Career," 384.

50. Brandon, *Fall of Jerusalem*, 91. One is reminded of the depths of depravity projected by some evangelical converts on to their apparently harmless and innocent pre-Christian lives to highlight the change they have experienced.

ponent of the nascent proto-Christian Movement—the ἐκκλησία τοῦ Θεοῦ in and around Jerusalem—an activity that may indeed have been a threat to their existence.

Philip Esler sees the persecution in the early days of the new movement as occasioned by the distinctive identity that caused offense to a zealous Israelite such as Paul.[51] Whatever the cause, this well-documented evidence (in Paul's letters and in Acts) of hostility in the early days/years following the execution of Jesus strongly implies that the *Jakobusgemeinde* was even then of a size, identifiable by its message and/or practice, and with a dynamic growth that could not be ignored (contra Gamaliel). Even more important for our purpose is to recognize that, whatever it may have involved, this outbreak of persecution is the *first* occasion the *Jakobusgemeinde* surfaces on the pages of history, and that is within a couple of years of Jesus' execution.

5.2.2 ταῖς ἐκκλησίαις τῆς Ἰουδαίας ταῖς ἐν Χριστῷ (1:22)

Paul uses the term ἐκκλησία as a descriptor for both the whole Movement and for its component groups (1:13 and 22). However, it must be very doubtful that those Judean proto-Christians in the early 30s CE would have used ἐκκλησία ἐν Χριστῷ as a self-description,[52] particularly with its qualification as ἐν Χριστῷ (1:22)—it is Paul's very distinctive phrase transposed onto them, and carrying with it the understanding, theology and connotations in process of maturing with Paul in the 50s CE in Asia Minor and Greece.

A further example of this retrojection from the Pauline mission of the 50s into the Judean setting of the early 30s, in the years immediately following the execution of Jesus, is in the description placed on the lips of the Judean believers: "The one who formerly was persecuting us is now proclaiming the faith . . . " (1:23). This is a rare example (even for Paul's letters) of the definite article being attached to "faith" as a body of teaching that can be proclaimed[53]—the Pharisees that the Lucan tradition describes as

---

51. Esler, *Galatians*, 123.

52. Du Toit, "*Paulus Oecumenicus*" 138–42 describes ἐκκλησία τοῦ Θεοῦ as "a prestigious self-designation which aligned the Jesus movement with the coveted tradition of Israel as the people of God (but) the claim to such a coveted title was still a drastic one. It should therefore rather be ascribed to the 'Hellenists,' that is the (more progressive) Greek-speaking Christian Jews in Jerusalem, than to the theologically conservative so-called 'Jewish Christians.'" Also, Treblico, "Why Did the Early Christians Call Themselves ἡ ἐκκλησία?" 440–60. Cf., riposte by Kooten, "ἐκκλησία τοῦ Θεοῦ: The 'Church of God'" 522–48.

53. "The faith" occurs more frequently in the later pseudonymous Pastoral Epistles, sometimes referring to the Christian way of living, but also referencing 'the faith' as a

being attracted into the *Jakobusgemeinde* (Acts 15:5; 21:20) are hardly likely to have used such language. We must remember that it is only with hindsight that we can identify "Jesus/Christ" as the unifying factor between the groups forming the proto-Christian movement(s): at the time, these groups are likely to have expressed their sense of "being together" in terms drawn from the praxis of late Second Temple Judaism.

What this does emphasize is that Paul affirms an integral continuity between that early movement in and around Jerusalem and the ἐκκλησίαι coming into existence in places like Galatia and Corinth, and a concomitant recognition that his ἐκκλησίαι could parade at this later date under the same banner as the ἐκκλησίαι of Judea and Jerusalem. Despite all his strident assertions of independence from Jerusalem and the *Jakobusgemeinde* (1:8–20) it is an acknowledgment of the origination and chronological priority of the *Jakobusgemeinde* and therefore of its primacy over the Pauline movement.[54]

We do need to note that Paul can refer, almost in the same breath, to both the ἐκκλησία of God and the ἐκκλησίαι of Judea that are in Christ. It is a hint that as early as the early 30s CE the proto-Christian Movement already had a significant following not only in Jerusalem but also in the surrounding territory of Judea—and also that they met together in some form of συναγωγή to be identifiable.[55]

As noted above, ἐν Χριστῷ is a characteristic and distinctive Paulinism retrojected back onto the *Jakobusgemeinde* of two decades earlier. There is a strong echo of this descriptor (also with a persecution topos) in *one* other place of Paul's writings—1 Thess 2:14—a letter generally recognized as a strong candidate for being the earliest of Paul's letters that we possess. It is there applied to the contemporary Judean ἐκκλησίαι in c. 50 CE. This would reinforce that sense of identity that Paul felt between his ἐκκλησίαι and the *Jakobusgemeinde*. However, doubt must be cast on its authenticity.[56]

---

body of teaching. This is particularly noticeable in 1 Timothy (1 Tim 3:9, 13; 4:1–6; 5:8; 6.:10–12, 20. 2 Tim 2:18; 4:7. Tit 1:1, 4, 14).

54. The notion that chronological priority conferred status was a problem faced by the early proto-Christian movements when confronted with the incontrovertible fact that the Baptist came before Jesus (see § 3. 3.).

55. We have to leave it as an open question whether of not all these groups were embraced within the *Jakobusgemeinde* or if some looked, for example, to Cephas who could have been the presiding figure of an associated proto-Christian assembly in Jerusalem. Cf., Bruce, *Galatians*, 99—"James was perhaps already the leader of one group in the Jerusalem church. About nine years later 'James and the brethren' seem to form a distinct group from those associated with Peter (Acts 12:17)." It remains however that James, Cephas and John were together the Pillars of the Movement in Jerusalem.

56. The status of 1 Thess 2:13–16 does not carry a scholarly consensus, e.g., Brandon, *Fall of Jerusalem*, 92–93; Pearson, "A Deutero-Pauline Interpolation," 79–94—a

position contested by Taylor, *Paul, Antioch and Jerusalem,* 152–53; cf., Bockmuehl, "1 Thess 2:14–16 and the Jerusalem Church," 1–31; Grindheim, "Apostate Turned Prophet," 546–50. Although there is no textual support for an insertion, the internal evidence points strongly in one direction:

a) The hostile reference to "the Jews" (NB. definite article) is uncharacteristic for Paul. His own preferred language on the whole is "Israel" (cf., Rom 9—11), with "Jews" mainly as an identity-definer over against "Gentiles" or "Greeks" (cf., Rom 2—3; Gal 2:11–15). He is disturbed and distressed by the apparent obduracy of his own people and longs for their salvation (Rom 9—11). In his angst about those who would seek to impose circumcision on his Gentile converts Paul can even wish they "had their goolies chopped off" (Gal 5:12) or slag them as "dogs" (Phil 3:2), but nowhere does he turn on his people as "the Jews"—that is the language of the Fourth Gospel near the end of the century.

b) 2:16 seems to refer to the destruction of Jerusalem in 70 CE—an event which, in the succeeding years, was increasingly seen by Christians as an act of judgment by God vindicating their supersessionist claim to be the true Israel (Wilson, *Related Strangers,* 108).

c) The reference to Jews as "Christ killers" also suggests the post-apostolic period when formative Judaism and primitive Christianity were developing their respective self-identities largely in relation to each other (Wilson, *Related Strangers*). Jewish responsibility for Christ's death, of course, emerges in Matthew's passion narrative (c. 85–90) and the reference to "killing the Lord Jesus and the prophets" is an unequivocal targeting of allusions in the synoptic tradition (Mark 12:1—12; Matt 23:29–39, 27:25).

d) The finality of God's wrath in v.16 is totally at odds with Paul's hope for Israel's final salvation (Rom 11:25–32).

e) The description of his message (twice in one sentence) as "the word of God" (1:13) is not typical of Paul—it occurs in 1 Cor 14:36 (a passage whose authenticity is suspect—Barrett, *1 Corinthians,* 330–33; Moffatt, *1 Corinthians,* 230–34) and it occurs in a variant reading of Phil 1.14, with reference to some fellow Christians. He also distances himself from the "peddlers of God's word" (2 Cor 2:17—καπηλεύοντες τὸν λόγον τοῦ Θεοῦ. In 1 Thessalonians he otherwise refers to "the word of the Lord" (1 Thess 1:8), as a synonym for the message of the gospel (Pahl, *Discerning the "Word of the Lord,"* 105), and in 4:15 in referring to a Jesus-saying. Paul's characteristic description of his message is "(the) gospel (of God/Christ)" (Rom 1:1, 15—16; 15:16; 1 Cor 15:1; Gal 1:7, 11; 2:2, 5, 7; 4:13; Phil 1:12; 1 Thess 2:8–9. cf. 2 Cor 4:2–3). Variants of this are "the word (ῥῆμα) of faith" (Rom 10:8), "the word of life" (Phil 2:16), "the message (τὸν λόγον) of reconciliation" (2 Cor 5.19), "the word of the cross" (1 Cor 1:18), "preach Christ crucified" (1 Cor 1:23), or simply "preach Christ" (Phil 1:15). (Pahl, "'Gospel' and the 'Word,'" 211—27). It is in the later Deutero-Pauline pastorals that Timothy is exhorted to "preach the word" (2 Tim 4:2), and in the later *Acts of the Apostles* that "the word of God" (or variants) is a descriptor of early Christian preaching, particularly that of Paul (Acts 4:29, 31; 6:2, 4, 7; 8:4, 25; 11:1, 16, 19; 12:24; 13:5, 7, 44, 46, 49; 14:3, 24; 15:7, 35—36; 16:6, 32; 17:11, 13; 18:11; 19:10, 20).

5.3 Key Notes—I (§ 4. 4.–5.)

- From our earliest point of contact James, with Cephas, is a central figure in the *Jakobusgemeinde*.

- Already, within about five years[57] after the execution of his brother (evidently for potential insurrection) we find James apparently well settled in Jerusalem and accorded a leading position in a movement proclaiming his brother's vindication by God.

- James is identified and openly known as "the Lord's brother" (1:19).[58] Family relationship to Jesus was accorded status in the *Jakobusgemeinde*.

- Despite Paul's need to establish his authority and message [i.e., his "gospel" (1:9)] as being "through a revelation of Jesus Christ" and not "from a human source, nor was I taught it" (1:12), and despite his attempt to downplay the extent and purpose of his single visit "going up to Jerusalem"—the information for us is clear—that Cephas, and James were leading figures in the proto-Christian movement in Jerusalem and Judea with a measure of respect that could not be gainsaid, and an authority that was already extending with the movement beyond the Judaic heartlands.

- The sacred status of Jerusalem as the center of the Judaic world reinforced the *Jakobusgemeinde*'s authority as guarantor of the testimony to the risen Christ—Paul "went up" to Jerusalem.

- Paul has no doubts that the ἐκκλησίαι of his Gentile mission remain an integral part of the movement, which began and was nurtured by the *Jakobusgemeinde*.

- The fact of the persecution in which Paul was involved so soon after the events surrounding the execution of Jesus demonstrates that the *Jakobusgemeinde* was already at that time large enough, distinctive in belief or praxis, and significantly growing to be felt as a threat by the

---

f) Excision of the passage permits a smoother textual flow between 2:12 and 2:17.

I consider that this points strongly to the passage being a later insertion, reflecting the mood amongst some Christians in the early part of the second century CE, drawing on the literary reference in Galatians and telling us more about the context of Jewish/Christian relations at that later period.

57. Riesner, *Paul's Early Period*, 322.

58. Much later, James is identified as the brother of Jesus by Josephus in his account of James' execution (*Ant* 20.200).

priestly hierarchy and/or others with a "zeal for the Law" to be seen as a threat.

- Given that the tradition he "received and handed on" (1 Cor 15:3–7) specifically names only the same two people he exclusively met on this first visit raises the probability that the tradition-content of Paul's preaching is strongly informed from this occasion and sheds light on the *kerygma* of the *Jakobusgemeinde* (§ 7.).

6. Paul's Second Visit to Jerusalem (Gal 2:1–10)

It is with Paul's account of his next visit to Jerusalem and the following "Antioch Incident" that our methodological "tunnel vision" needs to be most disciplined to avoid contamination of our source from the ever-lurking Lucan tradition. Our interest here is not in the historical issues surrounding the Jerusalem Conference, but in what this particular source tells us of James and the *Jakobusgemeinde*: we shall need to live with tension.

Paul's semi-autobiographical account takes us on a decade and a half to the late 40s CE[59] when Paul again "went up" [ἀνέβην to Jerusalem (Gal 2:1–2)].[60] That, without further definition, Paul can immediately refer to a meeting with "them" (αὐτοῖς)—clearly intending his readers to understand the *Jakobusgemeinde*—is again strongly suggestive that the symbolic significance of Jerusalem, inherited from the Judaic tradition, is beginning to spread within the incipient Christian movements. Just as we might talk of "going up to Westminster" or "converting to Rome," "Jerusalem" is more than a geographical location and it seems here to be in process of becoming a shorthand referent for the proto-Christian community in that city, along with a consequent presumption and acceptance of some degree of primacy (§ 5. 11.).

This element of authority is underlined by Paul's own description[61] —"I laid before them" (2.2—cf. Acts 25:14):[62]

> Paul describes the events at the conference with considerable detail. The use of official political language shows that the event had an official and legally binding character . . . in Paul's

59. The precise chronology of Paul's life and its sequencing is a matter for Pauline studies and does not affect this study.

60. Betz, *Galatians*, 83–112.

61. Murphy-O'Connor, *Paul*, 136.

62. Esler, *Galatians*, 131 asserts that ἀνατίθημαι does not carry the connotation of "seeking approval."

argument the Jerusalem conference and its outcome have the importance of a *praeiudicium*.[63]

Paul may have written with "considerable detail" but there is still a lack of clarity in the *dramatis personae* and in the sequencing of events. This may of course be the memory blurring effect of recalling vital events (even, as here, fairly recent) involving internal conflict of critical import, centered around himself, that were (and still are) shot through with emotion and critical significance. For instance, Paul asserts that he presented his case in "a private meeting" (2:2) yet almost immediately refers to "false brothers secretly brought in" which presupposes a more public occasion. We must stay with these inconsistencies and tensions in his kaleidoscopic recollections of these days as they pour from his pen producing glimpses of the *Jakobusgemeinde* in the late 40s CE in a tantalizing and impressionistic collage:

6.1 Glimpses of *Jakobusgemeinde*: Leadership

The *Jakobusgemeinde* had a clearly recognized triumvirate leadership—that is all the more impressive as Paul cannot hide the fact that he needs their approval, yet goes out of his way to avoid giving unequivocal recognition. They are "the acknowledged leaders (τοῖς δοκοῦσιν)" (2:2);[64] "those who were reputed to be something (τῶν δοκούντων εἶναί τι)" (2:6)[65] though, "what they were makes no difference to me" (2:6); and "acknowledged Pillars (οἱ δοκοῦντες στῦλοι εἶναι)" (2:9). Paul cannot bring himself to recognize any legitimacy in their ultra-clear status and authority within the *Jakobusgemeinde* (let alone for the developing proto-Christian movement), other than what is accorded them by their group.

Both the acknowledgment of their legitimacy by the *Jakobusgemeinde* and Paul's need of the triumvirate's approval—"to make sure that I was not running, or had not run, in vain" (2:2)—with (almost by default) its implicit

---

63. Betz, *Galatians*, 86. Betz identifies Gal 2:1–10 with the Conference of Acts 15. However this "contamination" from the Lucan tradition does not affect the forensic imagery of Paul's language here.

64. Asano, *Galatians*, 95–96.

65. There is an ambiguity in τοῖς δοκοῦσιν which divides the commentators: e.g., Cousar, *Galatians*, 40–41, argues that it is not derogatory, it is simply affirming that God does not judge by appearance, whilst Longenecker, *Galatians*, 48, avers that "it seems hard to ignore at least a certain dismissive tone." Asano, *Galatians*, 94–97, has Paul emphasizing his distance and detachment from Jerusalem. The NRSV has replaced the pungent sarcastic tone and emotional nuance of Paul's writing (reflected in the older RSV rendition) with the more anemic "*acknowledged* leaders" in vv. 2, 6 and 9.

recognition of that authority should be noted. There is also a clear resonance with Essene priestly-triumvirate leadership.

It is in this context more than any other that we are alerted to the partiality of Paul's description of these fairly recent events through his very ungracious "those who were reputed to be something" (2:6) and in the derogatory description of his opponents who, he says, "slipped in to spy" (2:4).

The triumvirate is finally named (2:9) as "James and Cephas and John":

6.1.1 James

James—obviously "the Lord's brother" (1:19)—is named first. This suggests a position of primacy.[66] This may indeed reflect, as is sometimes asserted,[67] a shift in power within the *Jakobusgemeinde* from the situation of Paul's first visit to Jerusalem when Cephas is foregrounded,[68] but we must take care not to translate the most important contact *for Paul* on that earlier visit into an objective fact about proto-Christian power relationships in Jerusalem. For example, it is likely that there was a "history" between Paul and James from the time when he was a persecutor of ἡ ἐκκλησία τοῦ Θεοῦ for, as we noted (§ 4. 5.1), it was James' own brother who had been executed and whose veneration and memory had been calumnied by Paul. This may have made contact with Cephas much the easier option in what was probably a very tense situation, although James' position nonetheless rendered a courtesy visit at least advisable.[69] This more formal listing (2:9) is, however, a clear indication of James' leading position within the *Jakobusgemeinde* and for the extending proto-Christian movements during those mid-century years when Paul was writing (c. 48–56 CE).

---

66. As is the case with "Simon who is called Peter," consistently occupying the initial ordinal position in the lists of the Galilean Twelve (Matt 10:2; Mark 3:16; Luke 6:14; Acts 1:13).

67. Bruce, *Galatians*, 121–22; Lüdemann, *Paul*, 49–81.

68. The reversal of ordinal positions from that of the traditional listing in 1 Cor 15:5–7 may be more significant—but that recitation may simply reflect the well established primacy effect in listings, reflecting the order (Gal 1:18–19) in which Paul received the traditions.

69. Another possibility is that suggested by William Farmer that Paul found the more open Cephas/Peter a better contact point for him than James (Farmer, "James the Lord's Brother, according to Paul"); Hengel, *Acts*, 86, also suggests that "Paul may have used a middle man in making contact with the authorities in Jerusalem." Brandon, *Jesus and the Zealots*, 163; Painter, *Just James*, 60;

6.1.2 Cephas

Cephas is named first in Paul's recitation of the tradition of those to whom the risen Jesus appeared (1 Cor 15:5). He was present in Jerusalem on the occasion of Paul's previous visit (1:18) which, along with his inclusion in the "acknowledged Pillars" (2:9) suggest the probability that he was a Jerusalem resident. Indeed, if Cephas is a Jerusalemite, rather than one of the "men of Galilee" (Acts 1:11), it is consistent with this that the traditions Paul refers to having "received"—the Last Supper and Crucifixion/Resurrection appearances (1 Cor 11:23–26; 15:3–7)—both have a Jerusalem location (§ 7.).[70]

We glean from Paul that Cephas became itinerant, for we find him at Antioch (2:11) and later he is mentioned *en passim* as traveling in a vocation comparable to that of Paul himself and Barnabas (1 Cor 9:5). The existence of a "Cephas party" at Corinth (1 Cor 1:12) strongly suggests a stay in that city at some time.[71]

6.1.3 John

Of John, Paul tells us nothing—and *we* must leave it at that.[72] Tradition, of course, identifies him with John bar Zebedee—a member of the "inner three" from amongst the Galilean Twelve with Jesus. Betz refers to him as "a mysterious figure of whom we know little as far as reliable historical information is concerned, and too much as far as legends are concerned."[73] (See further § 9.)

With leadership vested in a triumvirate, seen also in the "inner three" of Jesus' disciple group, there is also resonance of a broader Judaic pattern of organization observed in the Qumranic tradition of "a council of twelve men and (i.e., including[74]) three priests,"[75] presided over by a *mebaqqer* (overseer).[76] (§§ 3. 1.; 5. 9.2).

70. David Catchpole, *Jesus People*, 105.

71. Taylor argues that it could be his eminence as a Pillar of the *Jakobusgemeinde* and prime witness to the resurrection that encouraged this particular Corinthian group to identify themselves with such an illustrious name—Taylor, *Paul, Antioch and Jerusalem*, 177–78, 183–87.

72. "John" is equally mute in the text of Acts.

73. Betz, *Galatians*, 101.

74. Bauckham, *Jude*, 75 n.89.

75. 1 QS VIII, 1.

76. 1 QS I, 1; CD XIII, 7–13. "It seems most likely, in fact, that this material represents the program of a group that was about to be formed and was to become the

6.1.4 The Identity of Cephas

One of the tensions *within* the Pauline text of Galatians that we have to live with in consequence of our "tunnel vision" methodology (§ 4. 2.) relates to the ambiguity surrounding the identity of Κηφᾶς and Πέτρος.

Although the problem was recognized in the second century by Clement of Alexandria[77] there is, nonetheless, a strong Christian tradition, enjoying consensual support amongst scholars,[78] identifying Peter with Cephas, the Pillar whom Paul specifically sought out on that earlier visit to Jerusalem in the mid-30s, and with whom he stayed for a fortnight (1:18). However, Paul himself never identifies Cephas with Peter or gives the slightest intimation of such an identity. In fact, to the contrary, in Paul's description of his meeting with the Pillars (2:7–9), where we have the only instance of the name of "Peter" in the extant writings of Paul, the most natural reading is that "Peter" is differentiated from "Cephas." As Kirsopp Lake commented many years ago: "To call the same man by two names in the same sentence is, to say the least, a curious device."[79]

Squaring this particular circle has taxed the lateral thinking of commentary writers. Betz lists a number of attempts,[80] which Bart D. Ehrman once described as "explanations that are as numerous as they are ingenious."[81] Prominent amongst these suggestions, supported by Oscar Cullman, is

---

nucleus of the Qumran community. The passage is marked by a high idealism, suggesting a movement in its infancy . . . " (Knibb, *Qumran Community*, 129).

77. *Hist. eccl.* 1.12.2. Peter and Cephas are also listed separately in the mid-second century *Epistula Apostolorum* (*Ep. Apos.* 2).

78. This is an understatement. Discussions and references to the Antioch Incident in Galatians by NT scholars invariably refer without qualification to *Peter* in preference to *Cephas*, and this practice is accorded virtual canonical status in several modern translations of the NT where the name *Cephas* is replaced by *Peter* in Gal 1 and 2 without comment (e.g., GNB, *TEV, NIV, Contemporary English Version*). It has been recognized as a problem from the early centuries with minor variations of textual tradition, e.g., Codex Bezae completely replaces *Cephas* with *Peter* in Galatians—a practice resurfacing in the early English translation of John Wycliffe (1388)—despite Wycliffe using the Vulgate text which has *Petrum* in 1:18, whilst retaining *Cephas* for both 2:9 and 2:11. Wycliffe retains *Cefas* for 1 Cor 1:12 and 9:5. The KJV translators followed the lead of the Geneva Bible (1560) and "hedged their bets," changing *Cephas* to *Peter* for Paul's first Jerusalem visit (Gal 1:18) and for the Antioch Incident (Gal 2:11), whilst retaining the distinction between *Peter*, the apostle to the circumcised, (Gal 2:7–8) and *Cephas*, the *Jakobusgemeinde* Pillar, for "the handshake" (Gal 2:9). It is an ambivalence continued in the NKJB, despite the RV reverting to the Greek text of Paul, to be followed by the RSV/NRSV and, more recently, the *Common English Bible*.

79. Lake, "Cephas, Peter," 95–97.

80. Betz, *Galatians*, 96–97.

81. Ehrman, "Cephas and Peter," 463–74.

that Paul is reflecting the language of a formal (written?) agreement which used the name of "Peter."[82] Aside from the fact that it hardly clarifies the passage in question (and raises the question of why, in a formal document produced by a dominantly Aramaic-speaking community, the Greek form of Πέτρος is preferred to the Aramaic Κηφᾶς—specifically for the "apostle to the circumcised"), this is purely a product of scholarly speculation, totally dependent on further unverifiable speculation about the conflict-resolution procedures of the *Jakobusgemeinde*. Speculation in such a case is inevitable and quite proper, providing it is grounded on events/statements that do have some degree of empirical verification. Dale C. Allison, in a response to Ehrman, makes his principal objection that it stretches "credulity to maintain that earliest Christianity had among its outstanding leaders two men with exceedingly rare (sur)names or nicknames with the same sense"[83] (see further: *Excursus*). This overlooks the possibility that it is precisely because there were two individuals sharing a common nickname that it became necessary to distinguish them—in this case with different (language) forms of the same name. What Allison fails to note is that both Κηφᾶς (in Paul) and Πέτρος (in Acts and the gospels) were the respective "Right-hand Men" of two brothers, one of whom at least, Jesus, is presented as having a fondness for bestowing nicknames on his friends and companions (Mark 3:17).[84] "Nick-names were necessary among first-century Jews because there was a relatively small number of proper names in circulation."[85] Given the fact that "rock" has a long history as a natural epithet,[86] is it then too much to suggest that this nickname for one's closest friend and confidant was in common use by young lads in the alleyways and fields of Nazareth and became an element in their primary language code? This is complete speculation, but it does suggest an explanation for the coincidence that Allison rightly highlights, and is founded on the demonstrable fact of the brothers' shared socialization.

---

82. Cullman, *Peter: Disciple, Apostle, Martyr*, 20.

83. Allison, "Peter and Cephas," 489–95.

84. Catchpole, *Jesus People* 102–104; Chilton, "Getting It Right," 111.

85. Mason, *Josephus and the New Testament*, 166.

86. E.g., (1) its repeated occurrence in the "Song of Moses" (Deut 32:4, 15, 18, 30) and by the Psalmists as a descriptor for God—Pss 18:2 (twice), 31, 46; 19:14; 27:5; 28:1; 31:2–3; 62:2 *et al.* (cf. Isa 17:10; 26:4; 30:29; 44:8; Hab 1:12); (2) the widespread NT usage of rock/foundation imagery for the church, Christ, and individual believers (e.g., Matt 16:18; Mark 12:10; Acts 4:11; Gal 2:9; Eph 2:20; 1 Pet 2:4–7; Rev 3.12 (Rojas-Flores, "From John 2:19 to Mark 15.29," 31); (3) one also recalls Paul Burrell recounting *ad nauseum* that his late employer, Princess Diana, used to call him "my rock";

The brute fact remains that in his writings, the only contemporary evidence we have, Paul consistently uses the name Cephas, and it is fifty years later (John 1:42) before we find the two names being fused into the one person:

> (I)f one were to read Paul without prejudging the issue in light of John 1:42 and the overwhelming consensus of Christian opinion through the ages, one would be hard pressed indeed to show that when Paul said Cephas, he really meant Peter.[87]

Despite the dissonance, we should "listen to our witness"[88] (see n.34 above) and *act* on the confession of Lake:

> . . . Paul nowhere says that Peter is Cephas, though commentators have the bad habit (to which I plead guilty myself) of constantly talking of Peter when he says Cephas . . . [89]

In this investigation we seek to respect our witnesses and therefore, without prejudice, use the names of Cephas and Peter as they occur in the text.

6.2 Glimpses of *Jakobusgemeinde*: Community

Further to the incontrovertible evidence that the *Jakobusgemeinde* vested its central authority to a group of three men, we have a fleeting glimpse of a section of the community over which James, Cephas, and John presided. Using the "language of political demagoguery" (Betz)[90] these "false believers" (2:4) . . .

> . . . are "secretly smuggled in" (παρεισάκτοι), like undercover agents and conspirators. Their activity is the "infiltration" (παρεισέρχεσθαι) and "spying out" (κατασκοπεῖν) of what Paul calls "our freedom which we have in Christ Jesus."[91]

These were those in Jerusalem who opposed his Antiochene preaching on the same grounds as those who were now disturbing his Galatian

---

87. Ehrman, "Cephas and Peter," 467.

88. Contra (1) Oscar Cullmann: "completely unfounded idea" (Cullmann, *Peter,* 18 n.7); and (2) Joseph Fitzmyer: "we cannot take it seriously." (Fitzmyer, "Aramaic Kepha," 125). Professor Festinger might wish to comment on their strategies of cognitive dissonance reduction.

89. Lake, "Cephas, Peter," 97.

90. Esler, *Galatians,* 130, 135, prefers the metaphor of military imagery, conveying the sense of conflict present in the meeting.

91. Betz, *Galatians,* 90; also, Longenecker, *Galatians,* 50–58; Esler, *Galatians,* 130.

ἐκκλησίαι. For Paul they were clearly not "ἐν Χριστῷ" and could not be accepted as such, or else his whole Galatian pack of cards would collapse. For him they were not legitimate participants[92] in the debate at Jerusalem: they were "ψευδαδέλφοι." But they were there.[93] Paul's very descriptor of them as ψευδαδέλφοι enshrines their recognition by the *Jakobusgemeinde* as ἀδελφοι (§ 5. 6.1) and may be a reflection of boundary porosity within the broader movement of Judaic renewal of the time: ψευδαδέλφοι is Paul's perception—they were not "in Christ"—but on the streets of Jerusalem they were probably seen as "fellow-travellers" with the *Jakobusgemeinde* within that broader contemporary movement for the restoration of Israel. Whatever, they were crucially involved in the debate—in fact there was no debate without them—their opposition to the developments at Antioch were the *precise* reason for Paul's presence with Barnabas in Jerusalem.

At the least, this indicates that the *Jakobusgemeinde* was extensive enough to embrace distinct pressure/interest groups, or possibly even distinct συναγωγαί—the ψευδαδέλφοι being one of these.[94] Their persuasion *was* part of the *Jakobusgemeinde*, but not all of it.

This has to be the deduction from the fact that the final decision was to give "the right hand of fellowship" to the Antiochene delegation—the Pillars led or at least had the support of their community. In a patriarchal/*gemeinschaft* culture the probability is that their authority was vested in their position with the ready assent of the great majority of their followers. We can note how in 2:2, Paul can describe the act of presenting the Antiochene case "privately before those who were of repute" as laying their case "before them" (i.e., the *Jakobusgemeinde*).[95]

Stephan Joubert distils the significance of "the right hand of fellowship" as indicating:

> . . . the beginning, renewal or strengthening of a relationship between individuals and groups. Often, the initiative in the

92. Bruce, *Men and Movements*, 37; Bruce, *Galatians*, 130.

93. Asano, *Galatians*, 117.

94. Taylor, *Paul, Antioch and Jerusalem*, 101; Watson, *Paul, Judaism and the Gentiles*, 50. Both suggest that the ψευδαδέλφοι were from Antioch and may have been either part of a broader based Antiochene delegation than Paul is willing to acknowledge, or an unofficial counter-delegation. Alternatively, it might be that Paul's reference to he and Barnabas going up to Jerusalem "in response to an ἀποκάλυψιν" (2:2) conceals the reality that it was they who took the initiative and went separately to ensure that their case was properly presented and heard. It seems the ψευδαδέλφοι nonetheless could find sympathetic ears within the *Jakobusgemeinde* (§ 5. 9.1). We also need to take care and not impose boundary markers on the *Jakobusgemeinde* that may be alien to their position.

95. Contra Taylor, *Paul, Antioch and Jerusalem*, 163.

extension of the right hand was taken by the superior party in the relationship, thus symbolizing a bestowal of honor upon the inferior party (usually also in conjunction with some tangible benefits).[96]

We note that the understanding of the "right hand of fellowship" as an agreement between equal partners,[97] approving Paul's "gospel" and the Antiochene mission activity is Paul's interpretation. Asano, following a suggestion of Philip Esler,[98] affirms that the phrase implies "the enforcement of *status quo* in the power balance from the powerful to the powerless" and continues:

> The demarcation of missions may have been a concession by both the Jerusalem apostles and Paul. For the Jerusalem apostles, while retaining a sense of superiority over the delegates of the Gentile mission represented by Paul, they allowed Paul to continue work among the Gentiles, to gain sympathizers among them. The "Right hand of fellowship" was for the Jerusalem apostles a gesture to permit the ministry of a secondary group of sympathizers attached to the authentic community of faith represented by the Jerusalem church. Paul, on the other hand, may not have been satisfied with the permission to establish groups that are only secondary and not authentic, so he accepted the "right hand of fellowship" and interpreted and reported it as a gesture of recognition of autonomously authentic mission.[99]

Through the fog of battle, however, we should not overlook recognizing that the *Jakobusgemeinde* was supportive of such as Peter who "had been entrusted with the gospel[100] for the circumcised" (Gal 2:7) and was actively spreading the message to other Jews. The *Jakobusgemeinde* was not an introspective navel-gazing holy club, but the Pauline mission was viewed as ancillary to the mission to Israel.

Peter's apostolate may well be rooted in the commissioning of Jesus to his disciples which Matthew understands as explicitly "to the lost sheep of the house of Israel" (Matt 10:5–6). But whatever its ultimate origin, it

---

96. Joubert, *Paul as Benefactor*, 100–01.

97. Betz, *Galatians*, 100.

98. Esler, "Making and Breaking an Agreement," 299–300; Esler, *Galatians*, 133.

99. Asano, *Galatians*, 128. Betz, *Galatians*, 100, dissents: ". . . any recognition of subjugation by Paul and Barnabas can be ruled out. The handshake does not automatically imply a recognition of supremacy as far as the Jerusalem apostles are concerned."

100. NRSV translation *et al.*—literally "καθὼς Πέτρος τῆς περιτομῆς"—it seems that Paul could not bring himself to describe Peter's message to Jews as "gospel."

is implicit in Paul's description of his encounter with the Pillars that the *Jakobusgemeinde* viewed Peter as an authentically commissioned agent, with a leading role in the prosecution of the mission to Israel. This points to him being dependent upon and accountable to the *Jakobusgemeinde* and of secondary status to the Jerusalem Pillars.

The description of the leadership as "the Pillars" has, particularly since the discovery of the Qumranic literature, raised the possibility of this usage reflecting a communal self-perception by the *Jakobusgemeinde* of them being the eschatological Temple on the model of the sectarians of Qumran.[101] The evidence is ambiguous,[102] but if "on track," it would not only further embed the *Jakobusgemeinde* in the world of late Second Temple Judaism but could help us to a better understanding of how their community was organized.

6.3 Glimpses of *Jakobusgemeinde*: Issues

Paul, writing with an evident degree of emotional *angst* triggered by the intrusion into his memory of the ψευδαδέλφοι from that earlier period, fails to state the reason for the consultation.[103] But the reason is clear—it concerned the issue of Gentile circumcision:

- "Titus . . . was not compelled to be circumcised" (2:3);[104]

- "when they saw that I had been entrusted with the gospel for the uncircumcised, just as Peter had been entrusted with (the gospel for)[105] the circumcised" (2:7);

101. Bauckham, "James and the Jerusalem Church," 441–450; Dunn, *Jesus Remembered*, 514–515.

102. Betz, *Galatians*, 99–100, asserts: "There is, however, no evidence that the epithet is connected with the notion of the church as a spiritual temple."

103. The sentence is "a grammatical anacoluthon" (Betz, *Galatians*, 89); Barrett, *On Paul*, 6–7.

104. O'Connor, *Paul*, 137–38; "any ambiguity surrounding ἠναγκάσθη περιτμηθῆναι does not obscure the clarity of the issue" (Barrett, *On Paul*, 43).

105. "There can be little doubt that in Gal 2:7 we must supply the words τό εὐαγγέλιον before ἡ περιτομή." (Barrett, *On Paul*, 9). *Au contraire:*

- it may be that Paul, having emphasized that "his gospel" is the only gospel (1:6–9), is refusing that ascription to the preaching of Peter. The eschatological incorporation of the Nations into God's covenant people is the essential climax of his understanding of the "gospel" he proclaims (cf., Rom1:1–7; 11:25–36) and therefore Peter's preaching, restricted to τῆς περιτομῆς, may not for Paul be "gospel";

- significantly, he similarly does not apply the concept of ἀποστολήν for himself (2.8) as he does for Peter—Paul claims that his mission as an ἀπόστολος is "through Jesus Christ and God the Father" (1.1), not from the Jerusalem authorities. (see

- "we should go to the Gentiles and they to the circumcised" (2:9).

This is clear too from the way this same demand (that Gentile converts should be circumcised) is threatening his work in Galatia (Gal 5:1–12)—a demand that must be being made by some who would at the very least be fully sympathetic (if not actually identical) with the ψευδαδέλφοι.[106] In his letter Paul describes his gospel as a call to *freedom* from "a yoke of *slavery*," against which they must (as he did at Jerusalem) "stand firm" and "not *submit* again" (5:1, 13), echoing his recollection of how "the ψεθδαδέλφους . . . slipped in to spy on the *freedom* we have in Christ Jesus, so that they might *enslave* us" and "we did not *submit* to them . . . so that the truth of the gospel might always remain with you" (2:4–5).

Although περιτομή had the wider reference of adoption and entry into the whole style of Judaic life than simply physical circumcision,[107] that brute physical connotation (for males) was *the* distinctive marker[108] of belonging to the House of Israel from the time of the Maccabees through to its proscription by Hadrian:[109]

> The Prohibition of the rite by Antiochus Epiphanes (1 Macc 1:48) had elevated circumcision to the status of fundamental principle, worthy of martyrdom (cf., 1 Macc 1:60–61), and it had accordingly become definitive for Jewish identity in a way that had not previously been the case.[110]

The uncircumcised were quite simply, especially for the Torah-zealous in the land of Israel, "not Israel."[111] Περιτομή was *the* mark of Judaic identity.

However, beyond the land of Israel there was a range of ways in which Gentiles might relate to the local συναγωγή and a comparable range of levels through which they might find incorporation into its community:

"Nature of Primitive Christian Apostleship" in Taylor, *Paul, Antioch and Jerusalem*, 227–28.)

106. Eastman, "Cast Out the Slave Woman and her Son," 311, refers to a "widespread" consensus that "the circumcising missionaries (are) sponsored by the Jerusalem church." However, the precise identity of the agitators amongst the ἐκκλησίαι in Galatia is not an issue here, it is a matter for Pauline scholarship.

107. Taylor, *Paul, Antioch and Jerusalem*, 99–101; Borgen, *Early Christianity*, 260–62. Garroway protests that περιτομή consistently refers to "Jews" (Garroway, "Pharisee Heresy." 23–27).

108. Borgen, *Early Christianity*, 259–60.

109. Goodman, *Rome and Jerusalem*, 485.

110. Taylor, *Paul, Antioch and Jerusalem*, 100.

111. VanderKam, *Book of Jubilees*, 125.

For Jews, the concept of Gentile incorporation encompassed a wide range of acculturation phenomena of Gentile sympathizers around and toward the boundary line. Gentile sympathizers demonstrate their varying levels of attachment to Jews and their religion, such as mere admiration of the culture, selective practice of customs and beliefs, and distancing from their original lifestyle. Some choose to integrate fully into the Jewish community through the rite of circumcision.[112]

But there is no indication of there being any significant deviance on this issue within the *Jakobusgemeinde* in the city of Zion with its predominantly Judaic population. The note (2:3) that "Titus . . . was not compelled to be circumcised" suggests that circumcision was the norm in practice for the *Jakobusgemeinde* whilst its application to Gentiles in the novel situation being created by their fellow-travelers in Antioch was less well defined, not needing to have been thought through previously. Although the position stridently espoused by the ψευδαδέλφοι was not to win the day at this time, it is likely that they were expressing the feelings of a much wider constituency within the *Jakobusgemeinde* and beyond.[113] The story was to be different in the more cosmopolitan Antioch, where Paul's narrative now moves.

6.4 Key Notes—II (§ 4. 6.)

The picture is beginning to emerge of the *Jakobusgemeinde* c. 20 years after the execution of Jesus:

- a community/movement whose authority in the developing proto-Christian movement was a simple assumption;

- large enough to have identifiable interest groups;

- with a common Judaic identity, though differing in understanding of the scope of Gentile attachment;

- the περιτομή, although a minority grouping, are accepted within the *Jakobusgemeinde,* possibly reflecting the latter's self-understanding as part of the wider movement for Judaic reform with an associated boundary porosity—ψευδαδέλφοι is Paul's description of them, reflecting his mission experience in the Diaspora;

---

112. Asano, *Galatians*, 112. Fredriksen, "Judaizing the Nations," 239–40.

113. Sim, *Matthew*, 92–93, suggests that James may have had strong sympathy with the ψευδαδέλφοι.

- a movement large enough to need and to generate its own authority structure:

    - which is clearly recognized and accepted—the triumvirate of James, Cephas and John, from which we can infer the likelihood of its being organized on a familiar Judaic pattern similar to that of the Essenes;

    - James is now clearly the prime leader of the *Jakobusgemeinde*;

    - a community with a sense of a common self-identity and common cause also with a wider proto-Christian movement, over which they had some degree of authority, along with growing anxiety over boundary issues;

    - and capable of vigorous debate.

7. The Antioch Incident (Gal 2:11–14)

7.1 Identity in an Ambivalent Context

The broader diasporan amplification of boundary markers such as περιτομή are immediately evident at Antioch—the third largest city of the Empire in the first century CE and the capital of Coele-Syria, although sacrally (and crucially) designated within the boundaries of the land given to Israel by Yahweh.[114] It enjoyed a multi-ethnic population. Josephus records that, at the time of its foundation four centuries earlier, significant numbers of Jews, Athenians and Macedonians were settled alongside the native Syrians.[115] Contiguity with the lands of Israel encouraged migration[116] and it is estimated that around 10 percent of its first century CE population were Jews.[117]

There seems to have been a degree of ambivalence about the status of Antioch for Jews. For the zealous Israelite it was within the boundaries of the land scripturally designated as the gift of Yahweh, although well beyond even the most northern extension of David and Solomon's kingdom, as well as the more recent Maccabean expansion.[118] It had never been subjected to Israelite rule. Seeing Antioch as part of the land of Yahweh may have fired

---

114. Bockmuehl, *Jewish Law in Gentile Churches*, 49–83; Bockmuehl, "Antioch and James the Just," 155–198; Asano, *Galatians*, 133; Freyne, "The Jesus-Paul Debate Revisited," 143–163.

115. *Ant.* 12.119; Schurer, *History*, III.1. 13.

116. *J.W.* 7.43.

117. Asano, *Galatians*, 129 n.57.

118. Wright and Filson, *Westminster Historical Atlas*, 47–51, 78–81.

the *Jakobusgemeinde*'s particular concern over what they perceived as the blurring of vital purity boundaries in the reported proto-Christian praxis in that city, as well as explaining the resulting confusion amongst the Antioch Christians,[119] and Cephas also, when "certain people came from James" (2:12). Bockmuehl has pointed out that we have no instance of James interfering in any of Paul's Gentile Mission ἐκκλησίαι,[120] only at Antioch which, although in the Roman province of Coele-Syria, was in this scripturally defined boundary of Israel where a more rigorous adherence to Torah was looked for than in the diaspora proper. This points to a substantial segment of the *Jakobusgemeinde* sharing the growing Judaic nationalist sentiment of the middle years of the first century CE.

Another agenda was normal to Antioch, where there was a very different social complex from Jerusalem. For, as occurred elsewhere in the Diaspora, a minority community of Jews inevitably developed a wider range of social and commercial relationships with their Gentile co-inhabitants[121] in an interactive process yielding evidence of significant Gentile attraction at differing levels to Judaism.[122]

These more complex established patterns of Judaic/Gentile relationship, combined with minimal awareness of their City's siting in Eretz Israel, no doubt fed into the developing proto-Christian movement(s) of that city, facilitating their transgression of Judaic purity boundaries with open table fellowship outwith any demand for full proselyte circumcision.[123] However, as Asano notes:

> From the perspective of the Jews looking out at the boundary line, the positive attraction and attachment of Gentile sympathizers to Judaism are both a source of pride and confidence in God's supremacy and at the same time cause for concern for the purity of the religion and the coherence of the ethnic community. . . . The rite of circumcision was one of the important requirements for this full integration of a sympathizer into the ethnic community. The degree of insistence on this important physio-cultural feature for Jewish ethnic identity seems to vary from one group to another.[124]

---

119. A term we can use at Antioch (Acts 11:26).

120. Bockmuehl, *Jewish Law in Gentile Churches*, 49–83.

121. Stegemann, *Jesus Movement*, 269.

122. *J.W.* 2.463, 7.45; Schurer, *History*, III.1 160–62; Asano, *Galatians*, 104–13.

123. Fredriksen, "Judaizing the Nations," 240–44.

124. Asano, *Galatians*, 112–13.

Asano's insight into the inner contradictions experienced by faithful Israelites through the presence within their συναγωγαί of Gentile God-fearers and proselytes is on target. To put it simply, a small number of Gentiles within their gatherings could be generally acceptable but a more significant number (especially if they have undergone the rite of circumcision and become fully "Judaized") inevitably threatens the essential Judaic self-identity of the community. In a largely mono-cultural Judaic community, such as Jerusalem, the issue would not be pressing until, that is, someone (e.g., a "ψευδαδέλφος") raises it as an issue—an issue to which those living in the shadow of the Temple would have their sensitivities the more finely tuned, especially as Judaic boundary markers and Gentile impurity were becoming more pressing issues under the Imperial presence and threat.[125]

In multi-cultural and multi-faith Antioch the issue structured itself very differently from Jerusalem.

7.2 Confronting Cephas

Cephas, the Jerusalem Pillar, is now found some time later at Antioch in what appears to be more than a passing visit for "he used to eat (συνήσθιεν) with the Gentiles" (2:12). We are not told why he had moved, nor how this stay might relate to his later itinerant existence (1 Cor 9:5), but it seems clear that he was "doing in Antioch what the Antiochenes do" (i.e., sharing in open table fellowship in conformity with their understanding of the Jerusalem agreement[126] between Judaic and Gentile Christians). This would have been understood by the Antioch ἐκκλησία (and certainly by Barnabas and Paul) as in line with their agreement in Jerusalem ["we to the Gentiles . . . they to the circumcised" (2:9)]. Paul (and presumably Barnabas who was also sharing open table fellowship) was interpreting the "right hand of fellowship" (2:9) as a recognition of approval by the *Jakobusgemeinde* leadership of their preaching and practice, particularly open table-fellowship[127] and possibly open eucharistic celebration,[128] at Antioch.[129] Paul and Barnabas were "not running . . . in vain" (2:2) and "(the Pillars) added nothing to me; but on the contrary . . . saw that I had been entrusted with the gospel to the uncircumcised . . . and gave . . . the right hand. . ." (2:6–9 RSV). It was an agreement of mutual acceptance and respect—or, so Paul represents it—but

125. Ibid., 119–20.
126. Esler, *Galatians*, 138–39.
127. Asano, *Galatians*, 142.
128. Esler, *Galatians*, 133–34.
129. Asano, *Galatians*, 125.

as virtually all commentators remark, it was a compromise that was bound to break down, and sooner rather than later.

And it broke down on this occasion when "certain people came from James" (2:12). This must have been some form of official visit sanctioned by James[130] for if they were just *Jakobusgemeinde* members[131] perhaps passing through and spontaneously objecting to the Antiochene practice, or if they were from the ψευδαδέλφοι proto-Christian group, Cephas, a member of the triumvirate that had debated and pronounced their support for Antioch, could have put them right with no difficulty.[132] It is also a recognition, the more significant by being unremarked, that the authority inherent in the *Jakobusgemeinde* as the ἐκκλησία in Jerusalem, the Holy City, is now unequivocally invested in and expressed by James (formerly of Nazareth).

We can only speculate on the content of the dialogue between those "from James" and Cephas[133] (presumably with Barnabas and other Judaic members of the Antioch ἐκκλησία), but its outcome was definite: ". . . (Cephas) drew back and kept himself separate for fear of the circumcision faction (simply τοὺς ἐκ περιτομῆς[134])," followed by Barnabas and "the other

130. Oakes, Review of *Paul, Jerusalem and the Judaisers*, 98–99; Robinson, following a P[46] variant reading, argues that "those who came from James were the decrees of the Jerusalem council." Head, Review of *Donald Robinson*, 3.

131. Lightfoot, *Galatians*, 112.

132. Esler (*Galatians*, 136–37) argues that in Cephas' absence the ψευδαδέλφοι, whose honor was badly damaged through their defeat by Paul, had prevailed upon the remaining Pillars to rescind the agreement (perhaps with a threat similar to that of Paul before his conversion); contra Taylor (*Paul, Antioch and Jerusalem*, 173–76) who argues that it was the disruption in relationships of Paul, Peter and James that created the vacuum into which the "false brethren" re-asserted their position in Antioch's daughter churches in Galatia.

133. Apart from the focusing point being on the Antiochene practice of table-fellowship, the precise issue raised by those "from James" is unclear and may have had much to do with the perception in Jerusalem of what was happening in Antioch. Cf., discussion in Crossley, *Date of Mark's Gospel*, 141–54—Crossley considers: "The problem may be more subtle. As mentioned, if large numbers of gentiles were eating food prohibited in the Torah, many people would identify the Christians at Antioch as a gentile movement. Jewish Christians involved in table-fellowship at Antioch would have been associated with such practices and this would have disturbed the men from James (153). [In response to Dunn, "Incident at Antioch (Gal 2:11–18)," 3–57; Esler, *Community and Gospel in Luke-Acts*, 77–88; Esler, "Socio-Redaction Criticism of Luke-Acts," 123–50; Sanders, "Jewish Association with Gentiles and Galatians," 170–88; Sanders, *Jewish Law from the Bible to the Mishnah*, 283–308; Tomson, *Paul and the Jewish Law*, 221–58].

134. The identity of the περιτομή ranges from ethnic Jews (Schmithals, *Paul and James*, 67; Asano, *Galatians*, 132) to the ψευδαδέλφοι (Lightfoot, *Galatians*, 112; Esler, *Galatians*, 136).

Jews" (2:13). However, Paul's description of how Cephas "kept himself separate (ἀφορίζειν)" . . .

> . . . is a Jewish technical term describing cultic separation from
> the "unclean." If Cephas' shift of position resulted in "separation," this must have been the demand made by "the men from
> James." If they made this demand it was made because of their
> understanding of the implications of the Jerusalem agreement
> (cf. 2:7–9).[135]

Paul accuses Cephas of "moving the goalposts" on the inclusion of Gentiles into the covenant community of Israel (2:14). Open table fellowship was a sign of acceptance outwith circumcision: to withdraw from such sharing was to exclude them unless they first "Judaize" (ie., undergo the rite of circumcision).[136] Paul saw the implication—Cephas' action bestowed second-class status on the Gentile members of the Antioch ἐκκλησία.

It is frequently suggested that the concern of James and the *Jakobusgemeinde* might have arisen from the intensifying nationalistic temper in Jerusalem during the decade of the 40s CE[137] where problems were being created for the *Jakobusgemeinde* through their known association with the Antioch ἐκκλησία whose practice on the issue of περιτομή was reputed to be decidedly "soft."[138]

Be that as it may, and however great the openness of many in the *Jakobusgemeinde* and its leadership to the practices developing in the diaspora might have been at the time of the earlier meeting (and still might be in sentiment): the reality in the Holy City was περιτομή. When theory and practice collide, it is the latter that supervenes.[139]

The language Paul uses to portray Cephas reactions to the "men from James" is highly colored and tells us nothing about Cephas' actual feelings,

---

135. Betz, *Galatians*, 108.

136. Sim, *Matthew*, 95, urges that the use of the verb ἀναγκάζειν (to compel) in Gal 2:14 (as also in 2:3 and 6:13) must include male circumcision.

137. *Ant.* 18.23, 20.102; *J.W.* 2.118; Schmithals, *Paul and James*, 67–68, suggests that Peter's fear was of the Jews, not Jewish-Christians—anachronistic in that it overlooks the *Jakobusgemeinde*'s self-identification as essentially a movement within Judaism.

138. Bruce, *Galatians*, 130–31; Fung, *Galatians*, 108; Cousar, *Galatians*, 47; Longenecker, *Galatians*, 74; Taylor, *Paul, Antioch and Jerusalem*, 120–21, 130; Schmithals, *Paul and James*, 67–68; Asano, *Galatians*, 142–43; Hengel, *Saint Peter*, 65.

139. The Antioch agreement may be an early example of ecclesiastical "fudge," with similarities to the current Anglican debate on homosexuality—whilst some traditionalists continue to hold that homosexuality is generically sinful, many have moved to accepting that there is no sin in being homosexual: sin is in the act. The crunch point comes when a *practicing* homosexual is ordained as Bishop.

or his reasons/rationalizations ["fear of those of the circumcision" (2:12) was Paul's summary invective]. But the motives of Cephas[140] do not concern us, our focus remains on what Paul's recounting of this critical incident in his life tells us (through all the smokescreen) about James and the *Jakobusgemeinde*:

7.3 Key Notes—III (§ 4. 7.)

- the right of James/the *Jakobusgemeinde* to intervene in Antiochene affairs is not contested—they belong to the same movement;

- this intervention is suggestive of strong sympathy within the *Jakobusgemeinde* for the growing nationalist agenda in Jerusalem;

- male circumcision was the norm within the *Jakobusgemeinde* community, but there was not yet a common mind on the issue presented by the success of the Gentile Mission;

- certainly at the time Paul is writing, and implicitly much earlier, the natural authority of the proto-Christian movement in the sacred city of Jerusalem is vested in the person of James;

- the "men from James" operated either at the instigation of James or at least with his support;

- notably, Cephas feels obliged to recognize the paramount authority of James;

- despite the positive spin Paul puts on his description of the confrontation, it cannot hide that Paul was out on a limb—"even Barnabas" deserted him (Gal 2:13);[141]

- the Jerusalem "hand-shake" had indeed been a fudge—and even Cephas was confused about it;

---

140. Commentators commonly relate Cephas' "fear" to the rising tide of nationalism in Jerusalem at this period, e.g., the Antiochene practice may be creating problems for the *Jakobusgemeinde* who are known, to be associated with them; or Cephas' practice in Antioch might be compromising his "mission to the circumcised": Bruce, *Men and Movements*, 35; Jewett, "Agitators and the Galatian Congregation," 198–212; Taylor, *Paul, Antioch and Jerusalem*, 133; Paget, "After 70 and All That," 359–60). Sim, *Matthew*, 92–93, considers this line of argument to be overstated. Hengel, *Saint Peter*, 57–65, attempts a reconstruction of Peter's position.

141. Dunn, *Unity and Diversity*, 254; Barrett, *On Paul*, 223; Esler, *Galatians*, 136–37; Chilton, "James, Peter, Paul," 6–7).

- the concern of those "from James" (and therefore, presumably, James himself) is with the essential maintenance of all the key purity boundary markers of Judaic identity in Eretz Israel (including the purity rules surrounding table fellowship) by Judaic members of the Antiochene ἐκκλησία. Incorporation of Gentiles into the Covenant People required their circumcision: it being assumed in any case that male Judaic genitalia were in ritually modified good order;

- table fellowship between Judaic and Gentile "followers of the Way" was not a problem in Judaic mono-cultural Jerusalem: neither was it in cosmopolitan Antioch—which is precisely what concerned the *Jakobusgemeinde* περιτομή!

8. Paul: Evaluation

Much commentary space is deservedly devoted to trying to identify who the teachers[142] of "a different gospel" (1:6) in Paul's communities in Galatia were. Many focus on a possible Jerusalem connection. This is a valid form of mirror-reading that contributes to the hermeneutics of Galatians, but as it is heavily dependent on the very evidence that is the focus of our concern here we must be cautious in our judgment.

However, the evident fact that Paul's experience with Jerusalem and at Antioch is so germane to the current situation in Galatia, centering on the same demand for circumcision (2:3–9 and 5.2–6; 6.12), with the same watchwords of "freedom," "standing firm," "no submission to the yoke of slavery" (2:4–5 and 4:31—5:1, 13), makes it certain that these teachers of "a different gospel" (1:6), whoever they might be, are in close sympathy with channels of thought and concerns that find strong expression within the *Jakobusgemeinde*.[143] Therefore we may assume that Paul's dialogue (albeit at a distance) with these teachers resonates with debates within the broader proto-Christian Movement.

This debate is fully within the boundaries of late Second Temple Judaism. The significance of Christ's coming and redeeming death, along with the Galatians' experience of the Spirit in response to that message is completely embedded, explicated and contextualized within the *Heilsgechichte* of God's covenant people to demonstrate that "in Christ Jesus the blessing of

---

142. J. Louis Martyn advocates the use of the description "Teachers" as a replacement for value laden terms such as "agitators," "Judaizers" and "opponents." They are separate from and independent of Paul and his mission. Martyn, *Galatians*, 117–26.

143. De Boer, "New Preachers in Galatia," 39–60.

Abraham might come to the Gentiles, so that we might receive the promise of the Spirit through faith" (3:14).

No matter how Paul might have preached and argued his message with thoroughgoing pagans, when debating with those of the περιτομή, as well as those of broader sympathies within the *Jakobusgemeinde*, Paul, grounded in Pharisaism, was thoroughly conversant with and literate in contemporary Judaic hermeneutics. The proto-Christian Movement and its various groupings (including the Pauline ἐκκλησίαι) were vital explorations and expressions of a common Judaic inheritance—a family relationship they shared—within the world of Imperial Rome. That shared sphere of discourse is the symbolic world also, crucially, of James and the *Jakobusgemeinde*.

Standing back a little from Paul's story in these opening chapters of Galatians one becomes aware of a little remarked feature of this narrative—that, both "before" and "after," Paul defines himself in relationship to the *Jakobusgemeinde*.

In his "earlier life in Judaism" he was a persecutor of "τὴν ἐκκλησίαν τοῦ Θεοῦ" (1:13), specifically "ταῖς ἐκκλησίαις of Judea that are in Christ" (1:22). We must not overlook the significance of this—Paul's first encounter with the proto-Christian message was the *kerygma* of the *Jakobusgemeinde*, a message he heard and reacted against. Then at this later time he struggles with affirming his independence of "human authorities" (1:1; also 1:11–12, 16–17)—the *Jakobusgemeinde* and its leadership—whilst simultaneously having to own a need for their approval and support (2:2, 6–9). There is continuity as well as discontinuity in this relationship. From a position of open hostility to the *Jakobusgemeinde* he comes "on side" but then (in the eyes at least of some in that community, as exemplified by the ψευδαδέλφοι) began to challenge them from within—in some eyes, a more insidious danger.

Similarly, his mission "to proclaim (Christ) among the Gentiles" (1:16) with its message in these "last days" (1:2; 4:4–7; 5:5) of inclusion of Gentiles into the covenant people of God (3:25–29) without submission to the rite of circumcision (5:6) had to be defined, developed and defended *vis-à-vis* the dominant, normative *tendenz* centering on James, Jerusalem and the *Jakobusgemeinde*. This message of πίστις Χριστοῦ (2:16) that we see polemically pressed in the Galatian situation is presented with greater care and breadth a few years later in writing "to all God's beloved in Rome" (Rom 1:7) where we catch a glimpse of Paul's continued tortured relationship with the *Jakobusgemeinde*. Referring to the completion of the collection for the "poor among the saints at Jerusalem" he emphasizes the indebtedness of Gentile believers to their Judaic parentage, whilst expressing a real fear for his life in how he will be received, especially by "the unbelievers in Judea" (Rom 15:25–33 § 5. 6.1).

What we have here is something akin to a parent/child relationship as adolescence supervenes: Paul cannot get away from his parentage, yet in the midst of affirming his independence he still needs the approval and acceptance of the parent—the *Jakobusgemeinde*—that he experiences as so suffocating.[144] Nothing proclaims the originating status and ongoing authority of the *Jakobusgemeinde* under the presidency of James with more conviction and clarity than the conflictual angst of this "least of all the apostles, unfit . . . because I persecuted τὴν ἐκκλησίαν τοῦ Θεοῦ"(1 Cor 15:9).

9. The *Jakobusgemeinde* through the Pauline Prism

Our interest however is not in Paul's theology *per se* but in the fragmentary glimpses he betrays of the life and self-understanding of that more established community—the *Jakobusgemeinde*:

- The proto-Christian movement in Jerusalem was well established and at home within the world of late Second Temple Judaism both in its beliefs, practice and self-understanding, reflecting some of the range of current Judaic responses to issues of Israelite self-identity (§§ 4. 6.4; 4. 7.3 Key Notes II and III).

- The central status and veneration of Jerusalem within the Judaic world, its position as the place of God's saving action and the residence of the "apostles," whose witness to the risen Christ is foundational to the proto-Christian movements, combine to underpin the unquestioned authority of the *Jakobusgemeinde* over the new movement—nowhere seen more clearly than in Paul's *angst* on the occasion of "the handshake" consultation (Gal 2.1–10; § 4. 5.3 Key Notes I; § 4. 8).

- James was a central originating figure in the *Jakobusgemeinde*. He is an openly recognized leader from the very earliest time, respected as "the Lord's brother" and probably as an "apostle" (Gal 1.19; § 4. 5.3 Key Notes I).

- The *Jakobusgemeinde* was of a size and age from our first encounters with it (Gal 1:18—2:10) to have needed and generated a significant level of organization with a legitimated leadership, following recognized Judaic structures (§ 4. 6.4 Key Notes II).

144. Dunn, "Relationship between Paul and Jerusalem," 461–78.

- That leadership was vested in the triumvirate of James, Cephas and John; with James able to assert an authority to which even Cephas had to yield (§§ 4. 5.3; 4. 6.4; 4. 7.3 Key Notes I, II, and III).

- From the time of the consultation which ended in the "handshake," and clearly from much earlier, James is the established leader and voice of the *Jakobusgemeinde* (Gal 2.6–9; § 4. 7.3 Key Notes III).

- The community was also large enough to reflect a range of opinion and debate, typical of contemporary Israelite discourse, particularly on issues of Judaic orthopraxis and identity (§ 4. 6.4 Key Notes II). Its size was sufficient for at least one identifiable grouping (οἱ ψευδαδέλφοι) to emerge—indicative of a significant minority position at that time within the *Jakobusgemeinde* on the key issue of the status of Gentiles responding to the Gospel in Antioch, probably reflecting the *Jakobusgemeinde's* self-understanding as within the broader movement of Judaic renewal and therefore with a degree of boundary porosity that was alien to Paul (§§ 4. 6.4; 4. 7.3 Key Notes II and III).

- The *Jakobusgemeinde* shared a sense of self-identity and common cause with the extending proto-Christian Movement, over which they exercised a degree of authority (§§ 4. 6.4; 4. 7.3 Key Notes II and III).

- Gentile circumcision was not an issue within the mono-cultural *Jakobusgemeinde* itself: circumcision of Jewish males could be assumed. The emergent practice in cosmopolitan Antioch raised a fresh issue, where the inclusion of Gentiles, as Gentiles, into a proto-Christian Movement understood as a "daughter" of the *Jakobusgemeinde,* was a destabilizing development. This concern for Judaic praxis in Eretz-Israel Antioch is suggestive of a strong nationalist sentiment developing within the *Jakobusgemeinde* community (§ 4. 7.3 Key Notes III).

- The core tradition around which Paul's *kerygma* is developed is grounded in that of the *Jakobusgemeinde* (§ 4. 5.3 Key Notes I; see § 7. 2–4).

Excursus: Cephas // Peter

Further to § 4. 6.1.4 *The Identity of Cephas:*

In his response to Bart Ehrman's "Cephas and Peter,"[145] Dale Allison sets out in tabular form "the *facts* about Cephas as related by Paul and the *traditions* about Peter as found in the canonical Gospels and Acts[146] (my italics):

I have made two modifications to Allison's table:

1. I have inverted Allison's columns to give priority to what he himself describes as "the facts about Cephas" as against "the traditions about Peter."

2. I have italicized the Lucan "traditions."

Cephas	Peter
1. His name means "Rock"	His name means "Rock"
2. The Lord appeared to him (Cephas) first (1 Cor 15.5)	*The Lord appeared to him (Simon) first (Luke 22.32; 24.34)*
3. He was a Jew and a prominent leader of the primitive Jerusalem community (Gal 1—2)	*He was a Jew and a prominent leader of the primitive Jerusalem community (Acts 1—15)*
4. He was associated with both James and John (Gal 2.9)	*He was associated with both James and John (Acts 3.1–26; 4.1–31; 8.14; 15.1–21)*
5. He participated in the Gentile mission (Gal 2; this is probably also implicit in 1 Corinthians)	*He participated in the Gentile mission (Acts 10—15)*
6. He was married (1 Cor 9.5)	He was married (Mark 1.30–31)
7. He was of fickle character (Gal. 2)	He was of fickle character (Mark 14)
8. He knew Paul personally (Gal 1—2)	*He knew Paul personally (Acts 15)*

145. Ehrman, "Cephas and Peter," 463–74.
146. Allison, "Peter and Cephas," 494–95.

Cephas	Peter
9. He was an itinerant missionary (1 Cor. 1.12; 3.22; 9.5; and Gal. 2.11, taken together, strongly imply this)	*He was an itinerant missionary (Acts 1—15)*
10. He came into conflict with Jerusalem Christians over eating with the uncircumcised (Gal. 2)	*He came into conflict with Jerusalem Christians over eating with the uncircumcised (Acts 11)*

Fig. 2 Cephas and Peter

Comment [References to Allison's list in brackets]:

1. That both names are rare (at that time) and carry the same meaning [1] is correct and the rock on which the almost universal tradition of their identity rests (if I may be excused the pun—and muse, further, if it could be a "stone of stumbling"?). But the fact that the most natural reading in our *only* contemporary evidence (Gal 2:7–9) is that they are different persons is equally fundamental.

2. To identify *Cephas/Peter* as a married [6] Jew [3] tells us nothing—the nascent Christian movement was of Judaic origin—in Palestine—and most adult male Jews would be married. That "he was of fickle character" [7] is a judgmental comment—the two situations indicated are very different, in neither case do we know anything of *Cephas/Peter's* intention and motivation, and in the earlier Markan incident *Peter* actually demonstrates considerable courage.

3. Crucially, most points of contact Allison identifies between the specifically Lucan tradition about *Peter* and Paul's references to *Cephas* cover more than they reveal:
   - In Gal 2:6–10 *Cephas* is part of the ruling triumvirate with James and John [4] whilst *Peter* is distinguished by Paul as active in leadership of the Judaic mission—a role akin to that ascribed to *Peter* in the Hellenist traditions included in Acts 8—9. *Peter* is described in Acts as becoming critically involved in the inception of the Gentile mission [5], though it records no instance of

him itinerating beyond Israel [9]; and whilst there is evidence in Paul's writings of *Cephas* traveling beyond Jerusalem and into the Diaspora [9], there is no evidence of him extending his commitment beyond the Judaic mission clearly stated in Gal 2:9.

- There is a further lack of fit hiding under the rubric of "associated with" in the relationship portrayed between James and *Cephas/ Peter* [4]—the only occasion that James and *Peter* are on the stage together in Acts is at the Conference of Jerusalem (Acts 15) where there is no sense of *Peter* being along with James a "founding Pillar" of the community in the way Paul said of *Cephas* (Gal 2:9; 1 Cor 15:5). Rather, *Peter* appears before the presiding presence of James testifying to his apostolic experience in missioning, in a way that would fit the status and role of *Peter* in Gal 2:7–8 and the reports of his role in the Hellenistic traditions of Acts 8—9.

- Similarly, it is true that *Cephas* and Paul knew each other personally (Gal 1:18; 2:9) [8]; but in Acts Paul and *Peter* are only on the stage together in that same Conference, and then only as fellow witnesses—a relationship that coheres more with *Peter* in Gal 2:7–8 than the intense face-to-face relationship of Paul with *Cephas* in Gal 1.18; 2:9.

- The issue surrounding table fellowship [10] was a widespread problem in the early decades and not unique to *Cephas/Peter*. Although there is the same purity context in the events at Antioch (Gal 2) and Caesarea (Acts 11), the situations and the outcomes could hardly be more different—at Antioch *Cephas* has to give way to the demands from Jerusalem causing a serious split with Paul who is left out in the cold, whereas *Peter's* initiative at Caesarea is ratified by the ensuing Conference, including an endorsement of Paul's Gentile mission.

4. The occurrence and distinction of the names of *Cephas* and *Simon* as privileged with the first resurrection appearance [2] may reflect Jerusalem- and Galilee-based traditions, with the added factor of a time lapse of nearly half a century.

In brief, when we focus on Allison's specific points of contact between *Peter* in the Lucan tradition and information about *Cephas* in Paul's writings, we consistently find more distance than similarity highlighted. Furthermore, apart from the "early days" narrative in Acts 1—5 there is significant consonance between the *Peter* of Acts 8—15 and the Pauline *Peter* of Gal 2:7–8. The (bi-lingual?) early proto-Christian movement may have used *Cephas* and *Peter* rather to distinguish two persons sharing the same nickname (and nicknames tend not to appear in the epigraphic and literary sites that are our main source of information about naming patterns in ancient societies).

Allison's paper provides a valuable focus for discussion—he specifically disowns the word "proof" for the parallels he offers—I suggest they support a different conclusion from the consensus he defends.

In a much earlier paper, Donald Riddle[147] had suggested a process to explain how the names of *Cephas* and *Peter* had merged, which Allison effectively demolished.[148] However, if we can extricate Riddles' argument from the thoroughgoing, but very dated, form-critical framework within which it is embedded it may point a way forward. Riddles focused on the key significance of names in the oral transmission of traditions, with stories and sayings becoming transferred from their original source to a more central figure (what I termed the "gestalt effect"— § 1. 4.1.1). The problem in differentiating and identifying the gathering of Mary's at the foot of the Cross demonstrates the ease with which confusion and uncertainty easily surrounds who is who in the process of oral transmission. In the Lucan identification of *Simon* as recipient of the first resurrection appearance [2] we may be seeing this process approaching its final phase.

A simpler solution to the fusion of the two names that starts to be found in later writings, such as John 1:42 [though not in the contemporaneous *1 Clement* (c. 95 CE)][149], may be that it followed on from the circulation of Luke's history with its strong focus on Peter in his foundation myth of the Jerusalem Church (Acts 1—5) § 9.

147. Riddle, "Cephas-Peter Problem," 169–80.
148. Ibid., 495.
149. *1 Clement* 5:4 and 47:3.

5

Tradition and Memories: Acts

LUKE'S WRITING IS ALTOGETHER more complex than Paul with a medley of voices exhibiting both harmony and discord.

1. Listening to Acts

"Acts is a History"[1]—the indefinite article in Pervo's sentence, whilst hinting at a "more than," underlines the qualitative difference between Acts and the letters of Paul.[2] Not only is this the difference between fervent outpourings in the heat of battle contrasted with a carefully constructed literary text, but also the testimony of Acts concerning James comes from a significantly later time than Paul and is that of a narrator, rather than a key participant. It reflects the issues and concerns of that later day.[3] *Acts of the Apostles* was probably written towards the end of the first or early in the second century, and bears witness to a stream of tradition at least a generation after Paul's death and forty or more years later than the latter's scorching self-defense to his ἐκκλησίαι in Galatia.[4]

1. Pervo, *Acts*, 15.

2. Full discussion on the issues of genre, style, sources, structure and historicity are in the standard commentaries: Bruce, *Acts of the Apostles*, 15–18, 29–34; Barrett, *Acts of the Apostles*, xxxiii-xlii; Pervo, *Acts*, 14–18. For a summary, see Powell, *What Are They Saying*, 9–13; Bernheim, *James*, 130–48. Regev, "Temple Concerns and High-Priestly Prosecutions," neatly summarizes divergent scholarly evaluation: "One is left to wonder whether to regard Luke's competence as a historian as an indication of his reliability, or of his rhetorical skill," 70.

3. Mason, *Josephus*, 194–201.

4. There has been a fair degree of consensus amongst scholars for a date in the latter

This time-lapse factor of a couple of generations also highlights an important distinction in the nature of this testimony contrasted with that of Paul: the latter has the immediacy that our generation accords to a live video-tape of a participant in the action, whilst the former has a family relationship with our present day historical documentary, bringing together memories and traditions, individual and communal, illustrated with flickering black and white images from earlier times. It is sometimes enlivened by dramatization, along with improved definition for more recent events. The whole is researched, selected, contextualized, composed and interpreted by the writer/producer.[5]

> The writing of history is a reconstructive rather than descriptive task, so its truth depends not on the factuality of the events recounted (although historians should keep to the facts) but on the interpretation that the historian gives to a reality that is always open to a plurality of interpretive options.[6]

Luke's theme is the growth of the early Christian movement, under God, from its origins within Judaism, the Galilean "Jesus movement," and Jerusalem to a developing network of dominantly Gentile communities symbolized by their presence in Rome[7]—a theme most clearly present in the linking and placement of traditions, the connecting narratives, and (consistent with accepted historiographical practice in the classical world) the content of speeches.[8]

years of the first century for the writing of Acts, typically c. 80–85 CE (Powell, *What Are They Saying*, 36–37; Barrett, *Acts of the Apostles*, xlii; James Dunn records the "current consensus" as "the 80s or early 90s" (Dunn, *Beginning from Jerusalem*, 67). A recent significant critique is Pervo, *Dating Acts*; see also his *Acts*, 5–7; Tyson, *Marcion and Luke-Acts*.

5. This remains true even if Luke is using the tantalizing "we" to indicate his presence in some of the events narrated, a suggestion discounted by many scholars who consider it either an indication of a source close to Paul or as a stylistic feature of Luke's writing. See Powell, *What Are They Saying*, 32–26; Barrett, *Acts of the Apostles*, xxvii; Doble, Review of *The "We" Passages*. That "(the) we-sections are unedited first-hand reminiscence by the author of Acts" is vigorously defended by Gilchrist in an (unpublished) paper presented at the 2009 Conference of the British New Testament Society at Aberdeen University.

6. Gregory, Review of *First Christian Historian*, 67.

7. It is in discussing how this clear theme fits into our conception of Luke's purpose in writing (i.e., the genre of the writing)—irenic, polemical, apologetic, evangelistic, pastoral, theological (Powell, *What Are They Saying*, 13–19)—that the world of Lucan scholarship divides. Gasque, *History of the Interpretation*, 305.

8. Building on observations of Horsley and Hemer (Horsley, "Speeches and Dialogue in Acts") Pervo, "Direct Speech in Acts," (285) asserts that "direct speech is one characteristic of popular literature and that, in this respect, Acts is more like popular

It is written a generation after the cataclysm of the Jewish War of 66–73 CE, the destruction of the Temple and the devastation of Jerusalem. It is written for a developing Christian movement in the Gentile world of the Diaspora whose normative membership is increasingly Gentile. It is a community emerging from a Judaic embryo, following the demise of the *Jakobusgemeinde* after the Revolution, which has a need for confidence in its own self-identity, especially in a world suspicious of its Jewish roots.[9]

Acts thus focuses its story on Peter and Paul—"the greatest and most righteous pillars" of the church (1 Clem 5:1–6).[10] It is a text in which the absence of James is more noteworthy than his presence.

2. Luke as Redactor

2.1 The Sound of Distant Drums

Despite the much more limited extent of tradition material available to Luke for his writing of Acts, compared with the Jesus material for his Gospel, we do nonetheless hear "the sound of distant drums" beneath the super-imposed narrative. These traces of tradition need to be listened to free (if possible) of their Lucan redaction, especially where inconsistency with the overriding theme is detected. Such dissonance can alert us to memories that had no perceived relevance to the Redactor who therefore uncritically "delivers" what he has "received."[11] At the same time they can serve to high-light the issues, concerns and message of Luke from within the text of Acts. Anomalies, dissonance and aporiae between those remembered stories and their redactional framing assume significance both for our assessment of those traditions and for alerting us to the redactor's method and theme.

2.2 A Portfolio of Traditions

Luke has used traditions of differing quality and provenance: for example, Martin Dibelius's contrast remains valid that in chapters 13—21 Luke has a sequential story involving a travel itinerary, whereas in chapters 1—12 he

---

narrative than learned historiography." Also, Mason, *Josephus*, 196–97.

9. Mason, *Josephus*, 197.

10. Later in the same letter (1 Clem 47:3) Clement, in an allusion to 1 Cor 1:12, refers to Cephas. Unlike John 1:42, from a broadly similar period, Clement does not link the two names together. Nienhuis, *Not by Paul Alone*, 20.

11. Customary terminology for the transmission of tradition, e.g., 1 Cor 11:23, 15:3.

has isolated stories of individuals and events, with Luke himself supplying the framework through his linking verses.[12]

A summary overview of Acts, using Luke's own organizing structure (Acts 1:8), does betray a distinct correlation in the balance typically occurring between received tradition and Lucan redaction/authorship:

- The Pauline Narrative (Acts 13 onwards):

  There is wide recognition that the Lucan narrative focusing on Paul includes roots in Pauline tradition. This statement is valid whether (as typified by Barrett[13]) we date Acts in the later first century with the ascription of no knowledge of Paul's writings but with material coming from sources close to Paul; or thirty years later,[14] and arguing for knowledge of Paul's letters.

- The Hellenist Mission (Acts 6—12):

  Luke is at a greater historical distance from the traditions at his disposal in the first half of Acts.[15] The reference to Paul and his party spending time with "Philip the evangelist who was one of the seven" (Acts 21:8–9) strongly hints at the provenance of some of Luke's material. Several cycles of tradition ("Petrine," "Stephen/Philip," "Antiochene"), suggestive of a source within the Hellenist Mission, have been identified—but their structuring and relationship is provided by Luke.[16]

- Early Days in Jerusalem (Acts 1—5):

  The effort of Adolf von Harnack a century ago to establish the presence of sources behind the opening chapters of Acts (e.g., in the doublet of Acts 2:1–12 and 4:31) has largely received the scholastic verdict of "not proven."[17] For the early days in Jerusalem, Pervo observed that "Even Ramsay regarded Acts 1—5 as largely legendary,"[18] concurring with Dibelius who noted that stories such as the healing of the cripple

12. Dibelius, *Studies in the Acts of the Apostles*, 126.

13. That Acts as a whole was written by one of Paul's immediate circle is very difficult to believe, that the author . . . was able to draw on one or two sources derived from that circle . . . is probable." Barrett, *Acts of the Apostles,* xxviii–xxix; Marshall, "New Consensus," 192.

14. Pervo, *Dating Acts*; Pervo, *Acts,* 5–7.

15. Dibelius, *Studies in Acts,* 105–06.

16. Hengel, *Acts,* 65–66; Hengel, *Between Jesus and Paul,* 4.

17. Harnack, *Acts of the Apostles,* 175–86.

18. Pervo, *Profit With Delight,* 130 n.100, citing Ramsay, *St Paul the Traveller,* 367–72.

(Acts 3:1–10) were in the form typical of the healing miracle, lacking the specificity of Luke's later material in Acts. They are (in form-critical terms) *"legend"* that he has had to build and link together to illustrate his thesis that all was under the control of God.[19] Dibelius further made the perceptive observation that the individual stories are older than Luke's connecting summaries, leading to the paradox that when Luke writes as a historian—seeing links, etc.—he diverges from the tradition.[20] Thus when Acts presents itself as "history" it is least "historical."

Dominated by Peter, these early stories function as the Lucan "foundation myth" of the birth of the Christian movement and are of limited historical value: they speak rather to the needs of his hearers in the emergent Gentile church at the end of the first century (§ 9.).

In general, given Luke's practice of respecting the traditions that are available to him, known from his handling of gospel material, the gaps, inconsistencies and signs of "humps and hollows"[21] remaining in his narrative definitively indicate the presence of a fragmentary level of source material of varied quality available to him, with Luke himself providing the overarching framework (and filling out the narrative in places where his sources were sketchy or non-existent).

2.3 Orality to Literacy: Tradition in Process

In an oral culture, with very limited technology for the widespread production and dissemination of literature, it is not possible to draw a firm boundary line between the preservation and development of tradition by oral communication and its eventual incorporation into embryonic written form; although the latter does mark a distinctive new phase.[22]

Thus a demarcation of tradition and redaction is no easy matter in Acts—we lack the necessary controls but that does not excuse us the task of sensitively tuning in to its narrative to hear the echoes of earlier days (from both original and later contexts) crackling through the ether, as well as Luke's formatting of them from within his later world. Both their

19. Dibelius, *Studies in Acts,* 102.

20. Ibid., 128.

21. I am indebted to Longenecker, "Lucan Aversion to Humps and Hollows," for drawing my attention to this phrase from Lucian of Samosata.

22. Kelber, *Oral and The Written Gospel*; DeConick, *Recovering the Original Gospel of Thomas,* 20–31, stressed that orality continued to function alongside literacy *and* to shape it; Rodriguez, "Reading and Hearing in Ancient Contexts," 169–70.

harmony and their dissonance are valuable data into the world of nascent Christianity, including the traditions keeping the memory of James and the *Jakobusgemeinde* alive. This is also the necessary prolegomena for assessing and valuing Luke's achievement as *author*.

3. Luke as Author

3.1 Beyond Redaction

The role of redaction in producing a work of literature goes beyond the faithful reproduction of tradition, suitably adapted for the perceived needs and interests of the intended audience, in the light of an overarching theme; and also beyond the linking together and framing of individual units or clusters (additional to links forged during the oral transmission process). It includes a degree of creativity, from modifications and developments to received tradition, through the structuring of units into a coherent pattern and setting, to the creation of narrative to bind, enhance and progress the whole product.

When there is a substantial body of communal memory, bolstered by and embedded within a strong, community-based oral tradition, as in the case of the Synoptic Gospels, the scope for such creativity is restricted. In the obverse case, with traditions few, fragmented and lacking an underpinning structure, the need for creative writing and imaginative narrative[23] moves beyond that we associate with the task of redaction to the point where the material demands that we view the writer as *Author*.[24]

The homogeneity of style throughout both the Gospel and Acts argues persuasively for a strong authorial direction, especially in this second volume where there are no previous related writings framing his structure and presentation. There is "a greater depth of original composition."[25] If in the Gospel Luke is *Redactor*: then in Acts he is, additionally, *Author*.[26]

---

23. Alexander, *Preface to Luke's Gospel*: 200. "(H)istorical accuracy . . . is not (and never was) coterminus with Greco-Roman historiography." Downing, "Ears to Hear," 97–121, however, cautions that "a contemporary Hellenistic audience would not expect a historian to make up incidents *de novo* to entertain or improve it." He appears not to take into account necessary authorial practice when source/tradition material is not available.

24. Pervo, *Profit With Delight*; Mason, "Chief Priests, Sadducees, Pharisees," 116–119).

25. Dibelius, *Studies in Acts*, 2.

26. Barrett, *Luke the Historian*, 27: "In the second volume, Luke is not merely a compiler of traditions, but an author." Pervo, *Acts*, 14: "In Acts, the author is, more than in the Gospel, the master of his sources." Dibelius, *Studies in Acts*, 103: "Luke's literary

3.2 The Lucan Counterpoint

Listening to Luke-in-Acts *is* a more complex task than listening to Paul-in-Paul—the difference between an orchestration and a solo. In listening to Acts we need to be sensitive to the counterpoint produced by the over-arching Lucan movement embracing melodic lines and phrases full of memory, generating both harmony and dissonance. That controlling Lucan statement, whilst using and foregrounding a medley of material (some evocatively nostalgic), provides the framework for the whole orchestration, at times asserting its own dominant theme, sometimes glorying in creative improvisation, but always providing the context within which its riffs and cadences are embedded, and it is those latter traces of earlier traditions, now blended into the broader composition that we need to be alert to.

Acts is *a* history—not principally as an account of "what happened" but a theological history, retrospectively identifying and highlighting the movement of God through the vicissitudes of human affairs.

What Theodore Weeden has written of the processes influencing the transmission of oral tradition would need little adaptation to describe Luke's task as a historian:

> The primary concern (of informal controlled oral tradition) is to preserve a community's social identification in its "present" consciousness—even if that means the alteration of its oral tradition, including the possible loss of authentic historical information related to the community's past history—in order to bring its oral tradition into congruency with the community's current self-understanding of its social identity, as well as to make its oral tradition congruently relevant in addressing the demands of new existential realities when they arise.[27]

---

and redactional activity is over all his material in Acts . . . a pioneer work of literature." Michael Goulder extends this descriptor to the Gospel of Luke as well: "I have spoken in this book of Lucan *creativity*, because I am proposing the thesis that Luke has written much of the Gospel himself, as against the standard view, where he is the *redactor*. . . . There is always a kernel of gospel tradition behind everything Luke writes: but it seems proper to speak of Luke as the author of the Luke 15 parable, and of his creativity rather than his editing." (italics original). Goulder, *Luke*, 1:123.

27. Weeden, "Kenneth Bailey's Theory," 37. Responded to by Dunn, "Kenneth Bailey's Theory"; Iverson, Review of *Structuring Early Christian Memory*, summarizes: "Rodriguez concludes that the dialectic between past and present as depicted in the Gospel traditions is inherent to all memory reconstruction and does not undermine the text's historical contribution" (44).

Such a process was not only embedded into the traditions Luke knew, it was also operative in its transmittance into writing.[28] We must take cognizance of the fact that in penning Acts, Luke was continuing this process of bringing this story of the beginnings of the Christian movement "into congruency with the community's self-understanding of its social identity" and was "addressing the demands of new existential realities," including the need for a certain distancing from the *Jakobusgemeinde* and re-evaluation of its origin "from Jerusalem" (§ 9.).

4. James in Acts

Luke exhibits an evident reluctance in speaking of James. Despite his status as an "acknowledged leader" in the *Jakobusgemeinde* (Gal 2:6–9) he occupies just eighteen verses of the text of Acts. There is also a passing mention of the mother and brothers of Jesus (without any names) as present in the Upper Room after the Ascension, but they are distinctly excluded from the Movement's leadership for the new situation (Acts 1:14, 21–23).

After looking at the first brief explicit reference to James (Acts 12:17), our approach will be to factor in his critical appearance on the occasion of Paul's final, fateful visit to Jerusalem (Acts 21:17–26), before a fuller consideration of the Jerusalem Conference (Acts 15:1–29)—the fulcrum around which Luke balances his story.

5. The Specter at the Door (Acts 12:17)

"James . . . is never introduced or identified in Acts. He just appears."[29]

The Lucan assumption seems to be that we all know who this James is after many pages filled largely with the heroic presence of Peter. In a story replete with Passover and Passion imagery,[30] and told with not a little humor, Peter, fleeing for his life after escaping from prison, is left knocking at the door which Rhoda (the maid) had in shock slammed in his face, to be told by the others that she was "seeing things."

---

28. The history of textual transmission demonstrates this as a continuing factor, certainly prior to the formulation and acceptance of the NT canon, and until the invention of printing. Epp (*Junia*) demonstrates that it can still be a factor in the modern age.

29. Eisenman, *James*, 97.

30. Pervo, *Profit with Delight*, 62–63; Pervo, *Acts*, 303–31.

When eventually admitted, his message was brief and to the point: "Tell this to James and to the ἀδελφοῖς."[31] With the exception of a brief appearance to testify at the Conference of Jerusalem, Peter is then abruptly dismissed as the central actor in the Lucan narrative: "He left and went to another place" (Acts 12:17).

It is common for commentators, with their eyes on Peter, to see in this verse an indication of how a transition of power within the *Jakobusgemeinde* came about: with Peter now permanently away, the stage was clear for the brother of Jesus to assume leadership (perhaps having had to keep a low profile in the dangerous period immediately following the execution of his brother).[32] In asking for the message to be given explicitly to James it is suggested that it involved a request (perhaps even a prior agreement) for James to take over the leadership in Peter's absence.[33]

This apparent surprising change of leadership thus results from James moving into the leadership vacuum caused by Peter's enforced exile from Jerusalem (an exile that did not prevent him from attending the Conference at Jerusalem). It is argued that the power and influence of James grew as that of Peter waned.[34] This is not convincing. The *Acts of the Apostles* presents the ἐκκλησία τοῦ Θεοῦ as a charismatic movement, originating in a charismatic explosion and centering around the charismatic personality of Peter. Charismatic leaders of charismatic movements do not suffer an erosion of status or a diminution of their charisma through exile—if anything, it is enhanced. Ayatollah Khomeini did not have to re-assert his leadership when he returned from exile to Tehran in 1979: he was acclaimed.

Surely, given Luke's earlier narrative, Peter's heir-apparent should have been the ever-present companion, John. We are told nothing about what happened to him—possibly because he has served Luke's purpose

---

31. The reference is probably to the community of believers—ἀδελφοί being a common Lucan descriptor. The possible reference to the *brothers* of Jesus is less likely, Luke would then have probably used ἀδελφοί αὐτοῦ. Painter, *Just James*, 43 and Hartin, *James of Jerusalem*, 53 express this alternative.

32. Bruce, *Galatians*, 121–22; Bauckham, "James and the Jerusalem Church," 431–41; Pervo, *Acts*, 374; Sim, *Matthew*, 81–82. Bruce Chilton adopts the variant position that Peter's increasing itinerancy created the space in Jerusalem for James "to become the natural head of the community there." Bruce Chilton, "Conclusions and Questions," 257; Bernheim, *James*, 202–12 provides a good overview.

33. Bruce's suggestion that Peter's words indicate James and Peter being leaders of different "house churches" in Jerusalem (Bruce, *Men and Movements*, 28, 88, 91; Bruce, *Galatians*, 99) has had few takers (Bauckham, "James and the Jerusalem Church" 440). It is also suspect as involving an anachronistic post-Reformation concept of ἐκκλησία as a "gathered congregation."

34. Bruce, *Men and Movements*, 90–92; Dunn, *Beginning from Jerusalem*, 1078–80; Bauckham, "James and the Jerusalem Church," 439–41.

of validating Peter's early dominant presence—or—given the importance Luke attaches to the Twelve in the opening scenes of Acts, one of the other original band of disciples. The "apostles" are described as still present in Jerusalem at the later Conference (Acts 15).

In fact, Luke both studiously avoids any suggestion of Peter being the President/*mebaqqer* of that early Jerusalem community, just as he later resists (Acts 15:13) any identification of James' status in that focal Conference, although it *is* clear from the narration. The name of James was still too well known to need identification, but Luke consistently declines any reinforcement of his position. He even attempts at the Conference to detract from that evident supremacy of James by describing Peter as giving his evidence and testimony first, apparently on his own initiative, rather than by invitation of its presiding figure (Acts 15:7).

James needs neither introduction, identification, nor justification, neither to the group in Mary's house, *nor to the reader*. It is simple fact that James is the unequivocally recognized leading figure of the ἐκκλησία τοῦ Θεοῦ in Jerusalem, even by Peter, and not simply by default following the latter's exile. This initial reference by Luke to James exemplifies by its brevity a feature that is also found on the other two occasions where James appears "on stage"—the Conference (Acts 15) and Paul's final visit (Acts 21). The towering authority of James cannot be overlooked, but Luke's presentation of him could hardly be more low-key. Memory and veneration of James was maintained long after the events of 62–70 CE, particularly amongst the traditions of "Jewish Christianity"[35]. This fitted ill with the Lucan evocation of the emergent Gentile Church: Luke cannot deny James, so he plays him in a very minor key.

The implication is clear—James was *from the earliest days* one of the leading figures (if not *the* leading figure) of the *Jakobusgemeinde*, a fact that was embarrassing for our author (§ 5. 9.3).

6. James and Paul—High Noon[36] (Acts 21:17–36)

Before questioning the Lucan story of this final, critical meeting between James and Paul it will be useful to review Paul's own understanding, his

---

35. I am using this term in a fairly conventional way to describe that spectrum of the church in the early centuries who continued to practice Torah as an essential part of their Christian faith. See Jackson-McCabe, *Jewish Christianity Reconsidered;* Skarsaune, "Jewish Believers in Jesus in Antiquity"; Skarsaune, "Jewish Believers in the Early Centuries," 747–49; and Paget, "Definition of the Terms," 22–54.

36. Echo of the classic 1950s Western film.

hopes and rising anxieties surrounding his collection project, as embedded in his writings at the time. It is the context which Luke knew (Acts 24:17), yet ignored—a response that cannot be open to us.

6.1 The Jerusalem Collection

That Paul saw his Gentile mission as integral with the faith and mission of the *Jakobusgemeinde* and wanted others (especially in Jerusalem) to view it also in that light is nowhere more clearly demonstrated than by the energy he poured into the project for a collection from his Gentile ἐκκλησίαι for the poor/saints in Jerusalem (1 Cor 16:1–4; 2 Cor 8–9; Rom 15:25–31).[37] He "put his head on the block" (metaphorically, and eventually literally) for this.[38]

I leave to one side questions of the precise relationship of this project to the rather low key request of the Jerusalem Pillars to "remember the poor" (Gal 1:10) on the occasion of the handshake. The collection's significance for Paul is variously expressed by scholars as expressing the unity of Gentile and Jewish Christians; legitimizing the Gentile mission; attempting to provoke the Jews into accepting the gospel out of envy for the Gentiles; an act of almsgiving replacing circumcision, or an act of patronage.[39] But the interpretation that has been most influential amongst scholars[40] is that of Dieter Georgi[41] that it was an eschatological demonstration to Jerusalem[42] of the nations bringing gifts to Zion in the Last Days.

Whatever the original understanding, Paul developed a rhetorical strategy and theological interpretation which lifted the collection to a new level of significance in his eyes which, whilst responding to "the initial expectations of the Jerusalem church to provide in the needs of their poor,"[43] at the same time was a new level of challenge to the *Jakobusgemeinde* during a period of increasing intra-Judaic nationalist sentiment and pressure. It

37. Barrett, *2 Corinthians*, 25–32.

38. "No one was more conscious of the profundity of the widening gap between those for whom Christ was central and those for whom he was not. Yet it was desperately important to fling across the abyss a fragile bridge of charity. He would risk all in the attempt." (Murphy-O'Connor, *Paul*, 343).

39. Joubert, *Paul as Benefactor*, 2–3.

40. Ibid., 3.

41. Georgi, *Remembering the Poor*.

42. Taylor, *Paul, Antioch and Jerusalem*, 215–16, notes that the collection might be seen as a demonstration of the success of his Gentile Mission, and "whatever primacy he recognized in the Jerusalem church, Paul was traveling to Jerusalem not in submission but in self-vindication."

43. Joubert, *Paul as Benefactor*, 7.

may even have been a challenge/invitation to the *Jakobusgemeinde* to come off the fence with a radically different understanding of the signs of the impending ἔσχατον, in the context of a Jerusalem gripped by ever increasing ethnic/nationalist fervor (§§ 2. 6.2; 4. 7.1).

In his correspondence with Corinth Paul initially used the word λογίας[44]—"collection for the saints" (1 Cor 16:1) that shortly became διακονία—"ministry to the saints" (2 Cor 8:4; 9:1, 12–13) "which will produce (in Jerusalem) thanksgiving to God through us" (2 Cor 9:11–14).[45] In writing to Rome it becomes more specific as a "ministry to . . . the poor among the saints at Jerusalem" (Rom 15:25–31, which must here denote at least the economically poor[46]).

Evidencing the developing theological superstructure now in Paul's mind as he prepares for this critical journey to the Holy City, he goes on to describe his activity in conveying the collection, whilst still a charitable act, as that of a "minister of Christ Jesus to the Gentiles in the priestly service of the gospel of God, so that the offering of the Gentiles may be acceptable, sanctified by the Holy Spirit" (Rom 15:16). Whether ἡ προσφορὰ τῶν ἐθνῶν refers to the monetary gift of the Gentiles, or (more probably) Paul's priestly offering of his Gentile converts,[47] it is a sign, pregnant with promise and challenge, that the dawn of the ἔσχατον be recognized as the nations come with their gifts to Zion.[48]

A shadow now falls across the scene. Writing to Corinth earlier the note of triumphalist expectation had been clear (2 Cor 9:13–15), and to those at Rome he is still writing with apparent confidence that:

44. Moffatt, *1 Corinthians*, 271. " . . . a term common in papyri and in inscriptions for religious funds raised to promote the worship of some god or temple."

45. Jones, "Rhetorical Criticism," 496–524.

46. This does not exclude the much-discussed possibility that "the Poor" was also a characteristic self-designation of the *Jakobusgemeinde*, as it was of the Qumran community and the later Christian Ebionites. See Betz, *Galatians*, 102; Bruce, *Galatians*, 126. But see O'Connor, *Paul*, 144.

47. Barrett, *Romans*, 275; Dodd, *Romans*, 230–31.

48. However, Joubert, *Paul as Benefactor*, 210, after noting the dynamic nature of Paul's conceptualization of the collection, argues that in facing the possibility of its rejection in Jerusalem, Paul finally (Rom 15:28) presents "(t)he delivery of the collection (as) the culmination of the agreement reached at the Jerusalem meeting a few years earlier." He concludes (contra Georgi and Munck): "(Paul) has no intention of turning the delivery of the collection into an eschatological pilgrimage of the nations to Jerusalem as a sign of the imminent end of the world. He also does not want to elicit a 'mass conversion' from the Judeans when they see Gentiles pouring into the Holy City with gifts."

> I am going to Jerusalem in a ministry to the saints . . . so, when I
> have completed this, and have delivered to them what has been
> collected . . . I know that . . . I will come in the fullness of the
> blessing of Christ. (Rom 15:25–29)

In his next words, however, a deep anxiety breaks surface, an anxiety that he may not have been able to share with his own ἐκκλησίαι:

> I appeal to you, brothers and sisters, by our Lord Jesus Christ
> and by the love of the Spirit, to join me in earnest prayer to God
> on my behalf, that I may be rescued from the unbelievers in Ju-
> dea, and that my ministry ["the offering of the Gentiles" (v.16)]
> to Jerusalem may be acceptable to the saints . . . (Rom 15:30–31)

Given the exuberance and flow of his language to his Corinthian ἐκκλησία we must doubt if this newly acknowledged anxiety about the Collection's reception in Jerusalem was significantly present, if at all, a year or so before writing this letter "to all God's beloved in Rome" (Rom 1:7) which, if the final chapter is indeed integral to the original epistle, contained a good number of people with whom he was not only acquainted but had been colleagues in his apostolic work. It is to such as these that he requests "earnest prayer." Paul has become very aware of a changed atmosphere in Jerusalem from the days when he was able to go there as a delegate from Antioch.[49] His reception, even by the *Jakobusgemeinde*, is very uncertain—though we should note that there is not the slightest hint of any strain in his relationship with James himself.

A further small but significant shift of language in this request for prayer is Paul's slippage from third to first person in his description of the collection project—it is no longer τῆς λογίας (1 Cor 16:1) or τῆς διακονίας (2 Cor 9:1) but ἡ διακονία μου.

The coincidence of the emergence into the open of this deep anxiety relating to his reception in Jerusalem and the culmination of the theological superstructure he imposed on the collection project (now "*my* ministry"), reaching its apex in his self-description as "a minister of Christ Jesus to the Gentiles in the priestly service of the gospel of God" (Rom 15:16),[50] strongly suggests a process of cognitive dissonance reduction whereby the stakes are raised (the heightening significance of the project) to offset the increasingly apparent threat (death?) that was one realistic possibility.

---

49. Schoeps, "Ebionite Christianity," 219.

50. Downs, "Offering of the Gentiles," 173–86. "Paul frames 'the offering of the Gentiles' as an act of cultic worship."

We are face-to-face, now at a critical level, with the tension between Paul's strong sense of his personal apostolic calling over against his recognition of the primacy of James and the *Jakobusgemeinde*; and between the autonomy of his Gentile mission over against an associated conviction of belonging together "in Christ" (as he would have phrased it) with the *Jakobusgemeinde*. It is a tension implicit also in the programmatic summary of his apostolate as extending "from Jerusalem and as far around as Illyricum" (Rom 15:19)—true geographically, historically *and* theologically, for the traditions on which he earthed his "gospel" were those of the *Jakobusgemeinde*, whilst his interpretative development was forged well outside that city's walls.

But now Paul has become aware of significant and dangerous opposition to him within Jerusalem, especially as he was bringing the gifts of Gentiles to the City of Zion, accompanied by their (Gentile) representatives. These were the days when nationalist sentiment was building up tension in the City, which eventually focused on the issue of Gentile gifts, for it was to be the refusal of Caesar's offering to the Temple that sparked the War of 66–70 CE within a decade,[51] Paul cannot even be sure of his reception by the *Jakobusgemeinde*—"pray . . . that my ministry to Jerusalem may be acceptable to the saints" (Rom 15:31).

Conditioned by his missioning experience in the diaspora where his ἐκκλησίαι seem to be largely distinct from their συναγωγαί of origin, Paul distinguishes between the "unbelievers" and the "saints." The reality on the ground in Jerusalem was different: as early as his Galatian letter, Paul had difficulties with this—he could not envision the περιτομή as authentically part of the *Jakobusgemeinde*—they were ψευδαδέλφοι. Paul is working with a different frame of reference.

Who then are "the unbelievers in Judea"? Barrett is crystal clear—"non-Christian Jews are meant,"[52] others finger the ψευδαδέλφοι of Galatians 2, or simply "the extreme elements in Jewish Christianity."[53]

All these suggestions create problems if we persist in thinking of "the saints at Jerusalem" (Paul's descriptor in Rom 15:26) as the Jerusalem *Church*—a term loaded by later Christian developments and theology. Recalling the dominant *Gemeinschaft* nature of first century society it is likely that, whilst the *Jakobusgemeinde* acknowledged an integral linkage with the growing proto-Christian movements (as evidenced by its intervention at Antioch, and possibly in Galatia and Corinth), its primary self-identification

---

51. The war of 66 CE was triggered by the refusal to accept the emperor's gift for sacrifice (*J.W.* 2.409–10).

52. Barrett, *Romans*, 279.

53. Dodd, *Romans*, 236.

remained within the family of renewal groups that flourished in late Second Temple Judaism. The *Jakobusgemeinde* was an integrated part of the total Judaic community within Judea, albeit with a distinctive stress on the significance of the death of their leader's brother. But this element was well within the bounds of Judaic covenant faith (unlike, by common report, the boundary-breaking advocacy of Paul). Indeed, the contextualization of that brother's death as a sign of the impending ἔσχατον was substantially consonant with rising nationalist sentiment, which, in the decades prior to the war of 66–73 CE, looked to the ἔσχατον as imminent, involving the liberation and purification of the City and Temple.[54]

The "unbelievers in Judea" therefore are those who don't see things Paul's way—those both within the *Jakobusgemeinde* and beyond who are profoundly troubled by reports of Paul's preaching and praxis, seeing it as a fundamental betrayal of their covenantal community. Distorted and misinformed though their perceptions of Paul might be, there would be a wide swathe of opinion throughout the city on a continuum from profound unease to contemplation of assassination as a pious duty (following the example of Phinehas). This pattern of thinking would flow across any incipient *Jakobusgemeinde* boundary, with an increasing proportion viewing Paul (in Thatcherite terminology) as "the enemy within."[55] Not only "the unbelievers" but "the saints" also might find his presence and that of his Gentile companions unacceptable, and for much the same reason.

Whereas Paul maintained a primary identity for his ἐκκλησίαι that transcended ethnic (and other) boundaries—"in Christ"[56]—the *Jakobusgemeinde* maintained a self-identity fashioned within Torah-observant Judaism (§ 5. 9.1). The περιτομή could live with that, and the *Jakobusgemeinde* could live with the περιτομή. To bring a gift from Gentiles in the strengthening nationalism of the late 50s CE was courageous, even foolhardy: to accept it might strain the cohesion of the *Jakobusgemeinde* to breaking point, in addition to the broader reverberations throughout the City.

Jacob Taubes, for example, describes the gifts being brought by Paul from his Gentile ἐκκλησίαι as "a tainted business":

> When it gets around that they received from Paul, that will in
> the first place be a legitimation of Paul's position, and the Jewish

---

54. E.g., the inscription on coinage in the revolutionary wars of 66 CE and 132 CE proclaim "Jerusalem is holy"; "Jerusalem the holy"; "Freedom of Zion"; "Of the Redemption of Zion"; "Of the freedom of Jerusalem" (Schurer, *History,* 1:605–06).

55. Eisenman, *James*, 221. The identity of Paul as "the enemy" in the later Jewish-Christian Pseudo-Clementine *Recognitions* could possibly have originated within the *Jakobusgemeinde*.

56. Asano, *Galatians*.

Christian groups will then pull the plug, the groups, that is, who are the constant support for the Jerusalem congregations.[57]

Paul's anxiety over his reception in Jerusalem not only illuminates our understanding of the *Jakobusgemeinde*'s self-understanding primarily within the movements for the restoration of Israel (Acts 1:6–7), but also of the changing ethos within their community in that period.

6.2 The Meeting

Returning to Acts—on the occasion of Paul's final visit to Jerusalem we encounter James and the *Jakobusgemeinde* for the last time in Luke's narrative (Acts 21:17–36). As with all such occasions—in this case the final meeting of the *mebaqqer* of the *Jakobusgemeinde* with the Apostle to the Gentiles—there is much debate about its historicity, especially the silence which surrounds the collection, the reason for Paul's visit (Rom 15:22–31; Acts 21:10–14). Contra Pervo's scepticism which centers on the repetition of themes from Acts 15[58], I consider that blended into the Lucan authorial themes in this scene there is evidence both of Luke's care with (1) "apostolic actualization" (§ 5. 7.): and (2) an echo of tradition-material:[59]

1. The issue of "Torah/Temple/gifts from Gentiles" in Jerusalem is consistent with what we know from Josephus about the sensitivities surrounding rising nationalism there in the years prior to 66 CE; and the hostility and accusations emanating from pilgrims from Asia is precisely what we might expect from some of the things we know Paul wrote to his followers in that part of the world (Gal 5:2–6, 12; 6:15; Phil 3:2–8);

2. Although possibly enabling Luke to finally re-affirm the Torah-faithfulness of Paul, the compromise proposal of James is awkward and irrelevant for dealing with the allegations of the Asian pilgrims. For example, if Luke had wanted a culminating example of his "rejection by Jews" thesis in Jerusalem itself (resulting in new opportunities in Rome), he only needed the Temple riot of vv. 27–36, or, simpler, a straightforward rejection of the collection. Further, if the Jacobean strategy were a Lucan authorial device it is left high and dry by

---

57. Taubes, *Political Theology of Paul*, 17–21.

58. Pervo, *Acts*, 542–43.

59. Lüdemann, *Early Christianity*, 230–37.

the pressure of events and the *vox populi* that takes over Luke's own narration.

The story telling is thus distinctively rough at the edges, but its central scenario is totally in tune with the *modus operandi* established a decade earlier (Gal 2:7–10):

> Luke's account in Acts 21:19 portrays Paul as the successful missionary to the Gentiles, reporting back to the Jerusalem church which is described as undertaking a successful mission to the Jews, a mission based on the acceptance of the demands of the Jewish law (Acts 21.20).[60]

6.3 Exit the *Jakobusgemeinde*

This final meeting of two of the most important names in early Christianity includes a fleeting glimpse of the *Jakobusgemeinde* that exhibits consonance not only with earlier Lucan portrayal and Paul's own Galatian writing, but also with the indication of a changing atmosphere in Jerusalem that we traced in Paul's references in his letters to the "collection for the poor at Jerusalem."

Confirmed is:

- the growth of the *Jakobusgemeinde* to a numerically significant size— "many thousands" (Acts 21:20). Allowing for the Lucan appetite to inflate numbers and the probability that James' enumeration of those "zealous for the Law" may be embracing a wider range of Judaic Reform fellow-travelers, the *Jakobusgemeinde kerygma* was finding a responsive audience in and around the City.

- the *Jakobusgemeinde* as large enough to embrace a range of views (§ 4.6.2). But the περιτομή, who, as a minority group, could be overridden earlier by the leadership (whether the Pauline "Pillars" or the Lucan "James, the apostles and the elders") is now in the clear ascendancy to the extent that the Jerusalem leadership have to resort to risky strategies (Paul and the four Nazirites) in an attempt to de-fuse the situation. Luke had prepared us for this by referring to the increased number of Pharisees in the movement at the time of the Conference (Acts 15:5). "You see, brother, how many thousands of believers there are among the Jews, and they are all zealous for the law." (Acts 21:20).

---

60. Painter, *Just James*, 55; cf., Pervo, *Acts*, 543.

- the *Jakobusgemeinde as* a Torah-observant community, but with increased intensity of concern over the maintenance of the boundary-marker of circumcision (§ *5. 9.1*) which may be a product of the increasingly nationalist sentiment on the streets of Jerusalem in the period leading up to the rebellion of 66 CE (§ 2. 6.2).[61]

- the *Jakobusgemeinde*-approved Gentile missions (especially that of Paul) who, along with the changing nature of diasporan based proto-Christian movements and known to have links with James, were undoubtedly muddying the water in Jerusalem and probably exacerbating tension on the issue. Luke takes care, by his reference to the Conference encyclical (Acts 21:25; cf. 15:19–29) to make it clear that the issue at stake is not Gentile believers in the Diaspora but the allegations current that Paul was persuading Jewish converts in his ἐκκλησίαι to turn their back on the Torah and not to circumcise their (Jewish) children. The affirmation of the Conference Concordat certainly looks like Lucan redaction but the format—"We have sent a letter with our judgment" (Acts 21:25)—is distinctly odd if Paul had been a Conference participant. It may derive from a tradition in which Paul was not at the Jerusalem Conference,[62] but Luke engages it to re-enforce the Torah-centeredness of the *Jakobusgemeinde*.

However, Luke's description of the welcome accorded him (Acts 21:17–20) is suspect of Lucan redaction[63] for it is in tension with the anxiety Paul expresses about his coming reception in Jerusalem (Rom 15:31) which did in actuality fulfill his worst fear.[64] If Paul did receive the welcome Luke records, it could be that James and significant proportion of the Elders were striving to maintain against the stream an earlier more open tradition.

6.4 A Charged Atmosphere

Paul was very anxious about his reception in Jerusalem, having become aware of changes in the atmosphere of the City that boded ill for his visit (Rom 15:30–31). The boiling pot begins to spill over with allegations about Paul, initially rumored (Acts 21:21), rapidly becoming specifically by "the

---

61. Bruce, *Men and Movements*, 97–107.

62. Barrett, *Acts of the Apostles*, 1014.

63. Lüdemann, *Early Christianity*, 231–32.

64. Consonant with his hard distinction between "Christian Judaism" and "Gentile Christianity," Sim, *Matthew*, 93, infers from the Antioch Incident that "James himself . . . stood largely or completely in agreement with this περιτομή party as well."

Jews from Asia" (Acts 21:27)—the very province where Paul had long worked, centered on Ephesus. They are clearly not Judaic members of a Pauline ἐκκλησία but simply and solely diasporan Jews on pilgrimage to their Holy City. *Paul is not seen as the preacher of a new religion but as a fellow Jew who is betraying the faith of Israel.*

Through its association with him, the *Jakobusgemeinde* was in danger of being tarred with the same brush as Paul. The *Jakobusgemeinde* did not see itself, *nor was it seen by its compatriots*, as a new religion, albeit rooted in Judaism; nor as a somewhat deviant cult within Judaism—tolerated but largely irrelevant; nor was it (to use a theological anachronism) a "gathered Church" or "gathered Congregation." As a growing movement with a self-identity, disciplined structure and respected leadership, the position of James and his people on such issues as περιτομή and relationships with Gentiles was critical for their future. The *Jakobusgemeinde* was a vibrant movement *within* the mainstream of Judaic reform and restoration hopes that was such a lively element in the street-culture of Jerusalem under the Imperial heel.

6.4.1 A Rubicon Moment

It was as a result of being thus embedded within the flow of Jerusalem life in the years leading up to 66 CE that the *Jakobusgemeinde* was inexorably being caught up with the general sentiment of the times.[65] Coherent with this rising tide of nationalism is the Jacobean policy of the primacy of the Judaic mission for the renewal and restoration of Israel (Gal 2:7–10; Acts 15:13–29) to "rebuild the dwelling of David" (Acts 15:16), with the significant growth of the *Jakobusgemeinde* that was occurring, clearly seen as an affirmation of this policy (Acts 21:20).[66] This was accompanied by a growing exclusivity that was threatening an earlier established practice of tolerance and accommodation to some of the developments occurring in the proto-Christian movement beyond Judea (Acts 7—12) and in the Diaspora (Acts 13—20) (§ 4. 7.2): an expression of a commitment to "zeal for the Law" (Acts 21:20) that was to bind the *Jakobusgemeinde* to the ultimate fate of the City.

Thus, in the immediate situation, to welcome Paul *and* receive his gift from Gentiles would be seen in Jerusalem as a fundamental act of

---

65. Bruce, *Men and Movements*, 97–107.

66. Butz, *Brother of Jesus*, 87: " . . . almost as if the elders of the Jewish Christians are trying to top Paul's achievement after he relates his great success amongst the Gentiles."

betrayal—seen not only so on the streets, but felt as such by many within the *Jakobusgemeinde* itself.

It was a rubicon moment for James and the *Jakobusgemeinde*.[67]

6.5 The Collection Silence

Our story of James seems to be littered with silences that have to provoke comment. In addition to the silence that reverberates round the person and role of James himself, there is this silence of Luke about the reception accorded Paul's collection, despite Luke betraying awareness of the collection itself (Acts 24:17).[68] It was the principal reason for Paul's visit, despite its dangers (Rom 15:25–32).

We simply do not know what happened to the collection. Speculation is our only recourse, and "it is hard to shake off the suspicion that the collection was *not* welcomed and possibly not even received by the Jerusalem church" (italics original).[69]

It seems most probable that Paul's collection was not received in Jerusalem in the way that he had hoped or with the significance that he intended—a thank-offering from the Gentiles, a peace-offering to heal the widening gulf between the Judaic and the Gentile Mission, the acceptance of his Gentile Mission as a sign of the inbreaking ἔσχατον, and of his Gentile converts as part of God's covenant people. The *Jakobusgemeinde* was not so much turning in on itself but turning with a narrowing focus to the vision of an exclusively renewed and restored Israel.[70] It was a vision and aspiration shared by (in current journalese) both "conservative," "moderate," and "liberal."[71]

---

67. As it would be also for Paul and his ἐκκλησίαι. (n.71 below); to which could be added, "and for the future of Christianity."

68. David Downs argues that Luke did not know of Paul's collection—Downs, "Paul's Collection Revisited." We must not import material from Paul's letters into Acts.

69. Dunn, *Beginning from Jerusalem*, 970–72; Downs, "Paul's Collection Revisited," 68; Painter, "James and Peter," 162; Bernheim, *James*, 187–90; Martin, *James*, xxxvii.

70. Bruce, *Men and Movements*, 105–08; Lüdemann, *Early Christianity*, 236–37; Pervo, *Acts*, 546–47

71. The question must also be raised about the effect on the Pauline ἐκκλησίαι on receiving news that their gifts had been rejected, if that is what occurred. May this have initiated a feeling of righteous indignation, developing into a sense of alienation from James and the *Jakobusgemeinde* which would ultimately lead to the replacement of the Jerusalem Pillars by "the greatest and most righteous pillars" of the emergent Gentile church (1 Clem 5:1–6)—Peter and Paul? (§ 9. 1.)

6.6 James: His Final Bow

The leadership of the *Jakobusgemeinde* is now simply "James and the el-ders" (Acts 21:18). All trace of the Lucan Galilean presence in the leader-ship, if it was ever there, has now gone. As with the two previous occasions when James is allowed on stage no explanation about him is offered: "No reason is supplied for this consultation. James' leadership is presumed and unchallenged."[72]

Things have come to a head and the characteristic conflict with the synagogues in Asia and Greece that Luke has repeatedly chronicled has now to be faced in Jerusalem itself. Paul's working compromise in the Diaspora "To those under the law I became as one under the law . . . To those outside the law I became as one outside the law" (1 Cor 9:19–23) can now be seen, in Jerusalem, for what it is—an impossible self-contradiction. It is "high noon," and James demands that Paul makes very clear where he stands—a Torah-observant son of Israel.

Unlike the earlier Conference (Acts 15) where Luke records discus-sion and debate before an agreed resolution is achieved, James is now acting under the pressure of events over which he has little control and responds in a way that is characteristic of those enjoying an autocratic authority that is under threat—he dictates: "What then is to be done? They will certainly hear that you have come. So do what we tell you" (Acts 15:22–23). It is the "Royal-We"—and Paul conforms.

This expression of his authority masks the reality that he is no longer in total control of the *Jakobusgemeinde*, whose people are significantly affected by the growing nationalism in the City and therefore less in sympathy with the earlier practices that James had advocated.[73] We must also recognize that the allegations circulating about Paul only have significance insofar as the *Jakobusgemeinde* has significance in Jerusalem. This final appearance of James on the Lucan stage is testimony to the success of the Judaic mission of the *Jakobusgemeinde*—it is a movement large enough to command notice and is seen, as it sees itself, as part of that wider Judaic movement for the restoration and renewal of Israel.

After this second brief appearance in Acts, James melts back into the obscurity Luke reserves for him. Many commentators muse on the absence of any indication of assistance from James and the *Jakobusgemeinde* for Paul

---

72. Pervo, *Acts*, 542.

73. We have to take the Lucan description of the warm welcome Paul received (Acts 21:17–20), even if it is mainly from the Hellenists (Acts 21:16), as suspect of redactional interest.

in his detention.[74] This assumes that James and his community were in a position to influence the wielders of power, Roman or Judaic.[75] Despite a growing membership and possibly significant influence in the streets, taverns and συναγωγαί of Jerusalem, they may not have had that influence where it was needed—with the high priesthood or the Roman establishment (for Paul was accused of a capital offense, Acts 21:28). In fact, only a few years later it was the Jewish High Priest Ananus who would deliberately embrace an opportunity to be rid of James, an act which did however provoke some influential Pharisees to object, and who were people of sufficient status to have Ananus deposed as the first act of the incoming procurator.[76] Like Joseph of Arimathea they "come out of the woodwork" too late, but it is a strong hint from between the lines of Josephus' writing that although not part of the *Jakobusgemeinde* they could identify with and support James. And for such support to be effective at the highest level of Roman administration it must be seen as expressive of a much wider body of support. But that support was for James: Paul would have been an unlikely beneficiary.

Bruce, recognizing that James' people did not have the position and influence to intervene on Paul's behalf, posits that they may have felt a sense of relief when he was removed to Caesarea for "(t)hey had to go on living in Jerusalem"[77] and to be associated with Paul would have seriously affected their mission to their fellow-countrymen.[78]

We hear no more from Luke about James. He comes on stage without introduction and departs without an *adieu*. He returns to the silence from which he came—Luke had even removed the only reference to him from the gospel story about Jesus' rejection in his hometown (Mark 6:3//Luke 4:22). It is difficult to avoid the feeling that there is a degree of embarrassment about his presence and position when Luke was writing in the years after 70 CE and that he only scripted James in when it was unavoidable because the story could not be told without him.[79]

---

74. Painter, *Just James*, 56–57; Sim, *Matthew*, 168; Bruce, *Men and Movements*, 108–10.

75. Hartin, *James of Jerusalem* 81.

76. *Ant.* 20.199–203.

77. Common-sense must be part of a scholar's tool-kit.

78. Bruce, *Men and Movements*, 110.

79. Western histories of 1939–45, particularly those aimed at a more general audience, are of a similar genre—they rarely mention the Eastern Front where by far the most fighting and dying (on both sides) occurred. Comrade "Uncle Joe" Stalin, as a key ally and principal architect of victory, is a historical embarrassment.

7. The Jerusalem Conference

The Conference in Jerusalem (Acts 15:1–29) is both chronologically and theologically central to Luke's account—and James holds center-stage in it. Although Luke's evident reluctance to feature James may hint at a hidden agenda, it should be acknowledged that his description of James, to be credible, had to be consonant with the memory of the Lord's brother within the early Christian communities of Luke's day. What David Nienhuis wrote about the phenomenon of pseudepigraphic writing in the post-Apostolic period is apposite to our task:

> Writers engaged in this task of "apostolic actualization" reinterpreted the tradition according to their own contemporary needs; but *the power of their literary creation was dependent on its corresponding veracity* to the authoritative source it sought to actualize.[80] (my italics).

A similar consonance with remembrances of the *Jakobusgemeinde* in pre-70 CE Jerusalem would also have aided credibility.

Nowhere is the "Lucan Counterpoint" (§ 5. 3.2) more in evidence than in this presentation of the content and procedures of the Jerusalem Conference. It has a firm historical foundation, being clearly related to consultations Paul describes in Gal 2. It is focused on the same issue concerning the circumcision of Gentile converts, a concern that originates within the *Jakobusgemeinde*, and an essential unity was preserved through the adoption of a compromise, proposed by the *Jakobusgemeinde* leadership.[81]

Yet there is not a trace of the *angst* so clearly experienced by all sides in the dispute, as evidenced in the near contemporary writing of Paul to the Galatians: it is replaced and overridden by the dominating melody of Luke's authorial theme of the unity and harmony of their early movement.

Although the Conference of Acts 15 has definite connection with the consultation of Gal 2 it is not relevant to our concern to follow the much-trodden path of attempting their detailed co-ordination. It remains, however, the most substantial narrative unit in the NT portraying the *Jakobusgemeinde*—its composition, ethos and practice. Our task is to glean from Luke's account what we can of James and the *Jakobusgemeinde*, whether

---

80. Nienhuis, *Not by Paul Alone,* 17; Kloppenborg, "Diaspora Discourse," 271, describes a similar process in the task of constructing a pseudepigraphical letter: "(t)he writer must take steps to minimize the gap by accentuating features that the actual audience shares with the ostensible one, that is, by drawing the real audience as close as possible to the fictive one."

81. Dibelius, *Studies in Acts,* 93–101; Barrett, *Acts of the Apostles,* 709–11; Barrett, *On Paul,* 87–91; Pervo, *Acts,* 367–70.

grounded in the traditions he accessed, his later perceptions of the much earlier situation seen across the great divide of 70 CE, or the implications of his authorial narration.

It will progress our study, also, if we use this Lucan portrayal to program in other indicators scattered through his narrative, and linking with other NT sites.

8. *Jakobusgemeinde* Issues, Practice and Ethos

Not many years after this critical Conference, Paul was to return to Jerusalem to be greeted by James with the information of "how many thousands of believers there are among the Jews, and they are all zealous for the Law" (Acts 21:20). It is a portrayal strongly reinforced by the tradition embedded in EpJas (whether authorial or pseudepigraphic makes little difference) concerning which Peter Davids summarizes:

> That the community this letter represents is a Judaism is clear, not only from the self-reference to the communities as "the twelve tribes" (i.e., Israel), but also from the unselfconscious use of the Jewish scriptures. Of course, it would be anachronistic to call them "Jewish-Christian." They were a variety of Judaism and in their own eyes surely the "true" variety, . . . they recognize the formation narrative of Israel, the Torah, as their scriptures . . . When it comes to citing his basic creed, he cites the *Shema* (2:19; cf., Deut 6:4) . . . The Law is "the perfect law, the law of liberty" (Jas 1:25). It is "the royal law" (2:8). There can be no doubt but that James's community was part of a movement that valued the Torah.[82]

Zeal for the Law was a feature of the many movements for the renewal and restoration of Israel. It was an enthusiasm shared by EpJas (above), expressed by the pre-Christian Pharisee Paul in his persecution of the church (Phil 3:6), and commandeered as a title of (dis)honor by the Zealot faction in the War of 66–73 CE. In a period when encroaching Hellenistic culture and Roman imperialism were threatening the very essence of their Judaic life, identity and tradition, the maintenance of ethnic and purity boundaries was considered a vital foundation for that renewal of Israel they sought, and from the time of the Maccabees περιτομή was the distinctive marker of the true Israelite (1 Macc 2:46). "Zeal for the Law" could focus down onto

---

82. Davids, "James's Message," 67–68.

this very issue of περιτομή, as it did in Jerusalem and provided the occasion for the Conference.

The historical ground is firm, for in both Galatians and Acts the issue raised at this conference, by members from the *Jakobusgemeinde*, was the Antiochene practice of receiving Gentiles into open table-fellowship without insisting on their being circumcised.

We can be confident in taking the strength of feeling surrounding περιτομή evidenced in Paul's Galatian narrative as indicative of a "zeal for Torah" in the *Jakobusgemeinde*. In one sense circumcision would not have been an issue *within* the *Jakobusgemeinde* whose following in the City of Zion would include few, if any, Gentiles. The bone of contention concerned the new situation that had surfaced in Antioch and (according to the Lucan timeframe) the diasporan ἐκκλησίαι of the Antiochene mission of Barnabas and Paul. We have noted that this level of concern for *halakah* in the Syrian capital of Antioch—understood as part of Eretz Israel—may reflect a strong nationalist sentiment within sections of the *Jakobusgemeinde* (§ 4. 7.1).

We should also note that in both Pauline and Lucan accounts the complainants are represented as a group within the *Jakobusgemeinde*: the community led by James was not monolithic, its understanding of the implications of this new situation *vis-à-vis* the requirements of the Law was not uniform. But we can be sure that there was complete unanimity, not only in Jerusalem, but in Antioch and throughout the early days of the movement, on the circumcision of ethnic Jews [Luke makes sure the reader/hearer understands this by highlighting the action of Paul in circumcising Timothy (Acts 16:3)]. Fidelity to the Law could, and did, embrace diversity of interpretation. In this the *Jakobusgemeinde* mirrored the broader Judaic society but, as Paul was to discover on his return to Jerusalem a few years later, it was a tolerance that was wearing ever thinner as the political situation began to unravel—and to be wobbly[83] on the issue of περιτομή threatened the very core of their Torah-commitment. It is not that zeal for the Law within the *Jakobusgemeinde* increased in the years after the Conference—adhesion to the Torah was a constant for them—it is that, once the issue had been raised, the boundaries of tolerance became ever more closely defined, reflecting the *tendenz* in broader Judaic society. The *Jakobusgemeinde* was experiencing the tension between its self-understanding and identification as belonging to the movement for Judaic renewal on the one hand, with its sponsorship of a movement in the Diaspora whose reported practice threatened their integrity and credence in Jerusalem, on the other.

---

83. Prime Minister Thatcher's word to President Bush on the occasion of the invasion of Kuwait by Iraqi forces.

The intensity of feeling that was invested in this issue within the *Jako-busgemeinde* had receded in Luke's post-70 CE world—a world from which that center of power and influence had been effectively eliminated in the blood and fire of the Roman war-machine. A pressing issue now in the latter years of the first century for the increasingly Gentile Christian movement was to stress its unity and define its relationship with the Judaic tradition. Through the Conference, Paul (and therefore the Gentile Mission) is inte-grated into the Lucan authorial theme of "from Jerusalem to Rome": his law-free mission is a true inheritor of the Judaic tradition and accepted by the *Jakobusgemeinde*, albeit with qualifications.

Although the fact of the περιτομή issue is foregrounded by Luke, his description of the Conference proceedings again lacks that intensity of feel-ing that Paul's Galatian correspondence so powerfully conveys. Whereas Paul describes a confrontation—"we did not submit to them even for a moment" (Gal 2:5)—Luke portrays a conference where the issue in con-tention is identified and the protagonists are named (Acts 15:1–5). Like Paul's reminiscence in Galatians (Gal 2:1–10) two meetings seem to blur into one with a preliminary hearing before the community's leaders (Acts 15:6), followed by a more general gathering which Luke describes as τὸ πλῆθος (Acts 15:12). Witnesses are called upon and listened to by the whole assembly (Acts 15:7–12) before a President gives his judgment and guid-ance (Acts 15:13–21) which is acclaimed by both the community's council and the general gathering, with considerable detail of the action which was agreed upon (Acts 15:22–29).

While the precise historicity of Acts 15 is a matter of debate amongst scholars[84] it is widely acknowledged that the description and presentation is a Lucan construction from a later period when the fundamental divisive-ness of the περιτομή issue, with the strengths of feeling it engendered, had receded post-70 CE and with the apparently widely adopted *modus vivendi* expressed in the Conference Concordat—a policy it is difficult to imagine the Paul of the Galatian epistle signing up to. Yet, this does not mean that it is bereft of valid insight into the ethos, concerns, and practice of the *Jako-busgemeinde*, for that very important community—possibly encountered on pilgrimages to Jerusalem—was within the living memory of very many and her distinctive ways would be reflected in the Jewish-Christian συναγωγαί she had nurtured. Credibility is enhanced when the description engages both the memory and the experience of the hearers.

---

84. Dibelius, *Studies in Acts*, 93–101; Barrett, *Acts of the Apostles*, 709–12; Barrett, *On Paul*, 87–89; Pervo, *Acts*, 367–70.

As in the rest of Acts, where Luke displays great attention to details of the historical context of his narrative[85] (which are frequently cited to support an argument for the total historical accuracy of Acts), Luke takes great care to describe a fully Judaic context for the Conference. Whilst acknowledging the testimony of Barnabas and Paul, and consistent with the Torah adhesion of the *Jakobusgemeinde* we have noted, James bases his judgment solely on an exegesis of the Judaic scripture. There is no reference to either the acts or the words of Jesus (§ 7. 8.1). We shall meet a similar pattern in Paul's letters, in Jude, and in EpJas.[86] The final word is with the Law and the Prophets.

Where Luke differs totally from Paul is in his description of the compromise settlement of the issue. Luke reads back into the time of Paul and James what probably emerged as a working *modus vivendi* in Christian assemblies with a mix of Judaic and Gentile believers.[87] Unless Luke possessed a copy of Galatians, he may well have assumed that the working compromise in mixed assemblies of his day was in line with the agreement of the Jerusalem meeting many years previously. His readers would also have understood that. But to have reported an arrangement such as that which Paul records—which had not worked—would have been confusing and against his authorial concern to present a harmonious picture of the one Christian movement.[88] Conflict was dealt with and reconciliation achieved by a proper and dignified method of consultation.

The origin of the concordat is much debated. Barrett advocates that it originates in the *via media* position of the Hellenist Gentile Mission, a practical and workable compromise between the Petrine and Pauline positions— a compromise that allowed the church to move forward.[89] Dunn considers that the policy describes the practice that evolved in the churches under Jerusalem and Antioch's jurisdiction,[90] whilst Painter favors the decree as a Lucan creation designed to present James as "the exemplary moderate" between two extremes.[91]

Luke—probably viewing the *Jakobusgemeinde*, which at the time of writing was only a communal memory, through his knowledge of contemporary Jewish/Christian assemblies and diasporan synagogue structures

---

85. Dunn, *Beginning from Jerusalem*, 77–81.

86. Despite echoes in the latter of sayings that surface on the lips of Jesus in the Gospel traditions (§ 7. 7.).

87. Wahlen, "Peter's Vision," 516–18.

88. Although both compromises could be described as variations on a "live-and-let-live" theme—provided you don't push it in Jerusalem.

89. Barrett, *On Paul*, 89–90.

90. Dunn, *Beginning from Jerusalem*, 467–68.

91. Painter, *Just James*, 52.

and practice—presents a picture of the *Jakobusgemeinde* as possessing a well-established organization and structure with accepted procedural systems for decision making, including conflict-resolution. But while allowing for a degree of anachronism, it nonetheless remains that in our earliest encounter with the *Jakobusgemeinde* we find a community with a recognized structure and clearly understood ways of dealing with its matters of concern. Its Judaic origin and ethos is patent.

Luke's narrative has a hint of this Judaic ethos in his description of James using the Semitic form of Peter's name—Συμεων (Acts 15:14).[92] Betz comments that it "is a touch of Aramaic local color (that is) atypical for Luke, who is more likely to Hellenize foreign names."[93] Barrett concurs: "(T)his form . . . was probably intended to give the passage a Semitic air, regarded as suitable for James."[94]

The speech of James, as would be understood by a first century reader/hearer, is a Lucan construction. It is difficult to see the connection between the quotation from Amos 9:11–12 and the decision James announces (Acts 15:19–21),[95] and the quotation is from the LXX. This differs from the masoretic text, which could not have been used to support the interpretation James gives—"(It) has nothing to do with the inclusion of gentiles."[96] However, Bauckham offers a detailed examination of James' speech to defend it as, in summary form, "a very precise exegetical argument as to the relationship of Gentile Christians to the Law of Moses."[97] The use of the LXX quotation "is quite comparable with many examples of deliberate 'alternative readings' in the Qumran *pesherim*." But the rhetorical question of Barrett still challenges: "Would James in a Jewish meeting held in Jerusalem, have used Greek?"[98]

Yet, even here, we can hear possible echoes of an earlier Judaic atmosphere for the emphasis of the scriptural quotation lies decidedly upon the restoration of the Davidic kingdom as the grounding for Gentiles seeking the Lord (Acts 15:16–17).[99] It is a Zion-centered position (although one that Paul sought to turn on its head through his Collection Project?). This

---

92. Dibelius, *Studies in Acts*, 96.

93. Pervo, *Acts*, 375.

94. Barrett, *Acts of the Apostles*, 723.

95. Pervo, *Acts*, 375.

96. Ibid., 375–76.

97. Bauckham, "James and the Jerusalem Church," 452–62. Cf., Ulfgard, "Branch in the Last Days," 239.

98. Barrett, *On Paul*, 19.

99. Bruce, *Men and Movements*, 93–97; Chilton, "James, Peter, Paul," 7.

is not the "all one in Christ Jesus" position of Paul. It pragmatically accepts the fact of Gentiles becoming part of the Movement without circumcision [" . . . we should not trouble those Gentiles who are turning to God . . . " (Acts 15:19)], but that is hardly a resounding affirmation of an aggressive Gentile Mission policy. For James, the mission to the Jews has priority.[100]

That this presentation of James and his theology does not cohere with Paul's "neither Jew nor Gentile" is further testimony to Luke's attempt to preserve contextual historical actuality in his narrative creation.

9. The *Jakobusgemeinde* Structure

The description of the procedures adopted for settling a dispute that had occasioned "no small dissension" (Acts 15:2) in Antioch reveals the *Jakobusgemeinde* as a maturely developed community with a structure not dissimilar to that which we encounter at Qumran of priests, elders and people, with a "Guardian of the Congregation" (*mebaqqer*) who controlled their meetings,[101] and who interpreted and applies the scriptures in their situation (§ 3. 1.). It was a mutually recognized authority effected through a simple yet effective hierarchical structure (in contemporary terms) of:

- An *"assembly"* (Acts 15:12), (§ 5. 9.1), of the *Jakobusgemeinde* people, described as:

    - τὸ πλῆθος[102] Acts 15:12; (cf. Acts 6:2, 5—where NRSV translates as "the community"). Also referred to as:

    - οἱ ἀδελφοὶ, (Acts 15:22, 23. cf. 9:30; 11:1; 12:17 and 21:17. cf. 1:14 τοῖς ἀδέλφοῖς αὐτοῦ— *his* brothers);

    - ἡ ἐκκλησία—within the Conference narrative (Acts 15:4, 22) the Pauline usage—ἡ ἐκκλησία—comes into play, perhaps betraying later composition.

They are portrayed as hearing all the arguments and consenting (along with "the apostles and elders") to the guidance of the President (Acts 15:22).

---

100. Barrett, *On Paul,* 63; Hartin, *James of Jerusalem,* 84; McKnight, "A Parting within the Way,"109–111, 126–29; Bockmuehl, "Antioch and James the Just," 155–98 (179–91); Chilton, "Conclusions and Questions," 260–64; Chilton, "James, Peter, Paul," 7–11; Langston, "Dividing it Right," 125–34.

101. 1QS VI. 8–13.

102. Barrett, *Acts of the Apostles,* 721: " . . . probably the mass of the people . . . as distinct from the apostles and elders . . ."

- *A Council*, (§ 5. 9.2), referred to as "the apostles and elders" (Acts 15:4, 22–23. cf. Acts 8:14 "the apostles"; Acts 21:18 "the elders"). They can meet (presumably with the President) for more detailed discussion, argument and advice (Acts 15:2, 6) and have expertise and authority— "Paul and Barnabas and some of the others were appointed to go up to Jerusalem to discuss this question with the apostles and elders." (Acts 15:2) We note that there is no mention of James, to whom the latter are clearly subservient in the full assembly.

- *A President* (Acts 15:13), (§ 5. 9.3), who leads, guides, and speaks for them; and (like a *Mebaqqer*) is their authoritative interpreter of scripture (Acts 15:13–21). Acts knows nothing of the Pillars, or of a leadership vested in a triumvirate.

Luke portrays what was probably a more developed form of organization, procedure and practice—but such things do not appear *ex nihilo*—they develop from earlier procedures such as those we can perceive through the blurring fog of Paul's *angst* in his near-contemporary description in Galatians; and that probably more authentic historical picture from the early days of the proto-Christian movement undoubtedly had its own roots in widely observed Judaic organizational practice.

9.1 The *Jakobusgemeinde* People[103]

We have noted (§ 4. 5.2.1) that from the very earliest period after the death of Jesus the *Jakobusgemeinde* was evidently of sufficient size and vigor to be felt as a threat by some Pharisees at least (Phil 3:5–6). Unfortunately, but typically, our main insight into the *Jakobusgemeinde* people is through the emergence of the internal conflict and strife, which was the occasion for the Conference and also fed into the trouble surrounding Paul's final visit to Jerusalem. The conservative protagonists, identified earlier (Acts 11:2) as the περιτομή (cf. Gal 2:12) are now more clearly identified as "some believers

103. In his description of the Conference Luke uses the Pauline ἐκκλησία to describe the *Jakobusgemeinde* prior to the Conference (Acts 15:4) and at its conclusion (Acts 15:22), but during his description of the Conference debate and proceedings (where we have seen that Luke seeks to portray a characteristically Judaic ethos) he uses τὸ πλῆθος (Acts 15:12)—a word that can refer to "a multitude," or, with the definite article a gathering of people. NRSV translates it as "the assembly," which encapsulates the latter meaning, but in the Hebrews/Hellenists dispute τὸ πλῆθος is translated as "the community," referring to a much wider grouping of people. I am using "the people" as a better word in contemporary usage that embraces much the same range of application as τὸ πλῆθος.

who belonged to the sect of the Pharisees."[104] It is significant that "labeling" occurs in both our narrative accounts (περιτομή / ψευδαδέλφοι). Not only does this suggest that the *Jakobusgemeinde* is of sufficient size for interest-groups to develop and be readily identified, but the existence of περιτομή predicates the existence also of "ἀπεριτομή"—not "non-circumcision," but those more open to the developing practice in the Antiochene community of Gentile inclusion.

The περιτομή are of sufficient size and influence within the *Jakobusgemeinde* for the Conference to be necessary, and the issue raised critical for a Torah-centered people, but in neither account could they carry the day—the more pragmatic position of the "ἀπεριτομή" proved more in tune with the general feeling and understanding of the community at that stage of their development. It represents a power balance within the community that was to shift to Paul's disadvantage when he came with the gifts of his Gentile ἐκκλησίαι a decade later—a shift that would not have been helped by the rumors about him that were coming back from the province of Asia (Acts 21:21, 27).

We should also note that the περιτομή did not withdraw from the *Jakobusgemeinde* nor were they excluded—Gentile incorporation into the *Jakobusgemeinde* in the City of Zion was not the agenda.

We hear of them because they persistently made their voice heard on a crucial issue. There were no doubt other groupings reflecting distinct "voices" within Second Temple Judaism who were also within the Jerusalem proto-Christian movement such as the Hebrews and the Hellenists (Acts 6:1–6).[105] We do not need to precisely delineate these two groups[106]—suffice to note that we have here a memory of a more richly textured community in the early days than the somewhat monochrome portrait of the *Jakobusgemeinde* we have on the occasion of its exit from our story (Acts 21:17–26).[107]

---

104. Chilton, "James and the Believing Pharisees," 19–49.

105. If Luke's portrayal of Hellenist theology as expressed in Stephen's speech (Acts 7:2–53) is anywhere near the mark, their legacy to the *Jakobusgemeinde* may well be found in their advocacy of that broader interpretation of Torah that the περιτομή were pushing against. The removal of the Hellenist leadership (which is probably what Luke's account of the persecution implies) would not have harmed the περιτομή cause.

106. Cf., Hill, *Hellenists and Hebrews*.

107. Luke, in one of his broad-brush summarizing statements, also reported that "a great many of the priests became obedient to the faith" (Acts 6:7). These were possibly from the lower orders of the priesthood. (Painter, *Just James*, 140, 250; Painter, "Who was James?" 50. cf., *Ant.* 20.205–07). Luke makes nothing of this—which may suggest a bit of fragmentary tradition, or is it Luke the author drawing a picture of the broad appeal of the movement (even priests!)? It certainly would support a tradition of Temple-loyalty which Luke authors into his idealistic picture of the early days in

The culture and self-understanding of the Qumranic/Essene movement does display remarkable affinity with that of the *Jakobusgemeinde* as portrayed by Luke. In addition to a close similarity of organization (§ 5. 9.2), both see themselves as being, in the shade of the ἔσχατον, the core of a renewed Israel. The Torah was central to their being, and maintenance of purity a high priority. They could both describe their movement as "the Way" and the practice of community of goods is recorded for both groups. The Essene self-description of themselves as "the Poor" is also echoed in Christian tradition about the *Jakobusgemeinde* (cf. also Rom 15:26; Mark 10:21) It is significant that all this is detailed not only in the library of Qumran but also in the *Damascus Document*—evidence that this "Way" was not only the ideal for the wilderness community but also sought pragmatic expression in the secular Essene camps living, as did the *Jakobusgemeinde* community, in the wider Israelite society.

The *Jakobusgemeinde* developed and changed during the four decades we know of its existence. This is to be expected—Christianity did not come ready-made from heaven, it had to be hammered out on the anvil of daily living in turbulent and troubled times.

Similarly, "Pharisees were unlikely to have been part of a monolithic religious system, and their beliefs and practices might have changed over time, as well as depending on geographical situation."[108] Some strands of Pharisaism, at least, evidently found little conflict in their *Jakobusgemeinde* involvement and by the time of Paul's final visit to Jerusalem with the collection they have become the dominant voice within the movement (Acts 21:20). At an even later date we find that influential members of the Pharisaic party had clear sympathy with James and the *Jakobusgemeinde* in Josephus' account of their reaction to the illegal execution of James in 62 CE at the instigation of the High Priest Ananus, whom Josephus, the Pharisee, "fingers" as being "of the sect of the Sadducees":

> Those of the inhabitants of the city who were considered the most fair-minded and who were strict in observance of the law were offended at this. They therefore secretly sent to King Agrippa urging him, for Ananus had not even been correct in his first step, to order him to desist from any further such actions.[109]

Jerusalem (Acts 2:46; 3:1–4:4; 5:12–26, 42), but which is more realistically preserved in the importance of the Temple location during Paul's final visit (Acts 21:23–30).

108. Rowland, *Christian Origins,* 69.

109. *Ant.* 20.201.

If the ἐκκλησίαι of Paul's Gentile Mission found their self-identity "in Christ," the συναγωγαί of the *Jakobusgemeinde* continued as loyal sons of Israel but with a belief that the process of the ἔσχατον had already begun with the rising of Jesus, and was in process of moving towards its near consummation.

9.2 The *Jakobusgemeinde* Council

Development in organization and authority in a growing Movement is reflected in the Lucan narrative: the reconstitution of the Twelve (Acts 1:12–26) followed by the appointment of the Seven (Acts 6:1–6) are both highlighted, whilst a group simply referred to as "the apostles" emerges in the narrative embedded in the traditions of the Hellenist mission (Acts 8:14; 11:1). In this setting it is "the apostles" as a group who display the authority within the *Jakobusgemeinde* to delegate the task of supervising the developments in Samaria to Peter and John, inverting the power relationship that is presented as the norm in the "early days" (Acts 1—5); whilst after Peter's boundary-breaking activity in Caesarea, it was before this same group of "apostles" that Peter has to defend his unsanctioned initiative in baptizing Gentiles in face of the critique of the περιτομή. Our contemporary term for such a group would be along the lines of "executive council."[110]

9.2.1 The Jerusalem "apostles"

This "apostles"/Jerusalem matrix enjoys a double attestation for it is also present in the writings of Paul. In recounting the visions of the risen Jesus to the Corinthians he dissociates "the Twelve" from "the apostles" by linking the former with Cephas and the latter with James (1 Cor 15:5–7; see 1 Cor 9:5). And to the Galatians he describes himself as "(not going) up to Jerusalem to those who were apostles before me" (Gal 1:17) with a further reference to these "apostles" being in Jerusalem three years later (Gal 1:19).

---

110. This differs from the referent of "Council" in Vermes' translation of the DSS (e.g., 1 QS VIII 1–12); where the application is to the whole community in its deliberative role (Collins, "Site of Qumran," 14). Cf., the earlier translation of Theodor Gaster: "In the *formal congregation* of the community there shall be twelve laymen and three priests schooled to perfection in all that has been revealed of the entire Law. . . . When these men have undergone, with blamelessness of conduct, a two-year preparation in the fundamentals of the community, they shall be segregated as especially sacred among the *formal members* of the community." *Scriptures of the Dead Sea Sect*, 64–65. Qumran gives no indication of the role of the "fifteen," though we can presume significant influence would be accorded to them on account of their training and separated status.

We noted (§ 4. 5.1) that the "apostles" Paul refers to as being in Jerusalem are probably not co-extensive with the Twelve.

Initially, in Acts, Luke fills the apostolic stage with Peter and John and the unqualified reference to "the apostles" at whose feet gifts of money were laid does not necessarily refer to other than these two names who had dominated the whole story to that point (Acts 4:33, 35, 37; 5:2). But in the cycle of tradition focusing on the Hellenist Mission "the apostles" are the group who, in addition to their delegation and adjudication activity over the Mission in Samaria, are the group to whom Barnabas turned to gain Paul's acceptance (Acts 9:27). They were part of a ruling praesidium (with "the elders") at the Jerusalem Conference (Acts 15:2, 6, 22). However, only "the elders" appear on the occasion of Paul's final visit (Acts 21:18).

For Luke the emphasis, as in his gospel (Luke 6:13), is on the Twelve as the uniquely accredited "Apostles," the validators and witnesses to the whole of Jesus' ministry from the days of the Baptist to his risen appearances (Acts 1:25)—re-iterating a widely recognized feature in both Luke's writings whereby "Apostle" is not (despite Acts 14:4, 14[111]) a role or activity, but a title or status, restricted to "the Twelve." Whenever the generic term "apostles" (as a group) occurs in Acts it refers to a group who play a significant authority role in the Jerusalem movement, with the clear *implication* of being identified with the Twelve (Acts 2:42; 4:33–37; 5:2, 12, 18, 29, 40; 8:1, 14; 9:27; 11:1; 15:6, 22). In the early period it can refer to named persons—Peter and John— explicitly (Acts 8:18) or implicitly (Acts 4:33, 35, 37; 5:2, 18, 29, 40). We should note that this equation of "the Twelve" with the later generic use in the text of "the apostles" is derived solely from Acts 1:12–26.[112]

Luke certainly meant his intended readers to understand "the apostles" as including, and probably comprising, the Twelve although that specific reference only occurs once (Acts 6:2).

9.2.2 A Matured Structure

The Jerusalem Conference as Luke describes it is a well organized, deliberative and commendable occasion. There is "'much debate" (v.6) but no space for the fierce confrontation ("we did not submit"), or the "slagging off" (ψευδαδέλφοι; τῶν δοκούντων εἶναί τι) Paul evokes (Gal 2:4–6). It is clearly a

---

111. An earlier functional understanding of "apostle" for those sent by their commissioning church is probably preserved here: "Luke never used the word 'apostle' of Paul in the sense that Paul wanted it to be used of himself." (Dr Barry Matlock, responding to questions at a Sheffield University Seminar—December 8, 2008).

112. Epp, *Junia*, 69–70.

Lucan construction designed to lay bare the problem (almost as an academic exercise) and advocate what had become a usable working compromise. It may reflect the structure and procedures of Judaic-Christian συναγωγαί known to Luke who had their roots in the developed policy and practice of their mother-church, the *Jakobusgemeinde*. Yet there are clear resemblances here between what can be perceived through the confusing fog of Paul's emotions as he lived again in his mind the meetings he attended in Jerusalem and this more controlled description by Luke of the Jerusalem Conference:

- there seems to have been meetings with both a ruling group ("the acknowledged leaders") and a more general meeting at which the ψευδαδέλφοι were present (Gal 2:4–5)—and, as in Acts (15:6 and 12) this distinction is blurred in the memory;[113]

- for Luke the "apostles and elders"[114] exercise a legitimated authority, in contrast to Paul's vaguer "acknowledged leaders" (Gal 2:2, 6) (or "those who were reputed to be something"— RSV);

- Paul makes separate mention of the three Pillars—James, Cephas and John—who make the final decision and act on behalf of the whole community (Gal 2:9–10), but it is not much later that James is the sole name that speaks for "Jerusalem" (Gal 2:11–12), as in Luke's Conference scenario (Acts 15:13–21).

We encountered in the Galatians narrative an organization and structure that is well beyond its embryonic stage and dynamically moving towards that which Luke presents (§ 4. 6.2)—and it may well be that the challenge and crisis presented by Paul's Gentile policy made a significant contribution towards that dynamic development.

In Luke's narrative, "the apostles" are gradually replaced by "the elders" (Acts 8:14; 11:1; 15:2, 4, 6, 22; 21:18) leading to the inference that "the elders" were progressively appointed to fill the spaces left by the Twelve either by death (like James bar Zebedee) or departure (like Peter).[115] This may indeed be Luke's intent for each reference is in a section where Luke's

---

113. The Lucan description does have affinity with Qumran practice where the whole community comprises the "Council," with the "twelve men and three priests" having a special status on account of their specialized training (1 QS VIII 1–13. Collins, "Site of Qumran," 13–15).

114. Pervo, *Acts,* 542, 543–44, following Hengel, describes Luke as associating "James with presbyters in an anachronistic manner."

115. Bauckham, *Jude,* 70–79; Bauckham, "James and the Jerusalem Church," 439–41.

redactional activity is evident.[116] In this, Luke is probably synthesizing the organization of the *Jakobusgemeinde* as he understood it to have been prior to 70 CE, with his theological task of establishing the Galilean Apostles as the founders of the *Jakobusgemeinde* (Acts 1:11, 21–22; 2:7 § 9.).

9.2.3 *The Pillars and Qumran*

Luke's description of the Conference betrays a structure not dissimilar to that which we encounter at Qumran of priests, elders, and people, with a "Guardian of the Congregation" (*mebaqqer*) who controlled their meetings,[117] and who interpreted and applies the scriptures in their situation (§ 3. 1.).

Although Luke gives no indication of the Pillars Paul had earlier encountered, that triumvirate may also reflect the Qumranic recognition of "twelve men and three priests."[118] This, as a likely historical scenario, is strengthened by Richard Bauckham's argument that the tradition of fifteen bishops of Jerusalem between James and the Bar Kokhba revolt may be a misunderstanding, which included a listing of twelve names that were known as co-workers of James—"a body of twelve presbyters."[119] We are firmly in the world of late Second Temple Judaism.

Further, Martin Hengel, commenting on the "striking" mention of "the twelve" in Acts 6:2–5— contrary to Luke's usual terminology of "apostles"— considers this to be indicative of the presence of a pre-Lucan source.[120] Similarly, Gerd Lüdemann accepts an underlying written tradition behind Luke's abrupt introduction of the widow's conflict, but asserts that the details are redactional: the passage "presupposes the constitution of Luke's church; the proposal made by the Twelve (= leaders of the community) meets with the assent of the mass of the disciples (= full assembly)."[121] Either way, a Council of twelve men attending to the mission and needs of a proto-Christian συναγωγή is inferred as common early practice, arising out of a common Judaic way of organizing themselves (e.g., the Essene "camps"— § 3. 1.). And could such a council be familiarly referred to as "the twelve"?

116. Lüdemann, *Early Christianity*, 96, 129–30, 166–69, 231–32.

117. 1 QS VI. 8–13.

118. 1QS VIII. 1–4.

119. Eusebius, *Hist. eccl.* 4.5.1–3; Bauckham, *Jude*, 70–76. Later independently supported by Eisenman, *James*, 782–"sounds suspiciously similar to the number of the Community Council at Qumran." Roose, "Sharing in Christ's Rule," 126–30.

120. Hengel, *Between Jesus and Paul*, 4.

121. Lüdemann, *Early Christianity*, 76–78.

We need to return to "the twelve":

9.2.4 A Jerusalem XII?

"Twelve" is a widely present typological theme in late Second Temple Judaism,[122] associated with hopes for the restoration of Israel in the final days.[123] This is a trace of a very early period of proto-Christian development when the renewal movements looked and acted for this fulfillment. It is a hope independently attested in the Q tradition of the sayings about the Twelve sitting on thrones judging the twelve tribes of Israel (Matt 19:28// Luke 22:28–30; cf. Jas 1:1; 1 Peter 1:1; Acts 26:6–7. See also the vision of the New Jerusalem, founded on the twelve tribes and twelve apostles, Rev 21:12–14[124]):

> That the earliest Christian movement thought of itself as a res-
> toration movement within Israel is quite clear and is attested in
> the letter of James, which is addressed "to the twelve tribes in the
> Dispersion" (James 1:1), or in 1 Peter, whose author speaks of
> his addressees as "the exiles of the dispersion" (1 Peter 1:1). The
> hope of the restoration of the twelve tribes of Israel is strong in
> Christianity's first generation, though in time it fades.[125]

And fade it did indeed. It was transmuted almost out of recognition in Paul's understanding of the Gentile Mission with its expression in his collection project, but it was never totally forgotten: e.g., there are echoes in the late first century Roman concerns about Davidic descendants, as reported by Hegesippus,[126] and in Acts itself—both in Paul's defense before Agrippa (Acts 26:6) and in James' judgment at the Jerusalem Conference (Acts 15:15–16); as well as in the preserved pericope in Q about the Twelve sitting on thrones "judging the twelve tribes of Israel" (Matt 19:28//Luke 22:29).

The earliest reference in Christian literature to "the twelve" is 1 Cor 15:5—the sole reference from Paul—and it is normal for this group to be identified with "the Twelve" of later Synoptic tradition. That could be a presupposition too far, for it is a fundamental principle of inter-textuality that, like "the arrow of time" in cosmology, it only flows in one direction and we

122. Evans, "Jesus, John, and the Dead Sea Scrolls," 45–62.

123. Theissen, *Gospels in Context*, 46; Sanders, *Jesus and Judaism*, 95–105; Allison, *Constructing Jesus*, 71–76.

124. Possibly an early association with Zodiac cosmology that became a feature in later Gnostic circles (DeConick, *The Thirteenth Apostle*, 155).

125. Evans, "Assessing Typologies," 60–61.

126. Eusebius, *Hist. eccl.* 3:12, 19–20.

must take care not to prematurely import later textual information from the Gospels or Acts into the much earlier text of Paul (§ 4. 2.–3.). We should also not overlook the obvious historical inaccuracy that there were for the resurrection appearances, as both Matthew and Luke recognize, only eleven disciples[127] (Matt 28.16; Luke 24.9, 33; Acts 1:26[128]).

Paul is here recounting (1 Cor 15:5—7), almost as a litany, information he had received. Given that the two named persons in the list of Christophanies—Cephas and James—are precisely (and in the same order) the two named persons he met on his first visit to Jerusalem after his conversion the probability becomes very high that it was on that occasion—c.33/34CE[129]— that he received their stories. This was thirty to thirty five years before the Galilean "Twelve" surfaces in the writing of Mark,[130] where it is used to indicate the group of twelve men that Jesus had gathered about himself to support him in his work (Mark 3:14–19).[131] Mark uses it as a descriptor in much the same way that he describes the disgruntled group of disciples as "the ten" when the two Zebedean boys tried to steal a march on their colleagues (Mark 10:41). It is similar to the way we talk of "the eleven" in a sporting context. These twelve were specifically empowered by Jesus for a ministry of preaching, exorcism and healing in Galilee (Mark 6:7–13),[132] but, although they were *his* twelve there is no suggestion of innovation or uniqueness in Mark's narration.[133] Indeed, as Craig Evans has pointed out, the number twelve, as indicating the "twelve tribes" (i.e., the fullness of Israel) occurs with frequency in the annals of Israel, including the Dead Sea

127. Eisenman, *James*, 699 makes too much of a meal of this. E. P. Sanders argues that "the Twelve" is a symbolic number for an institution, not a "head count"—Sanders, *Jesus and Judaism*, 98–106; Allison, *Constructing Jesus*, 67–76.

128. John confines himself to "the disciples" (John 20:19, 26).

129. Reisner, *Paul's Early Period*, 322.

130. Accepting a broadly consensual dating of the late 60s CE for Mark.

131. Neither the Q traditions nor the Gospel of Thomas refer to "the Twelve," even though the saying (Matt 19:28//Luke 22:29) about them judging the twelve tribes of Israel is found in Q material. Both simply refer to "the disciples." Indeed, when the disciples ask Jesus who is to be their leader after his departure, he points them to "James the Just." (G.Thos.12:1–2).

132. Unlike the later Matthean Gospel (Matt 16:18–19) Mark makes no mention of their having a future role in founding, guiding, and ruling the early church. That may be redactional, reflecting Mark's negative assessment of "the Twelve."

133. With many commentators I take "whom he also named apostles" (Mark 3:14) to be an assimilation to the text of Luke 6.13. e.g.,Taylor, *Mark*, 230. Calling, training and setting apart a group of twelve, like the Essenes appear to have done (§ 3. 1.) was what leaders of Judaic restoration movements may customarily have done in preparation for the realization of their hopes (n.110 above).

Scrolls: "The typology of twelve signifies the renewal of the whole of Israel, that is, all twelve tribes."[134]

However, undoubtedly because they were *his* "Twelve," set apart and taught by Jesus, we are witnessing in embryonic form "the Twelve" of developing Christian tradition, who were to be seen as being commissioned and receiving from him the title of "Apostles" (Luke 6:13),[135] becoming viewed as the foundation of the Church (Rev 21:14).

There can be little doubt about the historicity of Jesus gathering a nucleus of twelve men around him.[136] In the mid-twentieth century Vincent Taylor judged:

> The general impression we receive is that, while the existence of the Twelve and the nature of their original appointment were firmly rooted in the tradition, apart from Peter, James, and John, most of them had become a somewhat distant memory.[137]

Whilst fifty years later, James Dunn concurred:

> Once again, then, it was the memory of twelve which stuck; the detail of who made up the twelve was of much less significance.[138]

Yet we have already noted the Qumran organization with its similarity to the *Jakobusgemeinde*, involved a special group of twelve (or "twelve men and three priests"[139]), and at Ephesus Paul encountered a group who only knew John's baptism and were "about twelve . . . in all" (Acts 19:7). A group of twelve was probably a typical form of organization in Second Temple Judaism and, within the arena of Second Temple reform movements, embodied the hope of a full restoration "twelve tribe Israel."[140] David Flusser notes that

> the (Isaiah) Pesher uses the same terminology for the Pharisees as for the Qumran community (congregation, assembly,

---

134. Evans, "Assessing Typologies of Restoration," 45–62.

135. We have noted a similar process occurring with the designation of "apostle/ Apostle."

136. Casey, *Jesus of Nazareth*, 192.

137. Taylor, *Mark*, 229, 619–27.

138. Dunn, *Jesus Remembered*, 507–11. Bauckham makes a vigorous defence of the identity of all twelve names in the variant NT listings. (Bauckham, *Jesus and the Eyewitnesses*, 93-113). This does not affect our main contention that it is the symbolic number of twelve that is important, rather than any specific recollection of their names.

139. 1QS VIII 1.

140. Cf., 1 QS VIII 5: "When these (twelve men and three priests) are in Israel, the Council of the Community shall be established in truth."

council) and these terms are not particular to the Essenes, but rather appear to be part of the common Second Temple lexicon for religious congregations.[141]

A grouping of twelve is significant, but not unique.

Returning to the tradition Paul recounted in the mid-30s CE (1 Cor 15:5–7)—this "twelve" are associated with Cephas in a *Jerusalem* context. Whenever Paul mentions Cephas it is always in a Jerusalem context (Gal 1:18; 2:6–10) or with a Jerusalem link[142] (Gal 2:11–14;[143] 1 Cor 9:5[144]), never Galilee, and this "twelve" are a group in Jerusalem at that time.[145]

Without the information embedded in the much later Acts/Johannine texts, we would have no difficulty in understanding Cephas as a Jerusalemite, as well as being a Pillar of the *Jakobusgemeinde* (§ 4. 6.1.2 & 4). Also, if the Pauline *kerygma* was informed by Jerusalem traditions, not Galilean (§ 7. 2.–3.), *who would Paul actually be referring to at this early date* when he referred to the appearance of Jesus "to Cephas, then to the twelve"? Who are "the twelve" in that context? May they not be the "council" of a Jerusalem community associated with Cephas on a familiar Judaic pattern? If this has substance, the isolated reference to "the twelve" in Acts 6:2 may have been in Luke's source material, as Hengel argued,[146] but referring originally not to the "men of Galilee" but to the Council of the *Jakobusgemeinde*.

---

141. Flusser, *Judaism of the Second Temple Period,* 239.

142. Catchpole, *Jesus People,* 105.

143. Antioch is a daughter church of Jerusalem (Acts 11:19–26).

144. In 1 Cor 9:5 Cephas completes a grouping of "the other apostles and the brothers of the Lord"—all apparently "on the road," as was Paul: these are the same individuals/groups that Paul identified in Jerusalem on his first visit (Gal 1:18–19). It is possible that Cephas and the Lord's brothers may have been an official delegation from the *Jakobusgemeinde* to Corinth—Dungan, *Sayings of Jesus,* 7. We should note that the interposition of "the brothers of the Lord" separates Cephas out from "the apostles." Acolytes of Cephas are mentioned by Paul as belonging to the ἐκκλησία in Corinth, which strongly implies a period of ministry by Cephas in that city, as had been the case with Antioch, whilst his association with "the brothers of the Lord" (above) is indicative of a *Jakobusgemeinde* mission initiative.

145. The preposition εἶτα (1 Cor 15:5) raises the question of whether Cephas is to be included in the number twelve or not (as is also the case with "James, then all the apostles," 1 Cor 15:7).

146. Hengel, *Between Jesus and Paul,* 3–4.

9.3 The President of the *Jakobusgemeinde*

Despite Luke's reluctance *vis-à-vis* James, it remains that whenever he is on stage with them, James is presented as a more significant figure than either Peter or Paul. At the Conference James is found presiding, deliberating, and announcing[147] what later Quakers would call "the mind of the meeting"—"with the consent of the whole church" Acts 15:22—displaying an authority that the Essenes would have found consonant with that of their *mebaqqer*.[148] James chairs the meeting, calling it to order (v. 13), which probably included calling the witnesses to testify; summarizes the debate (v. 14); discusses the problem they face in the light of their guiding constitution (i.e., the Law and the Prophets) (vv. 15–17) and, on that basis, advocates the policy to adopt (vv. 19–21). Peter and Paul are present only as petitioners and witnesses.

In keeping with his practice elsewhere, Luke plays James phlegmatically in a very low key denying him both job title and role-description to distinguish him from, say, apostles and elders. Yet the very matter-of-factness of the resultant description quietly but forcefully affirms the strength of James' position. He is unequivocally accepted and recognized as the Guardian/*mebaqqer* of this assembly/πλῆθος and its extensions in the Diaspora. It is a position of authority to which both Peter and Paul have to yield. This status, and its general recognition, point to James having acquired and been accorded what I have described as Quasi-rabbinic status (§ 2. 6.2.4) within this community. It may go further than this and indicate that James had acquired some degree of scribal-literary accomplishment and recognition (§ 8. 2.2.2).

The description in Josephus of the reactions to the execution of James in 62 CE is a strong independent witness to the standing of James within Jerusalem. Objections to the legality of this act were sent to Herod Agrippa and a delegation traveled to meet the incoming Roman procurator, Albinus. That they could petition Agrippa directly and that Albinus not only received the delegation but acted upon its presentation speaks for the civic status of the petitioners, as does the fact of their action speak of the recognition that was accorded to James in the City. Josephus' description of the protestors as "the most equitable of the citizens, and such as were the most uneasy at the breach of the laws" suggests that they were probably Pharisees—and their

---

147. McKnight, "Parting within the Way," n.54: "That Luke describes James' decision in forensic terms (15:19 διὸ ἐγὼ κρίνω) clearly implies the stature of James in the Jerusalem community as well as his position as an arbiter of interpretation."

148. Chilton, "Formation of the Gospels," 20–28; Eisenman and Wise, *Dead Sea Scrolls Uncovered*, 215–17, 270–71.

clear respect for James is good support for the tradition of James being a recognized interpreter of Torah.[149]

So clearly is this established that the position of James requires no explication—neither on his initial entrance (Acts 12:17) nor on his "final bow" in the Lucan narrative (Acts 21:17–26). It is significant that both Paul and Luke concur in recognizing the role and status of James in the *Jakobusgemeinde*, despite their reluctance (for very different reasons) to do so on this particular issue.

10. The *Kerygma* of the *Jakobusgemeinde*

We do not to have to accuse Paul of special pleading when he claims a fundamental identity between his own preaching and that of the *Jakobusgemeinde* (1 Cor 15:11). Whatever further Christological development took place within his fertile mind as he struggled theoretically and in practice with the implications of his own experience and sense of call, his core message was grounded in the traditions he received—which included from the very beginning "event" and "theology" ("Christ died"/"for our sins"—1 Cor 15:3). There is no reason to deny a substantial harmony between the message of the *Jakobusgemeinde* and Paul's Gentile Mission, except on the crucial boundary issue between Jew and Gentile. Although that was to prove "a bridge too far," the dispute in fact arose out of a commonly held belief that they were living under the shadow of the ἔσχατον, signaled in by the death and resurrection of Christ—for the *Jakobusgemeinde* this underscored their zeal for the Law, whereas for Paul it marked a new life in the Spirit (e.g., Rom 8:9–11).[150]

In his seminal work on *The Apostolic Preaching* C. H. Dodd summarized the primitive *kerygma* which he quarried principally from Paul's writings as:

> The prophecies are fulfilled,
>
> and the New Age is inaugurated by the coming of Christ.
>
> He was born of the seed of David.
>
> He died according to the Scriptures, to deliver us out of the present evil age.
>
> He was buried.

149. *Ant* 20.197–203.

150. Possession of a common gospel does not exclude variation of interpretation. Goulder, "Jesus' Resurrection and Christian Origins," 189–91.

He rose on the third day according to the Scriptures.

He is exalted at the right hand of God, as Son of God and Lord of quick and dead.

He will come again as Judge and Savior of men.[151]

Aside from the echo of later credal formulation we can work with this as a broadly consensual framework shared by the *Jakobusgemeinde* and those who came within its orbit, including the ἐκκλησίαι founded by Paul. It does need some modification for the *Jakobusgemeinde*, for we probably need to include within the first item the significance of the Baptist's message that the ἔσχατον is imminent, along with its call for repentance with baptism. The impact of the Baptist on many in Jerusalem is firmly embedded within the synoptic tradition (Mark 1:5) and may account for both the practice of baptism within the Christian movement from the very beginning (§ 3. 5.1), as well as the enthusiasm for Torah observance ("fruit that befits repentance" Matt 3:8). This commitment was both response and preparation for the final consummation and was a noted characteristic of the *Jakobusgemeinde*. If that is correct we should take note that the strength of commitment to the Torah with a concomitant emphasis on purity issues, particularly in the Holy City, was itself perceived as a necessity in the light of the ἔσχατον as it moved to its climactic finale. The death/rising of Jesus, a sign of the ἔσχατον, was integrated into hopes for the restoration of Israel that were widespread in late Second Temple Judaism: there is no sense of the Pauline "new creation in Christ" (2 Cor 5:17) or of a sea-change from being "under the Law" to living "in the Spirit" (e.g. Gal 3—4; Rom 7—8).

The Davidic descent of Jesus is almost certainly a product of the *Jakobusgemeinde*. It is part of the tradition Paul recounts, albeit moving his emphasis onto Christ's divine sonship consequent on his resurrection (Rom 1:3—4). Luke embeds the hope for the rebuilding of "the dwelling of David" at the heart of James' speech at the Jerusalem Conference (Acts 15:16), and it is remembered in the tradition which Eusebius attributes to Hegesippus "that after the capture of Jerusalem Vespasian issued an order that, to ensure that no member of the royal house should be left among the Jews, all descendants of David should be ferreted out."[152] Belief in Davidic messiahship is closely linked to the hope and expectation of the temporal restoration of the twelve-tribe Israel under the leadership of the House of David.

There was also probably a commonality between the *Jakobusgemeinde* and Paul on the central significance of Jerusalem in the eschatological

151. Dodd, *Apostolic Preaching*, 17.

152. *Hist. eccl.* 12.1.

drama in which they all felt they were participating. Paul's collection from his Gentile ἐκκλησίαι "for the saints/poor in Jerusalem" was an expression of his reading of the situation, that the response of Gentiles to the gospel being experienced through his mission is a sign that they are living in the shadow of the ἔσχατον, whereas the priority accorded the Mission to the Jews by James and the elders was a contrasting response. The narrative of Acts (§ 5. 6.4.) strongly suggests that the body (τὸ πλῆθος) of the *Jakobusgemeinde* was increasingly influenced by the populist drift towards that more radical nationalist position which found its tragic denouement in 70 CE. The restoration of the twelve tribes as part of a renewed Israel under God was a shared aspiration of the Judaic movements of the late Second Temple period (§ 5. 9.2.4).[153] In that opening scene of Acts, the Apostles give voice to this fundamental component of the scenario of the ἔσχατον for it to be peremptorily dismissed by Jesus. The priority accorded this interaction by Luke is itself evidence that these dreams of the temporal restoration of the nation of Israel were central for τὸ πλῆθος of the *Jakobusgemeinde*, certainly in the run up to the outbreak of the War.

11. The Status of the *Jakobusgemeinde*

There is a problem in Antioch. Rather, the *Jakobusgemeinde* has a problem over what is happening in Antioch; but it is Antioch who must journey to Jerusalem to seek its resolution. Staring us in the face, filling our horizon, is that most obvious fact—so obvious that it is taken for granted and never questioned or challenged—that the place for the resolution of the problem in Antioch is with James and the *Jakobusgemeinde* in Jerusalem. This is particularly significant if the tradition Luke records is correct that attributes the foundation of the Antioch ἐκκλησία to the initiative of the free-wheeling Hellenists (Acts 11:19–20).[154] Nothing expresses the significance of the *Jakobusgemeinde* more completely. It is a position of eminence also clearly expressed through Paul's collection project.

153. Casey, *Jesus of Nazareth*, 420. The Twelve judging Israel (Mark 10:35–40) must be early tradition as there was no reason for the church to create it.

154. Luke does not record the Hellenists as seeking approval from Jerusalem for their entrepreneurial evangelization in Samaria through to Caesarea (Acts 8:4–40), Phoenicia, Cyprus, and Antioch (Acts 11:19)—it is the "apostles at Jerusalem" who have to follow in their pioneering footsteps to maintain some supervision over these new developments (Acts 8:14; 11:22), and this may indeed have been a reason for Cephas' presence in Antioch (Gal 2:11).

11.1 A Capital Location

The status and respect accorded the *Jakobusgemeinde* is a reflection of its location in the Holy City itself—the very center of the Judaic world[155] and location for the anticipated consummation of all things at the ἔσχατον.[156] It was natural for Jews to talk of "going up" to Jerusalem (e.g., Luke 2:42; cf., v. 51) and Luke, like Paul, uses the pilgrimage language of ascent to describe how "Paul and Barnabas and some of the others were appointed to *go up* to Jerusalem to discuss this question with the apostles and elders" (Acts 15:2 § 4. 5.1). Given that the early proto-Christian communities were an integral (if slightly deviant) part of the greater Judaic presence both in Palestine and in the Diaspora, the *Jakobusgemeinde* can be expected to have attracted to itself in the eyes of its followers some of the prestige associated with Jerusalem for all Israelites.

And reinforcing this position of Jerusalem for proto-Christian movements is that the City was also the place of their Lord's suffering, death and exaltation.

11.2 The Family Presence

A second factor contributing to the *Jakobusgemeinde*'s eminence in the proto-Christian movement is the presence and leadership in Jerusalem of members of Jesus' family[157] with James at the head, which is strongly attested in the early traditions gathered by Eusebius[158] and confirmed by the occasional casual NT reference (Acts 1:14, 12:17; 1 Cor 9:5; Gal 1:19, 2:9). It is an eminence that would be further reinforced if James were indeed the elder brother to Jesus (§ 6.).[159]

---

155. Bauckham, "James and the Jerusalem Church," 417–27; Hengel, *Pre-Christian Paul*, 54.

156. DiTommaso, "Jerusalem, New," 797–99.

157. Esler, *First Christians*, 26–27. In first century Mediterranean society family members share in the honor of a significant family member.

158. *Hist. eccl.* 3:11–12, 19–20, 22.

159. Eusebius describes the *Jakobusgemeinde* (presumably a very fragmented remnant post-70 CE) as continuing the leadership of the dominical family, but he is completely silent about it being accorded any wider authority in the embryonic "Great Church." See Bernheim, *James*, 216–22 for an overview.

11.3 The Primacy of Age

Yet we must recognize that all the proto-Christian communities about which we have anything approaching hard information are those of Acts and the recipients of Paul's correspondence—all of whom, in one way or another, could trace their origin back to the *Jakobusgemeinde*. These would all have a natural allegiance to their "mother-church."[160]

In contrast, if the emphasis on Galilee as the location for Jesus' continuing presence and activity within the Synoptic tradition (Mark 14:28; 16:7[161]; Matt 26:32; 28:7, 10, 16–20. cf. John 21:1–23), is any guide, we must question whether the continuing proto-Christian community in Galilee, to whom we almost certainly owe the preservation and transmission of much of Jesus' words and deeds in that northern territory, felt such an indebtedness and relationship with Jerusalem.[162]

If Drury is right in identifying Jerusalem and Galilee as the two locations for "the beginning of the good news" (§ 3. 5.) then the *Jakobusgemeinde* must, in some sense at least, be rooted in, and perceived as, in continuity with the originating Baptist movement in Jerusalem.

Therefore, if the *Jakobusgemeinde*, in some form, was already in Jerusalem within the movement(s) for Judaic reform before the start of Jesus' ministry in Galilee, or as an outcome of the Baptist movement within the City contemporary with Jesus' activity in Galilee, and recognized as a continuing social entity, then its status would also derive from the fact of it being the senior movement, consolidating its eminence amongst developing ἐκκλησίαι in both Eretz Israel (apart from Galilee?) and the Diaspora. Its seniority derived from both its earlier beginning and direct connection to the ministry of John the Baptist compared with the derivative origination of the Galilean movement under the leadership of one of John's disciples—Jesus.

160. Our understanding of early Christian history would be greatly enriched if we were better informed of the origins of the movement in a wider range of places such as Alexandria. cf., Bruce, *Men and Movements*, 71–76.

161. " . . . there (Galilee) you will see him" (Mark 16:7) may not be referring to a Christophany but to Galilee as the location for the parousia. Marxsen, *Mark the Evangelist*, 75–95; Lightfoot, *Locality and Doctrine*, 52–65, 73–77.

162. It may be significant that the commission in Acts 1:8 is silent about Galilee ("witness in Jerusalem . . . Judea . . . Samaria . . . ends of the earth') and the sole reference to an ἐκκλησία in Galilee is in the Lucan summary of Acts 9:31.

6

The Family and the Brothers

OUR SEARCH TO THIS point has been dominated by what our limited texts reveal/suggest about the *Jakobusgemeinde*, and about James in his relationship with that lively community. It is time to focus on James as a person with a biography. From the first century CE nearly all the information we have is in fragments of tradition preserved within the gospels—and those fragments are included within the flow of the narratives because the gospel writer wants to tell us about Jesus, not James. We are bringing questions to a text that is essentially not interested in them.

I want to begin with a speculative flight of fancy:

1. Echoes of Family

1.1 The Elder Brother

I find myself haunted by the figure of the elder brother in the parable of the Prodigal Son—he is a "dead ringer" for James (Luke 15:11–32).

The popular title for the parable misleads—the story is about *two* sons, and while the preacher waxes eloquently about the returning son, many in the congregation reserve their sympathy for his unappreciated brother: " . . . you have never given me . . . so that I might celebrate" (15:29).

No scholar of James—famous for his Torah adherence—should miss the allusion: "For all these years I have been working like a slave for you, and I have never disobeyed your command" (15:29).[1]

1. The only references I have found are by Bruce Chilton: (1)"His (James) seniority

This allusion becomes a near certainty in the often-overlooked climax to the story: "Son, you are always with me, and all that is mine is yours . . ." (15:31). The challenge of the Form Critics to identify the *Sitz im Leben* of this parable within the life of the early Christian communities remains valid. One distinct probability is that it is an appeal to proto-Christian groupings such as the περιτομή within the *Jakobusgemeinde* to be more open to the Gentiles who were responding to the early Christian message.[2] It echoes the theology of James himself at the Conference (Acts 15:13–17) that Gentiles should be welcomed as a people of God, whilst Israel neverthe-less has primacy as God's special people,[3] and is also consonant with Paul's theodicy in Rom 9—11.[4]

In addition to its resonance with the problem of the relationship be-tween the mission to the Jews (the particular interest of James, *cf* Gal 2:9) and the mission to the Gentiles that was a continuing problem throughout the early decades, may there not also be here an echo of family history? It may be judged overly speculative, but there is nothing intrinsically improb-able in memories/stories about the earlier years of the two brothers who were central to the new faith continuing to be in circulation amongst their followers, albeit strongly colored by their later relationship and significance.[5]

---

relative to Jesus might just be reflected in the parable of the prodigal." (Chilton and Evans, *James the Just*, 15); (2) "(I)t was only natural (in contrast to Jesus) for James to sound increasingly like the prodigal's older brother." (Chilton, *Rabbi Jesus*. 78). In *Rabbi Jesus*, 63, 71–72—an imaginative venture into a biography of Jesus—Chilton further suggests that the welcome home Jesus received after long years in the wilderness with John the Baptist fed in to his description of the Prodigal's return.

2. Evans, *Luke*, 233–34.

3. Crossley has drawn attention to the way that the parables of "the lost" in Luke 15 all portray repentance as "re-turn" to God—where ἐπιστρεφω [= *shuv* (Heb)] would have been expected (consistent with what he demonstrates was the probable usage of both John the Baptist and Jesus)—yet μετανοέω is used (Luke 15:7, 11), the word characteristically used in the NT with reference to Gentile conversion, in preference to ἐπιστρεφω (Crossley, "Semitic Background to Repentance"): " . . . the problem of the unusual Greek translation in the gospels can be solved because the evangelists or earlier writers in Greek had one eye on the inclusion of gentiles in the Christian community." I would add that this "spin" on the Jesus tradition may well have its origin during oral performance of that tradition.

4. E.g., Kirk, "Why Does the Deliverer Come," 81–99.

5. Robert Funk lifts the parable out of its Lucan framework and does recognize "autobiographical overtones" in that the "parable mirrors the journey of Jesus," leaving home and possessions to become itinerant etc.—Funk, *Honest to Jesus*, 186–89. Ken-neth Bailey has argued that the interpretive framework for the parable is to be found in the story of Jacob in Genesis (Webb, Review of *Jesus and the Prodigal*, 109). This does not exclude a biographical origination—the suffering and crucifixion of Jesus is recounted and interpreted through the prism of OT imagery such as Ps 22 and the

1.2 The Younger Brother

If so, and if James is the elder brother, who is the younger brother?[6] In a situation of increasing economic pressure for the family (§ 2. 3.1.3) with debt and the threat of dispossession never further than one failed harvest away, did the younger son ask for an advance on his inheritance[7] so that he could do what some others were doing (the parable of the Talents/ Pounds, Matt 25:14–30//Luke 19:11–27)—seeking to break out of the cycle of poverty by taking what capital they could raise and seeking to increase it like the servants in the parable of the talents?[8] Does his saying about a son leaving home (Mark 10:29–30) preserve a personal memory? Did Jesus,

---

Suffering Servant of II Isaiah without negating its historical facticity.

6. Moxnes, *Jesus in His Place*, 97, notes that in many cultures there is pressure on the eldest sons to stay at home, safeguarding the family inheritance and caring for aging parents, whilst "younger brothers are more prone to leave home." In Galilee, this might involve joining one of the bandit-groups in the hills, and Moxnes muses on whether Jesus and his disciples might be "a movement of younger sons, who would have less to lose than their elder brothers." He is silent on the clear inference that Jesus may also be a younger brother.

7. The setting of the parable is a large farm (with servants and hired hands—Luke 15:19, 26)—Moxnes, *Jesus in His Place*, 44. The father can assign his property to his sons, but he retains the right of occupation and benefit unless he converts the assignment into a gift, which is what he seems to do here. In this case the recipient forgoes any further claim on the inheritance. Hence the assurance to the Elder Brother that "all that is mine is yours" (Luke 15:31) is legally correct—Manson, *Sayings of Jesus*, 286–87; Kloppenberg, "Parable of the Prodigal Son," draws on a wide range of evidence from Greco-Egyptian papyri to illustrate the normalcy of the procedure; Richardson, *Herod*, 45, notes that the eldest son inherits the largest share, which would result in younger sons feeling more pressure to leave the family home.

8. Herzog II, *Parables as Subversive Speech*, 150–68, locates the parable of the Talents/Pounds in the household world of rich owners using their retainers to further enhance their wealth at the expense of the peasantry. The setting for the parable of the Prodigal is different and although the father is comparatively well-off it is not he but one of his sons who takes the initiative in asking for a part of the estate to be liquidated for him. Commentators note the legality of the younger son's request (Num 27:8–11, 36:7–9; Deut 21:17); Green, *Gospel of Luke*, 580, whilst morally disapproving—"an act of grossest disregard and disloyalty"; Evans, *Luke*, 236. Mc Knight, on the basis of Matt 11:19, comments that " . . . it is most likely that Jesus was accused, during his lifetime, of being 'a rebellious son'" (McKnight, "Calling Jesus *Mamzer*" 74). The parable itself makes no such criticism, which is reserved for the perceived reason for the younger son's failure to make good—"dissolute living" (v. 13) maturing in the righteous imagination of the elder brother into "devoured your property with prostitutes" (v. 30). The parables of Jesus are being increasingly recognized as important material for our understanding of the social world of first century Israel as experienced and observed by the peasantry. Rohrbaugh, "Dysfunctional Family and its Neighbours," 141–64 and Moxnes, *Jesus in His Place*, 63–64, both locate the Prodigal within the context of household and village social relationships, but neither notes the familial resonances of the two sons.

the younger son, attempt this and dismally fail? That would add edge to his riposte when asked to arbitrate on an inheritance issue, particularly as it was between two brothers—"Friend, who set me to be a judge or arbitrator over you?" (Luke 12:13–14).

The younger son is described as going to "a distant country" (15:13), which is the same phrase (εἰς χώραν μακράν) used by Luke in his introduction to the parable of the Pounds where there is a clear historical allusion to a visit to Rome by Archelaus.[9] Is that where the younger son set out? Failing in his enterprise, and in his destitution finding himself living amongst those who were "outside the Law," did Jesus find there a level of humanity amongst them that he had not known before? Could his characteristic stance of being "a friend of sinners" and eating with them (e.g., Mark 2:16; Luke 15:2), which is so different from the tradition of Torah fidelity associated with his elder brother James ("the Just/Righteous"[10]), have its origin in such an experience?[11]

Embedded in the finale of the parable there lurks an understandable element of sibling alienation ("this son of yours . . . ," Luke 15:30) which could have led to Jesus not settling back at home, becoming a τέκτων (i.e., a builder[12]) and why, a few years later, we find him domiciled in Capernaum (Mark 2:1) whilst his brothers, with Mary, may for a time be in Cana (John 2:1–11) but then in Jerusalem (Acts 1:14).

Amongst parables reflecting many aspects of life on the margins in rural Galilee, the parables of Jesus reveal an intimate and wide knowledge and contact with the problems, challenges, anxieties, and rewards of farming. Historical Jesus scholarship has seen in this a possible clue to the socioeconomic status of the family of Jesus (§§ 2. 3.1.3 and 2. 4.1), and Richard Horsley detected the possibility that the family had lost their land in the cycle of debt that was shared by many at this time,[13] which may also be reflected in Jesus being a τέκτων, described by Dominic Crossan as a member of the artisan class who were "below the Peasants (subsistence farmers)

---

9. *Ant.* 17.208.

10. *Hist. eccls.* 2:23.4–8—"James . . . was called the 'Just' by all men from the Lord's time to ours . . ."

11. Crossley, *Why Christianity Happened*, 57–58, following Kautsky, notes that one factor that can facilitate the movement of a peasant into a position of leadership is experience of the world beyond the local village. Crossley examples pilgrimage visits to Jerusalem, contact with John the Baptist and knowledge of the Essenes. Had Jesus also been to "a far country"?

12. See § 2. 4.1 n.54.

13. Horsley, *Hidden Transcripts*, 16. Cf., Charlesworth, Review of *Settlement and History*, 283. Galilean archeology indicates the dominance of larger estate-farms over smaller peasant-subsistence farmers in the first century.

in social class because they were usually recruited and replenished from its dispossessed members."[14] The younger son's diversion of resources into his failed entrepreneurial endeavor may have been a factor in the loss of the family's land, and have led to his brothers (with Mary) having to move to Jerusalem, perhaps to seek the work that was available there on Herod's Temple Building project, whilst Jesus himself moved to Capernaum (§§ 2. 3.1.3; 2. 4.; 6. 2.2).

This is inevitably speculative. Richard Bauckham in a similar context, defended the disciplined use of . . .

> . . . historically informed imagination to draw possible infer-
> ences from the evidence but stopping short of the kind of imagi-
> native speculation that goes far beyond the evidence.[15]

Unlike the tendency of an earlier period of historical Jesus research,[16] this use of Luke's parable does not psychologize, nor does it feed back into Nazareth the social practice and family values of the writer's contemporary world.[17] It is speculation, framed by a story centering on two brothers coming from the peasant world of first century Galilee, that at every point links with and makes connections between the known socio-economic scenario of first-century rural Galilee and the facts about James and Jesus and the other family members as we encounter them in the text of the NT.

1.3. " . . . call him Jesus" (Matt 1:21)

One inference from this family portrait is that Jesus is not the eldest sibling but a younger son to James.[18] For very different reasons, already in the second century from the *Protevangelium of James*[19] we find the suggestion (to be linked from the fourth century with the name of Epiphanius)[20] that the

---

14. Crossan, *Jesus*, 25; Tabor, *Jesus Dynasty*, 89–90.

15. Bauckham, *Gospel Women*, 194.

16. Rubio, "The Fiction of the 'Three Quests,'" for a severe critique of the notion of 'First Quest.'

17. As, for example, in the delightful and deservedly popular book *Jesus of History* by T. R. Glover (1917) which sold 100,000 copies within ten years of publication.

18. Clearly implied in the mid- to late-second century *Inf. Gos. Thom.* 16:1–2. (Hock, "Infancy Gospel of Thomas" 369–79).

19. *Prot Jas* 9.2. Although very relevant in the second century, the issue of Mary's virginal status is irrelevant to this current discussion.

20. Painter, *Just James*, 208–13; Bernheim, *James*, 19–20.

siblings of Jesus were in fact the offspring of the widowed Joseph from his first marriage.[21] Crossan speculated:

> I wonder, in fact, if the emphasis given to James, who is known to both Paul and Josephus as Jesus' "brother," might indicate that James was the eldest in the family and that his prominence after the death of Jesus was due not just to his renowned piety but to his leadership position in a family whose father, Joseph, may well have been long dead.[22]

This possibility does not "go beyond the evidence": consideration of the naming pattern of the five brothers strongly supports its credibility:

Four brothers (Mark 6.3)	One brother (Matt 1.21)
Named after four of the patriarchs	Named after the one who led Israel into the Land
Jacob (= James);	
Joseph (= Joses);	Joshua (= Jesus)
Judah;	
Simon.	

Fig. 3 The sons of Joseph and Mary

---

21. Schofield, *In the Year 62*, 25. For a review of the evidence concerning the relationship between Jesus and his brothers, see Bauckham, *Jude* 19–32. He cautiously concludes that "the Epiphanian view has a better claim to serious consideration than is often nowadays allowed." This led to a fuller exchange of papers with a riposte in Meier, "Brothers and Sisters of Jesus," replied to by Bauckham, "An Epiphanian Response." Support for Jesus' siblings as Joseph's children, but not Mary's, comes also from Tarrech, *Jesus: An Uncommon Journey*—Downing, Review of Tarrech, 36–37. Alternatively, Tabor, *Jesus Dynasty*, 77–81, has proposed that Joseph died without fathering any children other than Jesus, and that Mary was taken in a Levirate marriage by his brother Clopas who fathered James and the other brothers. This leaves Jesus as the eldest of the brothers, and Tabor claims that it further solves the multiple "Mary's" conundrum in the Empty Tomb narratives (though it does nothing for the dogma of Mary's perpetual virginity).

22. Crossan, *Jesus*, 23–24.

James/Jacob, also named "Israel" (Gen 32:28), was the father of the twelve tribes that traditionally constituted the people of Israel and therefore was a more fitting name for the eldest son of a family than the much later Jesus. Judah and Simon were also popular names at this period through their identification with two of the heroes of the Maccabean revolution.[23] This may be an indicator of the political/religious sympathies of Joseph with the renewal and restoration movement within Israel and may add significance to the choice of the key name of Jesus/Joshua, born of his new and much younger wife/betrothed, from the much later epoch of Israel's history when the Israelites took possession of the Land.[24] At least this choice of name marks a break with the established family naming pattern and may well indicate a new family development.[25]

If Mary was Joseph's second wife, that may also be the simplest explanation of Jesus' identification (in a patriarchal society) as "the son of Mary" (Mark 6:3).[26]

23. Bernheim, *James*, 34–35.

24. Joshua led the Israelites in possessing the Land Yahweh had set aside for them. It was therefore a name that might well indicate an identification by the family of James and Jesus with the aspirations for a restoration of Israel within the Land.

25. If James was the eldest of four brothers, all born before Jesus (born c. 4 BCE), we have to factor in the implication for the age of James at the time of his death in 62 CE— probably in his mid-70s. This is not insuperable, but we need to be aware of it. However, this is eased if Chilton is correct, in modifying the traditional Epiphanian view that all the brothers (and sisters) of Jesus were Joseph's progeny from his first marriage, when he refers to the two younger brothers—Judah and Simon— as Mary's sons, by Joseph (Chilton, *Rabbi Jesus*. 23, 72). This retains the significance of the break in the naming pattern with the introduction of "Joshua." The younger sons names were very popular in late Second Temple Judaism from their additional association with the Maccabees, so all three of Mary's sons were then named after heroic figures in Israel's liberation.

26. It may be a reflection of the fact that Mary was a prominent figure in the early Christian movement, especially in Jerusalem. That Jesus was illegitimate can probably be discounted—McGrath, "Was Jesus Illegitimate," 81–100. Bauckham, "Brothers and Sisters," 698–700, draws attention to genealogical evidence in the OT and rabbinic literature that "sons of men who had children by more than one wife can be designated by their metronymic, instead of the usual patronymic" and concludes: "It is easy to suppose that, whereas outside Nazareth Jesus would have to be identified as 'the son of Joseph', in Nazareth, where the family was known, the children of Joseph's two wives would be distinguished by their metronymics. Jesus would be called 'the son of Mary' precisely because James, Joses, Judas, and Simon were not sons of Mary." See Casey, *Jesus of Nazareth*, 144, 152–58.

2. A Synoptic Interlude

2.1 A Dysfunctional Family?

The Gospel records are somewhat ambivalent about the relationship of Jesus to his family during his ministry.[27] The Fourth Gospel records his disciples along with his mother and brothers at a family wedding in Cana (John 2:1–12),[28] whilst the brothers of Jesus seem to be journeying with him in Galilee even though their faith is (in Johannine perception) seen as inadequate (John 7:1–5). The strong and overt theological structuring of the Fourth Gospel regularly affects confidence in the historicity of its traditions—in this instance bringing a focus on the Johannine theme of the καιρός of Jesus. The introduction of "the brothers" in this setting with the reference to their imperfect faith may thus carry an inference by the evangelist of the inadequacy of "the brothers'" understanding of the significance of Jesus, and likewise therefore of the *Jakobusgemeinde*, with whom they are associated. It need not be ruled out as containing valid tradition about family relationships during Jesus' ministry, but at his death this writer has Jesus place the care of Mary, not into the hands of his brothers, but into the care of "the beloved disciple" (John 19:26–27).[29]

It is the Markan narration that raises questions about the relationship between Jesus and his family. In the only gospel incident where James is actually mentioned by name (Mark 6:1–6) Mark describes how Jesus was rebuffed when he returned to his hometown of Nazareth. He records Jesus as specifically including his kin amongst his unbelieving fellow townsfolk. However, both Matthew and Luke distance themselves from their Markan source: Matthew omits the reference to "his own kin," whilst Luke totally blurs out the implication (Luke 4:22–24) to create the space for his retrojection of the later Gentile Mission experience into the ministry of Jesus (Luke 4:25–30).

In the Synoptic record, outside the Nativity narratives, the family of Jesus make their only appearance when they respond to alarming reports about Jesus' mental state, described by Taylor as "based on the best historical tradition" for no gospel writer would have invented an allegation that Jesus was mad (Mark 3:19b–22; 3:31–35).[30] James is not named but presumably

27. Martin, *James*, xl–xli; Brandon, *Fall of Jerusalem*, 194.

28. Jesus' abrupt address to his mother of "Woman" (γύναι) (John 2:4) often interpreted as a sign of distance between them may be translated as "Madam" or "Lady"—Bulembat, "Head-Waiter and Bridegroom."

29. Unless Tabor is right in identifying "the beloved disciple" as James. *Jesus Dynasty*, 165, 206–07.

30. Taylor, *Mark*, 235. Mark 3:21 describes "those with him" (οἱ παρ' αὐτοῦ) which

included in "your mother and your brothers." Neither Joseph (deceased?) nor Jesus' sisters are mentioned.

Redaction criticism has highlighted the strong contrast Mark makes in this pericope between Jesus' new family seated around him who "do the will of God" (v. 34) and his natural family who are specifically "outside" (v. 32)—a phrase which gains significance in the explanation attached to the parable of the Sower that immediately follows, where it is "those outside" who do not understand "the secret of the kingdom of God" (Mark 4:11).[31]

This may be a later Markan critique of the dominical family and of their leadership through the *Jakobusgemeinde*, (akin to the Johannine critique, above) but it has nonetheless nurtured a widespread perception of an historical alienation between Jesus and James during the time of the former's ministry.

Thus, commenting on the way "Mark goes out of his way to present the family of Jesus as dysfunctional and disunited," David Catchpole suggests that:

> He could hardly have ventured to do so if the historical family in general and the historical Mary in particular had been sympathetic to Jesus and supportive of his mission.[32]

On the other hand Painter points out that Mark is equally assertive about the disbelief of the Twelve, affirming:

> that the evidence used to document the unbelief of the family, the brothers in particular, will not bear the weight of the case that has been built on it.[33]

He rejects the notion that James was a late convert through his vision of the Risen Jesus (1 Cor 15:7), arguing for him being a prior disciple of his brother.[34] Unfortunately, he fails to consider the alternative possibility of James being independently active in Jerusalem.

However, reading the story by itself, we see a family who, whatever gremlins might be lodged within its relationships, shows natural concern over the health and well-being of one of their number; and Jesus, who knows the pain involved in turning away from his family of birth in order to fulfill

---

NSRV now translates (contextually—v. 31) as "family" in place of the RSV "friends." Painter, *Just James*, 27, preferring this latter translation, considers vv. 19b–21 to be Markan redaction.

31. Crossan, "Mark and the Relatives of Jesus."

32. Catchpole, *Jesus People*, 115.

33. Painter, *Just James*, 11–41; Painter, "Who was James?" 24–31.

34. Painter, *Just James*, 42; Bernheim, *James*, 94–100.

his sense of call in an itinerant ministry (Matt 10:37–39//Luke 14:26–27), keeps them at a distance. We need to remember that the love of those closest to us can sometimes be very difficult to deal with, especially if we are having to handle emotional stress within whilst dealing with demands from a situation to which we are committed.

Jesus has moved away from his family of origin and is now following a somewhat deviant course, but whatever strains are present in the relationship they do not override a shared, stronger underlying sense of kinship.[35]

Bruce Chilton describes it as "not a picture of family bliss,"[36]—but a more nuanced understanding of the complex of emotions involved in intra-family relationships is required. We have here a picture of a family of a (widowed?) mother and her sons, one of whom (Jesus) now lives away from them in Capernaum (Mark 2:1—ἐν οἴκῳ; also, Mark 3:19b)[37] from where they hear disturbing rumors about him. They hear—and respond.

I submit that the reaction of Jesus in not letting his family get too close to him is precisely one form of coping strategy that may be used by a person facing a conflict between the strongest of human ties clashing with an intense personal sense of divine calling. The strength of the family tie is evidenced both by their journey to see him, and the difficulty he has in receiving them. Intra-familial strains pre-suppose recognition and valuing of kinship.

The weight of evidence does not support the Markan topos of alienation between Jesus and his family: neither does it support the notion that some of his brothers were members of the close disciple group.[38] At best (John 7:1–6) they were "around" in Galilee at times during his ministry.

In the light of this suspicion that has been attached to James and his brothers we might also note that Paul (our earliest witness) appears to be in total ignorance of it. In all the fractious arguments in his Corinthian ἐκκλησία (2 Cor 10—13) about his status as an "apostle" he makes no reference to James, and any tradition about James being at odds with his brother during the latter's lifetime would surely have been "grist to the mill" of Paul's argument. In all Paul's writings, the validity and status of James' position remains inviolate.

---

35. Moxnes, *Putting Jesus in His Place*, 15, counsels that most studies of Jesus' family impose anachronistic family concepts.

36. Chilton, "Getting It Right," 107–24.

37. Kilpatrick, "Jesus, His Family and His Disciples."

38. Tabor, *Jesus Dynasty*, 164–65; Eisenman, *James*, 864–65.

2.2 Nazareth . . . to Jerusalem?

When Jesus returns to Nazareth[39] (Mark 6:1–6a) we encounter the only reference to James in the canonical gospels: "Is not this the τέκτων . . . brother of James . . . " (v. 3). And it is implicit in the disbelieving response of its inhabitants that his brothers (and mother) no longer live there—" . . . are not his sisters here with us (ὧδε πρὸς ἡμας)."[40] Presumably they had married local men and remained in the village.[41]

That the girls were old enough to marry while the family were still living in Nazareth suggests that the brothers would also be grown men when they left Nazareth with Mary. If Jesus was about thirty when he commenced his ministry (Luke 3:23) the family exodus from their native village must have been within a decade or so prior to that date. We know that Jesus eventually domiciled in Capernaum[42] (§ 6. 1.2). We know nothing of the whereabouts of the rest of the family (other than the Johannine tradition of a family wedding at Cana) but it is significant that within about five years[43] following this Nazareth incident we find one brother at least—James—in a leadership position (a Pillar) in Jerusalem (Gal 1:19) over a group of people that were sometimes referred to as "Nazarenes" (Acts 24:5.; § 8. 2.1.5).[44] Further, to

---

39. Moxnes, *Jesus in His Place*, 35–36, commenting on Matt 2:23 notes that "the author had difficulties in finding memories and establishing a history for Nazareth, . . . since there were no references to the town of Nazareth in Scripture . . . the most likely reason is that it was known to him that Jesus came from Nazareth."

40. John Meier, defending the Helvidian position that the siblings of Jesus were the later natural offspring of Joseph and Mary, draws attention to "the structure of Mark's questions: there is no mention of Jesus' father; the designation 'woodworker' (applied to Jesus), the name of the mother, and the name of the four brothers are all placed in one question; *and the (unnamed) sisters are referred to in a separate question.*' (my italics). (Meier, "Brothers and Sisters of Jesus" 11–12). In focusing on the implications of Mark's first question, he fails to note the significance of the latter question. Taylor also fails to note the significance of ὧδε πρὸς ἡμᾶς for its placement of the sisters, whilst recording its possible inference that "the brothers were not resident in Nazareth at this time" (Taylor, *Mark*, 300–01).

41. Hengel, *Saint Peter*, 109.

42. Malbon, "Τῇ Οἰκια αὐτοῦ: Mark 2:15 in Context"; Kilpatrick, "Jesus, His Family and His Disciples."

43. Following the chronology proposed by Riesner, *Paul's Early Period*, 322—taking a mid-term date (28/29 CE) within the ministry of Jesus for the Nazareth incident and the appearance of James (Gal 1:19) as a *Jakobusgemeinde* leader in 33/34 CE.

44. "The term 'Nazarene' is almost certainly linked with 'Nazareth'" (Bruce, *New Testament History*, 214; Dunn, *Jesus Remembered*, 313 n.272; Dunn, *Beginning from Jerusalem*, 14–15). There are 3 words/phrases that are translated (NRSV) as "(Jesus) of Nazareth": (1) ἀπο Ναζαρέθ (Mark 1:9; Matt 21:11; John 1:45–46; Acts 10:38). (2) Ναζαρηνός (Mark 1:24//Luke 4:34; Mark 10:47; 14:67; 16:6; Luke 24:10). (3) Ναζαραῖος

be in the role of Pillar—comparable to the Essene's role of *mebaqqer*—infers a recognized degree of competence for James in the interpretation of Torah with an associated level of literacy that could only be acquired over a period of time in Jerusalem itself.

Crossan, musing on the apparent high standing James achieved in Jerusalem itself, as evidenced in Josephus' account of his execution, its ensuing reaction, and outcome in the dismissal of the high priest,[45] has raised the question of how long James had lived there:

> (W)as he in Jerusalem long before Jesus' death, and did his presence there invite, provoke, challenge Jesus' only journey to Jerusalem?[46]

As James had apparently left Nazareth sometime before the occasion Mark narrates he could have been in Jerusalem for up to ten years, and therefore in Jerusalem (with his mother[47] and the other brothers) well before

---

(Matt 26:71; Luke 18:37; John 18:5, 7; Acts 2:22; 3:6; 4:11; 6:14; 22:8; 26:9. Only in Acts 24:5 does Ναζαραῖος carry the translation "(the sect of the) Nazarenes" which continued for some time to be the term used particularly in Jewish circles (e.g., the twelfth benediction " . . .may the Nazarenes and the heretics perish . . . " (Schurer, *History*, 2.461). Matthew understood Ναζαραῖος as a reference to Nazareth. (Matt 2:23). Throughout the Gospels and Acts Ναζαρηνός / Ναζαραῖος are variously but consistently translated as either 'Nazarene' or 'of/from Nazareth'. In most cases it is an identifier for Jesus. (Dunn, *Jesus Remembered*, 313 n.272). Exegetes have strained with little success to find a scriptural basis to legitimize Matthew's "quotation" (e.g., Plummer, *Matthew*, 18–19; Filson, *St Matthew*, 62). The earliest exegetes who sought for a deeper meaning in the epithet than the obvious geographical one are probably those Jacobean enthusiasts behind the traditions of James being a Nazirite that Hegesippus so fulsomely reports (*Hist. eccl.* 2.23.4). Bruce Chilton is a minority voice arguing that Jesus was a Nazirite. Noting that the LXX uses different transliterations for the Hebrew "Nazirite," similar to the uncertainty the Gospels show in (2) and (3) above, he only accepts ἀπο Ναζαρέθ as referring to Jesus' home-town (Chilton, "Yakov in Relation to Peter," 155–56; Chilton, "Getting it Right"; Chilton, "James, Peter, Paul," 23–25); Chilton, *Missing Jesus*, 118–23; cf. § 2. 5.2.5 n.104.

45. *Ant.* 20.197–203.

46. Crossan, *Jesus*, 135–36; Butz, *Brother of Jesus*, 53–54.

47. Brown suggests that Mary may have been living in Jerusalem during her pregnancy with Jesus—*The Birth of the Messiah*, 332. Stanley Porter has presented evidence that the census (Luke 2) was actually a property return, suggesting that Joseph and Mary may have owned property in Bethlehem—Lalleman, Review of *Paul, Luke and the Graeco-Roman World*, 90–91. Ehrhardt, *Acts of the Apostles*, 52, notes Mary's possible connections in Jerusalem. Pearson, "Q Community in Galilee?" 476–94, n.64, opines, "it is quite probable that Jesus' family had relatives in Jerusalem." James Charlesworth states: " . . . we now have abundant evidence of ethnic discontinuity in Galilee that began with a massive migration following the Hasmonean conquests of Galilee . . . Most of the migrating Judeans (perhaps Jesus' family) moved to lower Galilee before Herod." (Charlesworth, Review of *Settlement and History*, 283); Carlson, "Accommodations of

the period of Jesus' activity in Galilee. The Gospels, in very casual ways, refer to assistance that Jesus was able to call upon from within Jerusalem in getting a colt for his Entry into the City (Mark 11:2–6), and then acquiring a "large room upstairs, furnished and ready" for his Passover celebration (Mark 14:15).[48] If James, Mary and his brothers, were already established within the City, do we need to look any further for the most likely contact and source of assistance?

3. The Brothers

James (Jacob) was a popular Judaic name in the first century, and there are a number of men called James amongst the early followers of Jesus who get a mention in the NT.[49] When Paul describes James as "the Lord's brother" (Gal 1:19) it is probably a matter mainly of identification, for James' authority is principally expressed in his recognition as a Pillar of the *Jakobusgemeinde* (like Cephas and John).

However, Paul's passing reference (1 Cor 9:5) to the "brothers of the Lord" as distinct from "the other apostles" indicates both their involvement in the mission of the *Jakobusgemeinde* and that membership of the family of Jesus did carry status—Eusebius records the tradition that after his death, a cousin—Symeon—was elected to succeed James.[50] That being "the Lord's brother" enhanced James' authority in Jerusalem and (from that pinnacle of influence) into the Diaspora cannot be gainsaid, but it can be overrated.[51] For instance, his authority did not carry over to his brothers: in his lifetime a chasm exists between the position of James and that of his other brothers who briefly appear as James' itinerant envoys, whilst he remains firmly in charge at the center (1 Cor 9:5).

This is confirmed in the salutations of the letters from within the Jacobean tradition in the NT—EpJas and Jude. Like James, Jude was a popular name in the first century, but one of the other brothers of Jesus is clearly meant; whether its ascription is authorial or pseudonymous makes little difference. It is probably a writing from that strand of the early Christian movement that had its origins somewhere close to the *Jakobusgemeinde*. Jude describes himself (or, is described) first as "a servant of Jesus Christ"

Joseph and Mary," 336–42).

48. We also noted the admittedly late tradition in the *Gospel of the Hebrews* implying the presence of James at the Last Supper (§ 4. 4.1).

49. Painter, *Just James*, 2–3.

50. *Hist. eccl.* 3.11; 3.22; 4.22.4.

51. Bauckham, *Jude*, 125–30.

but significantly identifies himself, not as a "brother of Jesus," but as the "brother of *James*." His identity and status lay neither in himself nor in his sibling relationship to Jesus but as the brother of James. Such was the standing of James.

A similar perception occurs in EpJas where the opening salutation (whether authorial or pseudonymous is again not relevant) makes no reference to his sibling relationship to Jesus nor, for that matter, to his episcopal position (if I may be permitted an anachronism)—unlike the long self-descriptions Paul sometimes found it necessary to use in his letters, especially Romans and Galatians. It is simply "James, a servant of God and of the Lord Jesus Christ." The name "James" is sufficient, and, unlike Jude, carries a distinct authority of its own.

There is resonance here with the tradition preserved in the *Gospel of Thomas*:

> The disciples said to Jesus, "We know that you are going to leave us. Who will be our leader?" Jesus said to them, "No matter where you are, you are to go to James the Just, for whose sake heaven and earth came into being."[52]

In the following post-apostolic period, unlike James who continues as a revered figure, particularly in the writings of the Judaic-Christian and the Gnostic-Christian trajectories,[53] and is recognized as the first bishop of Jerusalem by the emerging "orthodox" tradition,[54] the other brothers of Jesus simply "drop off the radar."[55]

The authority of James is certainly not the authority of one whose leadership position came by default following the flight of Peter.[56] It is not simply that of a brother of Jesus.[57] It is not derived solely from his position as leader of the Judaic proto-Christian movement in the Holy City—that is what needs explanation.

James had no *real* successor. The authority vested in the *Jakobusgemeinde* ended when James' was stoned to death. It was an authority that was inextricably linked to James and vested in him as a person. It is the sort of

---

52. *Gos. Thom.* 12.

53. Reaching its apex in the third–fourth century Pseudo-Clementine literature.

54. Painter, *Just James*, 177–81.

55. A scan of the Christian names occurring in the titles of codices in the Nag Hammadi library makes the point: Peter (4 times); James (3 times); Paul and Philip (twice each); John, Thomas, Silvanus, Mary (once each). Nothing in the names of Jude or the other brothers (Robinson, *Nag Hammadi Library*, V—VIII).

56. Bauckham, "James and the Jerusalem Church," 439–41.

57. Contra Brandon, *Fall of Jerusalem*, 47–52.

authority often associated with initial charismatic leadership, blending into what I described as "Quasi-rabbinic Leadership" (§ 2. 6.2.3–4).

It is an authority that is unique to James. It is non-negotiable. It is non-transferable. It is the authority that adheres without qualification to the founder of a movement. When John Painter raises the question: "James as Convert or Foundation Leader?"[58]—there is just one answer. It only leaves the question of whether the *Jakobusgemeinde* over whose fortunes he presided for thirty years was created *ex nihilo* following on the events surrounding the execution of Jesus of Nazareth, or whether the *Jakobusgemeinde* was an already existent group founded and led by James within the spectrum of Judaic Reform movements, but profoundly influenced at some point by the message of John the Baptist.

---

58. Painter, *Just James*, 42–44.

7

A Black Hole at the Galactic Center?

1. Focused Listening

When I was a practicing counselor I knew it was important not only to listen intensively to the details, but also to tune in to the music of the story, with its themes and cadences, phrasings and riffs, underlying harmonies, surprising turns, rests and discords. Focused listening likewise tunes in to broader patterns, feelings, gaps, underlying agendas, personal constructs and quasi-Freudian echoes, as well as *allowing what is not being said to register.*

2. The Foundational *Kerygma*?

From both a confessional and academic viewpoint one of the frustrating elements in reading the letters of Paul, especially those to Galatia and Corinth, is that much of their content is problem-centered and focused on that which divides. This does provide much of the sheer human vitality of his writing, but, apart from a clear acceptance of a common Judaic inheritance, what is held in common is simply, (and frustratingly—though understandably) taken for granted. The very passion of Paul's contention with those he identifies as representing the *Jakobusgemeinde*, allied with the commitment and high level of personal risk he took with the Collection, evidences the strength of his conviction that at the most fundamental level his ἐκκλησίαι and the *Jakobusgemeinde* shared a common identity that distinguished them from other movements of Judaic renewal.

Writing to the Galatians, Paul claims the support of the Pillars for "the truth of the gospel" he proclaimed (Gal 2:5–9). Unfortunately (for us) he has no need to explicate further. Martinus de Boer has urged that Paul's phrase in Gal 2:16—"yet we know that . . . "—introduces a shared Jewish-Christian tradition—that " . . . a person is justified . . . through faith in Jesus Christ . . . ". He further claims it "is a direct citation of a formula."[1] However, it is more probably in the salutation of his letter where Paul writes that Jesus Christ was "raised . . . from the dead . . . (and) gave himself for our sins to set us free from the present evil age . . . " (Gal 1:1–4) that we find a deliberate recall of his "gospel" and, given its echoes elsewhere,[2] this looks like a christological formula which must be pre-Pauline.[3]

It is almost identical with a similar call to remembrance which, in addressing the Corinthian ἐκκλησία, he explicitly identified as "I handed on to you . . . what I had in turn received . . . the good news that I proclaimed to you . . . that Christ died for our sins . . . that he was buried . . . that he was raised on the third day in accordance with the scriptures, and that he appeared to Cephas . . . et al." (1 Cor 15:1–5). We have observed that the source of that tradition was almost certainly mediated through the *Jakobusgemeinde* (§ 4. 4.)

Charles Cousar makes the important observation that we must distinguish "gospel" from "tradition containing historical and interpretive statements about Christ's death and resurrection."[4] Recalling (§ 4. 8.) that Paul's relationship with the proto-Christian Movement both before and after his conversion was with the *Jakobusgemeinde*, we have a strong probability (despite his Galatian protestations[5]) that whilst the understanding and interpretation of the *significance* of that tradition ["the gospel that was proclaimed through me" (Gal 1:11)] was "through a revelation of Jesus Christ" (Gal 1:12), on both geographic and biographic grounds the initiating prov-

---

1. De Boer, "Justification Tradition in Galatians." Walker, "Does the 'We' include Paul's Opponents?"; see also, Watson, "Paul the Reader": " . . . the shaky hypothesis that a traditional pre-Pauline formulation in preserved in Gal 2.16." 368; Scott, "Common Ground?."

2. Gal 2:20; Rom 4:25, 5:6, 8:32, 10:9; 1 Cor 6:14, 15:15; 2 Cor 4:14; 1 Thess 1:10; also Eph 5:2, 25; Titus 2:14.

3. Bruce, *Galatians*, 75–77; Betz, *Galatians*, 41; Longenecker, *Galatians*, 7–8.

4. Cousar, *Galatians*, 28–29. Kim, *Origins*, who, arguing in great detail that the seed of Paul's message (his "gospel") and theology all derive from the Damascus Road Christophany, distinguishes between "the essence and the form (or the formal expression) of the gospel" (69). Paul's vision "confirmed (to him) the primitive Church's proclamation . . . Paul also confirmed at the Christophany the primitive Church's confession of Jesus as the Son of God. But at the same time he realized that Jesus was the Son of God not just in the sense of the Davidic Messiah who was confessed by the Christians as having been installed as God's Son through his resurrection, but more profoundly" (330–31).

5. Gal 1:18–19 "I saw no-one, only Cephas and James"—*only*?

enance of that core tradition as he knew it was the *Jakobusgemeinde*.[6] He heard their preaching and (initially) sought to crush it—but he had heard. Betz comments on Gal 1:4:

> "Christ gave himself up for our sins" implies an old christology which understood Jesus' death as an expiatory self-sacrifice. *This christology is likely to have originated in Judaism.* Jewish theology could have interpreted the death of Jesus in this way because according to Jewish belief the righteous man, when he suffered martyrdom, would expiate the sins of others. We may suppose that in the pre-Pauline period Jewish Christianity interpreted Jesus' death in this manner,[7] so that we have here one of the oldest christologies of the New Testament, *perhaps the oldest one of all.*[8] (italics mine)

Given that Paul's initial hearing and reaction to the Christian *kerygma* was through the *Jakobusgemeinde* I submit that we can go further than Betz and affirm not simply that "(T)his christology is likely to have originated in Judaism" but, specifically, that it was received by Paul *via* the *Jakobusgemeinde*.

It is implicit in his activity as a zealous opponent of the ἐκκλησία τοῦ Θεοῦ that Paul had gained familiarity (even if partial and distorted) with the proclamation of that community. "Damascus" was not so much the acquisition of new data, it was a paradigmatic shift of perception.[9]

Betz continues:

> The phrase "for our sins" (plural!)[10] suggests a pre-Pauline concept of sins as individual transgressions of the Torah.[11]

Through these antecedent formulae we are hearing, as in a primitive phonograph, through all the atmospherics, the authentic voice of the *Jakobusgemeinde*, the echo of the foundational *kerygma*.[12] Paul himself concurs:

6. Recognized, but not developed, by Jervell, *Luke and the People of God*, 34.

7. Nicklesburg, "Genre and Function of the Markan Passion Narrative."

8. Betz, *Galatians,* 41–42; also, Weeden, *Mark—Traditions in Conflict,* 145, 165.

9. Fung, *Galatians,* 42–43.

10. Also plural in 1 Cor 15:3.

11. Betz, *Galatians,* 42; Cousar, *Galatians,* 16. Betz refers to Paul's "concept of the demonic power of 'sin'" (42) and comments, "The plural 'sins' is not typical for Paul and points to a Jewish (Christian) concept of sin" (n.15); Longenecker, *Galatians,* 7–8.

12. DeConick, *Thirteenth Apostle,* 8–9. Paul Barnett goes much further in arguing for a "high Christology" received and maintained (with little development) by Paul from the early church. (Barnett, *Birth Of Christianity.*) This stretches the evidence too far (see Betz above). Paul's characteristic Christology more likely derives from the

"Whether then it was I or they, so we proclaim and so you have come to believe" (1 Cor 15:11).

That "the Lord Jesus Christ . . . gave himself for our sins to set us free from the present evil age" (Gal 1:4) was probably a significant part of the common ground that facilitated the "right hand of fellowship" (Gal 2:9). We cannot know exactly what such a phrase would have meant to the two parties at the time, but the phrase ὑπὲρ τῶν ἁμαρτιῶν has all the ambiguity needed for ecclesiastical fudge/creativity (whether recognized or not) and we do find early indications of Paul beginning to develop sacrificial interpretations of Christ's death (1 Cor 5:7)—reflecting a trend that would stamp itself on Christian theology and liturgy to this day—a long way from the "righteous martyr"[13] ideal that might well have been the understanding of the *Jakobusgemeinde*, and since the days of the Maccabean revolution had been well within the ideology of late Second Temple Judaism.

3. The Galilean Silence

Focused listening notices silence. Arguments from silence are dodgy: yet the sound of silence can be deafening. It is a matter of context. In Paul's correspondence the silence thunders.

For example, in Galatians "Christ" is central to the letter, and there is the rub—it is the metanarrative of the mythic "Christ," whom "(God sent) in the fullness of time . . . to redeem" (Gal 4:4–5), who "gave himself for our sins to set us free from the present evil age" (Gal 1:3), that is central to Paul's thinking (see *Fig. 4*). References to "Jesus Christ" in Galatians occur in nearly a third of the verses and in exactly half of these occurrences (twenty-two times) it is "Christ" alone that is used. By contrast, the name "Jesus" without qualification occurs just once (Gal 6:17).[14] There are ten references/allusions to the dying of Christ in Galatians, of which only three are grounded in the historical event (Gal 3:1; 6:14, 17), the remainder alluding either to the redemptive understanding of his death or to the experience of believers.

---

experience he describes as God revealing "his Son to/in me" (Gal 1:16). See also, Kim, *Origin*, 67–232.

13. If the fierce condemnation of the rich in Jas 5:1–6 preserves a trace of strong "zealot" sympathies within the *Jakobusgemeinde* (§ 2. 2.3 n.24) its concluding reference to the condemnation and murder of "the righteous one who does not resist you" is a clear statement of this early "righteous martyr" perception of the execution of Jesus.

14. Similarly, Dunn notes that in the whole Pauline corpus "Jesus" (alone) only occurs sixteen times and "the great majority of these refer to Jesus' death and resurrection" (Dunn, *Theology of Paul*, 6).

A scan through Galatians shows the following naming pattern used by Paul:

Name	Occurrences	Comment
Christ	22	mainly as shorthand for the fuller titles
Christ Jesus	8	
Jesus Christ	5	
Lord Jesus Christ	3	Two of which are in Salutations/ Blessings
Son of God	3	Including "his Son" (twice)
the Lord	2	1:19 "James the Lord's brother"; & 5:10—reference to God (?)
Jesus (n.14)	1	6:17 "the marks of Jesus on my body"

This usage reflects the centrality of the "mythic" Christ in Paul's thinking, which is further reinforced by the lesser number of (quasi-)historical references:

crucifixion/death of Christ	10	only 3 have an event-reference (3:1; 6:14, 17)
birth of God's Son	1	highlights the mythic event, qualified by "born of a woman" (4:4)
"the Lord's brother" (1.19)	1	

Fig. 4 References to Lord / Jesus / Christ in Galatians

Noticeably, there is no reference centered in Galilee.

There is almost complete silence in Paul's letters surrounding the life and teaching of Jesus.[15] Even so conservative[16] a scholar as Bruce observes that:

> (F)rom the Pauline letters we should not know that Jesus ha-bitually taught in parables, that He healed the sick or performed other messianic "signs"; we should not know of His baptism and temptation, of His Galilean ministry, of the confession at Caesarea Philippi or of the transfiguration which followed a week later; and although we have clear and repeated references to His crucifixion, we should know nothing of the events which precipitated it.[17]

L. L. Welborn, basing himself on Paul's self-justifying statement that "even though we once knew Christ from a human point of view, we know him no longer in that way" (2 Cor 5:16), has dismissively asserted that the details of Jesus' life "never mattered to Paul in the first place."[18] How wrong can he be?—the details of the traditions we know he did receive—those of the *Jakobusgemeinde*:[19] the Last Supper and the appearances of the Risen Christ (1 Cor 11:23–26; 15:3–7)—did matter to him, and he freely related them in detail (including a recognition of their source), as he did on the two occasions when he had a definite saying of Jesus, identifiable within the synoptic Galilean tradition, available—1 Cor 7:10 (on divorce cf., Mark 10:6–9//Matt 19:4–6) and 1 Cor 9:14 (on paying preachers, cf., Mark 6:8–10//Matt 10:9–11//Luke 9:3–4. Cf., Acts 20:35). In the former

---

15. Bultmann, *Theology of the New Testament, Vol.1*, 35, 188–89.

16. Bruce himself disowned the label "*conservative* evangelical": "Many of my positions are indeed conservative; but I hold them not because they are conservative—still less because I am myself conservative—but because I believe they are the positions to which the evidence leads." (Bruce, *In Retrospect*, 309–10—quoted in Grass, *Bruce: A Life*, 152–53).

17. Bruce, *Paul and Jesus*, 16–17: " . . . a remarkable absence of reference to details of Christ's ministry" (51).

18. Welborn, "Extraction from the Mortal Site." More convincingly, Lightfoot had argued that " . . . in the gospel proclaimed by St. Paul it was not necessary . . . to know of any single event between the birth and the passion of our Lord. . . . they were not necessary for him; they did not touch the essence of his gospel, which had a different basis, and a different kind of history. This history concerned a divine being, the pre-existent Son of God; . . . ' (Lightfoot, *History and Interpretation*, 210).

19. David Wenham, *Paul*, 396–97, nominates the Hellenists in Jerusalem as the specific group from whom "Paul had his first significant introduction to the traditions of Jesus, though he at first rejected their interpretation of Jesus fiercely."

case he is very careful to distinguish between the words of the Lord and his own guidance.[20]

It is reasonable to assume Paul was aware of other sayings and a number of possible allusions are noted:[21] for example, Dunn offers a list of fifteen "most striking" examples of echoes of Jesus tradition in Paul's letters (none of which are in Galatians).[22] In company with many scholars, Dunn finds it completely incredible that the recipients of these letters were unacquainted with Galilean traditions[23] and relates Paul's silence on this to their ready familiarity with this wider body of material so that allusion becomes an effective rhetorical strategy—Paul is using "insider" language.[24] The problem here is that "insider" language is essentially of uncertain parentage: it would not necessarily be exhausted by words of Jesus—Paul himself, for example, was no mean wordsmith.[25] In any case, one swallow doesn't make a sum-

20. Hengel, *Saint Peter*, 75–77 suggests that Paul's limited use of Jesus-traditions may reflect a lack of confidence *vis-à-vis* Peter, the close companion of Jesus.

21. Dungan, *Sayings of Jesus,* xxii–xxiv; Bruce, *Paul and Jesus,* 73–76; Bauckham, "In Response to My Respondents," 247.

22. Dunn, *Jesus Remembered,* 182 n.48.

23. Dunn, "Jesus Tradition in Paul," 155–78 (see also: Dunn, *Theology of Paul,* 183–195) prefaces his argument with an admitted *a priori* assumption: "It must surely be considered highly likely that the first Christian communities were interested in . . . the figure of Jesus." (156) and phrases such as "it would be surprising if" keep recurring. Wenham, strongly arguing for an extensive knowledge by Paul of Jesus' tradition, admits that "recognizing allusions can be a very subjective business: Some scholars see allusions everywhere and others fail to recognize them anywhere." Wenham, *Paul,* 6. Murphy-O'Connor admits that—"The existence of an allusion cannot be demonstrated. Its creation is an art, and its existence is 'sensed' or 'discerned'. The issue is so delicate that it can only be approached intuitively." (Murphy-O'Connor, "Origins of Paul's Christology," 121.) Some Philistines might observe that artistic merit has been claimed for Tracy Emin's unmade bed.

24. Dunn, *Jesus Remembered,* 183; Dunn, "Jesus Tradition" 173–78; Dunn, *Theology of Paul,* 189–95.

25. Dunn, "Jesus Tradition," 174, emphasizes the nature of what he labels as "the Jesus tradition" as a "*living* tradition" (italics original) such that "the force of each saying must have depended as much on the appropriateness to the situation addressed by the apostle" as in its origination with Jesus. Dunn fails to recognize that a "living tradition" is dynamic and creative and therefore, as form criticism rightly asserted, sayings could originate within the Christian communities in response to novel situations, only later becoming part of a "Jesus tradition." Some may have been crafted by Paul himself. This is not to discount the active agency of *aemulatio* in the oral transmission of the traditions of Jesus, but it can be pressed too easily into service (see discussion of the "Jesus sayings" tradition in EpJas— § 7. 7.). Even knowledge of authentic sayings of Jesus says nothing about their provenance: Did Paul learn them from Cephas during his two week stay in Jerusalem (Gal 1:18) as is often proposed, or were most picked up during the much longer period he spent working with the Antioch ἐκκλησία in the region just to the north of Galilee?

mer, and knowledge of two sayings of Jesus plus the possibility of a few others certainly does not add up to a knowledge or a valuing of the Galilean ministry of Jesus.[26] "Blink—and you miss them."[27]

This conviction that Paul and his churches *must* have known and valued the Galilean traditions of Jesus is an expression of commitment to the Lucan paradigm of the singularity of Christian origin (§ 1. 1.3), and the extent of scholarly energy and creativity expended on this problem distinctly reflects the process Kuhn recognized, that when confronted with anomaly "(scientists) will devise numerous articulations and *ad hoc* modifications of their theory in order to eliminate any apparent conflict" in preference to embracing a fresh paradigm.[28]

Writing half a century ago the observation of Brandon is still apposite:

> Many New Testament scholars have specially set themselves the task of showing that Paul was acquainted with all the chief moments of the Gospel tradition,[29] but the very undertaking is itself significant, for not only is the catena of references to the earthly life of Jesus which they succeed in culling singularly unimpressive when compared with the rich treasury of the Gospel narrative,[30] but the fact that the need of such an undertaking is felt clearly reveals a general recognition that Paul's writings constitute a real problem relative to what is believed to be the original emphasis of primitive Christianity on historical fact.[31]

26. Similar problems occur when Dunn affirms allusions to Jesus' example in Paul's writing. After acknowledging the *a priori* foundation of his argument, he strains exegesis to its limits on a very limited number of texts (Rom 6:17, 8:15–16, 15:1–5; 2 Cor 8:9, 10:1; Gal 1:18; Phil 2:5), where their characteristic reference is more to the example of the mythic Christ (which includes his salvific sufferings) than to any recollection of the Galilean peasant. Phil 2:5–8 is the exemplar (Dunn, "Jesus Tradition," 168–73).

27. Wenham, *Paul*, 3–7, provides a succinct summary of the problem.

28. Kuhn, *Structure of Scientific Revolutions*, 66–76, 78.

29. A thoroughgoing example of the genre is Wenham, *Paul*, who, on page 402 of a 410 page dissertation, still has to address the question of "Why Does Paul Refer to Jesus' Life and Ministry so Seldom?"

30. Jerome Murphy-O'Connor is able to present in about sixty words the information about the historical Jesus (in addition to his crucifixion/resurrection) that can be gleaned from Paul:

He was born into a Jewish family (Gal 4:4) of Davidic Descent (Rom 1:3). He had several brothers (1 Cor 9:5), one of whom was called James (Gal 1:19). He was opposed to divorce (1 Cor 7:10–11), and he taught that the gospel should provide a living for its ministers (1 Cor 9:14). On the night he was betrayed (1 Cor 11:23) he celebrated a meal of bread and wine with his followers, and directed that it become a commemorative ritual (1 Cor 11:23–25). Murphy-O'Connor, "Origins of Paul's Christology," 113–42.

That *is* pretty flimsy.

31. Brandon, *Fall of Jerusalem*, 3–4.

The words of Albert Schweitzer—"Even where they are specially relevant Paul passes over the words of the Lord"[32]—continue to bite.

Additionally, the traditions which Paul specifically states he had "received" and "handed on" from the *Jakobusgemeinde* (1 Cor 11:23; 15:3)—the Last Supper and the appearances of the risen Christ (1 Cor 11:23–25, 15:3–8)—have a Jerusalem location (the Supper) or a Jerusalem orientation (the key visions of Cephas and James).[33] In fact, the only saying of Jesus in Paul's writings with a secure setting are his words at the Last Supper (1 Cor 11:23–26)—distinctly not Galilean tradition.

With Paul's focus on the metanarrative of the mythic Christ, and highlighted by Paul's detailed recitation of Jerusalem tradition, the silence from Galilee *is* awesome.

4. The Critical Question

We recall that Paul, in referring back to the content of his preaching in Galatia, does so largely in the words of what were probably christological formulae that were held in common with the *Jakobusgemeinde* and were therefore *distinctive also of that community's preaching in Jerusalem and Judea.* (§§ 4. 5.3; 7. 2–3).

In support of this we also noted that through the years of his transformation, outside of his period of withdrawal (Gal 1:17—"Arabia"), it was the proto-Christian *Jakobusgemeinde* and its extensions, such as at Antioch (and Damascus?—Gal 1:17, 21),[34] with which he interacted whether as persecutor (Gal 1:13), advocate (Gal 1:23) or supplicant (Gal 2:1–10). Thus it was the same message as forged and expressed by this community in and from Jerusalem, initially received with hostility (§ 4. 8.), that Paul saw himself as developing in the Antiochene and diasporan setting. To the Galatians, he begins by reaffirming that basic original proclamation he shared with the *Jakobusgemeinde* (Gal 1:3; § 7. 2) and goes on to claim that in Jerusalem he received the full support of the Jerusalem Pillars (Gal 2:6); whilst later, to the Corinthians, he asserts an identity between his own and

---

32. Schweitzer, *Mysticism of Paul the Apostle*, 173.

33. Schmithals, *Paul and James*, 33 n.66, asserts that 1 Cor 15 does indicate Galilean appearances (cf. § 5. 9.2.4). Weeden, *Mark—Traditions in Conflict*, 50 and 117, claims that in Mark 16:8b "The sealed lips of the women deny Peter and the disciples' knowledge of the Easter event and its proclamation."

34. Taylor, *Paul, Antioch and Jerusalem*, 74.

their preaching (1 Cor 15:11). It was in its interpretation and practical application, particularly on the question of Gentile inclusion, where tension developed.

It is with this awareness that we highlighted two related and highly significant features of Paul's argument (characteristic of all his extant writings)—the awesome silence surrounding Jesus *of Nazareth* combined with a focus on the metanarrative of the mythic Christ who "gave himself for our sins to set us free from the present evil age" (Gal 1:3). Even when this Christ's human birth is acknowledged (Gal 4:4) it is under the rubric that "when the fullness of time had come, God sent his Son . . . to redeem . . . " (Gal 4:4–5). In brief, if this is a reflection of the basic message shared with, and therefore held by, the *Jakobusgemeinde* we have a proto-Christian community at the center of the newly developing movement, grounded in the Judaic tradition, believing that the ἔσχατον is upon them, which is *innocent of (or gives no value to) any knowledge of the ministry of Jesus in Galilee* which preceded and led up to his crucifixion.

A black hole at the Galactic Center?

5. Absence of Evidence or Evidence of Absence?

If evidence for knowledge of "Galilee" is largely absent in Paul's writing,[35] there is also evidence of a similar absence in the other major tradition trajectory in the NT that has its roots in the *Jakobusgemeinde*—EpJas and Jude—where the absence of "Galilee" (and more) echoes the Pauline silence in a way that demands attention.

The status of EpJas as a Christian document has often been challenged—apart from the two references to the/our "Lord Jesus Christ" (Jas 1:1 and 2:1)[36] it can be read as a completely Jewish document within the Wisdom tradition, referencing the OT scriptures for its argument.[37] Most significantly, it finds its example of fervent prayer in Elijah (Jas 5:17) and its encouragement for patience and endurance of suffering in the "prophets who spoke in the name of the Lord" and in "the endurance of Job" (Jas 5:10–11): unlike the author of the epistle to the Hebrews for whom Geth-

35. 1 Cor 7:10 stands out in his correspondence as the single occasion where he quotes a specific teaching of Jesus, with a very clear ascription, and in v. 25 there is a clear implication of knowledge of other words of Jesus relating to sexual relationships. Nowhere else is he so specific.

36. Dibelius, *James*, 21–23.

37. The presence of sayings that occur in EpJas (or are echoed) amongst the synoptic sayings of Jesus (e.g., Hartin, *James and Q*) is an issue we need to return to (§ 7. 7.).

semane was the overt exemplar of both fervent prayer and acceptance of suffering (Heb 5:7–8), or 1 Peter who paraded the sufferings of Christ as an example for Christian living (1 Pet 2:21–24). But EpJas displays no interest or knowledge in the life, death, or rising of Jesus—hence the perceived anomaly of the ascription in Jas 2:1.[38]

If EpJas is dated from the mid-1st century from sources close to James, as many scholars advocate (§§ 1. 2.4; 4. 1.3.2), this lack of Jesus-reference strongly supports the inference from Paul's writing about the limitations of the *Jakobusgemeinde* traditions.

It may be that if James had indeed been a founding figure of the *Jakobusgemeinde*, nurturing them from the period of Jesus' itinerancy (or even earlier)—rather than the disbelieving portrayal of the Markan and Johannine narratives—then neither he nor the members of the *Jakobusgemeinde* felt any need of deferring to the authority of his (younger?) brother for their teaching and guidance. Although being the "brother of the Lord" certainly enhanced his status and authority: it may not have originated it (especially in and for the non-Galilean *Jakobusgemeinde*). After all, being the innocent victim (= martyr) of Roman mis-justice (the principal personal experience of Jesus of most members of the *Jakobusgemeinde*) does not, of itself, validate the authority of Jesus' teaching.

Alternatively, if EpJas is dated much later—well in to the second century—this "Galilean silence" must reflect a tradition of immense strength and durability. Either way we are hovering on the blurred margin between "absence of evidence" and "evidence of absence" amongst the *Jakobusgemeinde* of significant knowledge or interest in the historical Jesus.

This "blurred margin" comes into clearer focus in the letter of Jude— the other letter in the NT from within the Jacobean tradition—despite its brevity. Its provenance has always been confused by its relationship with 2 Peter for which a date some time into the second century is widely affirmed. However, during the past century a broad consensus has developed maintaining the priority of Jude. Although a number of scholars continue to argue for the authenticity of Jude as an autograph, the majority of them judge it to be pseudepigraphal.[39] For our purpose it is also a sounder methodology to prefer a reading of it as a later pseudonymous letter, for that is more likely to make a specific reference to Jesus traditions, as occurs in 2 Pet 1:16–18. Bauckham advocates a date in the latter part of the first century, but situated within what he describes as "the milieu of apocalyptic Jewish

---

38. Kloppenborg, "Diaspora Discourse," 249–50.

39. Bauckham, *Jude*, 134–78; Green, *Jude and 2 Peter*, 1–26; Perkins, *Peter, James, and Jude*, 141–45; Brosend, *James and Jude*, 1–7.

Christianity"[40] or "Palestinian apocalyptic Christianity"[41]. It is a letter expressive of the conservative Jewish-Christian movement whose roots were in the *Jakobusgemeinde*, outwith Pauline/Lucan developments.

Unlike EpJas, there can be no doubting the Christian content and direction of Jude. In an exploration of the rhetorical strategies employed by Jude, Robert Webb describes how "Jude weaves narrative episodes from the Jewish scriptural tradition and from *the story of Jesus* into the story of the readers' Christian community . . . " (my italics).[42] Yet he confesses:

> Given the rich and varied use of story from Jewish scriptural tradition in Jude, it is somewhat surprising to note the paucity of references to the story of Jesus. In fact, we scour the letter in vain for any reference to an event in Jesus' life or even an allusion to his death or resurrection![43]

Overlooking his assumption that Jude's reference to "the salvation we share" (v. 3) refers to "a knowledge of the gospel story about Jesus Christ,"[44] Webb continues to assert that Jude "does in fact incorporate elements of Jesus' story in an interesting way"[45]—through an argument that Jude's usage of "Lord" consistently refers to Christ.[46]

Consequently, "Jude's use of narrative episodes concerning Jesus" includes earlier historical activity in the Exodus (v. 5), and supra-historical action such as keeping the rebellious Watchers in eternal chains (v. 6). In the present he protects from false teachers (v. 24a) and in the future will bring eschatological salvation and judgment (vv. 1b, 6, 14b–15, 21b, 24b).[47]

By default, Webb underlines the lack of the "gospel story" in Jude: it is the mythic Christ whose story is presented.

---

40. Bauckham, *Jude*, 161.

41. Bauckham, *Jude*, 155; Perkins, *Peter, James and Jude*, 142, perceptively notes: "The examples of God's judgment are all drawn from Jewish tradition. . . . Jude is not limited to canonical sources. The only direct quotations in the letter come from apocryphal traditions (vv. 9, 14b–15) and from the prophetic words attributed to the apostles (v. 18)."

42. Webb, "Use of 'Story.'"

43. Ibid., 66–67.

44. Ibid., 67.

45. Ibid.

46. Ibid., 67–69. If Webb is correct in *exclusively* equating "Lord" with "Christ" in Jude (which can be questioned), it is a usage which contrasts with EpJas where, for instance, the imminent "coming of the Lord" (Jas 5:7–11) almost certainly refers, as it does on the lips of John the Baptist, to the coming of God in judgment.

47. Webb, "Use of 'Story,'" 71–72.

How much more is needed before we have crossed that impercep-
tible boundary between "absence of evidence" and "evidence of absence"
with respect to significant awareness of the Galilean traditions in the
Jakobusgemeinde?

6. The Epistle to the Hebrews

To this slender amount of writing within the NT from sources sympathetic
to James we might also link the *Epistle to the Hebrews*, whose content and
early ascription reflects a probable context within the culture of a strongly
Judaic Christian community whose traditions and understanding are influenced by a *Jakobusgemeinde* tradition trajectory.

Even more than Paul, the writer of this letter exhibits a primary concern with the supra-mundane action of the risen/exalted Christ; whilst
the very historical suffering and crucifixion of Jesus are caught up into
this greater metanarrative in which his human birth and life are but a prologue—" . . . we do see Jesus who for a little while was made lower than the
angels, now crowned with glory and honor because of the suffering of death
. . . he himself likewise shared the same things, so that through death he
might destroy the one who has the power of death . . . " (Heb 2:9, 14). It is
the same metanarrative we noted in Galatians 4.4–5 (§ 7. 3.) and which is
found in the early Christian hymn embedded in Phil 2:6–11.[48]

As we noted, the writer (unlike EpJas) does draw on clear Jesus tradition in encouraging his hearers to remain faithful through suffering (Heb
4:14—5:10). However it is the story of Gethsemane to which he alludes—a
Jerusalem, not Galilean, tradition. The letter's focus on the salvific activity of
the mythic Christ (expressed in this instance through liturgical and priestly
imagery) is consistent with a similar orientation in Paul, as is its historical
referents being restricted within the Jerusalem-based Passion Narrative.

The "Galilean Silence" in the correspondence columns of the NT *is*
extensive and consistent.

---

48. The remembrance in Heb 2:3–4 to "signs and wonders . . . miracles . . . gifts of
the Holy Spirit" clearly refers to the traditions of early apostolic charismatic experiences understood as divine validation of their testimony to what "was declared at first
through the Lord . . . and attested to us by those who heard him." It evinces no interest
in the stories surrounding the Man of Galilee.

7. Echoes of "Galilee"?

There is one stumbling block—the widely recognized occurrence of echoes in EpJas of sayings found on the lips of Jesus in the Synoptic gospels. "(The) letter simply breathes the teaching of Jesus."[49] John Kloppenborg emphatically asserts that "the fabric of the letter is replete with allusions to and rhetorical emulations of the Jesus tradition."[50] Most commentators concur in identifying a tradition of the sayings of Jesus as one of its key resources. Indeed, "(I)t has often been thought that it contains recollections of sayings of Jesus not recorded in the Gospels."[51]

If EpJas is a pseudonymous product from the second century there would be little occasion for comment about these allusions and echoes, although lack of reference to any event in the letter, such as we find in 2 Pet 1:16–18 would still be notable. However, if EpJas is a much earlier first century product, even pre-70 CE, as a good number of scholars maintain, and is a document from the very heart of the Jacobean tradition trajectory, it would indicate a significant awareness of knowledge of "Galilee" (or, at least, a Q-like sayings tradition of Jesus) within the *Jakobusgemeinde.*

It would effectively checkmate any suggestion of a lack of knowledge/ interest in the Galilean activity of Jesus.

Patrick Hartin, introducing his examination of the textual relationship between EpJas and the Jesus tradition, states:

> While James makes no direct quotations of the words of Jesus, his writing does show a striking closeness to Jesus' words in the Gospels.[52]

Supporting this, a comparison of relevant passages in the Greek text reveals a very low level of verbal agreement but with a greater occurrence of examples where there is an agreement in sense.[53] We are therefore in the arena of oral rehearsal and performance rather than of literary dependency —a fact that is reflected in the uncertainty surrounding the boundaries of the problem. Hartin identified twenty-six examples of correspondences between EpJas and the Synoptic tradition whilst Dean Deppe surveyed over 180 possibilities before focusing down on just eight probables.[54]

49. Le Grys, Review of *James,* 114.

50. Kloppenborg, "Diaspora Discourse," 242–70.

51. Dunkerley, *Beyond the Gospels,* 22–23.

52. Hartin, *James and Q,* 140.

53. Kloppenborg, "Emulation of the Jesus Tradition," 143–50.

54. Deppe, "Sayings of Jesus," 219–21 (quoted in Kloppenborg, "Emulation," 124 n.12).

7.1 "It must be Jesus"

We need to be alert within the discussion of this EpJas/Synoptic phenomenon for an unacknowledged *assumption* of the primacy of Jesus.

For instance, in discussing the saying prohibiting oaths where EpJas and the Tradition ascribed to Jesus are at their closest, Hartin quotes with warm approval the words of Sophie Laws:[55]

> As the unqualified prohibition of oaths seems to have no precedent before the Christian tradition, and as it would be an extraordinary stand to take in the Jewish context, given the OT background, it seems most probable that it derives from Jesus himself.[56]

This is simple misuse of the criterion of double dissimilarity[57] (akin to the logical fallacy of the "undistributed middle"[58]). Aside from the inadequacy of that over-skeptical scholarly criterion which would strip Jesus of his Jewishness, given that someone within a Jewish context could make this "extraordinary stand," Jesus does not have to be the only candidate. There is a hidden assumption—in the immortal words of the young boy in response to the minister's question—"I suppose it must be Jesus."

To Law's credit she continues beyond Hartin's extract, betraying a certain sense of unease with her affirmation, though still uncritically holding to a dominical origin:

> James's lack of ascription is certainly no argument that it does not (derive from Jesus); though, equally, there can be no certainty that he himself knew that it did.[59]

Similarly in a characteristically careful and provocative study, Kloppenborg describes the practice and training of rhetoricians in paraphrase and *aemulatio* as a model for considering this EpJas/Jesus tradition phenomenon.

He stresses that in oral performance "the predecessor text is not a 'source' but rather a 'resource' for rhetorical performance"[60] in a new setting.

---

55. Hartin, *James and Q*, 190.

56. Laws, *James*, 224.

57. Laws is not alone—John Meier similarly misuses the criterion of dissimilarity (Meier, "Did the Historical Jesus Prohibit All Oaths?" 4–8).

58. "All cows are brown" does not mean "all brown things are cows."

59. Laws, *James*, 224.

60. Kloppenborg, "Emulation," 133.

Acknowledgment of the source finding fresh expression was not expected: the audience would recognize its presence.

Apart from the implications of the opening salutation, EpJas gives no ascription to any of its content, whether it is an original expression or a fresh rehearsal of sayings and teaching whose origin its audience could be expected to recognize. Yet Kloppenborg still writes under the rubric of "*The Emulation of the Jesus Tradition in the Letter of James*." Why Jesus? What we have in EpJas are words and phrases that resonate with sayings that in another (and later?) location are ascribed to Jesus, but here they have no ascription (other than the named writer of the letter). A question mark at the close of the title is the least we should expect.[61]

Similarly, Richard Bauckham[62] uses the way Ben Sira "re-expresses the wisdom of Proverbs" as a model for how EpJas draws on the wisdom tradition and offers "a *creative re-expression* of the wisdom of Jesus by his disciple the sage James" (italics original):

> My suggestion is that we should look instead for the ways in which James, *a wisdom teacher in his own right* but one consciously working in the tradition of his master Jesus, has worked creatively with the sayings of Jesus and the material in the Jewish wisdom tradition.[63] (my italics)

Bauckham demonstrates a process whereby a wisdom teacher, through reflection, absorbs sayings from wisdom traditions, then re-crafts and re-expresses them in his own words—a process we might describe as acquiring "ownership" of the tradition and its material.

Yet, despite recognizing James as "a wisdom teacher in his own right" and judging that the only "unmistakable allusion" to a saying of Jesus (Jas 5:12, on oaths) is "closer to the form in which he knew the saying of Jesus than it is to the only form in which we know it, that in Matthew"[64] the origination of the saying in the teachings of the Galilean is unquestioned. Professor Occam might wish to comment.

---

61. Shanks and Witherington, *Brother of Jesus*, 151, make the same assumption: "These parallels between the teachings of Jesus and James clearly show that James knows a collection of Jesus' sayings in some form." In the succeeding paragraph they then dig themselves further into the hole: "What is most striking about James's use of the Jesus tradition is that he rarely quotes it, nor does he attribute it to Jesus." There is a simpler explanation—the brother of Jesus himself.

62. Bauckham, "James and Jesus," 100–37.

63. Bauckham, "James and Jesus," 117.

64. Ibid.,118.

Whether we look to the rhetoricians or the sages for enlightenment, we have credible models for understanding the *process* of the transmission and expression of a sayings/teaching tradition: but neither can affirm its *source*. Also, the fact that leading NT scholars can offer different processes for the transmission of Jesus' sayings traditions [in both the Pauline (§ 7. 3.) and Jacobean literature] looks suspiciously like apologetics before scholarship.

In both cases, we are confronted with an unacknowledged assumption—the primacy of Jesus. It is even built into our terminology whenever we talk, for instance, of "The Sayings of Jesus in the Epistle of James." It is an assumption that stretches from the seminary through to the academy.

7.2 An Early Sayings Tradition

Meier, focusing on much the closest verbal Matt/EpJas parallel, records:

> In the end, all these comparisons and contrasts simply reinforce what is the common view among exegetes: Matt 5:34–37 and Jas 5:12 are two alternate literary forms (Gospel and epistolary paraenesis) of a common oral tradition.[65]

Luke Timothy Johnson and Wesley Wachob are more explicit:

> (T)he form of the saying in James is closer to the form of tradition commonly hypothesized as Q than to the final redaction of Matthew and Luke.[66] On this point, the instinctive assessment of Ropes[67] has been substantiated by all subsequent analysis. The most logical conclusion to draw about the composition of James, given this finding, is that it took place in a setting that was temporally and geographically *close to an early stage of the developing tradition.*[68] (my italics)

If that is correct, sayings recorded under the name of James are contemporary with, or even temporally prior, to that "developing tradition" indicated by scholarship as Q and ascribed to Jesus.

Notwithstanding, Johnson and Wachob argue:

---

65. Meier, "Did the Historical Jesus Prohibit All Oaths?" 194; Dibelius, *James*, 249–51.

66. Hartin, *James and Q*, 140–217, 220–44.

67. Ropes, *James*, 38–39.

68. Johnson with Wachob, "Sayings of Jesus in the Letter of James," 153–54.

> (T)hat there are four passages in James where not simply an echo of Jesus' teaching[69] but a specific use of *his words* is to be found.[70] (my italics).

This is a further example assuming the "primacy of Jesus"—given that there is no ascription of these words in EpJas, scholastic accuracy should have referred to "specific use of words *later* attributed to Jesus,"[71] especially when they go on to describe EpJas as being "close to an early stage of the developing tradition."

Of the remaining echoes, they continue:

> (T)here is no intrinsic reason why the author of James should not have been so deeply influenced by the teaching of Jesus that his inflections in each of these cases also echoed what had been said by Jesus. But we cannot show it.[72]

That, I submit, is a bit desperate, and feels like an echo itself of Theodore Zahn and Joseph Mayor.[73] Meier is not much better:

> *Knowing only stray oral traditions* that conveyed the teaching of Jesus, he would all the more readily absorb them into his own paraenesis.[74] (*my italics*)

The question must be asked: Whose echo are we hearing in EpJas?

The assumption of NT scholarship is Jesus. But there is no such ascription in the text. Was Jesus of Nazareth the only creative thinker within the early Christian movement, the only one with the confidence to pronounce on the actions and demands of God? The NT documentation itself is evidence against that.

---

69. Johnson, *Brother of Jesus*, 147–48. The clearest echo they assert is in Jas 2:5 (= QM 5.3)—the only occurrence of "kingdom" in EpJas, contrasted with its frequency in the sayings attributed to Jesus.

70. Johnson, *Brother of Jesus*, 153.

71. Earlier in their essay (143) Johnson and Wachob do take care to express themselves in a more careful way—"Our analysis supports the hypothesis that most probably Jas 5:12 is an independent source for the prohibition of oaths attributed to Jesus in Matt 5:34–37, and that—in agreement with Koester—the saying in James reflects an earlier stage of the tradition than the one in the Matthean SM (Sermon on the Mount)."

72. Johnson, *Brother of Jesus*, 153.

73. Zahn, *Introduction to the New Testament*, 1:114; Mayor, *James*, lxii. Critiqued by Kloppenborg, "Emulation" 125–26.

74. Meier, "Oaths," 2:13.

Jesus was an itinerant preacher whose ministry lasted for two to three years, mainly in Galilee. In marked contrast, his brother, James, was un-disputed leader of an established community in Jerusalem for more than twenty years at least (thirty years from his brother's death), or over thirty years if the *Jakobusgemeinde* does represent a founding proto-Christian movement that was contemporary with, or even antecedent to, the Galilean movement of Jesus. His leadership, judgment and teaching were, accord-ing to the brief glimpses we have of him in Acts and the writings of Paul, listened to and heeded. The *Jakobusgemeinde* may also have set higher store upon the teaching of their established leader and guru than that of his (pos-sibly) younger brother (§ 6. 1.2).

In all that time, did James not produce pointed chreiae, memorable aphorisms and apposite teaching that became part of the intellectual and cultural property of the *Jakobusgemeinde*? We cannot know, but if we can believe it of Jesus, why not of his brother, too—especially in the light of the actual content of EpJas? As with the sayings that clustered around the name of Jesus, would there not be a similar valuing of sayings linked to the name of James within the *Jakobusgemeinde*?—oral tradition that would be lost in 70 CE, had part of it not become melded into the Sayings tradition of Jesus.

Canon Streeter, in his landmark book on Christian origins,[75] sug-gested that the unique material in Matthew's Gospel ("M") may have been brought to Antioch (a probable location for the Gospel's origin) by Chris-tian refugees from Jerusalem, fleeing before its investment by Titus. If that is somewhere near the mark, it can explain how sayings originating with James became absorbed into the now more comprehensive collection of Sayings of Jesus, especially with the loss of the *Jakobusgemeinde* following the events of 70CE.

There is a tendency for memorable sayings and deeds to fasten on to the name of a more famous person, particularly if they have almost mythical status for their community (§ 1. 4.1.1 n.127) and we have seen reason to believe that some of the preaching of John the Baptist has been incorporated into that of Jesus especially within the Matthean tradition (§ 3. 5.2):

> The Gospel writers do not seem to have felt any concern about similarities between Jesus' and John's teaching, but they ensured that John's teaching was completely eclipsed by Jesus' and incor-porated into the *kerygma* of the early Church . . .[76]

75. Streeter, *Four Gospels*, 511–15 supported more recently by Painter, *Just James*, 86–88; Painter, "James and Peter," 191–206.

76. Taylor, *Immerser*, 151.

Would not sayings/teachings of James be drawn into the process of Christian paraenesis in the same way that is widely affirmed for the sayings of Jesus, especially if, as Kloppenborg and others argue, the sayings traditions (plural) became part of the total tradition through oral rehearsal where each occasion of utterance was a fresh expression?

John Meier, in his examination of the parallel sayings prohibiting oath-taking (Jas 5:12//Matt 5:34–37) which, according to Ropes, Johnson and Wachob, and Bauckham (above), has its earlier form in EpJas, does raise the question of "the ultimate origin of this first-generation tradition" and asks if "it is a case of an early Christian creation (transmitted and developed by James) being secondarily placed on the lips of Jesus (as depicted by Matthew)? (and he suggests) two criteria argue for origin from the historical Jesus: discontinuity and (by a circuitous route) multiple attestation."[77] The problem is that his first criterion shares the same logical fallacy already noted in Laws (§ 7. 7.1), whilst his "argument from the criterion of *multiple attestation*" which he admits is "necessarily more roundabout"—is so roundabout that it is even circular! In a footnote he claims to have refuted "the idea that the prohibition is an invention of the early church."[78] He doesn't even address the more obvious alternative to the historical Jesus—his brother.

Working within a different agenda outside of EpJas, Betz, in his erudite commentary on the Sermon on the Mount,[79] which of course is a major depository of sayings such as the prohibition of oaths, proposes the origination of the "Sermon" in written guidance for Jewish Christians (paralleling similar guidance for use with the Gentile mission that underlies the Lucan Sermon on the Plain). These two versions he sees as consequent upon the Jerusalem decision (Gal 2:6–10) to sponsor distinctive missions to Jews and Gentiles, therefore deriving from a date c. 50 CE. Further, recognizing "the important role the city of Jerusalem plays for the SM (Sermon on the Mount)" with an array of specific Jerusalem and more general urban references, " . . . one may conclude that the author was an inhabitant (of Jerusalem) and that the community for which the SM served originally was the early church in Jerusalem." (162).

Similarly, Painter (following Streeter) saw in the sayings about the immutability of the Law (Matt 5:17–20) a "strand of tradition . . . which stems

---

77. Meier, "Oaths" 2:4.

78. Ibid., n.61.

79. Betz, *Sermon on the Mount*, 70–88.

from James and Jerusalem but became embodied in what was to become ultimately a Petrine Gospel."[80]

That a saying is eventually ascribed to Jesus does not, of itself, tell us of its origin and growth through the processes of oral transmission. If EpJas is a very early NT document, as many of its scholars believe, then the "Jesus sayings" to which we now see allusions more probably originate in the historic ministry of James in Jerusalem. We may be witnessing the gestalt effect where sayings of others are attracted into the orb of the ultimately dominant historical person (§ 1. 4.1.1).

In brief, the presence of passages in EpJas which resonate with sayings ascribed to Jesus in the Synoptic tradition cannot be used to offset the consistent evidence of the "Galilean Silence" in the traditions flowing from Jerusalem, both Pauline and Jacobean.

8. A Lucan Perspective

From the immediacy of the letter-writers we can turn to the more reflective activity of Luke in writing his history of the movement, remembering that he certainly knew and valued the Galilean traditions:

8.1 The Conference Lacuna

Attention must be drawn to the fact that in Luke's recitation of the debate at the crucial Conference of Jerusalem (Acts 15) about the status of Gentile believers there is no reference to the teachings and actions of Jesus—the decision and recommendations of the Conference are presented as being solely and exclusively determined through the exegesis by the presiding figure of James of a passage in the Judaic scriptures (Amos 9:11–12) (Acts 15:6–21).[81]

This is significant from the pen of a writer who had embedded the inclusion of Gentiles into the account of Jesus' programmatic speech, delivered when he announces the beginning of his ministry in Galilee (Luke 4:14–30); who records Jesus' acclamation of the faith of a Roman centurion (Luke 7:1–10); and who constantly emphasized Jesus' inclusiveness as "a friend of sinners" towards those who lived outside Torah.

80. Painter, *James*, 91.

81. It has been suggested that an original Jesus-logion (Matt 19:28) may have been used during the Jerusalem Conference debates by advocates of the restriction of their mission to the περιτομή. Roose, "Sharing in Christ's Rule," 136–37. This would make Luke's lacuna even more remarkable.

This omission could be because that is what actually occurred. More likely is that it was Luke's understanding of how the *Jakobusgemeinde* would have made its decision (perhaps influenced by awareness of how contemporary Judaic-Christian communities operated), or even that he wished to emphasize the distance between James and the Galilean teaching which was entrusted in Acts to Peter and the "men of Galilee" (Acts 1:15–22; 2:7, 14).

8.2 The *Kerygma* of Peter and Paul

Complementing the primary evidence reviewed in this chapter for the *Jakobusgemeinde*'s lack of interest or knowledge of the Galilean ministry of Jesus can be placed the secondary evidence of the summary examples of apostolic preaching in Acts.

Luke includes a number of instances of early Christian preaching in Acts. It is widely recognized that historians in the Greco-Roman world constructed the speeches found on the lips of their principal characters. The best amongst them took care to ensure that the speech was "true" to the character and the situation and was appropriate within its historical context.[82] Luke is no exception. For example, Paul's sermon in the synagogue of Pisidian Antioch is rich in scriptural story (Acts 13:16–41), whilst a little later faced by a pagan Gentile crowd at Lystra, he drew on what later theologians might describe as the "theology of nature" (Acts 14:8–18). In Athens, Paul draws on Greek philosophy and literature (Acts 17:22–31). It is an example of the care Luke took with "apostolic actualization" (§ 5.7.), and while not recording the actual words used may well reflect traditions about the style and emphases of the leading figures.

Dunn makes the important observation of the Lucan speeches in Acts that:

> (T)here is an individuality and distinctiveness of material used which points to the conclusion that *Luke has been able to draw on and incorporate tradition*—not necessarily any record or specific recollection as such but tradition related to and, in Luke's considered judgment, representative of the individual's views and well suited to the occasion.[83] (italics original)

Dunn supports this with a detailed analysis of the three speeches of Peter [Pentecost (Acts 2:14–39); in the Temple (Acts 3:11–26); and at Caesarea (Acts 10:34–43)] demonstrating the remarkable range of features

---

82. Dunn, *Beginning from Jerusalem*, 87–88.
83. Dunn, *Beginning from Jerusalem*, 89.

and theology that belonged to a very primitive period of Christian formation from which the church he was familiar with had moved on by the time
Luke was writing.[84]

That Acts is written around a Peter/Paul duality is clear and the legacy
of the Tubingen School is an awareness of the many doublets (e.g., a miraculous escape from prison) that link the two men together. Given the care
Luke exercises in his portrayal it is therefore of interest to see how Luke portrays their use of the Jesus-tradition in his presentation of their preaching.

Luke has placed in close juxtaposition the last speech of Peter in Acts
addressed to the waiting group at the house of Cornelius (Acts 10:34–43), and
the first speech of Paul, to the gathered congregation in the synagogue at Pisidian Antioch (Acts 13:16–41). Thus we have exemplars of the two apostles,
speaking in both cases by invitation to an expectant, listening audience (albeit
one Gentile and the other Judaic)[85], permitting a structured format that invites comparison, especially of their presentations of Jesus-traditions.

They both begin with a preamble that is appropriate to the particular
audience and situation which they address before they draw on their distinctive Jesus-traditions:

Acts 10:36–41	Acts 13:23–31
(36) You know the message he sent to the people of Israel, preaching peace by Jesus Christ—he is Lord of all.	(23) Of (David's) posterity God has brought a Savior, Jesus, as he promised;
	(24) before his coming John had already proclaimed a baptism of re- pentance to all the people of Israel. And as John was finishing his work, he said, "What do you suppose that I am? I am not he. No, but one is coming after me; I am not worthy to untie the thong of his sandals on his feet.

84. Ibid., 90–96.

85. A further interesting contrast is that the "apostle to the περιτομή"(Gal 2:7)
addresses a Gentile audience whilst the "apostle to the Gentiles" addresses a συναγωγή
of Jews.

Acts 10:36–41	Acts 13:23–31
(37) That message spread throughout Judea, beginning in Galilee after the baptism that John announced: how God anointed Jesus of Nazareth with the Holy Spirit and with power; how he went about doing good and healing all who were oppressed by the devil, for God was with him. (39) We are witnesses to all that he did both in Judea and in Jerusalem.	
	(26) My brothers, you descendants of Abraham's family, and others who fear God, to us the message of salvation has been sent. Because the residents of Jerusalem and their leaders did not recognize him or understand the words of the prophets that are read every sabbath, they fulfilled those words by condemning him.
They put him to death by hanging him on a tree;	(28) Even though they found no cause for a sentence of death, they asked Pilate to have him killed. When they had carried out everything that was written about him, they took him down from the tree and laid him in the tomb.
(40) but God raised him on the third day and allowed him to appear, not to all the people but to us	(30) But God raised him from the dead; and for many days he appeared to those who came up with him from Galilee to Jerusalem,

Acts 10:36–41	Acts 13:23–31
who were chosen by God as witnesses, and who ate and drank with him after he rose from the dead. . . .	and they are now his witnesses to the people. . . .

Fig. 5 The Kerygma of Peter and Paul according to Luke

The spaces speak volumes:

- **Galilee:** The good people of Antioch are told absolutely nothing about what Jesus did—only what was done to him. As in Paul's letters, a blanket of silence descends on Galilee, in contrast to its focal positioning in Peter's speech, which we are presumably to understand as only a summary of the greater detail by which preachers in the Petrine mode would have illustrated their message. C. H. Dodd, contrasting these two speeches,[86] cautioned that "it would be rash to argue from silence that Paul completely ignored the life of Jesus in his preaching,"[87] and, in summation: "For it seems clear that within the general scheme or the *kerygma* was included some reference, however brief, to the historical facts of the life of Jesus."[88] But the silence of Paul specifically surrounding Galilee is there: it is coherent with the evidence in his epistles, and is never otherwise on Paul's lips throughout Acts. Additionally, in the samples of apostolic preaching Luke has scattered throughout his text it is only on the lips of Peter that there is a proclamation of God's activity in "Jesus of Nazareth" in Galilee (Acts 2:22; 10:38). To men crippled from birth Peter commands, "in the name of Jesus Christ of Nazareth, walk" (Acts 3:6): Paul simply says, "Stand upright on your feet." (Acts 14:10). That these references are not incidental is supported by the concentration of Galilee/Nazareth references Luke clusters on the lips of Peter.[89]

86. Dodd, *Apostolic Preaching*, 27–31.

87. Ibid., 28.

88. Ibid., 31.

89. Acts 2:22: "Jesus of Nazareth, a man attested to you by God with mighty works and wonders and signs which God did through him in your midst"; Acts 3:6 " . . . in the name of Jesus Christ of Nazareth, walk"; Acts 4:10 " . . . by the name of Jesus Christ of Nazareth . . . this man is standing before you well"; Acts 10:37–38 " . . . beginning from Galilee . . . how God anointed Jesus of Nazareth with the Holy Spirit . . ." It was a focus that was apparently echoed by Stephen - " . . . we have heard him (Stephen) say that

- **John the Baptist:** Paul prefaces his Galilean lacuna with a surprisingly full reference to the work and words of the Baptist, precisely recalling his words (v. 25//Luke 3:16) and the heart of his message—a baptism of repentance (v. 24). John's preaching is the beginning of the fulfillment of God's promise of a Savior (vv. 23–24): whilst Peter, under the rubric of "beginning in Galilee," focuses on the experience of Jesus at his baptism leading to the ensuing Galilean ministry (vv. 37–38). This contrast resonates with the dual origin of the gospel embedded in the prologue of Mark (§ 3. 5.).

- We should recall that the Baptist's preaching was a Jerusalem/Judea phenomenon (Mark 1:4–5//Matt 3:5–10//Luke 3:3).[90] It is reasonable to presume that a considerable number of John's baptizands continued to live out their repentance and were part of that Judaic renewal/restoration ferment in Jerusalem within which the *Jakobusgemeinde* emerged. The preaching of the Baptist was therefore probably part of the tradition that Paul initially received from the *Jakobusgemeinde*.

- **Jerusalem:** From this detailed presentation of the Baptist Paul glides immediately into a similarly detailed recitation of the Jerusalem traditions about his final days (Acts 13:16–41), whereas Peter uses just six words [(ὅν καὶ ἀνεῖλαν κρεμάσαντες ἐπὶ ξύλου (Acts 10:39)]. This is consistent with the dominance accorded to the traditions from Jerusalem that we have observed in Paul's writings.

- Only at this point do Peter and Paul begin to sing in unison—ὁ Θεὸς ἤγειρεν—and it is the Galileans who are the guarantors of the Jesus-traditions and sole witnesses to the resurrection (Acts 10:41 and 13:31. Cf., Acts 1:11, 21–22; 2:7; § 9. 2). James is "yesterday's man."

Thus Luke, writing many years later, preserves in his presentation of the Pauline message, over against the Galilean Peter, key elements and *omissions* that we have identified both in Paul and in the other tradents of the *Jakobusgemeinde's* traditions—a clear case of multiple attestation. It speaks for the strength of that tradition.

---

this Jesus of Nazareth will destroy this place" (6:14). In contrast, it is only in one of his Damascus Road encounter testimonies that Paul expands the self-reference of Jesus to "I am Jesus of Nazareth whom you are persecuting" (22:8), which is complemented by a later reference to the focal point of his persecuting activities as "I myself was convinced that I ought to do many things in opposing the name of Jesus of Nazareth." (26:9). Consistently with his letters there is no reference to the Galilean context of Jesus in any of Paul's mission speeches, conversations, and healings in the narrative of Acts.

90. In fact, the only Galilean on record as coming to John for Baptism is Jesus (Mark 1:9//Matt 3:13).

9. Thinking the Unthinkable

Writing in 1965, Walther Schmithals asked:

> Did decisive differences exist between Paul and the Jerusalem Christians in their attitude to the historical Jesus? In view of the fact that Paul practically ignored the historical Jesus this seems to have been the case. So far as I know, *no one has yet given consideration to the fact that the Jerusalem Christians might be equally ignorant.*[91] (my italics)

It is time to take up the gauntlet.

Are we to believe that this community, evidencing no information about the life and teaching of Jesus of Nazareth, was called into being and nurtured by the preaching and teaching of Peter and his Galilean colleagues? Are we to believe that this community, called into being according to Acts 2 by those who had been with Jesus throughout his time in Galilee, was not instructed in the life and teaching of Galilean Prophet? Are we to believe that their Galilean "fathers in God" did not draw extensively in their teaching and nurturing of this nascent Christian community upon their months and years of journeying, listening and talking with Jesus—or were singularly unsuccessful in this task? Are we to believe that receiving this information they gave it zero value? Are we to believe . . . ?

The question is critical.

---

91. Schmithals, *Paul and James,* 87. Lietzmann, *Geschichte der alten Kirche,* 58, had seen James as belonging "to those who remained alien from Jesus and his teachings" (Myllykoski, "James the Just," 75).

Evaluation

8

Review

I RETURN TO MY originating question (*Preface*)—when Jesus challenged the rich man to "go, sell what you own, and give to the poor" (Mark 10:21) was he advocating general charitable largesse, or was he more specifically directing this affluent would-be disciple to benefit the group in Jerusalem that was sometimes called "the poor"—the group, led by Jesus' brother, James, to whom Paul later brought a gift of money (Rom 15:26)? It proved a catalyst that triggered my quest—was James, and the group he led, already active in some way in Jerusalem, contemporaneous with Jesus' activity in Galilee?

Drawing on imagery derived from the discipline of archeology, I described our task in the following words:

> So it is that in approaching a study of James we immediately confront a problem—a distinct lack of data—a few fragmentary pieces of information and allusions caught up and dragged along like flotsam into a diverging and strengthening stream of tradition. Their evaluation is determined within that current, rather than from the source which gave them original significance (§ 2. 1.).

Within the sites we outlined (§ 4. 1.) we collected a small number of artifacts (texts) of remarkable quality, but generally treated within the setting of a later depositional layer (the overarching Lucan history), which may not be their originating location.

In Pauline studies we learned from John Knox the fallacy of using the much later history of Acts as the controlling framework for contextualizing Paul's letters. These letters are the primary historical evidence for Paul and therefore:

(A) fact only suggested in the letters has a status which even the most unequivocal statement of Acts, if not otherwise supported, cannot confer.[1]

We have yet to learn this lesson in our discussions of James. Most writings on James contextualize the primary evidence we have into the Lucan framework of Acts, particularly over the question of how and when James acquired the leadership of the Jerusalem movement. This is understandable—the hard primary information we have on James is very limited and mainly incidental, while the book of Acts is the only cohesive writing we possess on the origins and growth of the Christian movement during its first decades.

1. The Evidence

It is important to emphasize that the hard information we have on James and the *Jakobusgemeinde*, although fragmentary, is of good historical value, being found in prime historical material such as the letters of Paul or in traditions that have multiple attestation. Having interrogated our sources, we can identify the most relevant and promising threads of evidence:

1.1 The Primary Evidence of Paul

These are reactive writings (that themselves are an active part of the developing historical process) from one who knew James face-to-face; and who was a significant figure in some of the key events of *Jakobusgemeinde* history, including:

- **Meetings and Confrontations in Jerusalem and Antioch**, involving Paul, related in connection with an immediate problem in his Galatian ἐκκλησίαι. Paul describes his contacts with James and the *Jakobusgemeinde* leading up to the consultation/conference in Jerusalem (which receives a degree of complementary attestation in Acts 15) and the ensuing conflict in Antioch (Gal 1:13—2.14) (§ 4. 5.–7.).

- **Persecution** of the *Jakobusgemeinde*, with which Paul strongly identified himself, in the years immediately following the execution of Jesus. (Gal 1:13–14, 22–24; 1 Cor 15:9)—with double attestation by Luke (Acts 6:7—8:3; 9:1–19. § 4. 5.2.).

---

1. Knox, *Chapters in a Life of Paul*, 33.

- **The Collection**—the hurried notes embedded in his letters advocating and organizing his collection project—surely the first century equivalent of emails (1 Cor 16.1–11; 2 Cor 9:1–15; Rom 15.22–33. § 5. 6.1.).

To these historical events in which he was a principal participant, we can add two contrasting pieces of evidence from his writings:

- **Oral tradition**, datable to the early 30s CE, of the founding event of the Christian movement. A rare (unique?) specimen of an oral tradition, heard or received (probably from eye-witnesses) within a few years of the originating event, and committed to writing within a couple of decades (1 Cor 15:3–7. § 4. 4.).

- **The Galilean Silence**—Paul's extensive correspondence contains no reference to the details of Jesus' Galilean ministry, just a couple of sayings, in marked contrast to his very ready use of Jerusalem tradition (§ 7. 2.–3.).

This receives multiple attestation in the NT:

  – **The Jacobean Epistles**—EpJas and Jude (§§ 7. 5; 7. 7.).

  – **Acts**—Luke, very conversant with Galilee tradition, nonetheless excludes it from the lips of James and Paul in Acts. Only Peter speaks of Galilee (§ 7. 8.).

  – **Hebrews** - only Jerusalem located tradition (§ 7. 6.).

1.2 Secondary Evidence

1.2.1 A Teacher of Wisdom

There is a strong tradition, with multiple attestation in Acts 15 and the Epistle attributed to James, of James having competence in the Judaic tradition of a Wisdom teacher and recognized interpreter of Torah. Also, there is a measure of independent support in Josephus' description of the response to James' execution (§§ 5. 9.3; 7. 7.).

1.2.2 Tradition Fragments

- Brief appearances and mention of the dominical family in the canonical gospels, together with tradition from the early Christian centuries (§ 6).

- Tradition embedded in the history writing of Acts especially where James appears, albeit very briefly—the Conference of Jerusalem and the occasion of Paul's final visit to the City with his collection—both incidents gaining illumination from their links with passages in Paul's letters. Other tradition material in Acts relates to Peter and Paul (§ 5).

1.3 Baptist Tradition

The continuing impact of the Baptist proved relevant for our study and receives strong multiple attestation:

- the preservation of texts with a high view of John in the canonical gospels that otherwise exhibit a generic *tendenz* to confine John to a secondary role *vis-à-vis* Jesus—the criterion of embarrassment (§ 3. 3.);
- the independent evidence of Josephus that Herod feared John's hold over the people (§ 3. 2.1);[2]
- the incidental reference to the strength of John's influence amongst the people (Mark 11:27–33. § 3. 5.);
- the secondary evidence of continuing movements venerating John in Ephesus and Alexandria two decades later (Acts 18:24–19:7. § 3. 4.).

It is important that we evaluate these "artifacts" free, as far as possible, of our mental "default setting" in the Lucan context.

1.4 The Lucan Stream of Tradition

> . . . a few fragmentary pieces of information and allusions caught up and dragged along like flotsam *into a diverging and strengthening stream of tradition.*(§§ 2. 1; 8.)

We sought to remember the complexity of the task Luke set himself, blending a patchwork of traditions into a coherent narrative for his largely Gentile Christian audience, for Acts was written several decades later than the period of its subject with an agenda driven by the needs of that later time (§§ 5. 1.–3; 9. 1.). Since space does not permit a detailed discussion, suffice it to say that Luke was writing for the emergent Gentile church in the decades after the Jewish War when the parentage of their movement in a Judaic group committed to a Restoration ideology very close to that

---

2. *Ant* 18:116–19.

which fired the rebellion (Acts 1:6) was a problem. We have noted how Luke appears to avoid mention of James except where the story can't be told without him—"It is a text in which the absence of James is more noteworthy than his presence." (§ 5. 1.). Luke, highlighting Peter and Paul, is writing in the period when the emergent Gentile church has started the process of replacing the historic Pillars of James, Cephas, and John with Peter and Paul (1 Clem 5:1–6). This process is also seen in the contemporary writing of Matthew identifying Peter as the "rock" on which Christ would build his church (Matt 16:18) and in this very same period that the church in Rome was developing its own foundation myth of Peter and Paul as the founding apostles of their increasingly important church,[3] although we know from Paul's letter to Rome that this is historically incorrect.

In similar fashion the author of Acts focuses on Peter and Paul, and builds his foundation myth of the Christian movement (Acts 1—5) around the preaching and actions of the dominating figure of Peter the Galilean. In one sense, Luke was correct because the emergent Gentile church was finding its roots in the message of Paul and of those who had traveled with Jesus in and from Galilee to Jerusalem (Acts 1:21–22), rather than the post-70 CE suspect *Jakobusgemeinde*.

Although Painter has pointed out that Luke describes Peter as an evangelist and carefully refrains from describing Peter as the leader or president of the Jerusalem community in the "early days" narrative, Painter does not challenge that narrative itself.[4] But the fact is that the *only* evidence we have for Peter's dominant role in Jerusalem is the Lucan foundation myth of Acts 1—5 (see further § 9.).[5]

2. Evaluation

Inevitably, the focus of our study has been bifocal: the figure of James on the one hand, and the community in Jerusalem with which his name is vitally linked on the other. Given the fragmentary, imperfect, partial (in more senses than one) and frequently allusive nature of the evidence at our disposal definitive conclusions are not possible. Much depends on the

3. Goulder, "Did Peter Ever Go to Rome?"

4. Painter, *Just James*, 44—contra Cullman, *Peter*, 234."In the New Testament Jerusalem is the only church of which we hear that Peter stood at its head."

5. Peter is referred to by Paul as having a role in connection with the *Jakobusgemeinde* in the early period—a commission (ἀποστολή) to the περιτομή (Gal 2:7–8)—a delegatory role consonant with that portrayed for Peter in the traditions embedded in Acts 8—9.

questions we bring to our evidence, the quality of the inferences we draw out and degree of convergence of outcomes. We have identified the most promising threads of evidence, noting their quality (§ 8. 1.), so our focus must now be on evaluating it with the inferences that can reasonably be made (§ 8. 2.), before finally considering if a coherent picture emerges (§ 8. 3.).

Although it is rather like "dividing the indivisible," to aid clarity we will first review the evidence concerning the *Jakobusgemeinde* and then bring in James.

2.1 The *Jakobusgemeinde*

2.1.1 Persecution, Take-Off and Ethos

The earliest clear evidence we have of the existence of the *Jakobusgemeinde* refers to its presence and activity in the early 30s CE—the years following the execution of Jesus. It occurs in the unsolicited confessions/admissions of Paul, in his correspondence fifteen to twenty years later, of his role, prior to his conversion in the mid-30s CE, in persecuting what he described as τὴν ἐκκλησίαν τοῦ Θεοῦ (Gal 1:13; 1 Cor 15:9; Phil 3:6) or ταῖς ἐκκλησίαις τῆς Ἰουδαίας ταῖς ἐν Χριστῷ (Gal 1:22). This very solid testimony of early persecution receives corroboration from Acts, if the judgment of many scholars is correct that Luke did not have access to the letters of Paul in compiling his narrative.

Movements are persecuted when they are perceived as a threat through advocacy of new ideas (or a freshly invigorated old idea) combined with significant numerical growth. The persecution in which Paul seems to have taken a prominent role testifies to the presence in Jerusalem and Judea of such a growing movement attracted by a novel message centered, according to the primitive tradition Paul "received," on the death and rising of Jesus (1 Cor 15:3–4). Scholars have only been able to speculate on the reason for the persecution, though many cite the offense of a crucified Messiah (1 Cor 1:23) as a likely candidate.

What the persecution does not tell us is whether this movement was brought into being *ex nihilo* by the impact and experience of those days or (more likely) grew out of and around an existent group newly energized by that experience, such as the group who came down from Galilee with Jesus. However, we have chronicled a problem here in the lack of any Galilean reference in any of the gospel trajectories rooted in Jerusalem (§ 7.): we need to keep open therefore the possibility that the movement in

Jerusalem with which James is uniquely associated may have its core in a Jerusalem based group who, prior to their experience during the fatal visit of Jesus to Jerusalem, had a fairly low profile in the City with little to distinguish it by size or message/ideology from other groupings within late Second Temple Judaism.

There is a good deal of coherence between the impressions of the *Jakobusgemeinde* we encountered in the immediacy and heat of Paul's letters and the more measured later portrayal of Luke. We encountered a movement that was fully expressive in its ideology, concerns and organization of a movement for the Restoration of Israel within late Second Temple Judaism. Whilst the issue of Gentile inclusion into Yahweh's covenant community in the present allowed for some variety of interpretation, the community of James in Jerusalem held steadfastly to the success of its Judaic mission as *the* priority (§ 5. 8.). The historic ministry of Jesus in Galilee appears to have evoked little interest; rather, the focus was on this son of David's death, probably seen as the innocent suffering of a righteous martyr followed by his rising into the divine presence, validating his vindication by God. This was the new decisive factor in their message but it is understood, proclaimed and integrated into their hope of the Restoration of Israel by God (§ 5. 10).

Circumcision remained the critical marker of male inclusion in the covenant with adherence to Torah marking both individual and community life (§ 5. 8.). We found indications of a form of organization comparable to that of Qumran and the Essenes, with a ruling triumvirate and council of twelve under the overall guidance of a *mebaqqer* that may have been typical of groups looking for the restoration, through divine intervention, of the twelve tribe Israel within its God-given boundaries (§ 5. 9.2.2–4.). Derived from shared understandings within Restoration Judaism, the organization and culture of the *Jakobusgemeinde* is what would naturally be set up and developed by such a group whatever the time and occasion of their beginnings. However, the Galilean movement initiated by Jesus, whilst likewise exhibiting the "twelve with three" pattern of leadership seems to have been geared more to a focus on itinerant preachers traveling through the varied settlements in the land with their message, rather than the settled urban community we find around James.[6] The developed organization of the *Jakobusgemeinde* is more likely to have been of indigenous origin within Jerusalem than an import from Galilee. The integration of the death and rising of Jesus into an existent Restoration ideology is consistent with this.

6. E.g., Theissen, *Sociology of Early Palestinian Christianity*; Crossan, *Historical Jesus*.

2.1.2 Origination

In reflecting on what we can discover about the community of James from the limited historical evidence available, we find a community that is born of the concerns for the Restoration of Israel that are common amongst many in late Second Temple Judaism. Integrated into this pattern of understanding is their distinctive message concerning the death and rising of Jesus of Nazareth. This latter element, combined with the movement's growth, was the key triggering the persecution in which Paul was involved and obviously "post-Jesus." But there is nothing in the ideological setting of this message, nor in the organization of the *Jakobusgemeinde* that demands a community originating solely from that Jesus-event.

There are other indications:

2.1.3 The Baptist Connection

We drew attention to the parallelisms delineating "the beginning of the good news" (Mark 1:1) in the prologue to Mark's gospel as including not only the persons of John and Jesus but also the contrasting locations of Galilee and Jerusalem which suggests two locations of significance for the origins of the later Christian movement (§ 3. 5.). The hyperbolic statement that "people from the whole Judean countryside and all the people of Jerusalem were going out to him" (Mark 1:5) has historical verisimilitude as the region of Israel which is in closest proximity to where John was operating, and the impact of John on the streets of Jerusalem finds strong confirmation not only independently in Josephus[7] but also in the later challenge of Jesus to the chief priests, scribes and elders about their view on the baptism of John—they could not answer him for "they were afraid of the crowd, for all regarded John as truly a prophet" (Mark 11:27–33). It was thus amongst *these* people in Jerusalem that the proclamation of the dying and exalted Christ found fertile ground.

There is no evidence that John, any more than Jesus in Galilee, sought to organize his baptizands into any form of distinctive community (unlike the Essenes)—his call was to the whole of Israel to repent in preparation for the imminent ἔσχατον (§ 3. 2.1). But they did not return to Jerusalem to live as isolated individuals and inevitably some degree of clustering of his followers would occur—both informal and formal (a process that must have occurred at a much earlier time amongst the Essenes). We have seen that

---

7. *Ant* 20.197–203.

the Lucan presentation of the preaching of Paul, embedding the traditions he received from Jerusalem, began with an emphasis on John the Baptist (§ 7. 8.2) and the provenance of the hymns celebrating John's birth in his nativity narrative (Luke 1:47–55, 68–79) may well have been in such a Jerusalem grouping (§ 3. 3.2). It is likely that the initial core membership of that community we associate with James was one (or more) of these clusters, perhaps possessing the beginnings of a more formal structure.

That something of this order was occurring may be borne out by the anomaly surrounding baptism—that baptism was the entry rite into the Christian movement from the earliest times when it is totally absent from the accounts of Jesus' ministry in Galilee (§ 3. 5.1). The most likely resolution of this anomaly is that, probably after the execution of John, some of his followers, taking advantage of the ubiquitous *miqva'ot* within the city, continued his practice of baptism. The case of Apollos from Alexandria who "knew only the baptism of John" (Acts 18:25) and the "disciples" in Ephesus who also only knew of "John's baptism" is evidence that this practice did indeed continue amongst John's followers (Acts 19:1–7) merging, for some, into a continuing practice of baptism within the proto-Christian movements—though its signification ("in the name of Jesus") would at some point alter—a process routinized in that same Ephesus account. If this process makes sense, we must note that the practice of baptism, which, by its claim to uniqueness, goes beyond the repetition of routine Judaic purificatory rites, will incur the development of some level of more formal organization in the practicing baptist clusters and groups.

The *Jakobusgemeinde* as we encounter it in the pages of the NT exhibits markers from within the world of late Second Temple Judaism whose distinctiveness betrays an ancestry with the movement initiated by John (§§ 3. 2.1; 3. 6.):

- a life commitment underpinned by a belief in the imminence of the ἔσχατον, with hope for the restoration of twelve-tribe Israel within the Land;

- the practice of baptism;

- the commitment to a strenuous individual and corporate life lived under the rule of Torah, "bearing fruit worthy of repentance" (Matt 3:8; Luke 4:9);

- advocacy and acceptance of *zekhut*[8]—"the protecting influence of freely chosen good conduct over and above what was required by the Law" (e.g., Matt 5:17–48)—some of the sayings embedded in EpJas

8. Taylor, *Immerser*, 124. § 3. 2.1.

(§ 7. 7.) and in the Sermon on the Mount which may derive from the Jerusalem Jacobean tradition (see Betz[9]. § 7. 7.2) are consonant with this demand of the Baptist.

This infers that the originating core of what we later meet in the NT as the *Jakobusgemeinde* was not only birthed within the Baptist movement in Jerusalem but more specifically in one of the clusters/groups that would naturally develop as the baptizands sought to understand and live out their new commitment. It is in this context we suggested that, contributing to the unquestioned eminence of the *Jakobusgemeinde* in the new movement, was its identifiable continuity with a grouping—συναγωγή—developing within the movement flowing from John and prior to (or contemporary with) Jesus' Galilean ministry. This continuity would have given it temporal seniority to the Galilean based movement (§ 5. 11.3).

Indeed, the tradition exalting the Baptist that the prologue to the fourth Gospel so clearly challenges may well have is its roots within, or close to, the *Jakobusgemeinde* (§ 3. 3.3). This is even more likely given the presence of the cultic/liturgical material embedded in the Lucan nativity narrative which is ascribed by a number of scholars to that early Jerusalem community (§ 3. 3.2 n.74 and n.75).

More speculative is that if my challenge to the general assumption of a Galilean reference in 1 Cor 15:5 is valid, then we have supportive evidence from the very earliest strand of oral tradition indicating a degree of formal organization already present in the nascent proto-Christian movement in Jerusalem prior to the first Easter—"(Christ) appeared to Cephas, then to the *twelve*" (§ 5. 9.2.4).[10]

2.1.4 The Galilean Silence

Further, embedded within the traditions that have their roots in the *Jako-busgemeinde* there is preserved evidence of that community's own history— the "Galilean Silence." This is not just a case of one maverick witness, but the consistent and coherent testimony of several independent witnesses, reflecting different tradition trajectories. At the risk of some repetition I summarize the evidence, for this is critical:

9. Betz, *Sermon on the Mount*, 70–88.

10. I must emphasize that the thesis I am presenting is not dependent upon the distinction of "Cephas" from "Peter." Following Kirsopp Lake's confession/advocacy (§ 4. 6.1.4) as a *modus operandi* does however yield an outcome that is coherent with our fragmentary evidence (§ 4. Excursus) and opens possibilities for fresh exploration (see further § 9).

Remembering that the core tradition Paul knew was that of the *Jako-busgemeinde* (§§ 4.9; 7. 2.), we identified:

- Tradition Paul "has received" and "handed on," each enshrined in a Jerusalem context (1 Cor 11:23–26; 15:3–7), (§ 4. 4.);

- Recitations and allusions to primitive kerygmatic and Christological material—pre-Pauline Palestinian formulae, probably of Jerusalem provenance/agency (Gal 1:1–4; 2:20; Rom 1:3–6; 4:25; 5:6; 8:32, 10:9; 1 Cor 6:14; 15:15; 2 Cor 4:14; 1 Thess 1:10), (§ 7. 2.);

- Paul's almost complete lack of use of Galilean traditions—his "Galilean Silence" (§ 7. 3.), with complementary attestation:

  - in the Jacobean letters and Hebrews (§§ 7. 5 and 7),

  - and within the Lucan presentation in Acts (§ 7. 8.).

None of these writings taken by themselves is significant, but coming from different tradition trajectories the cumulative effect of their consistent and complete coherence in sustaining a "Galilean Silence" within the dominant metanarrative of the mythic Christ, revealing knowledge only of Jerusalem located tradition of the closing days of Jesus' life—multiple attestation—is impressive and persuasive.

We examined the arguments which affirm that sayings of Jesus in Paul's letters and in EpJas are embedded in the literature without attribution. Whilst accepting that there may be examples of this, what is common to all who argue on these lines is the *a priori* assumption that a Christian community *must* know the story of Jesus, including its Galilean dimension (§ 7. 7.). We possibly lack the empathic imagination into the world of late Second Temple Judaism to envision how a renewal group in Jerusalem, "looking forward to the consolation of Israel" (Luke 2:25) and "looking for the redemption of Jerusalem" (Luke 2:38), would integrate the dying and rising of Jesus experience into their ideology, with little concern for the details of his prior human life.

The weight of this evidence for the Galilean Silence"—consistent, coherent, and from a range of tradition trajectories—argues emphatically for the *Jakobusgemeinde* having no knowledge of the Galilean ministry of Jesus (or, at the very least, accorded it no significant value) (§ 7. 4.). For the *Jakobusgemeinde*, I suggest that Jesus of Nazareth only came over the horizon for that last fateful week of his life—and those days *did* effect change.

Other indications of a "life before Jesus" for the *Jakobusgemeinde* may be judged as only permissive—this demands it.

Whatever the "men of Galilee" (Acts 1:11) were doing in the weeks following that event, it is inconceivable that *this* community was founded by the preaching of Peter, the fisherman from Galilee. It is inconceivable that *this* is the community who, according to Luke, "devoted themselves to the apostles' teaching" (Acts 2:42)—that is, the very Galilean Apostles who had all journeyed with Jesus from the days of the Baptist right up to the ascension (Acts 1:21–22).

What is conceivable, indeed probable, is that the "Galilean Silence" preserves a trace of the history and historical experience of an existing group (not disparate individuals) in Jerusalem—the *Jakobusgemeinde*, the community of James. Although no doubt aware of the Prophet from Galilee (who was their leader's brother), in the main they had no direct encounter with him until that one fateful week. The events and possible involvement in that roller coaster of a week injected a new factor and fresh understanding into their Restoration vision. Whilst reinforcing their thoroughgoing Judaic commitment, their experience *as a group* precipitated its transformation, supplying a new confidence, dynamic and direction.

Identification and definition of that transformation is inevitably less hard-edged than recognition of such a happening, but something of this order is needed to satisfactorily account for the *Jakobusgemeinde*'s Jerusalem-centered traditions matched by an equal ignorance (or complete non-valuation) of traditions emanating from Galilee.

If this is the case, then the belief that the crucifixion and exaltation of Jesus had inaugurated the beginnings of the ἔσχατον—which was speeding to its consummation and fulfillment "within this generation"—may also have encouraged a lack of interest amongst the *Jakobusgemeinde* in Jesus' teaching in Galilee.[11] After all, in the Torah was all the instruction and guidance they needed—and they also had, like the Essenes, their own "teacher of Righteousness,"[12]—the brother of the Lord, "called the 'Righteous' by all men from the Lord's time to ours."[13]

2.1.5 The Nazarenes

The "Galilean Silence" also raises a question about the original reference of the term "Nazarenes" (Acts 24:5). This seems to have been an early descriptor for the Christian movement, which continued in use for some

---

11. Fortunately it was an interest to a wide swathe of people as evidenced by the Synoptic gospels.

12. This is not a vote for Robert Eisenman!

13. *Hist. eccls.* 2:23.4–8; *Gos. Thom.* 12.

time amongst Judaic Christians in the East, whose roots were probably in the original Judaic Mission of the *Jakobusgemeinde*. It occurs as the name for Christians in the Judaic "Twelve Benedictions" (Cf. § 6. 2.2 n.44).

It is normal to assume that the name was given "to designate Jesus' disciples as followers of the man from Nazareth, the Nazarene."[14] But if the movement centered in Jerusalem had little knowledge and no interest in the human antecedents of their crucified and exalted lord it seems unlikely that the "Nazarene" epithet would become readily attached to them.

This is speculative, but if the indicators outlined above of "the church of God" in Jerusalem growing out of and being in continuity with a grouping/συναγωγή of disciples of the Baptist it opens up also the question of the origin of the epithet "Nazarene." James was a leader of the *Jakobusgemeinde* at the very least from our earliest encounter with him (1 Cor 15:7), in association with his brothers (1 Cor 9:5), and probably from much earlier, if the *Jakobusgemeinde* was already in existence. But if they were a bunch of Baptist enthusiasts, coming together after receiving his baptism, why were they not so labeled, why "Nazarenes"? Migrants into a metropolis typically group themselves according to their trade or place of origin (§ 2. 5.2.5) and this group may have formed originally around the men of this family from Nazareth, perhaps attracting other migrants from that region of Galilee, earning the label "Nazarenes." The confusion between Ναζαρηνός and Ναζαραῖος in our texts clearly points to its *origin in an oral culture* rather than a literary one (§§ 2. 5.2.5 n.104; 6. n.44)—and the streets of Jerusalem are a much more likely breeding ground for the adoption of the name for a group of people than the Galilean fields close to the village itself. Further, the acquisition of the label "Nazarenes" rather than, say, "Baptizers" is suggestive of the group initially forming in a period before John appeared in the wilderness of the Jordan, when their region of origin was the most distinctive thing about them—perhaps the natural coming together of migrants from the same region who are now in a strange city, and it was only later that they came strongly under the influence of John and his message.

2.2 James

2.2.1 A Foundation Figure

We must begin with the very early primary evidence found in Paul's writing, always remembering Knox's dictum (§ 8. above).[15] Further, this evidence

---

14. Dunn, *Beginning from Jerusalem*, 14–15.

15. Knox, *Chapters in a Life of Paul*, 33.

is almost casually yielded in passages (1 Cor 15 and Gal 1—2) where Paul's focus is on issues current in his Galatian and Corinthian ἐκκλησίαι, and therefore it is less liable to have suffered distortion.

We noted that in the very earliest oral tradition, "received" by Paul within three or four years of Jesus' crucifixion, James alone is alongside Cephas in having received an individual appearance of the risen Christ (1 Cor 15:3–7; § 4. 4). There is not the slightest hint of this being a "conversion-experience," nor does it need the Hegelian assumption of an early power struggle within the Christian movement to confuse it. "What is sauce for the goose is sauce for the gander"—their visions validated the status of both Cephas *and* James as foundation figures for the *Jakobusgemeinde* and the proto-Christian movement that was starting to flow from it, just as Paul claimed validation for his own apostleship on the grounds of his vision of the risen Lord. The notion that James emerged at a later date into leadership of the *Jakobusgemeinde* on the basis of his sibling relationship to Jesus after the departure of Peter is a scholarly inference from the much later Lucan Acts narrative. This earliest of traditions clearly indicates that James was a foundation figure in Jerusalem from the very dawn of the Christian movement at the very least, if not earlier.

This is supported by the earliest literary evidence:

In Paul's Galatian correspondence we have contemporary evidence about James from one who knew and had met and debated with him—evidence of the finest kind—and we note that although not extensive, its quality as testimony from the actual pen of an eye-witness to those events in which both he and James were participants is far superior to any of the testimony we have about Jesus which has all been through the mill of cultic usage.

On Paul's first visit to Jerusalem after his conversion (in the mid-30s), probably the occasion when he became cognizant with the early *Jakobusgemeinde* tradition (above), James is one of only two significant named people (the other being Cephas) that Paul recounts as having met, whilst on his later visit James is the first name in the triumvirate of Pillars of the *Jakobusgemeinde*, along with Cephas and a "John," who are clearly the authority figures, both pronouncing their judgment and extending the hand of fellowship. This is coherent with the position of Cephas and James, at least, as foundation figures of the Jerusalem community (§ 4. 5.–4. 6.).

James' position as head of the *Jakobusgemeinde* becomes crystal clear in the "Antioch Incident" (Gal 2:11–14) when it is "people from James" who challenge Cephas, and therefore it is to the judgment and authority of James that Cephas, followed by Barnabas and other Judaic Christians, submitted.

The slightly later date of this standoff may indicate a growing consolidation of power into the person of James from the triumvirate of the Pillars, but that cannot detract from his status as a founding figure of the community (§ 4. 7.).

There can be little doubt that his sibling relationship to Jesus was also a factor in the respect paid to James, but it was a status at a level never shared by Jesus' other brothers, nor by Simeon, the cousin of Jesus who succeeded James' in leadership of the *Jakobusgemeinde* (§ 5. 11.2.). In the salutation of the brief epistle in his name, Jude/Judas, a brother of Jesus (Mark 6:3), is identified as "brother of James" (Jude 1)—only James is "*the* Lord's brother" (Gal 1:19). There is more to James' position than family kinship: "It is an authority that is unique to James. It is non-negotiable. It is non-transferable. It is the authority that adheres without qualification to the founder of a movement" (§ 6. 3.).

We also examined the evidence that can be gleaned, mainly by inference, about James and the *Jakobusgemeinde* from Paul's letters, including his hurried notes as he organized the collection from his Gentile ἐκκλησίαι and anxiously contemplated its reception in Jerusalem (§ 5. 6.1)—throughout his letters the position and authority of James in the *Jakobusgemeinde* and the mission that flowed from it is inviolate, much to Paul's chagrin on one occasion (Gal 2:6). When Paul did actually challenge it, in the "Antioch Incident," he lost. (§ 4. 7.2).

Consistent with this is the position assumed for James in the traditions embedded in the history of Acts, even in his somewhat low-key introduction by Luke (Acts 12:17). On the occasion of Paul's final visit to Jerusalem it is James alone who speaks for the *Jakobusgemeinde*, whilst at the earlier Conference, with Peter and Paul in a secondary role, James is portrayed as quietly assuming the mantle of a *mebaqqer*, presiding over the gathering, interpreting the scripture, and pronouncing the resolution. We noted that both Peter and Paul testify "by default," in Luke's presentation, to this position of James through their acceptance of the subordinate role of witnesses and petitioners to the Conference (§ 5. 9.3).

Luke had cast a veil of silence over James in his foundation myth of the Christian movement in Jerusalem (Acts 1—5) for, although the presence of the family of Jesus is recognized in the post-Easter gathering (Acts 1:14), James is not named. Also, by clear implication, James is excluded by Luke from any foundational role in the church by the "apostolic cv" laid out for the replacement of Judas (Acts 1:21–22). Thus it is significant that both on the occasion of Paul's final visit, and in constructing his account of the Conference, Luke portrays James exercising a firm authority to which all accede. It suggests a strong communal memory surrounding the role and status of James.

Thus, both contemporary evidence and ongoing tradition cohere in testifying to the unique status and authority of James in, and from, Jerusalem whilst the earliest evidence clearly points to this status being grounded in James as a founding figure of the *Jakobusgemeinde*.

The only challenge to this conclusion is the silence of Luke. I leave comment to Professor Knox.

2.2.2 Earlier Residence?

Nothing in the early oral tradition or the contemporary writings of Paul *absolutely* requires James' association with the *Jakbusgemeinde*, or the foundation of the latter, to be any earlier than Jesus' final days in Jerusalem. *Neither do they preclude an earlier presence in the city.* It is often suggested that James, along with other Galilean followers of Jesus, moved to Jerusalem after the latter's dying and rising to await his final, fairly imminent, return on Zion, but little attention is paid to their economic livelihood in the interim—not much work for fishermen in Jerusalem, though a τέκτων might fare better.

Yet, built into Luke's presentation of James as the *mebaqqer* of the *Jakobusgemeinde* (Acts 15) is a clear acceptance of him having achieved a significant measure of competence as an interpreter of Torah—a memory that is supported by the existence of the general epistle of James (wherever we place it on the autograph-pseudepigraph continuum), a writing well within the Judaic Wisdom tradition. As Bauckham commented: "a wisdom teacher in his own right."[16] The increasing demand for literate retainers provided one of the few opportunities for artisans to improve their social standing (§ 2. 3.1.2) and we noted evidence that points to the possibility of someone such as James acquiring a level of competence indicative of a degree of scribal literacy (§ 2. 6.2.4). That requires time and opportunity to achieve.

If this tradition is firmly grounded in the history it raises a critical question of how, when, and where he gained it. The home of an artisan family in the village of Nazareth in Galilee is an unlikely location—Jerusalem, as Crossan recognized, was a more likely scenario:

> Did he come there only after the execution of Jesus, or *had he been there long before it?* . . . much more explanation for James's presence and standing in Jerusalem needs to be given than is

---

16. Bauckham, "James and Jesus," 117.

usually offered. Did he leave Nazareth long before and become both literate and involved within scribal circles in Jerusalem?[17]

This concurs with indications in the gospels that Mary and the brothers had left Nazareth some years before the time of Jesus' ministry, along with the indication from Paul's letters that James was firmly established in the leadership of the *Jakobusgemeinde* from the earliest period following Jesus' execution (§ 6. 2.2). It also coheres with the opportunity in those years for young men of artisan parentage to be recruited into the scribal retainer class (§ 2. 3.1.2). However, competence in Torah interpretation, whether formally or informally acquired, requires some years of preparation in a setting that is conducive to this process, which all points to the probability of James having been in Jerusalem for some years prior to the dying and rising of Jesus and before John "appeared in the wilderness" (Mark 1:4).

We can only hypothesize about possible reasons for a move from Nazareth to Jerusalem. Economic problems for the family would no doubt play a part, and there may well have been family roots in Judea, as for many of the Judaic population in Galilee, and hinted at within the nativity legends (§ 6. 2.2 n.47).

Outlining the social/economic framework of the times in § 2. "The World of James," I explored the significance of Herod's Temple Building project with its huge demands for a range of both skilled and unskilled labor. This could have provided the occasion for the family of a τέκτων to move to Jerusalem, or if the family had made the move for other reasons the Temple project would have provided opportunity for the employment of the brothers. This can only be a suggestion, but it is one that meshes with the problems and opportunities of the day that would be faced by an artisan family from Galilee contemplating migration to Jerusalem. It does also have that one fragile yet tantalizing piece of tradition in Hegesippus in its support—the marked callosity of James' knees, typical of what is found within the building trade (§ 2. 4.2).

3. Towards a History of the *Jakobusgemeinde*

The concluding stage of evaluation focuses on "the degree of convergence of outcomes" (§ 8. 2.). In doing this we need to draw inevitably on a disciplined use of the faculty of creative imagination as described by Taylor:

> It goes without saying that in any recreation of the past much has to be supplied by the imagination; but there is all the difference

17. Crossan, *Jesus*, 135–36.

in the world between idle fancy and the historical imagination controlled by facts which have been patiently investigated.[18]

The identification of James with the early "church" of Jerusalem is a *sine qua non* for any study of James and his place within the beginnings of the Christian movement. Projecting back from fairly firm, albeit limited, foundations into the separate pasts of James and the *Jakobusgemeinde*, these two vistas (above) merge and mesh together to suggest a more rounded three-dimensional picture:

Very dimly seen is the migration, several years before the execution of Jesus, of James and his brothers (except Jesus) from Galilee to Jerusalem where, perhaps with others from the same region, they gathered around James into a distinctive enough group to be labeled "the Nazarenes." Jerusalem and its Temple may have provided both the stimulus and the opportunity for this son of a devout family from Galilee to begin acquiring the knowledge and skills that later enabled him to be recognized as a competent interpreter of Torah.

Much clearer is the impact of John the Baptist, from the wilderness onto the streets of Jerusalem, empowering groups such as the Nazarene brothers with a new vision, a refreshed commitment to live by Torah, and a new hope. Although of low profile, and probably not the only grouping affected by or brought into being by the message of John, some degree of organizational expression would occur, probably on a pattern familiar in late Second Temple Judaism, including a council of Twelve. After John's death they may also have continued his practice of baptism.

"Take-off" for the *Jakobusgemeinde* occurred following the experiences surrounding the final visit of Jesus to Jerusalem—an act of prophetic symbolism culminating in his death—an event in which "the Nazarenes" may have been involved (§ 6. 2.2). Following his suffering and death, visions of the risen Christ experienced by a number of people, including their leader James, became interpreted as the fulfillment of John's message—the ἔσχατον John had announced as imminent was now in process of realization, beginning with the eschatological suffering and exaltation of the Messiah. It was this fresh element, integrated into their hope for the restoration of Israel, in a city where the message of John had struck deep chords, that drew in new adherents, triggering the persecution in which Paul was involved, and marking the emergence of the *Jakobusgemeinde* onto the page of history. With James as their established leader and founder, little need or interest was felt for the activity and teachings in Galilee of his younger brother. With her primary self-identification continuing within the Judaic renewal movement, she grew

18. Taylor, *Formation of the Gospel Tradition*, 168.

in strength and influence in the climate of an increasingly nationalist Jerusalem giving birth to a range of ἐκκλησίαι in the Diaspora of both East and West, including those of her deviant offspring, Paul, before largely sharing the fate of the city with whom she was so closely identified.

Unlike Paul who, at a time of confrontation with some of his critics, could hyperbolically "write-off" all his Judaic inheritance and practice as rubbish—"in order that (he) may gain Christ" (Phil 3:2–11): the *Jakobusgemeinde* saw the events culminating in the exaltation of Jesus as *the* fulfillment of their Judaic faith, validating the message of John the Baptist: For Paul, the Christ-event marked a break with the past—"in Christ, there is a new creation, everything old has passed away; everything has become new!" (cf. 1 Thess 1:9), whereas the *Jakobusgemeinde* experienced it as in continuity with their past and were empowered to sing and proclaim (in the memorable phraseology of the KJV):

> Blessed be the Lord God of Israel,
>
> for he hath visited and redeemed his people
>
> (Luke 1:68)[19]

But, in embedding their faith within the hope for the Restoration of Israel, which was endemic in late Second Temple Judaism, the *Jakobusgemeinde* largely shared the fate of Jerusalem in 70 CE: the future lay elsewhere.

---

19. The *Benedictus* "is a more or less radical rewriting of a Jewish or Jewish Christian original . . . a poem of the Baptist's movement." Bovon, *Luke 1*, 32. All three of Bovon's descriptors could attach to the *Jakobusgemeinde*.

9

Thirty Years On

1. Pillars for a Movement in Transition

THAT JAMES OF JERUSALEM was a person of major importance and influence during the first decades of the Christian movement is *fact*: that he is not accorded the prominence in the text of the NT that should have been his due cannot be gainsaid. Unlike Matthias (Acts 1:26), however, his presence cannot be removed from the story.

I have argued that the kernel of the community associated with James, which we meet in the NT and refer to as the Church of Jerusalem, was a group earlier gathered around the brothers of Jesus, under the leadership of James, that at some point came under the inspiration of the preaching of John the Baptist.

This does not fit well with the normative portrayal of Christian beginnings in *The Acts of the Apostles*.

It is important to recognize that Luke was writing towards the end of the first century when the originating linkage of the emergent Gentile Christian church with the *Jakobusgemeinde* was a likely source of embarrassment in the decades following the War of 66–73 CE. It was similar to the need felt by Josephus in the same period in writing his apologetic *Wars of the Jews* for his Gentile audience.

Emerging from its Judaic embryo, the growing Gentile-dominant Christian movement had a need to clarify its sense of self-identity as a Gentile-inclusive movement free of the tutelage of Jerusalem. Most likely sharing a common Gentile perception of widespread Judaic responsibility for the War (a perception Josephus faced head on), their roots in the

Jakobusgemeinde under the leadership of the Jerusalem Pillars of James, Cephas and John, though undeniable, were distinctly suspect. Indeed, a degree of alienation from Jerusalem and the *Jakobusgemeinde* may well go back to the latter's probable rejection of their gift, conveyed by Paul on his final ill-fated visit there. Scholars have frequently discussed what happened to their gift—little consideration seems to have been given to the effect a rejection would have had on the givers in places like Corinth, Philippi and Thessalonica, as well as on the delegates who were the bearers of their gift. How did they all feel? What was the "message" they read into this rejection? How did they react when their delegates who had travelled with Paul returned with their reports? What did it do to their respect for the Pillars of Jerusalem?

We lack the evidence to answer questions like these, but given the energy and importance invested by Paul and his ἐκκλησίαι in gathering and taking this gift to Jerusalem, its rejection would have repercussions commensurate with their investment in the project. News of the co-incident arrest of Paul, in Jerusalem with their gift, would hardly have helped.

What we do know is that c. 95 CE Clement, bishop of Rome, could refer to Peter and Paul as "the greatest and most righteous pillars" without any sense of innovation (1 Clem 5:2); whilst a decade earlier Matthew had introduced into his Gospel the tradition that identified Peter as the "Rock" on which the church would be built (Matt 16:17–19). It was also during these years that the church in Rome was nurturing the tradition of the martyrdom of both Peter and Paul in Rome to enshrine its claim on them as its founding Apostles.[1] By the second decade of the second century Ignatius can simply "twin" the two names (Ign. Rom 4:3). Though not extensive, this testifies to a process within the emergent Gentile Christian church of replacing the Jerusalem Pillars with the names of Peter and Paul.

It was during this same period that the *Acts of the Apostles* saw the light of day, highlighting the role and acts of Peter[2] and Paul as the founding apostles of the Gentile-inclusive Christian church, now becoming centered in Rome. The parallels between Luke's presentation of the two men that were seen by the Tubingen School in the nineteenth century, under the influence of the dominant Hegelian philosophy of the time, as evidence of

---

1. Goulder, "Did Peter Ever Go to Rome?" 391–92.

2. Additionally, Luke, in the call of Jesus to his disciples to be "fishers of men" at the beginning of his mission in Galilee, changes the Markan setting of the story to that of the miraculous catch of fish (John 21: 1–19—symbolic of the future mission of the church) and addresses the charge directly and specifically to Peter (Luke 5:1–11. cp. Mark 1:16–20). Bauckham comments, "Luke already in this passage portrays Peter as called to a preeminent role in the community's future mission." Bauckham, *Jesus and the Eyewitnesses*, 171.

conflict within the early church (a perception that still influences exegesis) are better understood as a presentation evaluating Peter and Paul together as founding fathers.

This is the context within which we need to re-read the account of Christian beginnings in Acts. We need to re-visit the Lucan text, particularly his telling of the "early days" and of the Hellenist mission, before the better-informed saga of the later Pauline mission takes over.

2. The Men of Galilee

When discussing Luke's work as redactor (§ 5. 2.1) we noted the potential significance of breaks, anomalies and inconsistencies in his narrative. These are like the signs of disturbance in the ground that are a magnet to the archeologist's eye with their indication of earlier significant human activity. In my work as a counselor I knew that exploration of any dissonance—cognitive and/or affective—in a client's presentation of his/her situation was likely to be productive of a positive outcome, though it could be a painful process. In reading Acts we need to be similarly alert to the tensions, dissonance, and aporiae in Luke's presentation, for it is at these points that the traditions he is blending into his story are at odds either with each other or with his guiding thesis (or with both). Dissonance with the much earlier primary evidence within Paul's letters also attracts attention.

Tension in Luke's text commences on Easter morning.

This comes into focus if we register intriguing Synoptic testimony, where "Galilee" is more than a geographic locale. It is both the locus for the ministry of Jesus and, according to both Mark and Matthew, *it is the place to which the disciples were directed to go to meet the risen Jesus* (Mark 16:7; Matt 28:7).[3] The sheer abruptness of the ending of Mark, followed by Matthew, takes the close disciples of Jesus firmly away from Jerusalem and into Galilee. That would certainly help to explain the "Galilean silence" in Jerusalem-based traditions.

Luke dissents. He places all the appearances of the risen Jesus in Jerusalem in line with his fundamental thesis of "Beginning from Jerusalem." He changes the message of the Markan "young man" (Mark 16:7) into an

---

3. Lightfoot, *Locality and Doctrine*. This followed the seminal work of Lohmeyer, *Galiläa und Jerusalem*. Discussion of the questions raised has moved from the historical-critical position of Lightfoot and Lohmeyer to the redaction-critical approach of Marxsen, *Mark the Evangelist*, 102–11, and the literary-critical analysis of Malborn, "Galilee and Jerusalem."

angelic direction to "Remember how he told you, *while he was still in Galilee*, that the Son of Man must be handed over . . . " (Luke 24:6–7)—they are to "stay here in the city . . . " (Luke 24:49) and "he ordered them not to leave Jerusalem . . . " (Acts 1:4) until the empowerment of the Spirit. This leaves absolutely no space for Galilee, and is a determined and resolute rewriting by Luke of an existent tradition that located critical encounters between the risen Jesus and his remaining disciple-group back in their home territory of Galilee.[4]

Additionally, Luke, alone amongst the NT writers, separates out the event of the "Resurrection" from that of the "Ascension." In doing so he has created a space extending to the Day of Pentecost when the action begins in earnest with the coming of the Spirit. This is not an "event-space" to be filled with details of the "many convincing proofs" (Acts 1:3) that Jesus was alive, but a "literary-space"—a prologue—for Luke to set out central themes in his narrative.

Into this literary space, the Galileans are moved onto the center of the Jerusalem stage. It is clear who we are talking about—"the apostles whom (Jesus) had chosen" (Acts 1:2), that is, the Galilean Twelve (Luke 6:13). Following their empowerment through the Holy Spirit it is *they* who "will be my witnesses" (Acts 1:8). This grounding is further reinforced at the close of this introductory section when, after witnessing the Ascension, they are addressed as "Men of Galilee" (Acts 1:11). In case we missed it, Luke repeats this identification on the lips of the bewildered crowd at Pentecost. "Are not all these who are speaking Galileans?" (Acts 2:7).

Given the evidence of the "Galilean Silence" in the *Jakobusgemeinde kerygma* and tradition this must be considered a deliberative narrative ploy by Luke to retrospectively insert the "Galileans" with their knowledge of the full ministry of Jesus in Galilee as well as the final days in Jerusalem into the generating point of his foundation myth of the church.

Luke seeks not only to make good this omission in the *Jakobusgemeinde* message but also to neuter one of its distinctive expressions:

> The restoration of the twelve tribes as part of a renewed Israel under God was a shared aspiration of the Judaic movements of the late Second Temple period (§ 5. 10).

This shared hope for a renewal of the whole people of Israel under God is embedded in the belief system of the *Jakobusgemeinde*. It is repeated twice by Luke, forming a link between his volumes, and disavowed by the risen

4. Lightfoot, *History and Interpretation*, 207–08. Luke also seems to have transposed an original Galilean resurrection appearance story (John 21:1–23) into the context of Jesus' historical ministry there (Luke 5:1–11).

Jesus on both occasions (Luke 24:21; Acts 1:6–7). It is a rejection by Luke of a crucial dimension in the Jerusalem *kerygma* that was also at the heart of the Restoration ideology endemic in the growing nationalist movement in Israel in those mid-century years, which ultimately found its violent expression in the Judaic rebellion. In the Gentile world beyond Palestine few distinctions would be made—all Jerusalem was guilty.

This was a heart-rending problem for the increasing number of Gentile Christians in the Empire who had looked to the *Jakobusgemeinde* and its Pillars as their mother-church. It would have been a problem, too, for many Jews in the Diaspora (including "followers of the Way" in diasporan synagogues). Luke is placing clear blue water between the emergent Gentile movement and the *Jakobusgemeinde* whilst maintaining the undeniable historical origination of their movement in Jerusalem. Their Pillars are Peter and Paul; and the preaching of Peter that is the foundation of their faith is vested in the sayings and deeds of Jesus the Galilean who was martyred in Jerusalem by its leaders. It is no accident that the Lucan Acts is preceded by his Gospel, and significant that the dismissal of the question about the "restoration of the kingdom to Israel" at the beginning of Acts (1:6) forms an *inclusio* with its final verse where Paul's "proclaiming the kingdom of God" (a very rare phrase in Acts) is in parallel with "teaching about the Lord Jesus Christ" (28:31).

Luke is writing up into formal literature as history a process that was probably already well under development amongst the emergent Gentile Christian communities towards the end of the first century. I recall (with slight adaptation) Weeden's words:

> (A) primary concern (of history writing) is to preserve a community's social identification in its 'present' consciousness—even if that means the alteration of its . . . tradition, including the possible loss of authentic historical information related to the community's past history—in order to bring its . . . tradition into congruency with the community's current self-understanding of its social identity, as well as to make its . . . tradition congruently relevant in addressing the demands of new existential realities when they arise.[5] (cf. § 5. 3.2)

For Luke (and his readers/hearers), it was essential that the "men of Galilee" were both in Jerusalem and the bearers of the Message in the birthing of the church.

---

5. Weeden, "Kenneth Bailey's Theory," 37.

3. Twelve *in absentia*

Definition of "the men of Galilee" becomes more specific as the reconstitution of the Twelve is described—at considerable length—culminating in the appointment of Matthias for his fifteen minutes of fame (Acts 1:15–26). The requirement for Judas' replacement to have been present through the whole period from John's baptism through to the Ascension specifically ruled out James and other family members, although they are recognized as part of the movement in Jerusalem (Acts 1:14). This recognition of the Twelve is declared a scripturally required prolegomenon for the task now imminently before them (Acts 1:16–20)—the task of worldwide evangelization. It was that important.

Which brings us to the aporia that underpins the structure of the succeeding narrative:

After prioritizing this absolute importance of an identifiable twelve Names, all from Galilee, who have witnessed the whole train of events from the Baptist to the Ascension as guarantors of the tradition and message, *they then disappear from the story.*[6] Apart from one passing reference to a group so titled (Acts 6:2; cf. § 5. 9.2.4), Luke then allows the Twelve to slip away from his text like ships in the night, except James, brother of John [who raised his head only to lose it (Acts 12.2)] and Peter. The Twelve, whose names are recalled (Acts 1:13), are left (apart from Peter) to merge into a rather faceless group of "apostles" (§ 5. 9.2.1) whilst the real action is centered (in addition to that of Peter) on the "acts" of Stephen, Philip, and (above all) Paul.

As the Lucan narrative unfolds it becomes clear that this focus on the reconstitution of the Twelve is to legitimate the person and role of Peter in the foundational stories as the authorized and representative bearer of the message of the Galilean prophet.

This aporia of the reconstitution of the Galilean Twelve followed by their subsequent absence flows as an undercurrent in the narrative of Acts through to the founding and approval of the mission to the Gentiles (Acts 2—15).

We noted (§ 5. 2.2) how Dibelius contrasted the generalized healing story in the "early days" narrative (Acts 3:1–10) with the more specific and inconsequential detail in, e.g., the story of the healing of Dorcas (Acts 9:36–43) to point up the fact that in the corpus of tradition gathered around

---

6. As they are from Paul's accounts in Gal 1:18—2:10; Patterson, "Can You Trust a Gospel?" 200.

the Hellenist Mission (Acts 6—12) Luke did have some tradition—units available to blend into his story. However they are framed in a narrative flow provided by Luke, enabling him to move the locus of his story from Jerusalem to Antioch in line with his controlling thesis of "Jerusalem . . . Samaria . . .to the ends of the earth" (Acts 1:8).

This blending of fragments of tradition centering around the Hellenist Mission within its Lucan narrative framework facilitates the identification of the interests and strategies of the author which can then illumine our reading of the earlier Jerusalem story. What we find in a well-constructed narrative is a series of aporiae, all of which arise out of that underlying tension between the essential role of the Twelve with their absence from the ensuing story.

3.1 The "Seven"

The appointment of the "Seven" to "serve tables" (Acts 6:1–6) contrasts markedly with their subsequent activity as pioneering preachers and evangelists (Acts 6:8—8:40). The whole thrust and direction of Luke's story in the succeeding chapters demonstrates that the purpose in interjecting from nowhere this tradition of problems with the "daily distribution" is to bring the Seven, especially Stephen and Philip, leaders of an apparently independent charismatic movement,[7] into the foreground of the escalating action. But Luke uses the irrelevant memory of the widows to place the origin of this movement in Jerusalem—initiated and commissioned by the "apostles" (v. 6), and under their continuing supervision.

3.2 The Mission to Samaria

Peter and John are sent to make good what was lacking in the successful Hellenist Mission into Samaria (Acts 8:14–25). That Luke himself was aware of this continuing fault-line between his theme of the primacy and singularity of origin in Jerusalem and the traditions emanating from the charismatic Hellenist Mission is betrayed by the inclusion into the narrative of the story of Peter and John being sent to legitimate and complete the Samaritan mission of Philip through the imposition of apostolic hands "that they may receive the Holy Spirit" (Acts 8:14–17).

Jerusalem origination and the unity of the Movement is secured, but at a price: baptism "in the name of the Lord Jesus" (Acts 8:16) is evidently

---

7. Pervo, *Profit With Delight*, 40

deficient—"they had *only* been baptized in the name of the Lord Jesus." Reception of the Spirit (nowhere else in Acts) required the hands of Peter and John, the commissioned representatives of the apostles in Jerusalem. Reception of the Holy Spirit is a Lucan theme (Acts 1:8), though not normally conditional upon correct liturgy (Acts 2:1–4; 4:31; 10:44–48). Cover one crack, and another appears—the Lucan template (Acts 1:8) does not match the traditions of what actually happened on the ground and the aporiae hover around the introduction into the narrative of the apostles, especially the "big fisherman."

We might also note a degree of tension here in the presentation of Peter as commissioned by the "apostles at Jerusalem" contrasting with his completely dominant presence in Luke's own foundation myth. In fact the description of "Peter" in Acts 8:14–25 and 9:32–43 is more consonant with the "Peter" in Gal 2:7–8 than with the "Peter" of Acts 1—5.

3.3 The "Eye of the Storm"

When severe persecution ravages the church in Jerusalem (Acts 8:1)—"all except the apostles (i.e., the leadership) were scattered"—an intrinsically unlikely scenario. This anomaly occurs within Lucan framing of the Philip and Antiochene traditions, rather than in the content of those traditions themselves. It integrates into the narrative the controlling thesis that the gospel flowed progressively outwards through Judea and Samaria from its beginnings in Jerusalem (Acts 1:8). Luke is concerned to retain "the apostles" (= the Galilean Twelve, with Peter) as a continuing presence in Jerusalem, which, in accordance with his template, remains the generative point for the unified Christian mission under the guidance of Peter and the Twelve.

3.4 The Gentile Mission

The bold programming of Peter into the inception of the Gentile Mission (Acts 10:1—11:18; 15:7) is at odds with the Hellenist tradition, within which it is embedded, of Gentiles responding to their preaching (Acts 11:19–26); and at odds with his own (thrice repeated) telling of the significance of Paul's Damascus road encounter as a "light to the Gentiles" (Acts 9:15; 22:15, 21; 26:16–18). It is more seriously at odds with the contemporary evidence of Paul concerning the division of responsibility between Peter (to the circumcised) and himself (to the Gentiles), as agreed with the Jerusalem Pillars (Gal 2:7–9). In the Lucan scheme (Acts 1:8) this first full-blooded Gentile convert marks the transition to the third and final phase of the risen Christ's commission to be "witnesses . . . to the ends of the earth" and it is therefore of critical importance for Luke that this occurs, following incontrovertible divine guidance, through the agency of Peter alone (not even the apostles at Jerusalem), completing with the bold assertion by Peter himself at the Conference of Jerusalem that it was common knowledge that he was the one chosen by God from "the early days . . . to be the one through whom the Gentiles would hear the message of the good news and become believers" (Acts 15:7)—a statement that flies brazenly in the face of the contemporary documentary evidence we have from Paul (Gal 2:7–9).

This complete disjunction in telling the story of the origins of the mission to the Gentiles originates from Luke's insertion of Peter into the center of the picture.

Consistently, each example occurs in redactional linkages and inclusions where Luke is framing traditions of the Hellenist mission within the guidelines of his controlling thesis of the temporal, theological and ecclesial role of Jerusalem as the originating and nurturing center of the nascent Christian movement through the continuing presence and guidance of the Galilean Apostles—and his template does not fit. Peter and (to a lesser extent) "the apostles" are consistently and systematically found associated with each example of Lucan aporiae we have identified. It is here that we are seeing exposed most clearly our author's underlying narrative strategy of integrating Peter and the Galilean traditions he represents into the center of his story. This insight can then inform our understanding and interpretation of his "early days" narrative, where there is little tradition available to guide or constrain. (§ 5. 2.2)

4. The Early Days

Consonant with Luke's adoption of the strategy of complete excision of James from his "early days" narrative is his broader veil of silence over the *Jakobusgemeinde* Pillars of Gal 2:9.[8] Were it not for this account of Christian beginnings written around the end of the first century we would have little difficulty in recognizing from the near contemporary evidence of Paul that it is to James, Cephas and John we should attribute the origin and nurturing of that first Christian community. They were the recognized and respected Pillars who were confidently embedded as the Jerusalem leaders on the occasion of Paul's visit in the middle to late-40s CE (Gal 2:6–9) and, by inference, much earlier (Gal 1:18–19) in the mid-30s CE during his first visit.

---

8. In the whole of Acts James occupies a total of 18 verses out of 1007 = 1.75 percent.

Painter has registered a note of caution about Peter's role in Acts:

> It seems that the prominence of Peter in Acts has been interpret-
> ed in terms of his leadership. But that prominence is described
> more in terms of his activity in relation to those outside the
> believing community than in terms of leadership of the com-
> munity. Peter, like Paul, is portrayed as a "missionary" rather
> than as the leader of a settled community.[9]

Given Luke's pattern of intruding Peter into the narrative where some
source material is available from the Hellenist Mission, we are compelled
to challenge the presentation of Peter in the section on the early days in
Jerusalem (Acts 2—5) where Luke had much greater authorial freedom,
unconstrained by any solid traditions.

However, despite Peter completely dominating the Jerusalem story,
Luke is scrupulously careful in these opening chapters to avoid any explicit
recognition of Peter as having a status within the *Jakobusgemeinde* comparable to that held by James (Acts 15:13–21; 21:17–25); although we do know
(Gal 2:7) that Peter was associated with the *Jakobusgemeinde* at the time of
Paul's second visit there in the late 40s CE, exercising a key role, though
probably itinerant beyond Jerusalem,[10] in their mission to the περιτομή.
Consistent with this Luke presents Peter's programmatic speech at Pentecost as being specifically addressed to "devout Jews from every nation under
heaven" (Acts 2:5–11).

As well as playing on the growing identification of Cephas/Peter towards the end of the first century[11] I suggest that Luke enhances Peter's occupation of this role of ἀποστολή in the opening chapters (whether in the
earlier, pre-Pauline sense, or his own later usage) to the point where Peter
seems to be bursting through the very seams of the narrative: he assumes
the leadership (Acts 1:15; 2:14), is the authoritative interpreter of scripture
(1:16–22), thousands respond to his preaching (and we hear of no other
proclaimer) (2:14–41; 3:12–26), he heals (3:1–10; 5:12–16) and even his
shadow is therapeutic (5:15). He boldly confronts the Chief Priests in defense of the movement (4:1–22; 5:27–32) and his disapproval can be fatal
(5:1–11)!

9. Painter, *Just James,* 44—contra Cullman, *Peter,* "In the new Testament (Jerusalem) is the only church of which we hear that Peter stood at its head." 234.

10. The ἀποστολή of Peter in Gal 2:8 probably carries the earlier, broader usage that
we find in Acts 14:4 and 14 where Paul and Barnabas are ἀπόστολοι of Antioch—they
have been sent as agents of the commissioning group.

11. The specific identification of Cephas as Peter is first found in John 1:42. Roughly
contemporary is 1 Clement which knows of both "Peter" (5:4) and "Cephas" (47:3) yet
displays no awareness of identity.

But what about John, Peter's totally silent companion?[12] What role does he play? He does nothing, he says nothing.[13] Just like John, the Pillar in Galatians, he is mute. He never appears without Peter, and the pairing of Peter and the quiescent John in Acts is always a Jerusalem phenomenon: John is absent when Peter is further afield on the Mediterranean coastal strip (Acts 9:32—10:48).

"John" is identified by Luke as the brother of James whom Herod Agrippa I "killed with the sword" (Acts 12:2). We are surely intended to read this as a reference to the two Zebedean brothers of the Galilean Twelve, about whose martyrdom there is an early Christian tradition (Mark 10:38–39). Whatever the historicity behind the narrative, Luke here intrudes this tradition as a literary strategy to underline that the "James" he is about to introduce into the story in Peter's parting message (Acts 12:17) is most certainly not the "James" of the Galilean Twelve, whilst leaving the reader to infer "John" as a member of that critical group.

Can this "John"—the mute chameleon of Acts—really be the same person as the Son of Zebedee in the Gospels who, with his brother, was surnamed a "son of thunder" by Jesus (Mark 3:17); who took the lead in reprimanding an exogenous exorcist (Mark 9:38–40); and who with his brother (in Luke's own narrative), wanted to "nuke" the inhospitable Samaritans (Luke 9:51–56) and later with his brother sought to outsmart their colleagues, betraying a naked lust for power and control (Mark 10:35–41)?

The identity of John is left to the reader.[14]

---

12. The "faithful sidekick" is a common motif found in both contemporary novels and apocryphal Acts of Apostles (Pervo, *Profit With Delight*, 53).

13. Acts 4:1—Λαλούντων δὲ αὐτῶν is transliterated by NRSV as "While Peter *and John* were speaking to the people," but the preceding speech is Peter's, and as usual we are not told a word of what John was saying. Similarly in Acts 4:19—it is difficult to imagine the response to be other than that of Peter.

14. (1) Painter, *Just James*, 44 observed that: "The conclusion that Peter was the leader (of the Jerusalem church) at first is the consequence of the influence of an *interpretative tradition* that has no support in relation to Jerusalem." (my italics). The traditional identification of these two brothers with the Gospel's Zebedee brothers is similarly an "interpretative tradition." (2) This ambiguity is nurtured throughout the Lucan narrative—the specific identification of James and John as "sons of Zebedee" (Mark 3:17//Matt 10:2) is omitted from both Lucan lists of the Twelve (Luke 6:14; Acts 1:13), as is the whole Markan episode of the "sons of Zebedee" (or their mother in Matthew) seeking positions of power (Mark 9:35–45//Matt 20:20–28). The only occurrence of the Zebedean family name in Luke/Acts is in the Lucan version of the call of Simon which curiously refrains from following Mark, describing the call to the brothers as well (Luke 5:1–11//Mark 1:16–20//Matt 4:18–22).

Writing during the same period as Clement, John the Evangelist and Matthew, Luke is using narrative technique to program the Galilean Peter as a Pillar within the story of the "early days" in Jerusalem. He is described occupying a space comparable to that historically owned by Cephas who was remembered as the second Pillar of the mother church of Jerusalem. The ever-present silent companion, John, carrying the same name as the third Pillar (Gal 2:9), enhances that verisimilitude, facilitated by the tendentious repetition of the mantra-like "Peter and John" (Acts 3:1, 11; 4:13, 19; 8:14, 25) which evocatively draws back into being and transmutes fading memories of "the Pillars" from the early years.

In Luke's foundation myth of Christian origins, Peter does not replace James—he displaces him. All eyes are focused on Peter who is moved by Luke into the center of the action in Jerusalem and fills it—a gestalt effect—as the bearer and guarantor of the traditions of Jesus.

In the *Acts of the Apostles* the emergent Gentile church enjoys its lineage from the Galilean Peter, not from the *Jakobusgemeinde*. The message they have finally received and are nurtured in is founded on the comprehensive witness of the Galileans rather than the restrictive *kerygma* of the *Jakobusgemeinde* that is bereft of "Galilee." The latter's advocacy of the Restoration of Israel helped legitimize the nationalist ideology that drove the Jewish rebellion of 66-73 CE, or, at the very least, was much too close for comfort.

Whilst recognizing their origination in Jerusalem and their Judaic inheritance, Luke's projection of Peter into the birthing of the Christian movement, thirty years on from the death of James, guarantees a critical distance between memory of the *Jakobusgemeinde* and the contemporary formative Christian movement which was being shaped and nurtured by the life and teaching, as well as the dying and rising, of "the Lord Jesus Christ" (Acts 28:31).

Luke not only assured the emerging Gentile Christian church of the pedigree of its faith as truly grounded in the witness of those who walked with Jesus but, in doing so, has bequeathed to posterity the foundation myth of that continuing community who honor Jesus' remembrance and seek his continuing presence in *their* ever-changing present.

Epilogue

Like many mothers in that period, the *Jakobusgemeinde* died in childbirth: the future lay with her precocious, feisty and troublesome offspring, Paul.

Yet there remains an indelible signature of her historic role in the origins of Christianity: the vestigial remnants of her core message. Whenever the historic creeds of the Christian Faith are recited, we move smoothly from "born of the virgin Mary" to "suffered under Pontius Pilate." It has been memorably described by Robert Funk as the "Creed with an Empty Center."[1] That "Empty Center" is the "Galilean Silence." The *Jakobusgemeinde* has bequeathed us the very framework of the Christian confession of faith, and the echo of her voice can still be heard whenever Christians stand to repeat, "I believe . . ."

1. Funk, *Honest to Jesus*, 43.

Bibliography

Adamson, James. *The Epistle of James*. Grand Rapids: Eerdmans, 1976.

Ahmed, Akbar S. *Discovering Islam: Making Sense of Muslim History and Society*. London: Routledge, 1988.

Alexander, Loveday. *The Preface to Luke's Gospel: Literary Convention and Social Context in Luke 1.1–4 and Acts 1.1*. SNTSM 78. Cambridge: CUP, 1993.

Allison, Dale C., Jr. "The Continuity between John and Jesus." *JSHJ* 1 (2003) 6–27.

———. *Constructing Jesus: Memory, Imagination and History*. Grand Rapids: Baker, 2010.

———. *A Critical and Exegetical Commentary on The Epistle of James*. New York: Bloomsbury, 2013.

———. "Peter and Cephas: One and the Same." *JBL*. 111.3 (1992) 489–95.

Allsop, Kenneth. *The Bootleggers: The Story of Chicago's Prohibition Era*. London: Forum, 1961.

Arjomand, Said Amir. "Social change and movements of revitalization in contemporary Islam." In *New Religious Movements and Rapid Social Change*, edited by James A. Beckford, 87–112. London: Saye/UNESCO, 1986.

Armstrong, Karen. *Muhammad: A Biography of the Prophet*. London: Phoenix, 2001.

Asano, Atsuhiro. *Community-Identity Construction in Galatians: Exegetical, Social-Anthropological and Socio-Historical Studies*. London: T & T Clark, 2005.

Atwill J. and S. Braunheim. "Redating the Radiocarbon Dating in the Dead Sea Scrolls." *Dead Sea Discoveries* 11.2 (2004) 143–57.

Baigent, Michael, et al. *The Holy Blood and the Holy Grail*. London: Jonathan Cape, 1982.

Baigent, Michael, and Richard Leigh. *The Dead Sea Scrolls Deception: Why a Handful of Religious Scholars Conspired to Suppress the Revolutionary Contents of the Dead Sea Scrolls*. London: Jonathan Cape, 1991.

Bailey, Kenneth E. *Jesus and the Prodigal: How Jesus Retold Israel's Story*. Downers Grove, IL: InterVarsity, 2003.

Barclay, John M. G. "Mirror-Reading a Polemical Letter: Galatians as a Test Case." *JSNT* 31 (1987) 73–93.

———. "There is Neither Old nor Young? Early Christianity and Ancient Ideologies of Age." *NTS* 53 (2007) 225–41.

Barker, Margaret. *The Older Testament: The Survival of Themes from the Ancient Royal Cult in Sectarian Judaism and Early Christianity*. London: SPCK, 1987.

Barnett, Paul. *The Birth Of Christianity: The First Twenty Years after Jesus.* Grand Rapids: Eerdmans, 2005.

Barrett, C. Kingsley. *The Acts of the Apostles,* ICC, 2 Vols. London: T & T Clark, 1994.

———. *A Commentary on the First Epistle to the Corinthians.* BNTC. London: A & C Black, 1968.

———. *A Commentary on the Second Epistle to the Corinthians.* BNTC. London: A & C Black, 1973.

———. *The Epistle to the Romans.* BNTC. London: A & C Black, 1957.

———. *Luke the Historian in Recent Study.* Facet Books, Biblical Series 24. Philadelphia: Fortress, 1970.

———. *On Paul: Essays on His Life, Work and Influence in the Early Church.* London: T & T Clark, 2003.

———. Review of *Der Herrenbruder,* by Wilhelm Pratscher. *SJT* 45 (1992) 122–23.

Bauckham, Richard. "The Brothers and Sisters of Jesus: An Epiphanian Response to John P. Meier." *CBQ* 56.4 (1994) 686–700.

———. "The Economic Critique of Rome in Revelation 18." In *Images of Empire,* edited by Loveday Alexander, 47–90. JSOTSup 122. Sheffield: Sheffield Academic, 1991.

———. "For What Offence Was James Put to Death?" In *James the Just and Christian Origins,* edited by Bruce D. Chilton and Craig A. Evans, 199–232. NovTSup 98. Boston: Brill, 1999.

———. *Gospel Women: Studies in the Named Women in the Gospels.* Grand Rapids: Eerdmans, 2002.

———, ed. *The Gospels for All Christians: Rethinking the Gospel Audiences.* Grand Rapids: Eerdmans, 1998.

———. "In Response to My Respondents: *Jesus and the Eyewitnesses* in Review." *JSHJ* 6 (2008) 225–53.

———. *Jude and the Relatives of Jesus in the Early Church.* London: T & T Clark, 1990.

———. "James and the Jerusalem Church." in *The Book of Acts in its Palestinian Setting,* edited by Bauckham, Richard, 415–80. The Book of Acts in its First Century Setting. Vol. 4. Carlisle: Paternoster, 1995.

———. *James: Wisdom of James, Disciple of Jesus the Sage,* London: Routledge, 1999.

———. "James and Jesus." In *The Brother of Jesus: James the Just and His Mission,* edited by Bruce D. Chilton and Jacob Neusner, 100–37. Louisville, KY: Westminster John Knox, 2001.

———. "James, Peter, and the Gentiles." In *The Missions of James, Peter, and Paul: Tensions in Early Christianity,* edited by Bruce D. Chilton and Craig A. Evans, 91–142. NovTSup 115. Leiden & Boston: Brill, 2005.

———. *Jesus and the Eyewitnesses: The Gospels as Eyewitness Testimony.* Grand Rapids: Eerdmans, 2006.

Baumgarten, Albert I. *The Flourishing of Jewish Sects in the Maccabean Era: An Interpretation.* JSJSup 55. Leiden: Brill, 1997.

Bede. *A History of the English Church and People.* Translated by Leo Sherley-Price. Harmondsworth: Penguin, 1955.

Bermejo-Rubio, Fernando. "Why is John the Baptist Used as a foil for Jesus? Leaps of Faith and Oblique Anti-Judaism in Contemporary Scholarship." *JSNT* 11.2 (2013) 170–96.

Bernheim, Pierre-Antoine. *Jacques, Frere de Jesus.* Editions Noesis, 1996. Translated by John Bowden. London: SCM, 1997.

Best, Ernest. Review of *Der Herrenbruder*, by Wilhelm Pratscher. *ExpTim* 100.10 (1989) 377–82.

Betz, Hans Dieter. *Galatians: A Commentary on Paul's Letter to the Churches in Galatia.* Philadelphia: Fortress, 1979.

———. *The Sermon on the Mount: A Commentary on the Sermon on the Mount, including the Sermon on the Plain (Matthew 5:3—7:27 and Luke 6:20–49).* Edited by Adela Yarbro Collins. Minneapolis: Fortress, 1995.

Betz, Otto. "Jesus and the Temple Scroll." In *Jesus and the Dead Sea Scrolls*, edited by James H. Charlesworth, 75–103. ABRL New York: Doubleday, 1992.

———. "Was John the Baptist an Essene?" In *Understanding the Dead Sea Scrolls: A Reader from the Biblical Archaeological Review,* edited by Herschel Shanks, 205–14. New York: Random, 1992.

Bird, Michael F. "The Unity of Luke—Acts in Recent Discussion." *JSNT* 29.4 (2007) 425–48.

Blinzler, J. *Die Brüder und Schwester Jesu.* SBS 21. Stuttgart: Katholisches Bibelwerk, 1967.

Blok, Anton. "The Peasant and the Brigand: Social Banditry Reconsidered." *Comparative Studies in Society and History* 14 (1972) 494–503.

Blomberg, Craig L., and Mariam J. Kamell. *James.* ZECNT. Grand Rapids: Zondervan, 2008.

Bockmuehl, Markus. "1 Thess 2.14–16 and the Jerusalem Church." *TynBul* 52.1 (2001) 1–31.

———. "Antioch and James the Just." In *James the Just and Christian Origins,* edited by Bruce D. Chilton, and Craig A. Evans, 155–98. NovTSup 98. Boston: Brill, 1999.

———. *Jewish Law in Gentile Churches: Halakhah and the Beginnings of Christian Public Ethics.* Edinburgh: T & T Clark, 2000.

Borgen, Peter. *Early Christianity and Hellenistic Judaism.* London: T & T Clark, 1996.

Bolt Peter G. and Mark D. Thompson, eds. *Donald Robinson: Selected Works I; II; Appreciation.* Camperdown, NSW: Moore College, 2008.

Bovon, François. *Luke 1: A Commentary on the Gospel of Luke 1:1-9:50.* Translated by Christine M. Thomas Hermeneia. Minneapolis: Fortress, 2002.

Brandon, S. G. F. *The Fall of Jerusalem and the Christian Church: A Study of the Effects of the Jewish Overthrow of A.D. 70 on Christianity.* London: SPCK, 1951.

———. *Jesus and the Zealots: A Study of the Political Factor in Primitive Christianity.* Manchester: Manchester University Press, 1967.

———. *The Trial of Jesus of Nazareth.* London: Batsford, 1968.

Brooke, George J. *The Kittim in the Qumran Pesharim,* In *Images of Empire,* edited by Alexander Loveday, 158–59. JSOTSup 122. Sheffield: Sheffield Academic, 1991.

Brookins, Timothy A. "Luke's Use of Mark as παράφρασις: Its Effects on Characterization in the 'Healing of Blind Bartimaeus' Pericope (Mark 10.46–52/Luke.18–43)." *JSNT* 34.1 (2011) 70–89.

Brosend, William F., II. *James and Jude,* New Cambridge Bible Commentary. Cambridge: CUP, 2004.

Brown, Dan. *The Da Vinci Code.* New York: Bantam, 2003.

Brown, James A. C. *The Social Psychology of Industry: Human Relations in the Factory.* Harmondsworth: Penguin, 1954.

Brown, Roger W. *Social Psychology.* London: Collier-Macmillan International, 1965.

Brown, Raymond E. *The Birth of the Messiah: A Commentary on the Infancy Narratives in the Gospels of Matthew and Luke.* New York: Doubleday, 1977.

Brown, Raymond E., and J. P. Meier. *Antioch and Rome: New Testament Cradles of Catholic Christianity.* New York, 1983.

Brownlee, W. H. "John the Baptist in the New Light of Ancient Scrolls." In *The Scrolls and the New Testament,* edited by Krister Stendahl, 71–90. London: SCM, 1958.

Bruce, F. F. *The Acts of the Apostles: The Greek Text with Introduction and Commentary.* London: Tyndale, 1951.

———. *Commentary on Galatians.* Grand Rapids: Eerdmans, 1982.

———. *In Retrospect: Remembrance of Things Past.* London: Marshall Pickering, 1993.

———. *Men and Movements in the Primitive Church: Studies in Early Non-Pauline Christianity.* Carlisle: Paternoster, 1979.

———. *New Testament History.* Rev. ed. Bristol: Pickering & Inglis, 1982.

———. *Paul and Jesus.* London: SPCK, 1977.

Bryan, Christopher, *A Preface to Mark: Notes on the Gospel in its Literary and Cultural Settings.* Oxford: OUP, 1993.

Bulembat, Matand. "Head-Waiter and Bridegroom of the Wedding at Cana: Structure and Meaning of John 2.1–12." *JSNT* 30.1 (2007) 55–73.

Bultmann, Rudolf. *The History of the Synoptic Tradition.* Oxford: Blackwell, 1963.

———. *Theology of the New Testament, Vol.1.* London: SCM, 1952.

Butz, Jeffrey J. *The Brother of Jesus and the Lost Teachings of Christianity,* Rochester, VT: Inner Traditions, 2005.

Byrskog, Samuel. "The Transmission of the Jesus Tradition: Old and New Insights." *Early Christianity* 1.3 (2010) 441–68.

Campbell, Douglas A. "Galatians 5.11: Evidence of an Early Law-observant Mission by Paul?" *NTS* 57.3 (2011) 325–47.

Campbell, William Sanger. *The "We" Passages in the Acts of the Apostles: The Narrator as Narrative Character.* SBLSBS 14. Atlanta: SBL, 2007.

Capper, Brian J. "Essene Community Houses and Jesus' Early Community." In *Jesus and Archaeology,* edited by James H. Charlesworth, 472–502. Grand Rapids: Eerdmans, 2006.

———. "The Palestinian Context of Earliest Christian Community of Goods." In *The Book of Acts in its Palestinian Setting,* edited by Richard Bauckham, 323–56. The Book of Acts in its First Century Setting 4. Carlisle: Paternoster, 1995.

Carlson, Stephen C. "The Accommodations of Joseph and Mary in Bethlehem." *NTS* 56.3 (2010) 326–42.

Casey, Maurice. *An Aramaic Approach to Q: Sources for the Gospels of Matthew and Luke.* Cambridge: Cambridge University Press, 2002.

———. *Jesus of Nazareth: An Independent Historian's Account of His Life and Teaching.* London: T & T Clark, 2010.

Castelli, Elizabeth A. and Hal Taussig, eds. *Reimagining Christian Origins: A Colloquium Honoring Burton L. Mack.* Valley Forge, PA: Trinity, 1996.

Catchpole, David. *Jesus People: The Historical Jesus and the Beginnings of Community.* Grand Rapids: Baker Academic, 2006.

Cave, Andy. *Learning to Breathe.* London: Random, 2006.

Chancey, Mark A. "Disputed Issues in the Study of Cities, Villages, and the Economy in Jesus' Galilee." In *The World of Jesus and the Early Church: Identity and*

Interpretation in Early Communities of Faith, edited by Craig A. Evans, 53–67. Peabody, MS: Hendrickson, 2011.

———. *Greco-Roman Culture and the Galilee of Jesus*. SNTSMS 134. Cambridge: Cambridge University Press, 2005.

———. *The Myth of a Gentile Galilee*. SNTSMS 118. Cambridge: Cambridge University Press, 2002.

Charlesworth, James H. "Jesus Research and Archaeology: A New Perspective." In *Jesus and Archaeology*, edited by James H. Charlesworth, 11–63. Grand Rapids: Eerdmans, 2006.

———. Review of *Settlement and History in Hellenistic, Roman, and Byzantine Galilee: An Archaeological Survey of the Eastern Galilee*, by Uzi Leibner. *JSHJ* 8.3 (2010) 281–84.

Chilton, Bruce D. "Conclusions and Questions." In *James the Just and Christian Origins*, edited by Bruce D. Chilton and Craig A. Evans, 251–68. Boston: Brill, 1999.

———. "James and the Believing Pharisees in Acts." In *When Judaism and Christianity Began: Essays in memory of Anthony J. Saldarini—Vol. 1. Christianity in the Beginning*, edited by A. J. Avery-Peck, et al., 19–49. Leiden: Brill, 2004.

———. "James, Peter, Paul and the Formation of the Gospels." In *The Missions of James, Peter, and Paul: Tensions in Early Christianity*, edited by Bruce D. Chilton and Craig A. Evans, 1–28. Boston: Brill, 2005.

———. *Rabbi Jesus: An Intimate Biography*. New York: Doubleday, 2000.

———. "Recovering Jesus' *Mamzerut*." In *Jesus and Archaeology*, edited by James H. Charlesworth, 84–110. Grand Rapids: Eerdmans, 2006.

———. "Wisdom and Grace." In *The Missions of James, Peter, and Paul: Tensions in Early Christianity*, edited by Bruce D. Chilton and Craig A. Evans, 307–22. Boston: Brill, 2005.

———. "Yakov in Relation to Peter, Paul, and the Remembrance of Jesus." In *The Brother of Jesus: James the Just and His Mission*, edited by Bruce D. Chilton and Jacob Neusner, 155–56. Louisville, KY: Westminster John Knox, 2001.

Chilton, Bruce. D., et al., eds. *The Missing Jesus: Rabbinic Judaism and the New Testament*, Boston & Leiden: Brill, 2002.

Clarke, Peter B. "Japanese New Religious Movements in Brazil: From Ethnic to 'Universal' Religions." In *New Religious Movements: Challenge and Response*, edited by Bryan Wilson and Jamie Cresswell, 197–210. London: Routledge, 1999.

Collins, John J. "The Site of Qumran and the Sectarian Communities in the Dead Sea Scrolls." In *The World of Jesus and the Early Church: Identity and Interpretation in Early Communities of Faith*, edited by Craig A. Evans, 9–22. Peabody, MA: Hendrickson, 2011.

Cooper, Ben. "Adaptive Eschatological Inference from the Gospel of Matthew." *JSNT* 33.1 (2010) 59–80.

Cousar, Charles B. *Galatians. Interpretation: A Bible Commentary for Teaching and Preaching*. Louisville, KY: John Knox, 1982.

Cranfield, C. E. B. *The Gospel According to Saint Mark: An Introduction and Commentary*. London: Cambridge University Press, 1972.

Creed, J. M. *St Luke*. Basingstoke: Macmillan, 1930.

Crook, Zeba A. "Structure versus Agency in Studies of the Biblical Social World: Engaging with Louise Lawrence." *JSHJ* 29.3 (2007) 251–75.

Crossan, John Dominic. *The Historical Jesus: The Life of a Mediterranean Jewish Peasant.* San Francisco: HarperSanFrancisco, 1993.

———. *Jesus: A Revolutionary Biography.* San Francisco: HarperSanFrancisco, 1994.

———. "Mark and the Relatives of Jesus." *NovT* 15 (1973) 81–113.

Crossley, James G. *The Date of Mark's Gospel: Insight from the Law in Earliest Christianity.* Edinburgh: T & T Clark, 2004.

———. "The Semitic Background to Repentance in the teaching of John the Baptist and Jesus." *JSHJ* 2.2 (2004) 138–57.

———. *Why Christianity Happened: A Sociohistorical Account of Christian Origins.* Louisville, KY: Westminster John Knox, 2006.

———. "Writing about the Historical Jesus: Historical Explanation and 'the Big *Why* Questions,' or Antiquarian Empiricism and Victorian Tomes?" *JSHJ* 7 (2009) 63–90.

Cullen, Allen. *The Stirrings in Sheffield on a Saturday Night,* The Sheffield Crucible Theatre Company, 1973.

Cullman, Oscar. *Peter: Disciple, Apostle, Martyr,* Translated by Floyd V. Filson. Philadelphia: Westminster, 1953.

———. "The Significance of the Qumran Texts for Research Into the Beginnings of Christianity." In *The Scrolls and the New Testament,* edited by Krister Stendahl, 8–32. London: SCM, 1958.

Davids, Peter H. *The Epistle of James: A Commentary on the Greek Text.* Grand Rapids: Eerdmans, 1982.

———. "James and Peter: The Literary Evidence." In *The Missions of James, Peter, and Paul: Tensions in Early Christianity,* edited by Bruce D. Chilton and Craig A. Evans, 29–52. Boston: Brill, 2005.

———. "James's Message: The Literary Record." In *The Brother of Jesus: James the Just and His Mission,* edited by Bruce D. Chilton and Jacob Neusner, 66–87. Louisville, KY: Westminster John Knox, 2001.

———. "The Test of Wealth in James and Paul." In *The Missions of James, Peter, and Paul: Tensions in Early Christianity,* edited by Bruce D. Chilton and Craig A. Evans, 355–84. Boston: Brill, 2005.

———. "Why Do We Suffer? Suffering in James and Paul." In *The Missions of James, Peter, and Paul: Tensions in Early Christianity,* edited by Bruce D. Chilton and Craig A. Evans, 435–66. Boston: Brill, 2005.

Davies, Philip R. "James in the Qumran Scrolls." In *James the Just and Christian Origins,* edited by Bruce D. Chilton and Craig A. Evans, 17–32. Boston: Brill, 1999.

Davies, Rupert E. *Methodism.* Harmondsworth: Penguin, 1963.

Davies, W. D. and Dale C. Allison. *A Critical and Exegetical Commentary on the Gospel According to Saint Matthew.* Vol. 2. Edinburgh: T & T Clark, 1991.

De Boer, Martinus C. "The New Preachers in Galatia. Their Identity, Message, Aims, and Impact." In *Jesus, Paul, and Early Christianity: Studies in Honour of Henk Jan de Jonge,* edited by Rieuwerd Buitenwerf, et al., 39–60. Boston: Brill, 2008.

———. "Paul's Use and Interpretation of a Justification Tradition in Galatians 2.15–21." *JSNT* 28.2 (2005) 189–216.

DeConick, April D. *The Original Gospel of Thomas in Translation: With a Commentary and New English Translation of the Complete Gospel.* London: T & T Clark, 2007.

————. *Recovering the Original Gospel of Thomas A History of the Gospel and its Growth*. Library of NT Studies 286: Early Christianity in Context. London: T & T Clark, 2005.

————. *The Thirteenth Apostle: What the Gospel of Judas Really Says*. Revised. London: Continuum, 2009.

Deppe, Dean B. "The Sayings of Jesus in the Epistle of James." DTh diss., Free University of Amsterdam, 1989.

DiTommaso, Lorenzo. "Jerusalem, New." In *The Eerdmans Dictionary of Early Judaism*, edited by John J. Collins, and Daniel C. Harlow, 797–99. Cambridge: Eerdmans, 2010.

Dibelius, Martin. *From Tradition to Gospel*. London: Nicholson & Watson, 1934.

————. *James: A Commentary on the Epistle of James*. Translated by Michael A. Williams. Edited by Helmut Koester. Hermeneia. Philadelphia: Fortress, 1976.

————. *Studies in the Acts of the Apostles*. Translated by Heinrich Greeven. New York: Scribner, 1956.

Dixon, Norman F. *On the Psychology of Military Incompetence*. London: Vintage, 1994.

Doble, Peter. Review of *The "We" Passages in the Acts of the Apostles*, by William S. Campbell. *JSNT* 31.5 (2009) 67–68.

Dodd, C. H. *The Apostolic Preaching and its Developments*. London: Hodder & Stoughton, 1936.

————. *The Epistle of Paul to the Romans*. MNTC. London: Collins, 1959.

Downing, F. Gerald. "Ears to Hear." In *Alternative Approaches to New Testament Study*, edited by A. E. Harvey, 97–121. London, SPCK, 1985.

————. Review of *Baptist Traditions in Q*, by Clare K. Rothschild. *JSNT* 28.5 (2006) 35–36.

————. Review of *Jesus*, by Puig i Tarrech. *JSNT* 33.5 (2011) 36–37.

Downs, David J. "'The Offering of the Gentiles in Romans 15.16." *JSNT* 29.2 (2006) 173–86.

————. "Paul's Collection and the Book of Acts Revisited." *NTS* 52.1 (2006) 50–70.

Drury, John. "Mark 1.1–15: An Interpretation." In *Alternative Approaches to New Testament Study*, edited by A. E. Harvey, 25–36. London, SPCK, 1985.

Dungan, David. *The Sayings of Jesus in the Churches of Paul: The Use of the Synoptic Tradition in the Regulation of Early Church Life*. Oxford: Blackwell, 1971.

Dunkerley, Roderic. *Beyond the Gospels*. Harmondsworth: Penguin, 1957.

Dunn, James D. G. "Altering the Default Setting: Re-envisaging the Early Transmission of the Jesus Tradition." *NTS* 49.2 (2003) 139–75.

————. *Beginning From Jerusalem*. Christianity in the Making 2. Grand Rapids: Eerdmans, 2009.

————. "Did Jesus Attend the Synagogue?" In *Jesus and Archaeology*, edited by James H. Charlesworth, 206–22. Grand Rapids: Eerdmans, 2006.

————. "The Incident at Antioch (Gal 2 11–18)." *JSNT* 5 (1983) 3–57.

————. "Jesus Tradition in Paul." In *Studying the Historical Jesus: Evaluations of the State of Current Research*, edited by Bruce D. Chilton and Craig A. Evans, 155–78. Leiden: Brill, 1994.

————. *Jesus Remembered*. Christianity in the Making 1. Grand Rapids: Eerdmans, 2003.

————. "Kenneth Bailey's Theory of Oral Tradition: Critiquing Theodore Weeden's Critique." *JSHJ* 7 (2009) 44–62.

———. "The Relationship between Paul and Jerusalem according to Galatians 1 and 2." *NTS* 28 (1982) 461–78.

———. *The Theology of Paul the Apostle.* Grand Rapids: Eerdmans, 1998.

———. *Unity and Diversity in the New Testament: An Inquiry into the Character of Earliest Christianity.* London: SCM, 1977.

Du Toit, Andrie. "*Paulus Oecumenicus*: Interculturality in the Shaping of Paul's Theology." *NTS* 55 (2009) 121–43.

Duverger, Maurice. *Introduction to the Social Sciences, with Special Reference to their Methods,* Translated by M. Anderson. London: George, Allen & Unwin, 1964.

Eastman, Susan G. "'Cast Out the Slave Woman and her Son': The Dynamics of Exclusion and Inclusion in Galatians 4.30." *JSNT* 28.3 (2006) 309–36.

Ehrhardt, Arnold. *The Acts of the Apostles: Ten Lectures.* Manchester: Manchester University Press, 1969.

Ehrman, Bart D. "Cephas and Peter." *JBL* 109.3 (1990) 463–74.

Eisenman, Robert. *The Dead Sea Scrolls and the First Christians.* Shaftesbury, Dorset: Element, 1996.

———. *James the Brother of Jesus: The Key to Unlocking the Secrets of Early Christianity and the Dead Sea Scrolls.* London: Faber & Faber, 1997.

———. *James the Just in the Habakkuk Pesher.* StPB 35. Leiden: Brill, 1986.

———. *Maccabees, Zadokites, Christians and Qumran: A New Hypothesis of Qumran Origins.* StPB 34. Leiden: Brill, 1983.

———. "Paul as Herodian." *Journal of Higher Criticism* (1996) 110–22.

Eisenman, Robert, and Michael Wise. *The Dead Sea Scrolls Uncovered: The First Complete Translation and Interpretation of 50 Key Documents Withheld for over 35 Years.* Shaftesbury, Dorset: Element, 1992.

Elmer, Ian J. *Paul, Jerusalem and the Judaisers: The Galatian Crisis in its Broadest Historical Context.* WUNT 2.258. Tubingen: Mohr Siebeck, 2009.

Elliott, John H. "Jesus the Israelite was neither a 'Jew' nor a 'Christian': On Correcting Misleading Nomenclature." *JSHJ* 5.2 (2007) 119–54.

Epp, Eldon J. *Junia: The First Woman Apostle.* Minneapolis: Fortress, 2005.

Esler, Philip F. *Community and Gospel in Luke-Acts: The Social and Political Motivations of Lucan Theology.* Cambridge: Cambridge University Press, 1987.

———. *The First Christians in their Social World: An Introduction to Social-scientific Approach to the New Testament.* London: Routledge, 1994.

———. *Galatians.* London: Routledge, 1998.

———. "Making and Breaking an Agreement Mediterranean Style: A New Reading of Galatians 2.1–14." *Biblical Interpreter* 3.3 (1995) 285–314.

———. "Paul and Stoicism: Romans 12 as a Test Case." *NTS* 50.1 (2004) 106–24.

———. "The Socio-Redaction Criticism of Luke-Acts (1987)." In *Social-Scientific Approaches to New Testament Interpretation,* edited by David G. Horrell, 123–50. Edinburgh: T & T Clark, 1999.

Evans, Craig A. "Assessing Progress in the Third Quest of the Historical Jesus." *JSHJ* 4.1 (2006) 35–54.

———. "Jesus, John, and the Dead Sea Scrolls: Assessing Typologies of Restoration." In *Christian Beginnings and the Dead Sea Scrolls,* edited by John J. Collins and Craig A. Evans, 45–62. Grand Rapids: Baker, 2006.

———. *Luke.* Peabody, MA: Hendrickson, 1990.

———. "The Misplaced Jesus: Interpreting Jesus in a Judaic Context." In *The Missing Jesus: Rabbinic Judaism and the New Testament,* edited by Bruce D Chilton, et al., 14–27. Boston: Brill, 2002.

Fairchild, Mark R. Review of *The Birth Of Christianity,* by Paul Barnett. *RBL* 11/2005.

Farmer, William R. "James the Lord's Brother, According to Paul." In *James the Just and Christian Origins,* edited by Bruce D. Chilton and Craig A. Evans, 133–54. Boston: Brill, 1999.

Fee, Gordon D. *First Epistle to the Corinthians.* NICNT. Grand Rapids: Eerdmans, 1987.

Ferda, Tucker S. "John the Baptist, Isaiah 40, and the Ingathering of the Exiles." *JSHJ* 10.2 (2012) 154–88.

Fiensy, David A. "The Composition of the Jerusalem Church." In *The Book of Acts in its Palestinian Setting,* edited by Richard Bauckham, 213–36. The Book of Acts in its First Century Setting 4. Carlisle: Paternoster, 1995.

———. "Did Large Estates Exist in Lower Galilee in the First Half of the First Century CE?" *JSHJ* 10 (2012) 133–53.

Filson, Floyd V. *The Gospel According to St Matthew.* BNTC. London: A & C Black, 1960.

Fitzmyer, Joseph. "Aramaic Kepha' and Peter's name in the New Testament." In *Text and Interpretation: Studies in the New Testament presented to Matthew Black,* edited by Ernest Best and R. Wilson, 121–32. London: Cambridge University Press, 1979.

Flusser, David. *Judaism of the Second Temple Period. Vol 1: Qumran and Apocalyptism.* Grand Rapids: Eerdmans, 2007.

Foster, Paul. "Educating Jesus: The Search for a Plausible Context," *JSHJ.* 4.1 (2006) 7–33.

———. "Memory, Orality, and the Fourth Gospel: Three Dead-Ends in Historical Jesus Research." *JSHJ* 10.3 (2012) 191–227.

———. Review of *Greco-Roman Culture and the Galilee of Jesus,* by Mark A. Chancey. *JSNT* 28.5 (2006).

France, Richard T. "Jesus the Baptist." In *Jesus of Nazareth: Lord and Christ. Essays on the Historical Jesus and New Testament Christology,* edited by Joel B. Green, and Max Turner, 94–111.Grand Rapids: Eerdmans, 1994.

Fredriksen, Paula. "Judaizing the Nations: The Ritual Demands of Paul's Gospel." *NTS* 56.2 (2010) 232–52.

Frey, Jorg. "Essenes." In *The Eerdmans Dictionary of Early Judaism,* edited by John J. Collins, and Daniel C. Harlow, 599–602. Cambridge: Eerdmans, 2010.

Freyne, Sean. "Bandits in Galilee: A Contribution to the Study of Social Conditions in First-Century Palestine." In *The Social World of Formative Christianity and Judaism,* edited by Jacob Neusner, et al., 50–68. Philadelphia: Fortress, 1988.

———. "Galilee as Laboratory: Experiments for New Testament Historians and Theologians." *NTS* 53.2 (2007) 147–64.

———. "Herodian Economics in Galilee." In *Modelling Early Christianity in Social-Scientific Studies of the New Testament in Its Context,* edited by Philip F. Esler. London: Routledge, 1995.

———. "The Jesus-Paul Debate Revisited and Re-Imaging Christian Origins." In *Christian Origins; Worship, Belief and Society,* edited by Kieran J. O'Mahony, 143–63. JSNTSup 241. Sheffield: Sheffield Academic Press, 2003.

———. "Jesus of Galilee: Implications and Possibilities." *Early Christianity* 1.3 (2010) 372–405.

————. *Jesus, a Jewish Galilean: A New Reading of the Jesus Story.* London: T & T Clark, 2004.

————. *Retrieving James/Jakov, the Brother of Jesus. From History to Legend.* Annandale on Hudson, NY: Bard College, 2008.

Friesen, Steven J. "Poverty in Pauline Studies: Beyond the So-called New Consensus." *JSNT* 26.3 (2004) 323–61.

Fung, Ronald Y. K. *The Epistle to the Galatians.* NIC. Grand Rapids: Eerdmans, 1988.

Funk, Robert W. *Honest to Jesus: Jesus for a New Millennium.* New York: HarperSanFrancisco, 1996.

Funk, Robert, et al. *The Five Gospels: The Search for the Authentic Words of Jesus.* New York: Scribner, 1993.

Garroway, Joshua D. "The Pharisee Heresy: Circumcision for Gentiles in the Acts of the Apostles." *NTS* 60 (2014) 20–36.

Gasque, W. Ward. *A History of the Interpretation of the Acts of the Apostles.* Peabody, MA: Hendrickson, 1975.

Gaster, Theodor H. *The Scriptures of the Dead Sea Sect: In English Translation.* London: Secker & Warburg, 1957.

Geertz, C. *Islam Observed.* Chicago: University of Chicago Press, 1971.

Gellner, Ernest, *Postmodernism, Reason and Religion.* London: Routledge, Kegan & Paul, 1992.

Georgi, Dieter. *Remembering the Poor: The History of Paul's Collection for Jerusalem.* Nashville: Abingdon, 1992.

Gibson, Shimon. "The Trial of Jesus at the Jerusalem Praetorium: New Archaeological Evidence." In *The World of Jesus and the Early Church: Identity and Interpretation in Early Communities of Faith,* edited by Craig A. Evans, 97–118. Peabody, MA: Hendrickson, 2011.

Glover, T. R. *The Jesus of History.* London: SCM, 1917.

Goodacre, Mark. *Thomas and the Gospels: The Making of an Apocryphal Text.* London: SPCK, 2012.

Goodman, Martin. *Rome and Jerusalem: The Clash of Ancient Civilizations.* London: Penguin, 2007.

————. *The Ruling Class of Judaea: The Origins of the Jewish Revolt against Rome, AD 66-70.* Cambridge: Cambridge University Press. 1987.

Goulder, Michael D. "Did Peter Ever Go to Rome?" *SJT* 57 (2004) 377–96.

————. "Jesus' Resurrection and Christian Origins: A Response to N.T. Wright." *JSHJ* 3.2 (2005) 187–95.

————. *Luke: A New Paradigm,* 2 vols. JSNTSup 20. Sheffield: Sheffield Academic Press, 1989.

Grabbe, Lester L. *An Introduction to First Century Judaism: Jewish Religion and History in the Second Temple Period.* London: T & T Clark, 1996.

Grass, Tim. *F. F. Bruce: A Life.* Milton Keynes: Paternoster, 2011.

Gregory, Andrew. "Hindrance or Help: Does the Modern Category of 'Jewish-Christian Gospel' Distort our Understanding of the Texts to which it Refers?" *JSNT* 28.4 (2006) 387–413.

————. "The Reception of Luke and Acts and the Unity of Luke-Acts." *JSNT* 29.4 (2007) 459–72.

————. Review of *The First Christian Historian,* by Daniel Marguerat. *JSNT* 27.5 (2005) 67.

Green, Gene L. *Jude and 2 Peter.* Baker Exegetical Commentary on the New Testament. Grand Rapids: Baker, 2008.

Green, Joel B. *The Gospel of Luke.* Grand Rapids: Eerdmans, 1997.

Grindheim, Sigurd. "Apostate Turned Prophet: Paul's Prophetic Self-Understanding and Prophetic Hermeneutic with Special Reference to Galatians 3.10–12." *NTS* 53 (2007) 545–65.

Guelich, Robert A. *Mark 1–8.26.* WBC 34A. Dallas, TX: Word, 1989.

Gunther, Matthias. *Die Fruhgeschichte des Christentums in Ephesus.* ARGU 1, Frankfurt am Main, 1995.

Habermas, Gary R. "Resurrection Research from 1975 to the present: What Are Critical Scholars Saying?" *JSHJ* 3.2 (2005) 135–53.

Hanson, K. C., and D. E. Oakman. *Palestine in the Time of Jesus: Social Structures and Social Conflicts.* Valley Forge, PA: Fortress, 1998.

Harnack, Adolf von. *The Acts of the Apostles.* Translated by J. R. Wilkinson, 175–86. New York: G. P. Putnam, 1909.

———. "Die Verklärungsgeschichte Jesu, der Bericht des Paulus (1. Kor. 15,3ff.), und die beiden Christusvisionen des Petrus." *SPAW.PH* 5 (1922) 62–80.

Hartin, Patrick J. *James and the Q Sayings of Jesus.* JSNT Supp. 47; Sheffield: Sheffield Academic Press, 1991.

———. *James.* SP 14. Collegeville, MN: Liturgical, 2003.

———. *James of Jerusalem: Heir to Jesus of Nazareth.* Collegeville, MN: Liturgical, 2004.

Head, Peter M. Review of *Donald Robinson: Selected Works,* by Peter Bolt and Mark Thompson. *JSNT* 31.5 (2009) 3.

Hedrick, Charles W., and Robert Hodgson, eds. *Nag Hammadi, Gnosticism, and Early Christianity.* Peabody, MA: Hendrickson, 1986.

Hengel, Martin. *Acts and the History of Earliest Christianity.* London: SCM, 1989.

———. *Between Jesus and Paul: Studies in the Earliest History of Christianity.* London: SCM, 1983.

———. "Jakobus der Herrenbruder—der erste Papst?" In *Glaube und Eschatologie: Festschrift für W. G. Kümmel,* edited by E. Grässer and O. Merk, 71–104. Tübingen: J.C.B. Mohr, 1985.

———. *Saint Peter: The Underestimated Apostle.* Translated by Thomas H. Trapp. Cambridge: Eerdmans, 2010.

———. *The Zealots.* Translated by David Smith. Edinburgh: T & T Clark 1989.

Hengel, Martin, and Roland Deines, *The Pre-Christian Paul.* Translated by John Bowden. London: SCM, 1991.

Hengel, Martin, and C. Kingsley Barrett. *Conflicts and Challenges in Early Christianity.* Harrisburg, PA: Trinity, 1999.

Herzog, William R., II. *Parables as Subversive Speech: Jesus as Pedagogue of the Oppressed.* Louisville, KY: Westminster John Knox, 1994.

Hill, Craig C. *Hellenists and Hebrews: Re-appraising Division within the Earliest Church.* Philadelphia: Fortress, 1992.

Hobsbawm, E. J. *Primitive Rebels: Studies in Archaic Forms of Social Movements in the 19th and 20th Centuries.* New York: Norton, 1959.

Hock, Ronald F. "Infancy Gospel of Thomas," In *The Complete Gospels,* edited by R. J. Miller, 369–79. Santa Rosa, CA: Polebridge Press, 1994.

Hooker, Morna D. *The Message of Mark.* London: Epworth, 1983.

Horsley, G. H. R. "Speeches and Dialogue in Acts." *NTS* 32 (1986) 609–14.

Horsley, Richard A. *Archaeology, History and Society in Galilee: The Social Context of Jesus and the Rabbis*. Valley Forge, PA: Trinity, 1996.

———. *Galilee: History, Politics, People*. Valley Forge, PA: Trinity, 1995.

———, ed. *Hidden Transcripts and the Arts of Resistance: Applying the Work of James C. Scott to Jesus and Paul*. Semeia Studies 48. Atlanta: SBL, 2004.

———. "Jesus and the Politics of Roman Palestine." *JSHJ* 8.2 (2010) 99–145.

———. *Jesus and the Spiral of Violence: Popular Jewish Resistance in Roman Palestine*. San Francisco: Harper & Row, 1987.

———. "Popular Prophetic Movements at the time of Jesus: Their Principal Features and Social Origins." *JSNT* 26 (1986) 3–27.

———. *Sociology and the Jesus Movement*. New York: Crossroad, 1989.

Horsley, Richard A., and John S. Hanson. *Bandits, Prophet, and Messiahs: Popular Movements in the Time of Jesus*. Minneapolis: Seabury, 1985.

Hunter, A. M. *Saint Mark*. TBC. London: SCM, 1949.

Hurtado, Larry W. *Mark*. Good News Commentary. San Francisco: Harper & Rowe, 1983.

Iersel, Bas M. F., van. *Mark: A Reader-Response Commentary*. Translated by W. H. Bisscheroux. Sheffield: Sheffield Academic, 1998.

Iverson, Kelly. Review of *Structuring Early Christian Memory*, by Rafael Rodriguez. *JSNT* 33.5 (2011) 44.

Jackson-McCabe, Matt. *Jewish Christianity Reconsidered: Rethinking Ancient Groups and Texts*. Minneapolis: Fortress, 2007.

Jeremias, Joachim. *Jerusalem in the Time of Jesus: An Investigation into Economic and Social Conditions during the New Testament Period*. London: SCM, 1969.

Jensen, Morten H. "Herod Antipas in Galilee: Friend or Foe of the Historical Jesus? *JSHJ* 5.1 (2007) 7–32.

Jervell, Jacob. *Luke and the People of God: A New Look at Luke-Acts*. Minneapolis: Augsburg, 1972.

Jewett, R. "The Agitators and the Galatian Congregation." *NTS* 17 (1971) 198–212.

Johnson, Luke Timothy. *Brother of Jesus, Friend of God: Studies in the Letter of James*. Grand Rapids: Eerdmans, 2004.

———. *The Letter of James*. Anchor Bible 37. New York: Doubleday, 1995.

Johnson, Luke Timothy, and Wesley Wachob. "The Sayings of Jesus in the Letter of James." In *Brother of Jesus, Friend of God: Studies in the Letters of James*, edited by Luke Timothy Johnson, 136–54. Grand Rapids: Eerdmans, 2004.

Jones, Ivor H. "Rhetorical Criticism and the Unity of 2 Corinthians: One 'Epilogue', or More." *NTS* 54.4 (2008) 496–524.

Joubert, Stephan. *Paul as Benefactor: Reciprocity, Strategy and Theological Reflection in Paul's Collection*. Tubingen: Mohr Siebeck, 2000.

Juel, Donald H. *Mark*. ACNT. Minneapolis: Augsburg, 1990.

Kee, Howard C. *Christian Origins in Sociological Perspective*. London: SCM, 1980.

Keith, Chris. "The Claim of John 7.15 and the Memory of Jesus' Literacy." *NTS* 56.1 (2009) 44–63.

———. *Jesus' Literacy: Scribal Culture and the Teacher from Galilee*. LNTS 413. London: T & T Clark, 2011.

Kelber, Werner H. *The Oral and The Written Gospel: the Hermeneutics of Speaking and Writing in the Synoptic Tradition, Mark, Paul, and Q*. Philadelphia: Fortress, 1983.

Kennard, J. Spencer. "Judas of Galilee and his Clan." *JQR* 36 (1945-46) 281–86.

Kilpatrick, G. D. "Jesus, His Family and His Disciples." *JSNT* 15 (1982) 3–19.

Kim, Seyoon. *The Origin of Paul's Gospel*. Grand Rapids: Eerdmans, 1981.

Kirk, Alan. "Crossing the Boundary: Liminality and Transformative Wisdom in Q." *NTS* 45.1 (1999) 1–18.

Kirk, J. R. Daniel. "Why Does the Deliverer Come ἐκ Σιων (Romans 11.26)?" *JSNT* 33.1 (2010).

Kloppenborg, John S.

———. "Diaspora Discourse: The Construction of 'Ethos' in James." *NTS* 53 (2007) 242–70.

———. "The Emulation of the Jesus Tradition in the Letter of James." In *Reading James with New Eyes: Methodological Reassessments of the Letter of James*, edited by Robert L. Webb and John S. Kloppenborg, 143–50. Library of New Testament Studies 342. London: T & T Clark, 2007.

———. *The Formation of Q: Trajectories in Ancient Wisdom Collections*. Philadelphia: Fortress, 1987.

———. "Goulder and the New Paradigm: A Critical Appreciation of Michael Goulder on the Synoptic Problem." In *The Gospels according to Michael Goulder: A North American Response*, edited Christopher A. Rollston, 29–60. Harrisburg, PA: Trinity, 2002.

———. "The Parable of the Prodigal Son and Deeds of Gift." In *Jesus, Paul, and Early Christianity: Studies in Honour of Henk Jan de Jonge*, edited by Rieuwerd Buitenwerf, et al., 169–94. Boston: Brill, 2008.

———. "The Theodotus Synagogue Inscription and the Problem of First-Century Synagogue Buildings." In *Jesus and Archaeology*, edited by James H. Charlesworth, 236–82. Grand Rapids: Eerdmans, 2006.

Knibb, Michael A. *Cambridge Commentaries on Writings of the Jewish and Christian World 200BC to AD200. Vol.2: The Qumran Community*. Cambridge: Cambridge University Press, 1987.

Knox, John. *Chapters in a Life of Paul*. London: A & C Black, 1954.

Koester, Helmut, and Thomas O. Lambdin. "The Gospel of Thomas." In *The Nag Hammadi Library in English*, edited by James M. Robinson. New York: HarperSanFrancisco, 1990. 139–60.

Kooten, George H. van. "ἐκκλησία τοῦ Θεοῦ: The 'Church of God' and the Civic Assemblies (ἐκκλησίαι) of the Greek Cities in the Roman Empire: A Response to Paul Treblico and Richard A. Horsley." *NTS* 58.4 (2012) 522–48.

Kraeling, C. *John the Baptist*. New York: Scribners, 1951.

Kuhn, T. S. *The Structure of Scientific Revolutions*. Chicago: University of Chicago Press, 1962.

Lake, Kirsopp. "Cephas, Peter." *HTR* 14 (1921) 95–97.

Lalleman, Pieter J. Review of *Paul, Luke and the Graeco-Roman World*, edited by Alf Christopherson and Carsten Claussen, et al. *JSNT* 27.5 (2005) 90–91.

———. Review of *James*, by Dan McCartney. *JSNT* 33.5 (2011) 117.

Lane, William L. *The Gospel According to Mark: The English Text with Introduction, Exposition and Notes*. NICNT. Grand Rapids: Eerdmans, 1974.

Langston, Scott. "Dividing it Right: Who is a Jew and What is a Christian?" In *The Missing Jesus: Rabbinic Judaism and the New Testament*, edited by Bruce D. Chilton, et al., 125–34. Boston & Leiden: Brill, 2002.

Langworth, Richard M., ed. *Churchill's Wit: The Definitive Collection.* London: Ebury Press, 2009.

Lawrence, Louise J. "Structure, Agency and Ideology: A Response to Zeba Crook." *JSHJ* 29.3 (2007) 277–86.

Laws, Sophie. *The Epistle of James.* Peabody, MA: Hendrickson, 1980.

Le Grys, Alan. Review of *James*, by Craig Blomberg and Mariam J. Kamell. *JSNT* 32.5 (2010) 114–15.

Legasse, Simon. "Paul's Pre-Christian Career According to Acts." In *The Book of Acts in its Palestinian Setting*, edited by Richard Bauckham, 365–90. The Book of Acts in its First Century Setting 4. Carlisle: Paternoster, 1995.

Leibner, Uzi. *Settlement and History in Hellenistic, Roman, and Byzantine Galilee: An Archaeological Survey of the Eastern Galilee.* TSAJ 127. Tubingen: Mohr Siebeck, 2009.

Leuba, J. L. "Apostle." In *Vocabulary of the Bible*, edited by J. J. von Allmen, 21–23. London: Lutterworth, 1958.

Lietzmann, H. *Geschichte der alten Kirche I. Die Anfänge.* Berlin: W. de Gruyter, 1953.

Lightfoot, J. B. *The Epistle of St Paul to the Galatians.* Grand Rapids: Zondervan, 1957.

Lightfoot, Robert Henry. *History and Interpretation in the Gospels: The Bampton Lectures 1934.* London: Hodder & Stoughton, 1935.

―――. *Locality and Doctrine in the Gospels.* London: Hodder & Stoughton, 1938.

Lohmeyer, E. *Galiläa und Jerusalem.* Gottingen: Vandenhoeck und Ruprecht, 1936.

Longenecker, Bruce. "Exposing the Economic Middle: A Revised Economy Scale for the Study of Early Urban Christianity." *JSNT* 31.3 (2009) 243–78.

―――. "Lucan Aversion to Humps and Hollows: The Case of Acts 11.27—12.25." *NTS* 50 (2004) 185–204.

Longenecker, Richard N. "A Realized Hope, a New Commitment, and a Developed Proclamation: Paul and Jesus." In *The Road from Damascus: The Impact of Paul's Conversion on His Life, Thought, and Ministry*, edited by Richard N. Longenecker, 24–29, 65–70. Grand Rapids: Eerdmans, 1997.

―――. *Galatians.* Word Biblical Commentary. Vol. 41. Dallas, TX: Word, 1990.

Lüdemann, Gerd. "A Chronology of Paul." In *Colloquy on New Testament Studies: A Time for Reappraisal and Fresh Approaches*, edited by Bruce Corley, 289–308. Macon, GA: Mercer University Press, 1983.

―――. *Early Christianity according to the Traditions in Acts: A Commentary.* London: SCM, 1989.

―――. *Paul Apostle to the Gentiles: Studies in Chronology.* London: SCM, 1984.

―――. *Primitive Christianity: A Survey of Recent Studies and Some New Proposals.* Translated by John Bowden. London: T & T Clark, 2003.

Machin, Frank. *The Yorkshire Miners: A History.* Vol.1. Barnsley: National Union of Mineworkers, 1958.

Macintyre, Ben. *A Foreign Field: A True Story of Love and Betrayal during the Great War.* London: Harper Collins, 2002.

Mack, Burton L. *The Christian Myth: Origins, Logic and Legacy.* New York: Continuum, 2001.

―――. *The Lost Gospel: The Book of Q and Christian Origins.* San Francisco: HarperSanFransisco, 1993.

―――. *A Myth of Innocence: Mark and Christian Origins.* Philadelphia: Fortress, 1988.

MacNeill, H. L. "The *Sitz im Leben* of Luke 1.5—2.20." *JBL* 65 (1946) 126–27.

Malbon, Elizabeth Struthers. "Τῇ Οἰκίᾳ αὐτοῦ: Mark 2.15 in Context." *NTS* 31 (1985) 282–92.

———. "Galilee and Jerusalem: History and Literature in Marcan Interpretation." In *The Interpretation of Mark,* edited by William Telford, 253–68. Edinburgh: T & T Clark, 1995.

Malina, Bruce J. *The New Testament World: Insights from Cultural Anthropology.* Atlanta: John Knox, 1981.

Manson, T. W. *The Sayings of Jesus: As Recorded in the Gospels According to St. Matthew and St. Luke Arranged with Introduction and Commentary.* London: SCM, 1949.

Manson, W. *The Epistle to the Hebrews.* London: Hodder & Stoughton, 1951.

Marcus, Joel. "*Birkat Ha-Minim* Revisited." *NTS* 55.4 (2009) 523–51.

———. "Meggitt on the Madness and Kingship of Jesus." *JSNT* 29.4 (2007) 421–24.

Marguerat, Daniel. *The First Christian Historian: Writing the "Acts of the Apostles."* Translated by Ken McKinney, et al. Cambridge: Cambridge University Press, 2004.

Marshall, I. Howard. "A New Consensus on Oral Tradition? A Review of Richard Bauckham's *Jesus and the Eyewitnesses.*" *JSHJ* 6 (2008) 182–93.

———. "A New Understanding of the Present and the Future: Paul and Eschatology." In *The Road from Damascus: The Impact of Paul's Conversion on His Life, Thought, and Ministry,* edited by Richard N. Longenecker. Grand Rapids: Eerdmans, 1997.

Martin, Michael W. "Progymnastic Topic Lists: A Compositional Template for Luke and Other *Bioi*?" *NTS* 54.1 (2008) 18–41.

Martin, Ralph P. *James.* Waco, TX: Word, 1988.

Martyn, J. Louis. *Galatians: A New Translation with Introduction and Commentary.* New York: Doubleday, 1997.

Marxsen, Willi. *Mark the Evangelist: Studies on the Redaction History of the Gospel.* Translated by J. Boyce, et al. New York: Abingdon, 1969.

Mason, Steve. "Chief Priests, Sadducees, Pharisees and Sanhedrin in Acts." In *The Book of Acts in its Palestinian Setting,* edited by Richard Bauckham, 115–78. The Book of Acts in its First Century Setting 4. Carlisle: Paternoster, 1995.

———. *Josephus and the New Testament.* Peabody, MA: Hendrickson, 1992.

Mayor, Joseph B. *The Epistle of St. James: The Greek Text with Introduction, Notes and Comments.* London: Macmillan, 1892.

McCartney, Dan G. *James.* BECNT. Grand Rapids: Baker, 2009.

McGrath, James F. "Was Jesus Illegitimate? The Evidence of His Social Interactions." *JSHJ* 5.1 (2007) 81–100.

McKnight, Scot. "A Parting within the Way: Jesus and James on Israel and Purity." In *James the Just and Christian Origins,* edited by Bruce D. Chilton, and Craig A. Evans, 83–132. Leiden & Boston: Brill, 1999.

———. "Calling Jesus *Mamzer.*" *JSHJ* 1.1 (2003) 73–103.

Meeks, Wayne A. *The First Urban Christians: The Social World of the Apostle Paul.* New Haven: Yale University Press, 1983.

Meggitt, Justin J. "The Madness of King Jesus: Why was Jesus put to Death, but his Followers were not?" *JSNT* 29.4 (2007) 379–413.

Meier, John P. "The Brothers and Sisters of Jesus in Ecumenical Perspective." *CBQ* 54.1 (1992) 1–28.

———. "Did the Historical Jesus Prohibit All Oaths? (Part 1)." *JSHJ* 5 (2007) 175–204.

———. "Did the Historical Jesus Prohibit All Oaths? (Part 2)." *JSHJ* 6 (2008) 3–24.

Miller, Merrill. P. "Antioch, Paul, and Jerusalem: Diaspora Myths of Origins in the Homeland." In *Redescribing Christian Origins: Symposium*, edited by Ron Cameron and Merrill P. Miller, 177–236. Atlanta: Society of Biblical Literature, 2004.

———. "'Beginning from Jerusalem . . .': Re-examining Canon and Consensus." *JHC* 2.1 (1995) 3–30.

Moffatt, James. *The First Epistle of Paul to the Corinthians*. London: Hodder & Stoughton, 1938.

Moo, Douglas J. *The Letter of James*. Grand Rapids: Eerdmans, 2000.

Moxnes, Halvor. *Putting Jesus in His Place: A Radical Vision of Household and Kingdom*. London: Westminster John Knox, 2003.

Murphy-O'Connor, Jerome. "The Origins of Paul's Christology from Thessalonians to Galatians." In *Christian Origins; Worship, Belief and Society*, edited by Kieran J. O'Mahony, 113–42. Sheffield: Sheffield Academic, 2003.

———. *Paul: A Critical Life*. Oxford: Oxford University Press, 1997.

Myllykoski, Matti. "James the Just in History and Tradition: Perspectives of Past and Present Scholarship (Part 1)." *CurBS* 5 (2006) 73–122.

Neusner, Jacob. *The Rabbinic Traditions about the Pharisees before AD 70*. Leiden: Brill, 1971.

———. "Vow-Taking, the Nazirites, and the Law: Does James' Advice to Paul Accord with Halakhah?" In *James the Just and Christian Origins*, edited by Bruce D. Chilton and Craig A. Evans, 59–82. Leiden & Boston: Brill, 1999.

———. "What is a Judaism?" In *The Brother of Jesus: James the Just and His Mission*, edited by Bruce D. Chilton and Jacob Neusner. Louisville, KY: Westminster John Knox, 2001.

———. "What, Exactly, Is Israel's Gentile Problem? Rabbinic Perspectives on Galatians 2." In *The Missions of James, Peter, and Paul: Tensions in Early Christianity*, edited by Bruce D. Chilton and Craig A. Evans, 275–306. Leiden & Boston: Brill, 2005.

Nicklesburg, George W. E., Jr. *Ancient Judaism and Christian Origins: Diversity, Continuity, and Transformation*. Minneapolis: Fortress, 2003.

———. "The Genre and Function of the Markan Passion Narrative." *HTR* 73 (1972) 153–84.

Nienhuis, David R. *Not By Paul Alone: The Formation of the Catholic Epistle Collection and the Christian Church*. Waco, TX: Baylor University Press, 2007.

Nineham, D. E. *The Gospel of St Mark*. Pelican NT Commentaries. Harmondsworth: Penguin, 1963.

Oakes, Peter. "Constructing Poverty Scales for Graeco-Roman Society: A Response to Steven Friesen's 'Poverty in Pauline Studies.'" *JSNT* 26.3 (2004) 367–71.

———. Review of *Paul, Jerusalem and the Judaisers*, by Ian J. Elmer. *JSNT* 32.5 (2010) 98–99.

Oberlinner, L. *Historische Überlieferungen und christologische Aussage: Zur Frage der Brüder Jesu in der Synopse*. Stuttgart: Katholisches Bibelwerk, 1975.

Ong, Walter J. *Orality and Literacy: The Technologizing of the Word*. New York: Methuen, 1982.

Osiek, Carol. *What Are They Saying about the Social Setting of the New Testament?* New York: Paulist, 1992.

Paget, James Carleton. "After 70 and All That: A Response to Martin Goodman's *Rome and Jerusalem*." *JSNT* 31.3 (2009) 339–65.

———. "The Definition of the Terms *Jewish Christian* and *Jewish Christianity* in the History of Research." In *Jewish Believers in Jesus: The Early Centuries,* edited by Oskar Skarsaune, and Reidar Hvalvik, 22–54. Peabody, MA: Hendrickson, 2007.

———. "Marcion and the Resurrection: Some Thoughts on a Recent Book." *JSHJ* 35.1 (2012) 74–102.

Pahl, Michael W. *Discerning the "Word of the Lord": The "Word of the Lord" in 1 Thessalonians 4.15.* London: T & T Clark, 2009.

———. "The 'Gospel' and the 'Word': Exploring Some Early Christian Patterns." *JSNT* 29.2 (2006) 211–27.

Painter, John. "James and Peter: Models of Leadership and Mission." In *The Missions of James, Peter, and Paul: Tensions in Early Christianity,* edited by Bruce D. Chilton and Craig A. Evans, 143–210. Leiden & Boston: Brill, 2005.

———. *Just James: The Brother of Jesus in History and Tradition.* Columbia, SC: University of South Carolina Press, 1997.

———. *Mark's Gospel: Worlds in Conflict.* London: Routledge, 1997.

———. "The Power of Words: Rhetoric in James and Paul." In *The Missions of James, Peter, and Paul: Tensions in Early Christianity,* edited by Bruce D. Chilton and Craig A. Evans, 235–75. Leiden & Boston: Brill, 2005.

———. "Who Was James? Footprints as a Means of Identification." In *The Brother of Jesus,* edited by Bruce D. Chilton and Jacob Neusner, 10–65. Louisville, KY: Westminster John Knox, 2001.

Painter, John, and deSilva, David A. *James and Jude.* Paideia Commentaries on the New Testament. Grand Rapids: Baker, 2012.

Parsons, Mikael, and Richard I. Pervo. *Rethinking the Unity of Luke and Acts.* Minneapolis: Fortress, 1993.

Patrick, W. *James the Lord's Brother.* Edinburgh: T & T Clark, 1906.

Patterson, Stephen J. "Can You Trust a Gospel? A Review of Richard Bauckham's *Jesus and the Eyewitnesses.*" *JSHJ* 6 (2008) 194–210.

Pearson, Birger A. "1 Thess 2.13-16: A Deutero-Pauline Interpolation." *HTR* 64 (1971) 79–94.

———. "A Q Community in Galilee?" *NTS* 50.4 (2004) 476–94.

Perkins, Pheme. *First and Second Peter, James, and Jude.* Louisville, KY: Westminster John Knox, 1995.

Perrin, Jim. *The Villain.* London: Hutchinson, 2005.

———. *Visions of Snowdonia: Landscape and Legend.* London: BBC, 1997.

Perrin, Nicholas. *Thomas, the Other Gospel.* London: SPCK, 2007.

Pervo, Richard I. *Acts: A Commentary.* Hermeneia. Minneapolis: Fortress, 2009.

———. *Dating Acts: Between the Evangelists and the Apologists.* Santa Rosa, CA: Polebridge, 2006.

———. "Direct Speech in Acts and the Question of Genre." *JSNT* 28.3 (2006) 285–307.

———. *Profit With Delight: The Literary Genre of the Acts of the Apostles.* Philadelphia: Fortress, 1987.

Pixner, Bargil O. S. B. "Mount Zion, Jesus, and Archaeology." In *Jesus and Archaeology,* edited by James H. Charlesworth, 309–22. Grand Rapids: Eerdmans, 2006.

Plant, Raymond. "Community." In *The Blackwell Encyclopaedia of Political Thought,* edited by David Miller, 88–90. Oxford: Basil Blackwell, 1987.

Plummer, Alfred. *An Exegetical Commentary on the Gospel of Matthew.* London: James Clarke, 1910.

Powell, Mark Allan. *What Are They Saying about Acts?* New York: Paulist, 1991.

Pratscher, W. *Der Herrenbruder Jakobus und die Jakobustradition.* Gottingen: Vandenhoeck & Ruprecht, 1987.

Price, Robert, "Eisenman's Gospel of James the Just." In *The Brother of Jesus: James the Just and His Mission,* edited by Bruce D. Chilton and Jacob Neusner, 186–97. Louisville, KY: Westminster John Knox, 2001.

Pryor, John W. "John the Baptist and Jesus: Tradition and Text in John 3.25." *JSNT* 66 (1997) 15–26.

Puech, Emile. "Some Results of a New Examination of the Copper Scroll (3Q15)." In *Copper Scroll Studies,* edited by George J. Brooke and Philip R. Davies, 58–91. London: T & T Clark, 2002.

Ramsay, W. *St. Paul the Traveller and Roman Citizen.* London: Hodder & Stoughton, 1896.

Rappe, Donald. "Secret Book of James." In *The Complete Gospels,* edited by R. J. Miller, 332–42. Santa Rosa, CA: Polebridge, 1994.

Rawlinson, A. E. J. *St Mark: with Introduction, Commentary and Additional Notes.* Westminster Commentaries. London: Methuen, 1925.

Regev, Eyal. "Temple Concerns and High-Priestly Prosecutions from Peter to James: Between Narrative and History." *NTS* 56.1 (2010) 64–89.

Richards, Hubert J. *The First Christmas: What Really Happened?* London: Collins, 1973.

Richardson, Peter. *Herod: King of the Jews and Friend of the Romans.* Columbia, SC: University of South Carolina Press, 1996.

Riddle, Donald W. "The Cephas-Peter Problem, and a Possible Solution." *JBL* 59.2 (1940) 169–80.

Riesner, Rainer. "Jesus, the Primitive Community, and the Essene Quarter of Jerusalem." In *Jesus and the Dead Sea Scrolls,* edited by James H. Charlesworth, 198–234. New York: Doubleday, 1992.

———. *Paul's Early Period: Chronology, Mission Strategy, Theology.* Grand Rapids: Eerdmans, 1998.

———. "Synagogues in Jerusalem." In *The Book of Acts in its Palestinian Setting,* edited by Richard Bauckham, 179–211. The Book of Acts in its First Century Setting 4. Carlisle: Paternoster, 1995.

Robertson, Archibald, and Alfred Plummer. *A Critical and Exegetical Commentary on the First Epistle of St Paul to the Corinthians.* Edinburgh: T & T Clark, 1911.

Robinson, James M., and Helmut Koester. *Trajectories through Early Christianity.* Valley Forge, PA: Fortress, 1971.

Rodriguez, Rafael. "Reading and Hearing in Ancient Contexts." *JSNT* 32.2 (2009) 151–78.

———. *Structuring Early Christian Memory: Jesus in Tradition, Performance and Text.* London: T & T Clark, 2010.

Roetzel, Calvin J. *Paul: A Jew on the Margins.* London: Westminster John Knox, 2003.

Rofe, Alexander. "The Onset of Sects in Post-Exilic Judaism: Neglected Evidence from the Septuagint, Trito-Isaiah, Ben Sira, and Malachi." In *The Social World of Formative Christianity and Judaism,* edited by Jacob Neusner, et al., 39–49. Philadelphia: Fortress, 1988.

Rohrbaugh, Richard. "A Dysfunctional Family and its Neighbours." In *Jesus and His Parables: Interpreting the Parables of Jesus Today,* edited by George V. Shillington, 141–64. Edinburgh: T & T Clark, 1997.

Rojas-Flores, Gonzalo. "From John 2.19 to Mark 15.29: The History of a Misunderstanding." *NTS* 56.1 (2010) 22–43.

Roose, Hannah. "Sharing in Christ's Rule: Tracing a Debate in Earliest Christianity." *JSNT* 27.2 (2004) 123–48.

Ropes, J. H. *A Critical and Exegetical Commentary on the Epistle of St. James.* ICC. Edinburgh: T & T Clark, 1916.

Rothschild, Clare K. *Baptist Traditions in Q.* Tubingen: Mohr Siebeck, 2005.

Rowe, Kavin, "History, Hermeneutics and the Unity of Luke-Acts." *JSNT* 28 (2005) 131–57.

———. "Literary Unity and Reception History: Reading Luke-Acts as Luke and Acts." *JSNT* 29 (2007) 449–57.

Rowland, Christopher. *Christian Origins: The Setting and Character of the Most Important Messianic Sect of Judaism.* 2nd ed. London: SPCK, 2002.

Rubio, Fernando Bermejo. "The Fiction of the 'Three Quests': An Argument for Dismantling a Dubious Historiographical Paradigm." *JSHJ* 7 (2009) 211–53.

Saldarini, Anthony J. *Pharisees Scribes and Sadducees in Palestinian Society.* Edinburgh: T & T Clark, 1989.

Sanders, E. P. *Jesus and Judaism.* London: SCM. 1985.

———. "Jewish Association with Gentiles and Galatians 2.11–14." In *The Conversation Continues: Studies in Paul and John in Honor of J. Louis Martyn,* edited by R. T. Fortna and B. R. Gaventa, 170–88. Nashville: Abingdon, 1990.

———. *Jewish Law from the Bible to the Mishnah.* London: SCM, 1990.

———. *Judaism: Practice and Belief, 63BCE–66CE.* London: SCM, 1992.

Sawicki, Marianne. "Person or Practice? Judging in James and Paul." In *The Missions of James, Peter, and Paul: Tensions in Early Christianity,* edited by Bruce D. Chilton and Craig A. Evans, 386–408. Leiden & Boston: Brill, 2005.

Schmithals, W. *Paul and James.* Studies in Biblical Theology. London: SCM, 1963.

Schoedel William R., and Douglas M. Parrott. "The (First) Apocalypse of James." In *The Nag Hammadi Library,* edited by James Robinson, 260–68. San Francisco: Harper & Row, 1988.

Schoeps, Hans-Joachim. "Ebionite Christianity." *JTS* 4 (1953) 219–24.

———. *Paul.* Philadelphia: Westminster, 1961.

Schofield, Guy. *In the Year Sixty-Two: The Murder of the Brother of the Lord and its Consequences.* London: Harrap, 1962.

Schurer Emil. *The History of the Jewish People in the age of Jesus Christ.* Edited by Geza Vermes and Fergus Millar. Edinburgh: T & T Clark, 1973.

Schweitzer, Albert. *The Mysticism of Paul the Apostle.* Translated by W. Montgomery. London: Black, 1931.

———. *The Quest of the Historical Jesus.* London: SCM, 2000.

Scobie, Charles. *John the Baptist: A New Quest of the Historical John.* London: SCM, 1964.

Scott, Ian W. "Common Ground? The Role of Galatians 2.16 in Paul's Argument." *NTS* 53 (2007) 425–35.

Segal, Alan. *Paul the Convert: The Apostate and Apostasy of Saul the Pharisee.* New Haven: Yale University Press, 1990.

Shanks, Herschel, and Ben Witherington, III. *The Brother of Jesus: The Dramatic Story and Significance of the First Archaeological Link to Jesus and His Family.* San Francisco: HarperSanFrancisco, 2003.

Shaw, Brent D. "The Bandit." In *The Romans,* edited by Andrea Giardina, translated by Lydia G. Cochrane, 300–41. Chicago: University of Chicago Press, 1993.

Silberman, Neil Asher and Yuval Goren. "Faking Biblical History." *Archaeology* 56.5 (2003).

Sim, David C. *The Gospel of Matthew and Christian Judaism: The History and Social Setting of the Matthean Community.* Edinburgh: T & T Clark, 1998.

Skarsaune, Oskar. "The History of Jewish Believers in the Early Centuries—Perspectives and Framework." In *Jewish Believers in Jesus: The Early Centuries,* edited by Oskar Skarsaune and Reidar Hvalvik, 745–82. Peabody, MA: Hendrickson, 2007.

——. "Jewish Believers in Jesus in Antiquity—Problems of Definition, Method, and Sources." In *Jewish Believers in Jesus: The Early Centuries,* edited by Oskar Skarsaune and Reidar Hvalvik, 3–21. Peabody, MA: Hendrickson, 2007.

Sleeper, Freeman, C. *James.* ANTC; Nashville: Abingdon, 1998.

Smith-Christopher, Daniel L. "Peace." In *The Eerdmans Dictionary of Early Judaism,* edited by John J. Collins and Daniel C. Harlow, 1038–40. Cambridge: Eerdmans, 2010.

Smith, D. E. "Was there a Jerusalem Church?: Christian Origins According to Acts and Paul." *Forum* 3 (2000) 57–74.

Sprott, W. J. H. *Human Groups.* Harmondsworth: Penguin, 1958.

Stark, Rodney. *The Rise of Christianity: How the Obscure, Marginal Jesus Movement became the Dominant Religious Force in the Western World in a Few Centuries.* San Francisco: HarperSanFrancisco, 1997.

Stauffer, Ethelbert, "Zum Kalifat des Jacobus." *ZRGG* 4 (1952), 193–214. Translated by D. J. Doughty, "The Caliphate of James." *JHC* 4 (1997) 120–43.

Stegemann, Ekkehard W., and Wolfgang Stegemann, *The Jesus Movement: A Social History of its First Century.* Minneapolis: Fortress, 1999.

Steinmann, Jean. *Saint John the Baptist and the Desert Tradition.* Translated by Michael Boyes. London: Longmans, 1958.

Strange, James F. "Archaeological Evidence of Jewish Believers?" In *Jewish Believers in Jesus,* edited by Oskar Skarsaune and Reidar Hvalvik, 710–41. Peabody, MA: Hendrickson, 2007.

Streeter, B. H. *The Four Gospels: A Study of Origins Treating of the Manuscript Tradition, Sources, Authorship and Dates.* London: Macmillan, 1924.

Sumney, Jerry L. *Identifying Paul's Opponents: The Question of Method in 2 Corinthians.* Sheffield: Sheffield Academic Press, 1990.

Tabor, James D. *The Jesus Dynasty: The Hidden History of Jesus, His Royal Family, and the Birth of Christianity.* New York: Simon & Schuster, 2006.

Tarrech, Armand Puigi. *Jesus: An Uncommon Journey.* Studies on the Historical Jesus. Tubingen: Mohr Siebeck, 2010.

Taubes, Jacob. *The Political Theology of Paul.* Stanford, CA: Stanford University Press, 2004.

Taylor, Joan E. *The Essenes, the Scrolls and the Dead Sea.* Oxford: Oxford University Press, 2012.

——. *The Immerser: John the Baptist within Second Temple Judaism.* Grand Rapids: Eerdmans, 1997.

Taylor, Joan E., and Federico Adinolfi. "John the Baptist and Jesus the Baptist: A Narrative Critical Approach." *JSHJ* 10.3 (2012) 247–84.

Taylor, Justine. "The Original Environment of Christianity." In *Christian Origins; Worship, Belief and Society,* edited by Kieran J. O'Mahony, 214–24. Sheffield: Sheffield Academic, 2003.

Taylor, Justine, and Etienne Nodet. *The Origins of Christianity: An Exploration.* Collegeville, MN: Liturgical, 1998.

Taylor, Nicholas. *Paul, Antioch and Jerusalem: A Study in Relationships and Authority in Earliest Christianity.* Sheffield: Sheffield Academic, 1992.

Taylor, Vincent. *The Formation of the Gospel Tradition.* London: Macmillan, 1949.

———. *The Gospel According to St. Mark: The Greek Text with Introduction, Notes, and Indexes.* London: Macmillan, 1955.

Theissen, Gerd. *The Gospels in Context: Social and Political History in the Synoptic Tradition.* London: T & T Clark, 1992.

———. *Sociology of Early Palestinian Christianity.* Philadelphia: Fortress, 1978.

Thiede, Carsten Peter. *The Dead Sea Scrolls and the Jewish Origins of Christianity.* Oxford: Lion, 2000.

Thompson, E. P. *The Making of the English Working Class.* Harmondsworth: Penguin, 1963.

Tomson, P. J. *Paul and the Jewish Law: Halakah in the Letters of the Apostle to the Gentiles.* Minneapolis: Fortress, 1990.

Tönnies, Ferdinand. *Gemeinschaft und Gesellschaft.* Leipzig, 1887. *Community and Society: Gemeinschaft und Gesellschaft.* Translated by Charles P Loomis. East Lansing, MI: The Michigan State University Press, 1957.

Treblico, Paul. "Why Did the Early Christians Call Themselves ἡ ἐκκλησία?" *NTS* 57.3 (2011) 440–60.

Tuckett, Christopher M. *Q and the History of Early Christianity: Studies on Q.* London: T & T Clark, 1996.

Twelftree, Graham F. "Jesus the Baptist." *JSHJ* 7 (2009) 103–25.

Tyson, Joseph B. *Marcion and Luke-Acts.* Columbia, CA: Polebridge, 2006.

Ulfgard, Hakan. "The Branch in the Last Days: Observations on the New Covenant Before and After the Messiah." In *The Dead Sea Scrolls in Their Historical Context,* edited by Timothy H. Lim, et al., 219–33. London: T & T Clark, 2000.

VanderKam, James C. *The Book of Jubilees.* Sheffield: Sheffield Academic, 2001.

VanderKam, James C. and Flint, Peter, *The Meaning of the Dead Sea Scrolls: Their Significance for Understanding the Bible, Judaism, Jesus, and Christianity.* London: T & T Clark, 2002.

Vermes, Geza. *The Complete Dead Sea Scrolls in English.* London: Penguin, 2004.

Wahlen, Clinton. "Peter's Vision and Conflicting Definitions of Purity." *NTS* 51.4 (2005) 505–18.

Wainwright, Arthur W. *A Guide to the New Testament.* London: Epworth, 1965.

Walker, William O., Jr. "Does the 'We' in Gal. 2.15–17 Include Paul's Opponents?" *NTS* 49.4 (2003) 560–65.

Wall, Robert W. *The Community of the Wise.* Valley Forge, PA: Trinity, 1997.

Watson, Francis. *Paul, Judaism and the Gentiles.* Cambridge: Cambridge University Press, 1986.

———. "Paul the Reader: An Authorial Apologia." *JSNT* 28.3 (2006) 363–73.

Wearmouth, Robert F. *Methodism and the Struggle of the Working Classes 1850-1900.* Leicester: Edgar Backus, 1954.

———. *Methodism and the Trade Unions.* London: Epworth, 1959.

―――. *Some Working-Class Movements of the Nineteenth Century.* London: Epworth, 1948.

Webb, Robert L. *John the Baptizer and Prophet: A Socio-Historical Study.* JSOTSup 62. Sheffield: Sheffield Academic, 1991.

―――. Review of *Jesus and the Prodigal,* by Kenneth E. Bailey. *JSHJ* 4.1 (2006) 109.

―――. "The Use of 'Story' in the Letter of Jude: Rhetorical Strategies of Jude's Narrative Episodes." *JSNT* 31 (2008) 53–87.

Wedderburn, A. J. M. "Paul's Collection: Chronology and History." *NTS* 48.1 (2002) 95–110.

Weeden, Theodore J. "Kenneth Bailey's Theory of Oral Tradition: A Theory Contested by its Evidence." *JSHJ* 7 (2009) 3–43.

―――. *Mark: Traditions in Conflict.* Philadelphia: Fortress, 1971.

Welborn, L. L. "'Extraction from the Mortal Site': Badiou on the Resurrection in Paul." *NTS* 55 (2009) 295–314.

Wenham, David. *Paul: Follower of Jesus or Founder of Christianity?* Grand Rapids: Eerdmans, 1995.

―――. Review of *Discerning the "Word of the Lord,"* by Michael W. Pahl. *JSNT* 32.5 (2010) 105.

Wickham, E. R. *Church and People in an Industrial City.* London: Lutterworth, 1957.

Williams, Francis E. "The Apocryphon of James." In *The Nag Hammadi Library in English,* edited by James M. Robinson, 29–37. New York: HarperSanFrancisco, 1990.

Wilson, Bryan. *Religious Sects: A Sociological Study.* London: Weidenfeld and Nicolson, 1970.

Wilson, Stephen G. *Related Strangers: Jews and Christians 70-170 CE.* Minneapolis: Fortress, 1995.

Wink, Walter. *John the Baptist in the Gospel Tradition.* Cambridge: Cambridge University Press, 1968.

Witherington, Ben, III. *Grace in Galatia: A Commentary on St Paul's Letter to the Galatians.* Grand Rapids: Eerdmans, 1998.

―――. *Letters and Homilies for Jewish Christians: A Socio-Rhetorical Commentary on Hebrews, James and Jude.* Nottingham: InterVarsity, 2007.

Zahn, Theodore. *Introduction to the New Testament, Vol.1.* Edinburgh: T & T Clark, 1909.

Zangenberg, Jurgen K. "Archaeological News from the Galilee: Tiberias, Magdala and Rural Galilee." *Early Christianity* 1.3 (2010) 471–84.

Subject Index

Index of Modern Authors

Ancient Document Index

Greco–Roman Writings

Early Christian Writings

Lightning Source UK Ltd.
Milton Keynes UK
UKOW06f1004270515

252367UK00001B/37/P